Dietrich Bonhoeffer
1906–1945

Dietrich Bonhoeffer
1906–1945

Martyr, Thinker, Man of Resistance
Ferdinand Schlingensiepen

Translated by Isabel Best

t & t clark

Published by T&T Clark International
A Continuum Imprint
The Tower Building, 11 York Road, London SE1 7NX
80 Maiden Lane, Suite 704, New York, NY 10038

www.continuumbooks.com

The original edition was published as *Dietrich Bonhoeffer 1906–1945.*
Eine Biographie
© Verlag C. H. Beck oHG, München 2006

British Library Cataloguing-in-Publication Data
A catalogue record for this book is available from the British Library

Typeset by Fakenham Photosetting Ltd, Fakenham, Norfolk
Printed and bound in Great Britain by the MPG Books Group

ISBN: 978-0-567-03400-7 (Hardback)

In memoriam

Jean Freeman
and
Dr Harold Wilke

Contents

Acknowledgements

No one can write a book like this without good and kind helpers. Thus I owe my thanks to many persons.

Professor Andreas Dreß kindly allowed me to quote passages from the unpublished memoirs of his mother, who was Dietrich Bonhoeffer's youngest sister. These memoirs provide such a lively picture of childhood and youth in the Bonhoeffer home that they really ought to be published. I thank Peter von Wedemeyer for a photo of his sister Maria (p. 335). With Ruth-Alice von Bismarck, née von Wedemeyer, I was able to have a long conversation about her sister, whom I myself had met in 1976.

Several friends from the International Bonhoeffer Society read my manuscript or parts of it; I am thus indebted to Dr Ilse Tödt, Dr Christian Gremmels, Dr Jürgen Henkys, Martin Hüneke and Enno Obendiek for important suggestions and indications. The same is true for my friends Dr Rudolf Kreis, Dr Rainer Oechslen and Dr Jürgen Regul. To Dr Ekkehard Klausa of the Memorial to the German Resistance, and Peter Schünemann of the German Academy for Language and Poetry, I also owe thanks for their critical reading of the manuscript.

My warm thanks to two graduate students, Laura Cyron and Christine Hubenthal, who, after reading parts of the manuscript, asked to see the rest and declared that the biography was quite understandable and Bonhoeffer an important subject. Laura Cyron is now writing a thesis about him.

Without the friendship of Eberhard and Renate Bethge, which I have enjoyed for over fifty years, I would hardly have been likely to write this book. I also remember with gratitude conversations about the church struggle with my father, Confessing Church pastor Hermann Schlingensiepen, and with Bishop Kurt Scharf on whose staff I served for 10 years. My wife Elisabeth and our daughters Stephanie and Irmela have offered criticisms of my manuscript which ensured that I was always brought back to the necessary objectivity about my subject. Elisabeth also proofread each new version of the manuscript.

My sincere thanks go also to my lector, Dr Ulrich Nolte, as well as

Angelika von der Lahr at Verlag C. H. Beck, for their patient and knowledgeable fostering of my work.

A project such as this biography is like climbing a mountain. Towards the end, as the publisher's deadline approaches, it becomes ever steeper. But long before reaching this final phase, I had found in Dr Ulrich Kabitz a mountain guide who led me onward with an energy that belied his then 85 years. Decades ago he had also accompanied Eberhard Bethge in the writing of his Bonhoeffer biography; thus he had already been the guide on the first ascent. I remember the day when Eberhard Bethge gave me a copy of his biography, with the words 'I don't know what I'd have done without Ulrich Kabitz!'

For me, Kabitz was the friend who not only carefully read every new version of my manuscript, but also drew my attention to important bibliographical sources, kept me from misinterpretations and urged me to expand the most central points in the story. As the deadline neared and it was in fact getting harder, he telephoned almost daily to encourage and advise me. I shall never forget how he once said, 'My wife finds your new chapter exciting and well written, but I think there are a few things you should change.' In other words: Please write this chapter over again!

Ulrich Kabitz and I had become friends years earlier through our common interest in Bonhoeffer. But the guidance he provided through his knowledge of Bonhoeffer's works, the secondary literature and especially the Nazi period, of which he had been an alert witness, went far beyond what one expects from a friend. So I, too, now say, I don't know what I should have done without Ulrich Kabitz. To him above all I owe my heartfelt thanks.

List of Illustrations

Preface

I first heard the name Dietrich Bonhoeffer in 1948, when I was given the small volume *Zeugnis eines Boten* (Testimony of a Messenger), edited by W. A. Visser 't Hooft of the Netherlands, the first General Secretary of the World Council of Churches. Fascinatingly, it brought the man to life. Still, it never occurred to me to ask my father about Bonhoeffer. Years later I learned that my father had not only known him, but had once travelled in a police van with him, spending the time in animated conversation, after being arrested together with other pastors at Martin Niemöller's home. Throughout my time at university, Bonhoeffer remained for me a name from the time of the church struggle, to be mentioned respectfully along with the names of Paul Schneider, Lutz Steil, Werner Sylten, Friedrich Weissler and Friedrich Justus Perels, pastors and staff members of the Confessing Church who also were murdered by the SS in their concentration camps.

In 1952 Bonhoeffer's image changed almost overnight, when his letters from prison were published under the title *Widerstand und Ergebung* (Resistance and Submission – published in English a year later as *Letters and Papers from Prison*) and became *the* topic of conversation among us younger people. The generation ahead of us were probably no less fascinated, but almost all older theologians to whom we mentioned the book found Bonhoeffer's new theological ideas 'too fragmentary' and therefore impossible to evaluate. They had experienced much of the church struggle too, but the period of the the Second World War, which for Bonhoeffer ended in death, had been entirely different for them. His new theology must have appeared utterly strange and alien to them.

I feel fortunate to this day that in 1954 I was sent to Bradford, in the north of England, to serve as pastor to a German-speaking congregation, because that was how I came to know Eberhard Bethge, close friend of Bonhoeffer's and and his first biographer. He was working in London then, and in spite of the distance, we saw each other often and I was soon included in Eberhard and Renate Bethge's circle of friends. I knew about Bethge's laborious efforts to decipher the manuscripts of his friend in order to prepare them for publication. He was probably already working on the biography; but he was generous to any theologian who wanted to write about Bonhoeffer. He would photocopy texts, advise visitors in long conversations and provide hospitality to them. So the first researchers on Bonhoeffer came to see him through the eyes of Eberhard Bethge. This was true for me too.

To this day, most of what we know about Bonhoeffer stems from Bethge's long biography of him which was published in 1967 (the English edition appeared in 1970). All subsequent biographies, including the present one, have to build on it. Since Bethge was at his friend's side throughout the decisive years, his work is one of the most important sources on Bonhoeffer's life. It is all the more admirable that Bethge was nevertheless able to distance himself from his subject as every biographer must.

Eberhard Bethge was convinced that, at 1080 pages, the biography was far too long for most readers. He asked me back then if I would like to write a shortened version. I set to work eagerly, but had to stop when I accepted a new position in 1969. It is only now, in the book that lies before you, that I feel I have finally fulfilled the request of the man whose friendship has meant so much to me. A shortened version of Bethge's work would now no longer meet the need for an up-to-date biography of Bonhoeffer. Bethge himself, in his foreword to the fifth edition of his book in 1983, asked whether it wasn't time to revise the 'image that was set in 1967'. This question has become ever more valid since then.

We know more today than we did several decades ago about Bonhoeffer's life and his thinking. For example, the publication in 1992 (in English in 1994) of *Love Letters from Cell 92* makes it possible to portray Bonhoeffer's engagement to Maria von Wedemeyer in more detail than Bethge could do in 1967. At least as significant is the fact that we know, since the publication of the complete correspondence between Bonhoeffer and Bethge, how modestly, for decades, Bethge kept in the background, behind his friend. Yet he was an indispensable dialogue partner for Bonhoeffer, whether in helping him to clarify important ideas or even inspiring them.

When Bethge was writing his book, the period of the Third Reich was much more clearly present in the consciousness of the German people than it is today. Bethge could assume that people were familiar with experiences in the Church and with words that we now have to explain. On the other hand, we today know much more about the Third Reich and the resistance to it than was known in Bethge's time. But it is especially people's estimation of the Resistance which has changed fundamentally.

It is no longer regarded with suspicion, but rather positively for the most part. Commemorations of the attempted overthrow on 20 July 1944 had been held since 1946, but were still an embarrassment to many politicians in 1967. Adenauer, though he had been consistently opposed to Hitler, never attended these ceremonies. He knew how unpopular it would have been for him as Chancellor to do so. Very few Germans in Adenauer's time would have mourned Hitler, but scarcely any wanted to confront questions about their own Nazi past, or even worse, to think about how they should have behaved. So Bethge still had to protect Bonhoeffer from denigration. His biography can be read in part as a defence of Bonhoeffer as a member of the Resistance.

Today Bonhoeffer enjoys great respect, not least of all because his opposition to Hitler began well before 1933. The accusation that the nationalist, conservative Resistance didn't turn away from Hitler until late in his regime does not apply to Bonhoeffer any more than to his brother-in-law, Hans von Dohnanyi, or the other members of his family, just as it does not apply to Helmuth von Moltke and Adam von Trott. Bonhoeffer no longer needs to be defended.

Glad as one may be of this development, there is also a danger in it. A person whose hundredth birthday is ceremoniously celebrated, who died a martyr 60 years ago, can easily become the focus of universal veneration – all the more when he lived such a life as Bonhoeffer's, and when he left us a poem such as 'Von guten Mächten [Powers of Good]'. But Bonhoeffer did not want to be venerated; he wanted to be heard. Anyone who puts him up on a lonely pedestal is defusing that which, to this day, makes a thoughtful encounter with him worthwhile.

This includes the unique connection Bonhoeffer made between theology and political action, which still aroused mistrust during the postwar period. Thus, during the first decades after the Second World War, the Evangelical Church pastor Paul Schneider, murdered in Buchenwald concentration camp in 1939, was frequently held up as a 'genuine' martyr over against Bonhoeffer, who had been 'liquidated', not as a confessing Christian, but as a conspirator together with his companions in the Resistance. Hitler himself had given the orders, in his command bunker during the 'noon meeting' on 5 April 1945. Bonhoeffer is nevertheless a Christian martyr, because he did not enter into his role as a conspirator by chance; instead, it was theological thinking and decisions that made this Confessing Church pastor a member of the Resistance movement. He had already long been engaged in other ways in the political struggle.

And not least of all, his brother-in-law, Hans von Dohnanyi, and Colonel Oster persuaded him to join the conspiracy.

Bonhoeffer's attitude towards racism and colonialism was shared by few others in his time and was thus remarkably forward-looking. Before 1933 he had experienced, in a black church congregation in the USA, their acceptance of him as an equal in the midst of a racist society. He was hoping to travel to India to learn about the religions in that country shaped by colonialism. When he heard about Gandhi, it seemed to him that here was the quintessential teacher who stood up to the dangers of the time. That Bonhoeffer already had racism and colonialism in his field of vision was not the least of the reasons why he recognized, soon after Hitler came to power in 1933, anti-Semitism driven to the worst excesses as *the* issue, for church and politics, which would decide the future of Germany.

It is this vision, as clear-headed as it was committed, which makes Bonhoeffer interesting to people who want to look beyond the trends and interests of their day and sharpen their own perception of long-term developments. In September 1941 Bonhoeffer wrote from Switzerland, to his American friend Paul Lehmann, what we today can recognize as an astonishingly prophetic letter: 'The development that we believe is bound to come in the near future is world domination – if you will forgive me this expression – by America . . . But at any rate the power of the USA will be so overwhelming that hardly any country could represent a counterbalance' (DBWE 16, 219, original in English). Bonhoeffer was worried about this prospect, although he felt that 'world domination by America' was the only possible solution for the world in which he was then living. But what does this mean, if not that, decades ahead of time, he foresaw problems that have not been solved to this day. What he said about it challenges us to think further. This is also true, not least of all, for his ideas about guilt and how it should be handled.

'It would really be very interesting to study Islam on its own soil', he wrote in April 1924, aged 18, to his parents from Tripoli (DBWE 9, 120). Where are the theologians or the educational policymakers who are doing this today when it is urgently needed? But enough of such examples.

To be able to live, to act and to die as Bonhoeffer did requires traits that even he did not inherit, but rather acquired in youth, in his parents' home and during his time at university: intellectual curiosity, an incorruptible sense of right and wrong, and the courage to make uncomfortable decisions with potentially dangerous consequences. In these ways Bonhoeffer is an example for others, and of interest even to people who no longer expect anything from the Church. However, they must be prepared – with intellectual curiosity of their own – to become engaged with what, for Bonhoeffer, theology was. Bonhoeffer wanted to expose theology to 'the fresh air of modern thinking'. He insisted that the message of the Church must always apply concretely to the reality of the world. Timeless truths he considered useless, for 'what is always true is precisely what is not true today'.

It is the biographer's privilege not to need to write treatises on such ideas, but rather to tell a story which takes in all of that, and more.

Ferdinand Schlingensiepen
Düsseldorf-Kaiserswerth
Good Friday 2005

Preface to the English Edition

I am delighted that T&T Clark have decided to publish the English translation of my Bonhoeffer biography. My ties with the United Kingdom
and the United States over the years have been many, beginning as long
ago as 1950 with a scholarship from the Church of Scotland to study at
New College, Edinburgh.

As someone with a degree of knowledge about the country I was then
sent by the German Evangelical Church to Bradford/Yorkshire as minister
to the German-speaking congregation, in 1954. During our time there my
wife and I were able to form friendships that have lasted a lifetime and
three of our four children were born British citizens.

My experiences in Scotland and England led to my appointment, in
1959, as ecumenical advisor to the Evangelische Kirche der Union with
its headquarters in Berlin. This is the former 'Protestant Church in Prussia'
of which Bonhoeffer had been a member.

The 1960s were a time of very lively ecumenical exchange between
the many national churches that were members of the World Council of
Churches. Based in Berlin, my role was to lend a helping hand and bring
the relationships to life, with the Kyodan in Japan and the United Church
of Christ in the United States in particular. The dialogue with these two
churches, which began back then, endures to this day.

Another part of my job was to keep those congregations of our church
that were behind the Iron Curtain informed about ecumenical affairs.

The fact that over time we were able to include ministers of the churches
in (then) Communist East Germany (the German Democratic Republic) in
our mutual exchange programme for pastors from Germany, Japan and the
United States of America made my role all the more exciting.

On moving to a new post in Düsseldorf in 1969 I took a favourite
project with me. I had been trying to assist Eberhard Bethge in his efforts
to keep Bonhoeffer's ecumenical legacy alive. This is how in 1971 the
first International Bonhoeffer Conference and the foundation of the
Bonhoeffer Society in Düsseldorf-Kaiserswerth came about.

This Bonhoeffer biography, published in German in 2005, is the result
of my personal involvement in this work. I am very grateful to Mrs Isabel

Best that an English translation is now available. Our year-long, intensive working relationship via email has been a joy to me. Later on, as the book was taking shape, I entered into an equally enjoyable, slightly more hectic relationship with Thomas Kraft, Associate Publisher of T&T Clark. To him I am equally grateful. Special thanks go to our daughter Stephanie Schlingensiepen for her advice to me during this project and for reading through the final manuscript.

I dedicate this book to the memory of two people who have had a profound influence on my relationship with Britain and the United States: Mrs Jean Freeman, long-time resident of the City of Bath and the Revd Harold Wilke from New York. I am deeply indebted to both of them.

When I arrived in Bath in 1951 my friends teased me, gently, about my English, which they said was straight from the King James' version of the Bible, spoken with a Scottish accent. Jean Freeman began to introduce me to English literature by giving me the novels of Anthony Trollope and Jane Austen, and later the works of Lord Byron, to read. Our extended families are friends to this day.

Harold Wilke was the ecumenical advisor of the United Church of Christ. Together we developed the international exchange programme. He was one of the most impressive people I have ever met. Born without arms, he led his life as if his disability had not existed. After the thalidomide scandal he advised governments all over the world on the necessary support for those who had been affected

My friendship with Bonhoeffer's friend Eberhard Bethge and his wife Renate taught me to appreciate how vital personal friendships are in the life of the Church. I would like to include in my dedication all those who have made my life richer with their friendship.

Ferdinand Schlingensiepen
Spring 2009

Translator's Preface

This English translation of Ferdinand Schlingensiepen's biography of Dietrich Bonhoeffer is appearing over sixty years after Bonhoeffer's death at the end of the Second World War. Yet there is more interest than ever in Bonhoeffer and in early twentieth-century German history. The fall of the Berlin Wall 20 years ago made available a great deal of archive material previously inaccessible from the West, and a new generation of historians is at work. There is even a new Hollywood version, *Valkyrie*, of the last attempt at a military coup against Hitler.

A noteworthy contribution to these studies is being made by the Bonhoeffer Society's *Dietrich Bonhoeffer Works in English* (DBWE), published by Fortress Press, translating the German scholarly edition of Bonhoeffer's complete works, *Dietrich Bonhoeffer Werke* (DBW), published by Kaiser Verlag. Dr Schlingensiepen quotes generously from the DBW volumes, and from many other sources, so that general readers as well as scholars can hear Bonhoeffer and his contemporaries speaking in their own words. The challenge for the translator has been to track these quotations in DBWE or DBW and cite them clearly.

Volumes 1–10, 13 and 16 of the DBWE have already been published. Quotations from these volumes are cited in parentheses as follows: (DBWE vol. no., page nos.). For two of the forthcoming volumes, DBWE 8 and 12, final texts exist, and these have been kindly made available to the translator by Victoria Barnett, DBWE series editor; they have been cited as follows: (DBWE vol. no., section no./document no.). Texts from the remaining volumes 11, 14 and 15 could not be quoted from DBWE, and have therefore been translated provisionally from the DBW originals and cited as follows: (DBW vol. no., page nos.) See the complete DBWE series list, including forthcoming volumes, on pp. xxv–xxvii.

The numerous quotations from *Dietrich Bonhoeffer: A Biography* by Eberhard Bethge, in the English version of 2000, revised and edited by Victoria J. Barnett, Minneapolis: Fortress Press, are cited as (DB-ER page no.).

For quotations from other works which do not exist in English translation, of which English titles are given only in brackets in the endnotes,

English versions have been provided by this translator. In these cases, page numbers cited are those of the German original.

Biblical texts are quoted from the New Revised Standard Version, Anglicized edition (Oxford, 1995) except as indicated, or as used in a translation quoted from another work.

In translation from German to English, often no precise equivalents can be found for names of church governing bodies and titles of officials. *Oberkirchenrat* can be either a high-level council or the title of a member of such a council. A consistory can be the council with its administrative office at either national or regional level. Germans tend to think more hierarchically, express more respect for authority, and thus organize things differently from the style of most American churches. They also have a previous history of the churches of the Reformation (Lutheran, Reformed, United) being under government protection, and the laws that since the nineteenth century have guaranteed the rights of the churches were a major issue under the Nazi state.

The same lack of exact equivalents in English pertains to military ranks and commands. A *Generaloberst* such as Ludwig Beck, for example, is something like a four-star general and can be in command over many generals of lower rank. Field marshal is the highest rank, as in Britain. Hitler's military organization was confusing, and he often fiddled with it to keep it that way and guarantee his own power to micro-manage anything he wished.

The word 'minister' has been used for the head of a department in the national government, or in a provincial government, so Christian parish ministers are here called 'pastors', the usual Lutheran term in any case. 'Ordinands' are candidates for ordination in the final stage of their preparation as parish pastors.

The 'Chancellor' is, to this day, the 'Prime Minister' of the German national government.

Besides the Notes, Chronology, Bonhoeffer family tree and Index, five complete texts in English translation have been included in the Appendix. The most famous statement made by the Confessing Church of Germany under the Hitler regime is the Theological Declaration of Barmen. It was the basis for the resolutions made at Dahlem to organize the Confessing Church, which Bonhoeffer upheld and for which he struggled, as a 'Dahlemite', with friends and opponents. To this day, the Barmen Declaration is reprinted in hymnals of the German Evangelical Church, so that the witness of the Confessing Church may be easily at hand and may not be forgotten. The translation here is that of Arthur C. Cochrane, in his book *The Church's Confession under Hitler* (Philadelphia: Westminster, 1962).

Another text which German Protestants have in their hymnals is Bonhoeffer's last poem, written in prison at the end of 1944 for his fiancée, family and friends: 'By Powers of Good', here translated by Nancy Lukens. The 'Poems for Prisoners', which Bonhoeffer also wrote in prison, were duplicated and distributed by the prison chaplains as part of their ministry to the inmates of Tegel military prison, many of whom were condemned to death and executed. The translations here are by Lisa E. Dahill. All other translations of Bonhoeffer's poems quoted in this book are by Nancy Lukens. These English versions of the poems are all found in DBWE 8, *Letters and Papers from Prison*.

I would like to thank Victoria Barnett of the Bonhoeffer Society in the USA; Augsburg Fortress Press, Minneapolis; Andover Harvard Theological Library and Widener Library at Harvard College, both in Cambridge, Massachusetts, for their help with access to the Dietrich Bonhoeffer Works in English and other necessary texts.

Warm thanks also to the author, Dr Ferdinand Schlingensiepen, for his patient and genial accompaniment of my work; to our publisher, Thomas Kraft, at T&T Clark/Continuum Books, London; and for expert assistance, collegial counsel and support, to Clifford Green of the Bonhoeffer Society as well as Victoria Barnett, Nancy Lukens and my husband, Tom Best.

This is an important book for the peoples of Britain and the United States, especially in the churches. As Germany's opponents in the Second World War, it is good for us to know more about the courageous Germans who resisted the Nazi state from within – not only the martyrs and heroes such as Bonhoeffer, but the colleagues, church leaders, friends and families who helped. May our remembering them help to keep our peoples together in friendship, not least of all those of us who belong to the worldwide Church.

Isabel Best
Belmont, Massachusetts
Lent 2009

Dietrich Bonhoeffer Works in English (DBWE) Series List

Dietrich Bonhoeffer Works, English edition (DBWE). Victoria J. Barnett, Wayne Whitson Floyd, Jr and Barbara Wojhoski (general editors). Published by Fortress Press, Minneapolis.

A translation from the German of *Dietrich Bonhoeffer Werke* (DBW), edited by Eberhard Bethge, Ernst Feil, Christian Gremmels, Wolfgang Huber, Hans Pfeifer, Albrecht Schönherr, Heinz Eduard Tödt and Ilse Tödt (Gütersloh: Chr. Kaiser Verlag, 1996–).

Vol. 1 – *Sanctorum Communio: A Theological Study of the Sociology of the Church*; translated from *Sanctorum Communio* (German) ed. Joachim von Soosten; English edition edited by Clifford J. Green; translated by Reinhard Krauß and Nancy Lukens, 1998.

Vol. 2 – *Act and Being: Transcendental Philosophy and Ontology in Systematic Theology*; translated from *Akt und Sein*, ed. Hans-Richard Reuter. English edition edited by Wayne Whitson Floyd, Jr; translated by H. Martin Rumscheidt, 1996.

Vol. 3 – *Creation and Fall: A Theological Exposition of Genesis 1–3*; translated from *Schöpfung und Fall*, ed. Martin Rüter and Ilse Tödt; English edition edited by John W. de Gruchy; translated by Douglas Stephen Bax, 1997.

Vol. 4 – *Discipleship*; translated from *Nachfolge*, ed. Martin Kuske and Ilse Tödt; English edition edited by Geffrey B. Kelly and John D. Godsey; translated by Barbara Green and Reinhard Krauß, 2001.

Vol. 5 – *Life Together / Prayerbook of the Bible*; translated from *Gemeinsames Leben / Das Gebetbuch der Bibel*, ed. Gerhard Ludwig Müller and Albrecht Schönherr; English edition edited by Geffrey B. Kelly; translated by Daniel W. Bloesch and James H. Burtness, 1996.

Vol. 6 – *Ethics*; translated from *Ethik*, ed. Ilse Tödt *et al.*; English edition edited by Clifford J. Green; translated by Reinhard Krauß, Charles C. West and Douglas W. Stott, 2005.

Vol. 7 – *Fiction from Tegel Prison*; translated from *Fragmente aus Tegel*, ed.

Renate Bethge and Ilse Tödt; English edition edited by Clifford J. Green; translated by Nancy Lukens, 1999.

Vol. 8 – *Letters and Papers from Prison;* translated from *Widerstand und Ergebung,* ed. Christian Gremmels, Eberhard Bethge and Renate Bethge with Ilse Tödt; English edition edited by John W. de Gruchy; translated by Isabel Best, Lisa E. Dahill, Reinhard Krauß, Nancy Lukens and Martin Rumscheidt, forthcoming.

Vol. 9 – *The Young Bonhoeffer, 1918–1927;* translated from *Jugend und Studium, 1918–1927,* ed. Hans Pfeifer with Clifford J. Green and Carl-Jürgen Kaltenborn; English edition edited by Paul Duane Matheny, Clifford J. Green and Marshall D. Johnson; translated by Mary C. Nebelsick with Douglas W. Stott, 2003.

Vol. 10 – *Barcelona, Berlin, New York, 1928–1931;* translated from *Barcelona, Berlin, Amerika 1928–1931,* ed. Reinhart Staats and Hans Christoph von Hase with Holger Roggelin and Matthias Wünsche; English edition edited by Clifford J. Green; translated by Douglas W. Stott, 2008.

Vol. 11 – *Ecumenical, Academic and Pastoral Work 1931–1932,* translated from *Ökumene, Universität, Pfarramt 1931–1932,* ed. Eberhard Amelung and Christoph Strohm, English edition edited by Michael B. Lukens and Mark S. Brocker, translated by Nick Humphrey, Marion Pauck and Anne Schmitt-Lange, forthcoming.

Vol. 12 – *Berlin 1933,* translated from *Berlin 1933,* ed. Carsten Nicolaisen and Ernst-Albert Scharffenorth; English edition edited by by Larry Rasmussen, translated by Isabel Best and David Higgins, forthcoming.

Vol. 13 – *London, 1933–1935;* translated from *London, 1933–1935,* ed. Hans Goedeking, Martin Heimbucher and Hans-Walter Schleicher; English edition edited by Keith Clements, translated by Isabel Best and Douglas W. Stott, 2007.

Vol. 14 – *Theological Education at Finkenwalde 1935–1937;* translated from *Illegale Theologenausbildung: Finkenwalde 1935–1937,* ed. Otto Dudzus and Jürgen Henkys with Sabine Bobert-Stützel, Dirk Schulz and Ilse Tödt; English edition edited by Gaylon Barker and Stephen Plant, translated by Douglas W. Stott, forthcoming.

Vol. 15 – *Theological Education Underground 1937–1940,* translated from *Illegale Theologenausbildung: Sammelvikariate 1937–1940,* ed. Dirk Schulz; English edition edited by Victoria J. Barnett, translated by Victoria J. Barnett, Scott and Claudia Bergmann-Moore, and Peter Frick, forthcoming.

Vol. 16 – *Conspiracy and Imprisonment, 1940–1945;* translated from *Konspiration und Haft 1940–1945,* edited by Jørgen Glenthøj, Ulrich Kabitz and Wolf Krötke; English edition edited by Mark S. Brocker; translated by Lisa E. Dahill and Douglas W. Stott, 2006.

1. Ancestors, Childhood and Youth

Dietrich Bonhoeffer's life was bounded by the two world wars of the twentieth century. On 4 February 1906 – a few years before the First World War – he and his twin sister were born in Breslau, Silesia, then part of Germany, now in Poland. On 9 April 1945, a few days before the end of the Second World War, he was put to death, on Hitler's orders, in Flossenbürg, Germany.

At Dietrich Bonhoeffer's birth, Germany was an empire. He remembered this clearly, especially since the family moved to Berlin, the capital, in 1912. What war means entered, like nothing else, into his awareness with the death of his second-eldest brother Walter, in 1918, after being wounded in battle. His mother's grief over the death of this son was among Dietrich's most vivid childhood memories.

During his formative years at school and university, Germany was a republic which was increasingly bitterly resented by a majority of the population, though not in Bonhoeffer's parents' home or by the people who visited there. Thus to have a different political opinion from that of the majority was nothing unusual to him. He was at university during a time of political controversy. A year in Spain and another in the USA widened his view of the world, including his view of Germany. There then followed his first work experiences as a university lecturer and as a pastor, before Hitler came to power, bringing the dictatorship which was to last 12 years and during which Dietrich Bonhoeffer became a convincing witness for the 'other Germany'.

Ancestors

'After all, everyone's got a family tree,' Bonhoeffer said to colleagues in London when researching one's ancestors became fashionable in Germany.[1] For the Bonhoeffers it was taboo to talk about one's ancestors or put on airs about them. But on one occasion an interesting exception was made. When the Gestapo informed Dietrich Bonhoeffer, on 9 September 1940, that the SS's Reich Headquarters had banned him from speaking publicly anywhere in the Reich, he protested vigorously to the dreaded SS:

The reason for this ban is stated as 'activity subverting the people'. I reject this charge. My entire outlook, my work as well as my background, make it inconceivable for me to allow myself to be identified with groups warranting the stigma of such a charge. I am proud to belong to a family that has rendered outstanding service to the German people and nation for generations. Among my ancestors are Field Marshal Count Kalckreuth[2] and the two great German artists of the same name, the Jena church historian Karl von Hase, renowned in the entire scholarly world of the past century, and the Cauer family of sculptors; my uncle is Major General Count von der Goltz, who liberated the Baltic lands; his son, the state attorney Count Rüdiger von der Goltz, is my first cousin; Major General von Hase, currently on active military duty, is my uncle. My father has been a full university professor of medicine in Berlin for nearly thirty years and serves to the present day in distinguished public offices; his ancestors lived for centuries as highly esteemed craftsmen and councillors of the then Imperial City of Schwäbisch Hall, and even today our pictures hang proudly in the city's main church. My brothers and brothers-in-law serve in high government positions, and one of my brothers was killed in the First World War. It has been the aspiration of these men and their families to serve the German nation and people at all times and to risk their lives in this service. In conscious affirmation of this spiritual legacy and moral position of my family, I cannot accept the charge of 'activity subverting the people'. (DBWE 16, 75)

Thus we get to hear today, courtesy of the SS Headquarters, something about his ancestors from Dietrich Bonhoeffer himself.

An upper middle-class family

The sort of family in which Dietrich Bonhoeffer grew up is hard to imagine for all but a very few people today. Karl Bonhoeffer, about whose ancestors we have already heard a little, was from Württemberg in southwest Germany and a professor of psychiatry in Breslau and from 1912 onwards in Berlin; his wife Paula, née von Hase, came from a pastor's family. Her father had been chaplain in the court of Emperor Wilhelm II in Potsdam, but had asked to be discharged after two years. The family knew of two reasons which could have led to this: he had resisted the inclination of Wilhelm II to do his own preaching, and had dared to contradict the Emperor when he referred to the proletariat as a 'rabble'. After leaving his post, Karl von Hase became a church official, as a member of the consistory of the church province of Silesia, and an honorary professor in the theology faculty of the University of Breslau. His wife Clara, who had been born Countess Kalkreuth, made her home a meeting-place for scholars and artists. A junior doctor named Karl Bonhoeffer turned up there one day, and said later that on seeing Paula von Hase for the first time he knew immediately that he would marry her. It is said of Bonhoeffer's parents that on their golden wedding anniversary they counted up all the days they had been apart during 50 years of marriage, and it didn't even amount to one month.

The upper middle-class Bonhoeffer household employed five servants, and was later joined by a chauffeur. Even in those days this was unusually grand; but the mother spent a great deal of time with her eight children. She was a trained teacher and gave the older five children their first schooling herself, along with some of the neighbours' children. In her view, if at all possible, one should not turn one's children over to strangers during their early years, which are so important for the development of imagination and character. The Bonhoeffer family agreed with the saying that German boys 'had their backs broken' twice in life; first in school and then in the military. At the end of each school year, Paula Bonhoeffer's pupils did brilliantly in the state examinations, and were even able to skip years of school. Like his brothers and sisters, Dietrich took his *Abitur* (school-leaving exam) early. The best way to get a picture of this large family – which included Grandmother Bonhoeffer – is to look through the family album, in which many interesting photos are preserved.

'True Berliners come from Silesia,' people used to say, and this applies to Dietrich Bonhoeffer. He remembered Breslau (now Wroclaw in Poland), the city of his birth, as a paradise for children. The family lived in the suburb of Scheitnig, where his father was director of a psychiatric clinic, in a villa built in the 1870s, during the foundational period of modern industrial Germany. This house is now a guesthouse, and bears a plaque stating that Bonhoeffer lived there between the ages of three and six. The big garden was ideal for children to play in, and the house had, in addition to bedrooms and living room, a schoolroom where the mother taught the older children, a room for doing crafts and handiwork and, to the horror of the servants, also a room where live snakes, lizards, squirrels and pigeons were kept, and where a collection of bugs and butterflies was on display. This children's paradise also included a holiday house in Wölfelsgrund, where the children could have their father, too, all to themselves.

Family photo on the occasion of Karl Bonhoeffer's 75th birthday, 31 March 1943. Seated in front, left to right: Karl-Friedrich Bonhoeffer, Paula Bonhoeffer holding Walter Bonhoeffer, Karl Bonhoeffer holding Andreas Dress, Ursula Schleicher. Standing, first row, left to right: Dietrich Bonhoeffer, Christine von Dohnanyi, Christoph von Dohnanyi, Friedrich Bonhoeffer, Christine Schleicher, Susanne Dress with Cornelie Bonhoeffer in front, Barbara von Dohnanyi, Michael Dress in front, Dorothee Schleicher, Klaus von Dohnanyi, Thomas Bonhoeffer in front, Rüdiger Schleicher, Emmi Bonhoeffer, Klaus Bonhoeffer, Walter Dress. Back at left, Eberhard Bethge; to the left of the door, Jürg Zutt with his wife; in front of the right door-jamb, Hans Gerhard Creutzfeld and Ferdinand Sauerbruch; further right Maria Czeppan and Friedrich Justus Perels

For Dietrich Bonhoeffer, his family was the centre of his life, to which he returned again and again. In the above photograph we see him (far left) at his father's 75th birthday celebration. Not all of the Bonhoeffer parents' 18 grandchildren are to be seen here, but there are friends offering congratulations, such as Ferdinand Sauerbruch, then the most famous surgeon in Germany (back row, third from right). It is a photo which could illustrate an essay on the patriarchy of a bygone era. But if one knows the family history, this image of a big, happy gathering already foreshadows something quite different. Five days after the picture was taken, three members of the family, Hans and Christine von Dohnanyi and Dietrich Bonhoeffer, were arrested. Four family members were murdered, on Hitler's orders, shortly before the end of the war: Rüdiger Schleicher, Hans von Dohnanyi, and Klaus and Dietrich Bonhoeffer. The parents' faces, in the photograph taken little more than two years later, are deeply marked by their experiences.

But let us turn back to the early pages. The albums of almost all such large families of the time have photographs such as the one on the next page, when the Bonhoeffers were still leading a happy and carefree life in Breslau.

Eight children in ten years was not at all the rule even then. Karl Bonhoeffer wrote in 1909:

Dietrich Bonhoeffer's parents after the war

In spite of having eight children, which surprises many people at the present time, we do not have the feeling that it is too many. The house is spacious, the children have developed normally, we parents are not too old, and we try not to spoil them but to give them a happy childhood. (DB-ER 16)

The eldest was Karl-Friedrich (1899–1957). He was to become professor of physical chemistry at the early age of 31. Dietrich was particularly attached to him, and – as their lively correspondence showed – respected him all his life as the eldest brother. Walter (1899–1918), the second son, seems to have been his mother's favourite. The further history of this big family reveals that Dietrich, the youngest son, later occupied the place of this second-eldest brother in her affections. For many years, parents, brothers and sisters mourned Walter, who had died so prematurely, and began each year's Christmas celebration with a visit to his grave. Klaus (1901–1945) became a lawyer. His father found him 'the most difficult but also the most amusing and intelligent' of his children (DB-ER 18).

The three eldest sons were followed by two daughters, very different from one another. Ursula (1902–1983) took the part of 'mother' to the other children when they were on their own. She was warmhearted and had a strong sense of duty. In a novel that Bonhoeffer was trying to write while in Tegel Prison, he included a loving portrayal of this sister with whom he shared a deeply trusting relationship. The next younger sister, Christine (1903–1965) was altogether different; lively, intellectually curious and critical, she enjoyed outshining her schoolmates and fellow

Bonhoeffer's parents and their children

students. For Sabine (1906–1999) and Susanne (1909–1991), Dietrich was the 'big brother' who was fond of pointing out, as a child, that he was 10 minutes older than his twin sister. But both younger sisters said of him later that, from early on, he was their knight in shining armour who protected them, so they were happy to let him play the role of older brother.

In the picture, Dietrich with his chin in his hands, looks somewhat subdued, as if it wasn't that easy to have five older brothers and sisters

Dietrich at the age of 11

as well as his parents in authority over him. It was not easy, and would take a long time, for him to find his role in the family. There were always 'the older ones' who were already so far ahead of him, and could therefore attract their parents' attention in ways not yet open to 'the little ones'. And it is very possible for younger children in such a large family just to run along with the rest, and to develop feelings of loneliness without the parents suspecting it. The memoirs of Bonhoeffer's youngest sister Susanne

The Bonhoeffer home in Berlin-Grunewald, Wangenheimstraße 14 and the holiday home in Friedrichsbrunn/Harz

illustrate this very well.[3] In a 'New Year's Eve Journal' kept by their father to record the family history, the entry for 1911 says: 'The twins this year are not yet in school, both however want to be useful around the house and Dietrich is an avid learner. Hopefully this will remain so' (DB-ER 19). References to the younger children became shorter and shorter. Four years later, there is this brief entry: 'Dietrich does his work independently and tidily. He likes fighting, and does a great deal of it' (DB-ER 24).

If Bonhoeffer himself said later that he was terribly ambitious (DB-ER 204), this must have something to do with his role as sixth child and youngest son. It is a role against which one can rebel, but which nonetheless continues to be defining; one can catch up with the older ones in one area or another, but this will never happen without ambition. So, for example, Dietrich was astonishingly quick to take over from his eldest brother as accompanist on the piano. His sisters and mother enjoyed singing the songs of the Romantic period. At the age of 12, Dietrich was already playing Mozart sonatas, and not long afterwards he would take the leading role in musical evenings at home. When the siblings and their friends went hiking, he took his guitar along.

One of the most important persons in Bonhoeffer's life was, from his

The much beloved grandmother Julie Bonhoeffer

early childhood, his grandmother in Tübingen, Julie Bonhoeffer, née Tafel. She was politically alert, had been interested in women's issues from early on, and like his parents set an example for making one's own decisions as to what is right and what one should do. When, on 1 April 1933, the Nazis declared an official boycott of Jewish businesses, this 91-year-old lady went shopping at the leading department store in Berlin, the *'Kaufhaus des Westens'*, walking through the cordon of SA men in front of it to demonstrate against this injustice. She had moved to Berlin with her housekeeper in 1925, occupying a couple of rooms in the Bonhoeffers' house, where the

Dietrich Bonhoeffer with his guitar

grandchildren loved to be invited to tea. Since she was a great reader, they could also discuss the latest works of literature with her, for example those of Thomas Mann.[4]

At a commemoration of Bonhoeffer in Geneva, Switzerland in 1976, Carl Friedrich von Weizsäcker, the well-known physicist and philosopher, said of him:

Dietrich Bonhoeffer was one of those *homines religiosi* who make the decision to offer themselves to the service of God early in childhood, in a way that escapes the observation of their fellows. Certainly there were theological precursors in that cultivated, liberal, upper middle-class family; in its well-ordered but free family life, evening prayers with the children were still customary although Sunday church-going was no longer the practice … A child can, without detriment to his natural development as a child, have a silent and intensive life with God in which the environment only provides him with the culturally distinctive patterns in which he can interpret and cultivate this inner experience. Some such experience, begun in childhood and probably never fully disclosed to another human soul was, it seems to me, the vital spring of Dietrich Bonhoeffer's entire life right until his death.[5]

However, the youngest sister's memoirs show that the 'three little ones' had a sort of religious community amongst themselves from an early age, of which the rest of the family apparently were hardly aware. Their nanny, Maria Horn, affectionately known as 'Hörnchen' to the whole family, may have had something to do with this. She was considered a member of the family, was respected by all in her Moravian piety,[6] and for the twins and especially for Susanne was an important influence in their upbringing. 'She was teased a lot, and loved even more.'

In their make-believe games, the three youngest were 'always poor people, never kings or counts or fairies'. A special favourite was the 'criminal who is converted'. At bedtime they prayed together and agreed to 'think about "forever"', the last word of the Lord's Prayer. Dietrich had a phase in which he imagined himself dying in faith, and everyone mourning for him. But when Susanne had similar imaginings a few years later, he said to her, 'You'd just love that, wouldn't you, to lie in a box and do nothing all day. Life is pretty hard, but it gets better with practice.'

Their summer house in the Harz Mountains, which their parents had bought in place of the house in Wölfelsgrund, played a large part in the lives of all the Bonhoeffer children. It was the setting for the loveliest memories which Susanne Dress relates, for example how they came to know the family that looked after the house when none of them were there. Mother Bonhoeffer had told her daughter Susanne that she could celebrate her seventh birthday in Friedrichsbrunn and invite whomever she liked. In the end there were 57 children. It was 1916 and wartime, but the whole family helped to make it a day glowing with happiness. It ended with a procession with paper lanterns, then the parents came to collect the young guests, but five children were left. Paula Bonhoeffer took them home herself, and found Mr and Mrs S. arm in arm in front of a shack. They had not come to fetch their children because they were too poorly dressed. They were considered 'outsiders' because they came from another village, 10 kilometres away, and had no work and no money.

By the time she got home, my mother already had a plan. We could clear out the big washhouse … My big brothers didn't really need a workshop in there any more. By adding one interior wall we could make it two rooms plus kitchen, and would have people on the property who looked out for the curtains when we weren't there … As usual, Father was content with this.

The curtains and other things had been stolen in previous winters. But the S. family didn't steal anything, they simply 'borrowed'. He was a carpenter and probably also a locksmith. No matter how tightly we closed the shutters, or put safety locks on the doors, he could always get in during our absence … When we arrived, we would simply go and say, 'May I please have the big zinc tub and the white bucket, the grater and the big kettle, that you borrowed,' and we got it all back.

Not even when mattresses were borrowed and came back full of fleas did this disturb the Bonhoeffers' relations with the S. family, which by then had nine children. 'We loved them in spite of everything. They worked hard and didn't really have any vices, just never enough money.'

In the shadow of the Great War

The twins were taught by Käthe Horn, sister of 'Hörnchen', for their first year of school. After that Dietrich was sent, like his brothers, to the Friedrich Werder Gymnasium (college preparatory school) in Berlin, which also had a primary school. All the way through to his school-leaving examinations, he never found schoolwork very demanding.

The event which loomed over his early school years was the beginning of the First World War. Although his parents did not share in the enthusiasm for the war that was initially widespread among the population, eight-year-old Dietrich followed the early successes of the German troops with childish patriotism. His older brothers showed him how to mark the progress of the fronts from day to day on a map with coloured pins. From 1916 onwards, when it became harder to supply the population with food, he developed unexpected talents. His older brothers strictly refused to eat black market bread or meat, but Dietrich became, as his father noted in the 'New Year's Eve' book, the family's 'messenger and food scout' (DB-ER 26). For his mother, to whom it was more important that her patriotic sons be adequately nourished, he found out where things were available and soon knew all the black market prices. These activities of his were kept secret from his older brothers.

It was in these years that Dietrich became an expert on wild mushrooms. During holidays in Friedrichsbrunn one could gather mushrooms to one's heart's content, dry them and take them back to Berlin along with the berries which had been picked and made into jam. When Dietrich spent holidays with his cousin Hans Christoph von Hase, he gleaned ears of grain in the fields, had them milled and brought a sackful of flour home with him. That others were not so fortunate was something he always confronted anew on the way to school, and spoke of later in the United States.

The number of the suicides increased in a terrifying way. I remember very well, I had on the way to my school to pass by a bridge and in the winters from 1917 to 1919 almost every morning when I came to this bridge I saw a group of people standing on the river and everybody, who passed by, knew what had happened. These impressions were hard for young boys. (DBWE 10, 414, original in English)

None of this detracted from Bonhoeffer's school career; it was taken for granted that he was one of the best pupils. But it soon became evident that his interests were different from those of his scientifically inclined brothers. He liked to read 'exciting books', and developed very early a love of German literature. At 14 he read Theodor Fontane's *Der Stechlin* and was enthralled by its 'brilliantly portrayed' characters (DBWE 9, 36).

In March 1916 the Bonhoeffers moved to a large one-family house in Grunewald, not far from the Halensee city railway station. Towards the end of his rule, Bismarck, the nineteenth-century first Chancellor of the German empire, gave over the northern part of the state-owned forest between Berlin and the imperial city of Potsdam for the development of an exclusive residential district. Well-to do merchants built fine houses there and scholars and artists found properties to rent. The prominent publisher Samuel Fischer lived there, as did theologian Adolf von Harnack and his brother-in-law, the historian Hans Delbrück. The Bonhoeffers could hardly have found more stimulating surroundings in Berlin. But in 1916 it was the garden that attracted them most, where one could grow vegetables and even keep a goat to provide the family with milk. In the holidays the goat was taken along to Friedrichsbrunn on the train.

As clever as he was at helping to provide for the family, Dietrich was still a normal 10-year-old, as a letter to his cousin Hans Christoph shows. He urges his cousin to write to him, reminding him that he is counting on an invitation for the holidays, without which he can't come, and then what would become of 'our wonderful plans'?

We are building an underground cave and tunnel [in the garden] ... It's there so that in case we fight with Klaus again, we can either bring reinforcements from the cave ... or attack the enemy from behind. We're building a wall in front of the cave and a pit, and a very deep hole. Then when someone falls in, we can drag him into the hole. (DB-ER 28)

The expression 'bring reinforcements' came from reading the news from the front, and his rivalry, at age 10, with his 15-year-old brother Klaus is unmistakable. Karl-Friedrich and Walter were looking forward to joining the real army as soon as possible; it had been a long time since they had taken part in any battles in the garden.

The year 1917 was the one in which, through the entry of the United States into the war, it began to appear likely that Germany would be defeated. Starting with the 'turnip winter' (when there was nothing else but turnips to be had), it became a year of hunger which no one who experienced it could ever forget. Bonhoeffer later described this nationwide hunger to church groups in the United States, when he was studying there on a scholarship. But nobody in Germany wanted to believe that they could lose the war. General Ludendorff, Hindenburg's chief of staff, was the most powerful man in the empire and was then already trying to organize 'total war'. The propaganda left no one in doubt that the Emperor and Germany's just cause would be victorious in the end. During this time Karl-Friedrich and Walter were called up, and after a brief period of training were sent to the front. During an advance on 23 April 1918, Walter, an officer cadet, was severely wounded. On 28 April, three hours before his death in the field hospital, he dictated a last letter to his family:

My technique of not thinking about the pain had to serve here too. But there are more interesting things in the world at present than my wound. Mount Kemmel and its possible consequences, and today's news that Ypres has been taken, give us great cause for hope. I dare not think about my poor regiment, which has suffered so in the last few days, but wonder how it's going for the other officer cadets. Thinking of you with longing, my dears, every minute of the long days and nights. Love from so far away, Walter.

The death of this son was more than Paula Bonhoeffer could bear. For weeks she lay in bed, as if paralysed, in the home of the Schönes next door and was screened off from everyone. The father kept silent and quietly left the room whenever Walter's death was mentioned. For 10 years there were no more entries in his New Year's Eve Journal. Twelve-year-old Dietrich could never forget his mother's wild suffering. Family holidays ceased. The three youngest children were sent to the seashore, on the Baltic, with Maria Horn. His sister Susanne writes that Dietrich's behaviour there was 'rather rude', trying to get over Walter's death. In Boltenhagen they saw two air force pilots, both accompanied by their fiancées, take off in their areoplanes, gain altitude and then collide in mid-air. One of the pilots survived, but had to be stopped from trying to drown himself in the sea. Susanne Dreß, in her memoirs, remembered with admiration that Maria Horn did not gloss over this accident, but rather discussed it quite realistically with the three children. But one evening after their return to Berlin they heard 'Hörnchen' sobbing, and so they learned that the King had abdicated. Klaus had witnessed this as an 18-year-old soldier at General Headquarters. None of the Bonhoeffers shed a tear for King Wilhelm II. To the contrary: Karl-Friedrich, then in the Charité Hospital with less serious wounds, had become a USPD[7] sympathizer. A republic was now proclaimed in Germany.

Bonhoeffer had continued to attend the Friedrich Werder Gymnasium until 1918. Now he transferred to the elite Grunewald Gymnasium, to which he could walk. On his way there he saw some of the street fighting during the 'Spartacus Uprising' (November Revolution), and began to be interested in politics, with youthful excitement. He wrote to his grandmother that suddenly in the middle of the night the family had soldiers billeted with them, an officer with his private, and that they had been able to hear the fighting around Halensee Station.

Karl-Friedrich has been discharged from the Charité. He would like to be part of this somehow, but Mama and Papa are not yet ready to consent. At present, thank heaven, the government troops are getting the better of it. Our holidays have been extended to 17 January. Either because of the unrest or because of the coal shortage.

Dietrich Bonhoeffer at school

Coal was scarce everywhere. During that period the Bonhoeffers heated only two rooms in their house: the kitchen, where conversation was allowed, and a living room, which was kept quiet for study. Like most Germans, Dietrich at 13 was angered by Article 231 of the Treaty of Versailles, which he could still recite from memory years later.

The Allied and Associated Governments affirm and Germany accepts the responsibility of Germany and her allies for causing all the loss and damage to which the Allied and Associated Governments and their nationals have been subjected as a consequence of the war imposed upon them by the aggression of Germany and her allies.

He asked his parents: 'What do you think of the terms of peace? I hardly believe that one can accept them in their present form ... I hope that Ebert will call a general vote, so that he doesn't have to bear the responsibility alone ...' (DBWE 9, 29).

During this time Bonhoeffer joined the Boy Scouts. He wanted to do what his schoolmates were doing for once, instead of always following his brothers. At first he liked it. At ceremonies he was asked to play the piano, and he also enjoyed the sports and field games. But then he must have found that there was a bit too much marching, and when his family bought a collapsible rowing boat he left the Scouts and went along with his brothers and sisters again.

In the spring of 1921, the sum of reparations demanded by the Allies was settled at 132 billion Reichsmarks – in January they had still been saying 269 billion – but this time there was an ultimatum, that the Ruhr industrial region would be occupied if Germany did not accept this demand. Fifteen-year-old Dietrich mentioned this problem in a letter to his grandmother, in which he also asked what people in southern Germany thought about the assassination of the Roman Catholic 'Centre' politician Matthias Erzberger. The following year when Foreign Minister Walther Rathenau was assassinated, not far from Grunewald Gymnasium, Bonhoeffer expressed his opinion very decidedly both in class and in a letter to his twin sister: 'What a pack of right-wing Bolshevik scoundrels! He was murdered merely because he did not appeal to some conceited, idiotic ass. People are responding with crazed excitement and rage here in Berlin. They are having fistfights in the Reichstag' (DBWE 9, 49).

Marion Winter, later Countess Yorck and a member of the Resistance, was in Bonhoeffer's class and hers is one of the few accounts we have of his schooldays. In her memoirs she described her relationship with him.[8] For her, Rathenau's murder represented the shattering of an idyll. She wrote that about half the pupils at the Grunewald school were Jewish, but that religious loyalties played no part in their friendships. Like the Bonhoeffers, she herself had been brought up 'Christian, but not in the church'. Marion Winter's best friend, Ursula Andreae, was a niece of Rathenau. She sat in the same row in the classroom as Bonhoeffer, and Countess Yorck wrote that the three of them formed 'a nice clique'. Marion Winter was invited, with or without her friend, to dinner at the Bonhoeffers' about once a month, and Dietrich dined at their homes about as frequently.

Ursula Andreae, who was Jewish, decided like Bonhoeffer to take Hebrew as an elective subject, and like him she later also studied Protestant theology. Mr Kappus, the teacher of Hebrew, had been a tutor to princes before coming to the Grunewald Gymnasium. That sort of thing counted for something in those days. It was said that he spoke 11 foreign languages.

Going to the theatre together was an important activity for the three friends. For example, they saw Shakespeare's *Richard III* as produced by Leopold Jessner, with Fritz Kortner in the title role; both were famous names in the theatre at the time.

For a young person from an academically inclined upper middle-class family, which was 'Christian, but no longer in the church', to decide to study theology was as rare then as it is nowadays. Carl Friedrich von Weizsäcker thought of Bonhoeffer's father and brothers as 'intellectual exponents of the modern mind', a class of people who 'have moved further and further away from the substance of the Christian faith'.[9] However, it was not typical that the mother gave each of her eight children three years of serious religious instruction. She might well have been pleased, since she was a pastor's daughter, that her son Dietrich wanted a theological career; his father was surprised, and his brothers could be openly scornful. It didn't fit the family image. The children had lots of other opportunities open to them.

Bonhoeffer completed his schooling in March 1923, having been given a solid grounding in the humanities and a thorough familiarity with classical German literature. For his favourite teacher, Walther Kranz, an outstanding scholar of classical antiquity, he voluntarily wrote an essay on 'Catullus and Horace as Lyrical Poets'. He passed his *Abitur*, the school-leaving exam required for university entrance, with the top grade of 'very good'. Only his handwriting was considered 'unsatisfactory' by his teachers. He had just turned 17 a month before.

We have already spoken of the 'religious community' which the three youngest Bonhoeffer children had amongst themselves. The youngest sister has written of being deeply impressed by the celebration of the Lord's Supper following her confirmation. When she wanted to attend another communion service not long afterwards, her mother said, 'one doesn't go that often'. But when she asked Dietrich whether the Lord's Supper was something special, he said 'It is for me. I'm glad to be invited where someone is glad to have me.' After that, the brother and sister often went to church together.

Susanne loved to have Dietrich along as her protector when she wanted to go out. She had a friend, Bärbel Damaschke, who lived in Werder, near Potsdam. When Dietrich went there with her, Bärbel's father, a well-known commentator on public affairs and an early advocate of land reform, took them sailing and asked Dietrich to sit in the bow and sing with his guitar. Susanne Dreß writes, 'I can still see the tears in the eyes of that old, bearded campaigner when Dietrich sang: "Beaten, we head for home tonight. Our grandchildren will put up a better fight."'

The funniest story the youngest sister tells is another one about 'Hörnchen'. Maria Horn became engaged to a teacher, Dr Czeppan, whom Dietrich especially liked because he went bicycling with him and to the theatre. The Bonhoeffers held the wedding festivities for the couple just as they did later for their own children. But afterwards, an intensive search in which everyone joined couldn't come up with a place for them to live. Mrs Schöne next door had three spare rooms, but even the pleas of Mother Bonhoeffer couldn't persuade her to give them up. So Dietrich rang up Mrs Schöne, disguising his voice: 'This is the Grunewald Housing Office', and told her that tenants were being sent to her the next morning, since she still had three unoccupied rooms. 'Less than half an hour later, she came over and entreated us to get Hörnchen and her husband to move in with her, so she wouldn't have to let total strangers in.'

2.   University Studies (1923–1929)

From Protestant Tübingen to Catholic Rome

As Dietrich Bonhoeffer was beginning his study of theology, his father received the proceeds of a life insurance policy which had matured. That evening he brought home a small basket of strawberries; that was all it would buy. Inflation was about to reach its peak in Germany. If Karl Bonhoeffer had not had foreign patients who paid him in their own currencies, he would not have been able to keep four of his children at university at the same time. As it was, Dietrich enrolled at the University of Tübingen like his father and brothers before him. To save money, he made his way to Tübingen from Berlin by taking the cheapest seats on local train lines. Before the end of his first semester, a meal in the *Mensa*, the student dining hall, cost a billion Reichsmarks. But in October 1923, Treasury Secretary Helfferich instituted a currency reform, which stabilized the situation overnight. This meant that Bonhoeffer could have a second semester in the southern German city. His father wanted his children to get to know Württemberg, the home of their ancestors. But none of them adopted the Swabian culture of the region – the influence of their mother and of the Berlin area was too strong.

For the first semester Bonhoeffer found a tiny room such as students rented; for the second, he and his sister Christine, who was studying zoology and had moved from Heidelberg University to Tübingen, both stayed at Grandmother Bonhoeffer's house, which all her grandchildren knew well from holiday visits there. Dietrich doesn't seem even to have noticed that his sister, who in those days was expected to do his laundry and iron his shirts for him, resented the time she spent doing so, being as busy as he with her studies. After some heated quarrels with the owner of the house, a rough character who no longer wanted to have a tenant there, Dietrich recommended to his parents that they move Grandmother to Berlin. He had been especially fond of her since childhood, and enjoyed reading aloud to her, in the evenings, from Goethe's novel *Wilhelm Meister*.

Bonhoeffer's list of courses for the year in Tübingen shows that he devoted himself more to philosophy than to theology, and this was to be important for his later theological career. He attended lectures by Karl Groos in 'Logic' and 'History of Recent Philosophy', as well as a seminar in which Groos introduced students to Kant's *Critique of Pure Reason*. In those days most theology students came to Tübingen to hear Adolf Schlatter, and Bonhoeffer was among those who learned from him how to deal with New Testament texts. Schlatter was Swiss and had a full white beard, and many students from north Germany found it hard to understand his Swiss dialect. But it was close to the Swabian German which Bonhoeffer knew from his father and grandmother, so he didn't have that problem. He used Schlatter's commentaries diligently all his life.

For us today it seems odd that Bonhoeffer – unlike his brothers – joined the student fraternity to which his father and uncle had belonged. He seems never to have felt the need to distance himself from his father, as Karl-Friedrich and Klaus apparently did. Instead, in many ways he as the 'little brother' deliberately differentiated himself from his brothers, and becoming a member of the 'Hedgehogs [*Igel*]' seems to have belonged to this phase of his development. In Tübingen it would have been possible for him to find quite different social contacts and interesting people to talk with. Many people with whom he later worked closely during the church struggle had belonged, while studying in Tübingen, to the German Christian Student Association (DCSV), but Bonhoeffer seems not to have had any interest in it.

The Hedgehog members, from their founding onward, deliberately tried not to be like other students who belonged to fraternities. Instead of the usual student cap with a visor, they wore a sort of knitted grey wool cap with spines, and a grey ribbon instead of one with varicoloured stripes. 'Look at us, we're different,' they seemed to be saying. But that didn't stop them, in 1933, from expelling their Jewish members like the other fraternities. Bonhoeffer thereupon immediately renounced his Hedgehog membership and never mentioned it again.

At the time, however, he enjoyed the amenities of the Hedgehog House with its splendid view of the Neckar River, and since it had a good piano he often played music there with others. In the 1960s an acquaintance from this period remembered being impressed by Bonhoeffer as a theology student interested in philosophy, as a musician and as an agile conversationalist. 'He had a subtle way of teasing and a good sense of humour. He wasn't proud and could take criticism.'[1] Thus his conduct in the Hedgehog fraternity seems to have been much the same as among his brothers and sisters at home.

There was one other episode from Bonhoeffer's student days which seems equally out-of-the-way to us – one that took him and his Tübingen friends to the city of Ulm on the Danube. It can only be understood in the context of the times. In September 1923 Gustav Ritter von Kahr, who still mourned the Empire, became State Commissioner for Bavaria. He took strong measures against leftists, kept contact with Hitler, who was already head of the Nazi Party, and picked quarrels with the Reich government in Berlin. Hitler and General Ludendorff were preparing their attempted coup in Munich which became known as the 'March to the *Feldherrnhalle*'. In the west and north of Germany, on the other hand, there were communist uprisings, including one in Saxony. Separatists on the left bank of the Rhine, under French occupation since the First World War, dreamed of breaking their homeland away from Germany.

The student societies of all the German universities felt it was their duty to call upon their members to come to the rescue of the Reich. Thousands underwent training as volunteers; Bonhoeffer was among those who took a course offered by the Ulm Rifles troop.[2] He asked his parents afterwards for their consent to his having interrupted his semester's work. No one knew whether this training would still be possible after the end of the semester, he told them; the university was full of spies, and an Allied Control Commission was expected to investigate. According to the Treaty of Versailles, Germany only had the right to an army of a hundred thousand, which was not sufficiently equipped to deal with civil war. Thus even democratically minded groups were in favour of such training for students.

From this episode we can see that Bonhoeffer at that time was as conservative and nationalist as the great majority of his fellow students. His brother Karl-Friedrich was already seeing a danger in such undertakings. The reactionary mood among the *Reichswehr* teams in Ulm was not congenial to Dietrich either, but he was pleased to find that he could participate easily in the exercises, some of which were quite strenuous. He found the training personnel to be decent and good-natured. But, once back in Tübingen, he did appreciate sleeping in a bed with sheets and being able to wash in warm water.

On his eighteenth birthday Bonhoeffer found himself strictly confined to his bed. He was an enthusiastic ice skater, and had taken such a spill while skating that he was badly concussed. His worried parents came to see him in Tübingen on their way to Italy, and he told them that he too would like to visit that country. His father said that this could wait, but when Klaus passed his bar exams and asked for a trip to Italy to celebrate, Dietrich was allowed to go with him. Italy had long been a goal for holidays in the family. Great-grandfather Hase had been there 20 times and had a long conversation about Rome with Wolfgang von Goethe when, as Minister to the Grand Duke in Weimar, the famous poet had offered Hase a professorship at the University of Jena. The Bonhoeffer brothers had already been made familiar with Roman antiquity at the Grunewald Gymnasium. By chance they met their former teacher, Walther Kranz, to whom they owed a great deal of this knowledge, on a trip to the top of Mount Vesuvius.

When he crossed the border into Italy, Bonhoeffer knew his Baedeker guidebook 'by heart', and he kept a travel diary. Much of it sounds somewhat effusive, but it also contains very vivid descriptions.

It feels strange when one first crosses the Italian border. Fantasy begins to transform itself into reality. Will it really be nice to have all one's wishes fulfilled? Or might I return home completely disillusioned after all? But the reality is, quite certainly, more beautiful than fantasy. This was demonstrated for the first time in the Bozen rose garden. (DBWE 9, 83)

He enjoyed the liveliness of the southern Europeans, their noise and their kindness. In Bologna the two brothers wandered through the streets at night with two travelling companions. One of them, who was studying to be a Catholic priest, proved later on in Rome to be a well-informed guide. Dietrich was eager to try out his knowledge of the language. He had memorized some Italian from a book at home. 'To my astonishment, it went pretty well.' In Rome, where he was already conversing more boldly, he wrote: 'Our landlord and landlady speak only Italian. I find this very useful, particularly since Klaus doesn't begrudge me the opportunity to speak. He keeps himself in elegant ignorance of the language' (DBWE 9, 87). Bonhoeffer was fascinated with languages all his life. In Rome he was glad that the table of their guesthouse was 'a very Tower of Babel': 'Italians, Russians, Greeks, French, Britons and we Germans'. He noticed that the Russians especially had a good command of numerous languages, while the British usually could speak only their own language, and even the Germans only came next to last in this comparison.

Rome was the city Bonhoeffer loved best on that journey, and it remained so to the last. Even in his letters from prison in 1943–1944 he spoke of it often. He was entranced by the throngs and the noise in the streets, the children playing, the women with their baskets of flowers and the vendors with their carts. 'The later in the day, the louder grows the roar in the streets.' On the other hand, they could sit in the Colosseum, at that time still surrounded by greenery, in complete stillness, or wander in the Roman Forum. He wrote: 'Antiquity is not dead at all, the saying *'Pan ho megas tetheken* [The great Pan is dead]' is not true, that is completely obvious after a few moments ... I went home with the recurrent thought: the great god Pan is not dead (DBWE 9, 83).[3]

While Klaus was most interested in antiquity, it was Catholic Rome with which Dietrich Bonhoeffer became more and more enchanted each day. He kept being drawn back to the Basilica of St Peter. He did note a bit sullenly, 'At the entrance one always gets brought down to earth by some impudent vendor', but that didn't stop him from attending almost all the Holy Week services held in St Peter's.

This morning: Mass from 10 to 12:30 in St. Peter's, celebrated by a cardinal. The most incredible thing was the boys' choir. In some respects they had trained voices like women, as if they were eunuchs. To a marked degree, however, they still had splendidly expressive children's voices. It would be absurd to compare the choir of Berlin Cathedral with them. In the Catholic Church Palm Sunday is infused completely with the expectation of the Passion. The complete Passion story is read as a dialogue between the evangelist, Jesus, Pilate, etc., and the choir. In contrast, at home Palm Sunday is the day of greatest joy, even though the thought of the events that follow Palm Sunday naturally has an effect on the celebration ... In addition to the cardinal, many other important clergymen, seminarians and monks stood at the altar, illustrating the universality of the church in a marvellously effective manner: white, black, yellow – all in clerical robes united under the church. It truly seems ideal ... Well, now I have to go to the Trinità dei Monti to Vespers, sung by the nuns. (DBWE 9, 88)

Of this Vesper service he wrote:

With unbelievable simplicity, grace and great seriousness they sang Evensong ... The impression left by these novices was even greater ... because every trace of routine was missing ... it was worship in the true sense ... It was the first day on which something of the reality of Catholicism began to dawn on me – nothing romantic etc. – but I think I'm beginning to understand the concept of 'church'. (DBWE 9, 89)

He hastened to the Easter services in all the famous churches in Rome, and to a celebration of the Resurrection according to the Armenian rite, which seemed to him 'like an oriental fairy-tale play'; in short, he hardly missed anything. Klaus was urging him that they should travel on to Sicily, just when Dietrich could hardly tear himself away from Rome. The younger brother then described in his diary the crossing to the famous island, not without an ironic side-swipe. After a meagre meal in a grubby *trattoria*, the two of them bought things 'Klaus considered essential to keep us alive during the sea voyage: schnapps [spirits], lemons, chocolate, sardines, oranges; then we went to a restaurant – to have *pasta asciutta* one last time' – and climbed aboard the ship. 'Nothing was of any help for Klaus. After only 4 hours he lay there and had had more than enough; the sea was making great demands on him … It invited me to perform my duty only at the first sight of the magnificent sunny mountainous cliffs' (DBWE 9, 94).

Even in prison 20 years later, Bonhoeffer still remembered the heat in Sicily. He wrote to his friend Eberhard Bethge: 'I remember very well how, in June 1924,[4] I longed to be away from Italy, and could only breathe freely again on a hike in the Black Forest when it rained all day' (DBWE 8, III/170). But at the time this was probably only a passing mood, for the two of them even decided to cross the Mediterranean to Africa. An Italian military officer whom they had met on their journey obtained visas for them. They bought tickets for the 'tween-deck amid a colourful throng of many nationalities and races. It was 'the most delightful travelling company one could imagine', Klaus wrote to his parents (DBWE 9, 113). A man from Stuttgart found them a cheap hotel in Tripoli and guided them around the city. They entered a mosque barefoot, and on an excursion in the surrounding countryside, amid Arabs, blacks and Jews taking their donkeys and camels to drink at the wells, were reminded of scenes from the Old Testament (DBWE 9, 114f). But this side trip was suddenly spoilt by events about which they seem never to have told anyone. They were expelled from the country by the police, a most disagreeable experience. 'One should not spend a longer time in Africa without preparation, the shock is too great and increases from day to day, so that one is glad to return to Europe' (DB-ER 59).

While Klaus started for home again, his brother Dietrich was allowed to stay on in Rome for a few weeks' study. He attended lectures in Rome, but unfortunately we don't know where. He went to museums and was particularly interested in the early Christian art in the Catacombs. He saw the royal family, Mussolini and once even Pope Pius XI, but these were not highlights of his stay. Rome as a whole and St Peter's were the real experience. It was the Catholic atmosphere that attracted him.

The openness of this young Protestant's observations is astounding. One senses already something of his later ecumenical attitude. Things that repelled most Protestants at that time fascinated him, and thus he developed early on an understanding, which stayed with him, for the nature of the Roman Church. Of confession he wrote:

It is gratifying here to see so many serious faces; nothing that you can say against Catholicism applies to them. Even the children confess with a true fervour that is very touching to see. For many of these people confession is no longer a 'must' but has become a necessity ... Also it is not mere pedagogy, but is the only way for primitive people to be able to speak to God. For those people who are religiously astute it is the realisation of the idea of the church that is fulfilled in confession and absolution. (DBWE 9, 89f)

The young man studying for the priesthood whom he had met in Bologna often spent time with him and could explain a great deal. Bonhoeffer's eagerness seems to have led him to suppose he might have a potential convert before him. But when they discussed Kant, they found themselves quarrelling.

Following these discussions, I find I am once again much less sympathetic to Catholicism. Catholic dogma veils every ideal thing in Catholicism, without knowing that this is what it is doing. There is a huge difference between confession and dogmatic teachings about confession, unfortunately also between 'church' and the 'church in dogmatics'. (DBWE 9, 93)

In a letter to his parents we find a thought that is as characteristic of Bonhoeffer as it would have been considered bold on the part of a Protestant theology student in those days:

The unification of Catholicism and Protestantism is probably impossible, although it would do both parties much good. Catholicism will be able to exist for a long time without Protestantism. The people are still very devoted to it. The Protestant church often seems like a small sect compared with the tremendous scale of the ceremonies here. (DBWE 9, 111)

Bonhoeffer couldn't yet know what he had discovered here – which was not only to become the subject of his doctoral thesis, but was to occupy him all his life: the question of the nature of the Church. Four years later in a sermon in Barcelona, he referred directly to what he had learnt in Rome, and this résumé of his Italian experience is worth reading in full:

There is a word that evokes tremendous feelings of love and bliss among Catholics who hear it, a word that stirs in them the most profound depths of religious feeling, from awe and dread of judgement to the sweetness of God's presence, but assuredly also awakens feelings of home for them, feelings that only a child feels for its mother, of gratitude, reverence and self-surrendering love; the feelings that come over us when, after a long time away, we enter our childhood home again.

And there is a word that among Protestants has the sound of something infinitely banal, more or less indifferent and superfluous, that does not make their hearts beat faster; a word we often associate with feelings of boredom, a word that in any event does not lend wings to our religious feelings – and yet a word that will seal our fate if we are unable to find in this word a new or rather the original meaning. Woe to us if that word ... does not soon acquire significance for us again, if it does not indeed become a matter with which our very lives are concerned.

Yes, 'church' is the word whose glory and greatness we want to examine today. (DBWE 10, 505)

When he preached this sermon, he had already written his doctoral thesis on the Church as the *communio sanctorum*, the communion of saints.

Before travelling home again by way of Siena and Tübingen, Bonhoeffer went once more to St Peter's, where on 1 June he heard the great *Te deum*.

I had always hoped to have one more splendid experience in St. Peter's ... But I had not even dreamed it would be like this. The choir sang angelically. The whole congregation sang the antiphon. It made an enormous impression. Once again, at the end of my stay, I saw what Catholicism is, and once again I became truly fond of it. (DBWE 9, 107)

On the last possible date, 16 June 1924, Bonhoeffer registered for the summer semester at the University of Berlin.

Teachers in Berlin

Dietrich Bonhoeffer made his mark very early and unmistakably in theology, even as a young student in Berlin in 1924–1927, because he was pursuing two discoveries which none of his teachers had suggested to him. This gave him the sort of independence, from the professors, to which other students find their way only towards the end of their studies, if ever. At the age of 18 he had come back from Rome with his question concerning the church, so ecclesiology, the doctrine of the church, became the topic that interested him most. In Berlin, during the winter semester of 1924–1925, another topic gained importance for him: Karl Barth's doctrine of revelation, which was increasingly being discussed in Germany, but was being resolutely combated in Berlin.

During the horror of the First World War, Barth had begun rejecting all attempts to adapt Christianity to modern times and to propose any form of it which would have social uses. Instead, he placed the biblical message of Christ, the crucified and risen Son of God, in all its archaic strangeness, squarely in the middle of the theological debate as God's insistent word spoken 'vertically from above'. Bonhoeffer read Barth's lectures and his commentary on the Epistle to the Romans. Even his mother, who had begun reading Ernst Troeltsch, the famous sociologist and church historian, in order to learn about the interests of her son Dietrich, took up Barth's lectures in the autumn of 1924.

More and more students in those days were going to Göttingen because Barth was teaching there. According to Eberhard Bethge (DB-ER 75), typical of such students would be a 'youthful rebel driven or shattered by the postwar crisis', or 'a former pietist rebelling against his upbringing'. But he did not mean this in a derogatory sense, since the postwar generation then at university was seeking orientation in a way that no previous generation had had to do. The fact that Barth was being attacked by most of his colleagues in Germany made him that much more interesting to young people.

Barth had tackled a problem with which whole generations of theologians since the Enlightenment had struggled without finding a solution. This was the question of whether the Bible can still be called the word of God, since both Old and New Testament studies had clearly shown that the Scriptures were written by fallible human beings over the course of centuries. Since this question had been posed by Lessing and others, two views, irreconcilable with one another, had developed in the Church and among theologians. Biblical 'literalists' or 'positivists' said: 'We believe in God more than in scholarship; the Bible is the word of God.' Liberals, on the other hand, could no longer see the Scriptures as a source of revelation, only as a document which had to be interpreted respectfully, but by using the historical-critical method. They found in it a guide to 'genuine morality and love of humanity', but the First World War, with its fallback into barbarism, had thoroughly shattered this conception.

The crisis of the early 1920s cried out for a completely new beginning. Taking as his example the Apostle Paul and his letter to the Christians in Rome, Barth showed that the writers of the Bible were personally affected by the message they were conveying, and that the confession of a Paul, John or Jeremiah as to how deeply they were affected allows one to speak of revelation in a wholly new way. For Barth the Bible texts remain documents from antiquity which may, indeed must, be analysed as such.

At the same time, however, one may recognize in these texts – indirectly – a message from God, which the writers received and are passing on to anyone who is prepared to be affected by it in turn.

We today can no longer easily imagine how liberating and at the same time upsetting this new approach was. Such a teacher could be followed easily and with enthusiasm. To prove it, a sentence could have been quoted here in which Barth reproaches his opponents with 'defusing' the message of the Bible; their method of interpretation was as if they were 'carefully extracting each round of live ammunition from the barrel' of a gun. But this sentence, in which Barth keeps piling one metaphor on top of another, is 33 lines long.[5] His expressionist language, his Swiss accent and his humour, together with his critique of contemporary life and of the Church, enabled him to cast his spell over generation after generation of young theologians.

Of course there were also quite conventional people among Barth's listeners, such as Bonhoeffer's cousin Hans Christoph von Hase, who had gone to Göttingen to study physics but was so impressed with Barth's lectures that he switched to theology. What would have been more natural for Bonhoeffer too, electrified as he was by these new insights, than to go to Göttingen? He doesn't seem even to have considered it. Barth's discoveries fired him with enthusiasm, but he remained centred on his parents' home. He wasn't looking for a master, but rather seeking his own way. He wanted to acquire as much knowledge as possible as quickly as possible, and to show what he could do; for this, his own insights would serve. This is what he meant by saying, many years later as we have already seen, that he was 'very ambitious' (DB-ER 204).

Bonhoeffer soon attracted the notice of his teachers in Berlin as a very promising student, not least that of the most famous of them, the church historian Adolf von Harnack, who was widely known even outside his own field and who, as president of the King Wilhelm Society, was one of the educational policymakers of the time. Harnack was a neighbour in Grunewald and enjoyed travelling with young Bonhoeffer on the city train from Halensee Station to the university. He was already retired but still offered a lecture series and a seminar each semester for selected students, and here Bonhoeffer earned his spurs. To his very first seminar paper, on 'The Jewish Element in First Clement; Its Content and Relationship to the Whole Letter' (DBWE 9, 216), Harnack not only gave the top mark, but handed it back to him with a comment that Bonhoeffer still remembered many years later in prison:

I was eighteen years old, was coming from a Harnack seminar in which he had discussed my first seminar paper very graciously and had expressed the hope I would someday become a church historian; I was still quite full with this when I entered the Philharmonic Hall [to hear Bach's B Minor Mass]; then the great 'Kyrie eleison' began and at that moment everything else sank away completely. (DBWE 8, II/72)

Harnack could see how enraptured Bonhoeffer was with Barth, and this worried him greatly. He himself had certainly made efforts to understand this innovator, but came to the conclusion that scholarly theology would be shipwrecked if it followed Barth. In a polemic against him, Harnack said:

If it is certain that everything unconscious, numinous, everything to do with feeling, fascination etc. is not yet human until it is seized by reason, understood, purified ... how can one find fault with reason or want to eliminate it? ... Is there ... any theology other than the one which is firmly linked, and related by blood, with knowledge itself?

And Barth replied:

If theology regained the courage to be objective, the courage to witness to the word of God's revelation, of God's judgement and love, it could also be the case that 'knowledge itself' would appear to be 'firmly linked and related by blood' with theology, rather than the other way around.[6]

Even as a student, Bonhoeffer wanted to bring together scholarly precision as taught by Harnack with Barth's insights, and this seems to have led to discussions with the master in Harnack's seminar. After the Second World War, one of the other students described this:

I had already noticed Dietrich Bonhoeffer at the very first sessions. Not only that he surpassed almost all of us in theological knowledge and ability, really impressed me, but what stirred me even more and drew me to Bonhoeffer was that here was someone who ... thought for himself and already knew what he wanted, and presumably also wanted what he knew. I actually experienced (and for me it was rather alarming and a tremendous novelty!) seeing the young blond student contradict the revered polyhistorian, His Excellency von Harnack, politely, but certainly on objective theological grounds. Harnack replied, but the student contradicted him again and again. I no longer know the topic of discussion – Karl Barth was mentioned – but I still recall the secret enthusiasm that I felt for this free, critical and independent theological thinking. (DB-ER 67)

Harnack wrestled with Bonhoeffer. He would later write him a letter, in December 1929, in which he said:

Materialism, economics and sports are threatening our intellectual and spiritual existence, and our theological existence is additionally threatened by contempt for academic theology and by unscholarly theologies. Hence, all those loyal to genuine scholarship must hold its banner high all the more confidently, and they must build as kings, yet at the same time not shy away from the drudgery of cart drivers.[7] I am sure that you, dear Mr Bonhoeffer, will always be mindful of that, and I have the utmost confidence in your work and your progress along the right path. I hope you will come to see me often; let me encourage you to do so. (DBWE 10, 196f)

Harnack, as a person and as a scholar, left his stamp on Bonhoeffer and remained an example to him all his life. Another important teacher in Berlin was Karl Holl, who was breathing new life into research on Luther. Here the personal contact was lacking, but from Holl also Bonhoeffer earned an unusually high mark for a seminar paper, and he could, had he wished, have written his doctoral dissertation under Holl. For 150 years in Prussia, Germany's largest principality, Martin Luther had been falsely promoted as the epitome of whatever was considered convincing and good. In Napoleon's time he was seen as the defender against 'the wily French'; in the conventional Biedermeier period he became *the* exemplary husband and father. During the revolution of 1848 he appeared as the pure soldier of faith, who turned his back on any uprising against authority, but in the Franco-Prussian War of 1870, as well as in 1914, he went to war with the troops again. Karl Holl's precise interpretation of Luther's writings was epoch-making and tried to clear away the misuse which the churches of the Reformation had made of him. He had Bonhoeffer write a seminar paper on 'Luther's Feelings about His Work as Expressed in the Final Years of His Life, Based on His Correspondence of 1540–1546' (DBWE 9, 257ff.) This paper is exciting to read even today, and testifies to Bonhoeffer's psychological sensitivity to others.

It is understandable that both church historians, Harnack and Holl, would have liked to see him choose to work in their fields. Three months before Holl's early death – in 1926, shortly after his sixtieth birthday – Bonhoeffer wrote another paper for him on 'Luther's Views of the Holy Spirit, according to the Disputations of 1535–1545' (DBWE 9, 325ff.). The path that Bonhoeffer later pursued is unimaginable without what he learned from Holl about Luther. Both Harnack and Holl would have been glad to supervise doctoral dissertation.

This, however, he was to do under a third teacher in Berlin, the arch conservative Reinhold Seeberg. Like Harnack, Seeberg came from the Baltic States, but politically he belonged to a different camp. Harnack affirmed the republic, while Seeberg, along with the great majority of German theologians, still mourned the passing of the empire. But Seeberg represented Bonhoeffer's preferred field, dogmatics, and it was to be the very field in which Bonhoeffer almost ran aground. He wrote his first two seminar papers in it before he came across the work of Karl Barth. But then he wrote for Seeberg on the topic, 'Can One Distinguish between a Historical and a Pneumatological Interpretation of Scripture, and How does Dogmatics Relate to This Question?' (DBWE 9, 285ff.). Whether Seeberg devised this topic as part of his faculty's fight against the innovator in Göttingen, or whether Bonhoeffer himself proposed it in order to start a discussion in Seeberg's seminar of his latest insight, we do not know. In any case, when he read the paper it left Seeberg speechless.

Bonhoeffer at that time was trying to force a reconciliation between the historical-critical method, as it was taught in Berlin, and Barth's theology of revelation, without yet having any success. 'None of us can return to a pre-critical time' (DBWE 9, 294), but he was equally sure that one cannot get anywhere near the divine revelation by using the critical method, for after the 'total disintregration of the texts, historical criticism leaves the field of battle. Debris and fragments are left behind. Its work is apparently finished' (DBWE 9, 286). Bonhoeffer objects:

God can be understood only from God's spirit. This understanding is then a most remarkable experience, not an a priori one. It is only here that illumination can be achieved, without which all this is *nothing* ... Through this unique understanding, 'inspiration' is received by the believer. Thus the believer comes to understand the category of revelation and uses it as the foundation for all further interpretation. Here we recall Augustine: 'You would not seek me if you had not already found me.' (DBWE 9, 292)

We have from later years very impressive interpretations of biblical texts, especially in Bonhoeffer's sermons, but he never really mastered historical-critical work on ancient documents, and a few times he was justly criticized for this.[8] Seeberg's assistant, who had to mark the paper, seems to have been bewildered by such unscholarly thinking, and made it clear through innumerable short comments in the margins, question marks and passages crossed out. Seeberg agreed entirely and declared the whole thing merely 'adequate', thereby giving Bonhoeffer the lowest grade he had ever received. However, Seeberg found this student undeterred. Bonhoeffer had managed politely to evade Harnack's offer to supervise his doctorate. Barth's lectures he didn't even attend, afraid to let himself come under the spell of a master. Instead, half a year after the seminar paper which he had almost failed, he asked Seeberg to accept him for doctoral supervision, and proposed his own topic: 'Sanctorum Communio: A Dogmatic Enquiry into the Sociology of the Church'.

Bonhoeffer wrote this dissertation in less than two years, during which time he also submitted seven seminar papers, four catecheses and four sermons. And that was not all. Since discovering the Church as his topic, Bonhoeffer also wanted to keep open the possibility of parish ministry, besides that of an academic career. This meant that when he took his First Theological Examination, he would have to demonstrate to the church authorities that he had done 'field work' in a local church. He decided on the children's Sunday school programme at the Grunewald church in which he had been confirmed four years earlier.

Sunday school and family camaraderie

Bonhoeffer had never attended Sunday school as a child himself, since his mother had not wanted to send her children to church for this purpose. Long ago she had served as assistant to her pastor father and had concluded that unsuitable helpers in Sunday school could do a lot of harm. So while her children were small she preferred to show them Schnorr von Carolsfeld's picture Bible and tell them the stories that went with the pictures. Later she gave each of them three years of religious instruction, and that seemed enough to her. Bonhoeffer had thus learned from her how to tell Bible stories.

The assistant pastor of the Grunewald congregation who was in charge of the children's programmes was delighted with his new helper. Bonhoeffer had a definite gift for working with children. His group grew rapidly, and after a time he asked his sister Susanne if she would like to take over a group for girls. The older Sunday school helpers in the church did not want their girls to move to this group, so the boys in Dietrich's group brought their sisters, who invited their own friends, and soon Dietrich and Susanne had each gathered 30 children. When more and more children kept coming, Bonhoeffer persuaded a student to help with the group. The Sunday school helpers met once a week. They took turns being the one to introduce the story for the following Sunday, and then discussed as a group how it should be interpreted for the various age groups. Bonhoeffer really loved this work and did not give it up until 1928, when he went to Barcelona for his year as an assistant pastor.

In the Bonhoeffer family it was unusual to excuse oneself from family activities because of one's own work, and unheard of to complain of having too much work, and for Bonhoeffer musical evenings at home were too important to be missed. He enthusiastically attended concerts of the Berlin Philharmonic and Max Reinhardt's theatrical productions. But what really affected his life and work were the long walks with his brothers and sisters and their friends. Once again, it is Susanne Dreß who tells us:

The lakes, especially the most beautiful, the Müggelsee, were where we all, brothers and sisters, wanted to be on Sundays ... The first train to Erkner, a bit after four in the morning, was not yet full. We had our cooking equipment and food ready the day before, hoping the weather would hold so that we wouldn't have to get up that early for nothing. Rather sleepy-eyed, we all met at Halensee Station – 'all' included the Delbrücks, Dohnanyis, Brandts, Weigerts and ourselves as the core group, along with any friends and relatives anyone had brought along. Usually we filled two compartments on the train. Sometimes someone brought a guitar. We wore *Beiderwand* dresses and our hair in braids, short lederhosen and thick jackets; but we were nothing to do with the *Wandervogel*,[9] or any club, any part of the youth movement. We were a strictly private, arrogant band, and would have found it impossible to be allied with a group. Yet others observing us wouldn't have found us so distinct from the youth movement, even though we were an individualist club. Sunday after Sunday found us out there together, until the engaged couples began breaking away.[10]

The Brandts and the Weigerts were families whose children were friends with the Bonhoeffers during the 1920s.

Bonhoeffer's sister-in-law Emmi, his brother Klaus's wife, remembered that there were different ideals for bringing up children in different homes in the neighbourhood. She reports that when her father, the historian Hans Delbrück, had taken his school-leaving exams, his report card said: 'If he can restrain his impulse to make cheeky judgements, even though they are to the point, he will go far!'

At home, too, he enjoyed our cheeky judgemental remarks when they were to the point, no matter in what relation the judge stood to that which he was judging. This was one of the first differences we noticed between the Bonhoeffer home and ours. The Bonhoeffer children were brought up to be modest above all, and this included the way they expressed themselves. Pathos, pretentious vocabulary and foreign words, if they could be avoided, were taboo.[11]

One development from Bonhoeffer's Sunday school group was that, on outgrowing it, the first group of boy members formed a youth group, meeting on Thursdays at the Bonhoeffers' home on Wangenheimstrasse.

Here they were offered a demanding programme consonant with living in that area of Berlin. Bethge writes that it 'would have done credit to a college' (DB-ER 94), with theological, ethical, denominational, political and cultural topics. Not only Bonhoeffer, but also the participants presented introductory papers at the sessions. A number of very gifted boys from Jewish homes took part in these evenings. They went to operas and concerts together, Bonhoeffer giving them an introduction to Richard Wagner's *Parsifal* before they attended a performance of that work. When he left Berlin, these youngsters wrote to him and sent him their first poems. A young man named Götz Grosch, who later studied theology and during his pastoral assistant year was Bonhoeffer's student at the Finkenwalde seminary during his year as pastoral assistant, carried on with the Thursday group. Almost all the members of the group became victims of the persecutions during the Nazi period, and were killed; Götz Grosch fell as a soldier in the war.

Max Diestel as 'discoverer' of Bonhoeffer

'Christianity entails decision.' With these words began Dietrich Bonhoeffer's first sermon in 1925. One can either be wholly Christian or not at all is what that means. And what decides whether one is or not, is whether one follows up one's confession of faith with appropriate actions, whatever that may cost.

'Decision' was, from then on, one of the keywords in his theology. It may be observed that, according to the old Brockhaus German dictionary, decision-making can involve anxiety and therefore be avoided or put off. Newer editions of Brockhaus no longer take note of this. Bonhoeffer was to write in his doctoral dissertation of the 'boundless fear of making a decision'. The more important the issue to be decided, the greater one's fear, but the more necessary it is that the fear be overcome. These insights were to take on existential importance for him after 1933.

That first sermon, with its portentous opening, was given by the 19-year-old theology student at the request of Superintendent Max Diestel, his supervisor, who needed a substitute for a pastor who had suddenly fallen ill in Stahnsdorf, on the south side of Berlin. Bonhoeffer asked his superintendent to discuss the draft of the sermon with him, and Diestel, who had a canny feel for people and their particular gifts, kept an eye on him from then on. It is not saying too much to call him the discoverer of Bonhoeffer, as he was the first to consider how the young man's career could be furthered, without telling him so or influencing him in any way. The most Diestel did was occasionally to invite Bonhoeffer to his home, alone or with others, and, because Bonhoeffer was good with children, to have him play St Nicholas for his large family.[12] But as soon as the young theology student had earned his doctorate and passed his First Theological Examination, Diestel purposely sent him abroad to experience a world completely different from his upper middle-class home. And in case this was not enough, he made sure that, after taking his Second Theological Examination, Bonhoeffer was able to study in New York for a year, after which Diestel made him his colleague in international ecumenical work. For the young pastor, this last became an unexpectedly time-consuming volunteer position, but it helped to shape him both theologically and personally. Many years later he wrote to Diestel:

Most likely you have forgotten all about these 'interventions' in my life, since within the full scope of your work these were all, of course, extremely minor, secondary matters. But for me they were fundamental for my entire life and its formation. Later I was able to be with you at numerous ecumenical conferences; there, just from your way of speaking and manoeuvring, I learned to recognize and understand the full responsibility of the German church toward other churches. (DBWE 16, 368)

A 21-year-old Doctor of Theology

'Sanctorum Communio:[13] A Dogmatic Enquiry into the Sociology of the Church' was the title Bonhoeffer gave to his dissertation, and first of all it must be said that when he spoke of the 'communion of saints', he wasn't accepting any easy distinction between 'the visible and the invisible church'. He was speaking of the Church in the concrete sense. Only if it is the *communio sanctorum*, the congregation of the saints, is there a 'loving fellowship' within it. There were at that time in German Protestantism two theologically based views of the Church, and both were negative.[14] The first view was espoused by the liberal theologian and sociologist Ernst Troeltsch, who believed that the Church had 'all the hardness, afflictions and trivial thinking of an official institution'. It was to be used as a means to an end, and as such, 'as far as possible, to be made into a tolerable means to one's ends'.[15] This was the view familiar to Bonhoeffer from home. In a time of opposition between Christian tradition and contemporary culture, Troeltsch believed the Church could no longer be reformed.

The other view was the early opinion held by Karl Barth, in which the existing church had lost its credibility through its conduct before and during the Great War, and according to which a struggle against the old church, or for a new church, would not be worthwhile. For him the only important thing was preaching: 'We should speak of God, and yet cannot ... at once the necessary and the impossible task of the minister.'[16] Bonhoeffer, who saw great strength in the type of the Church (*Volkskirche*) as it had developed historically, objected:

Luther's love for the church and deep dogmatic insight into the significance of its historical nature made it very hard for him to tear himself away from the church of Rome. We should not allow resentment and dogmatic frivolity to deprive us out of hand of our historical Protestant church.[17]

He did see, however, that this church should not remain as it now was. 'The church of the future will not be bourgeois [*bürgerlich*]' he said of its future development. 'We want to take the church to the proletariat.'[18]

Carl von Weizsäcker said, in his above-mentioned speech in Geneva, that Bonhoeffer's dissertation 'in two respects ... marks the beginning of the journey towards reality, beyond liberal theology and beyond Barth', on one hand by speaking of 'religious existence in the concrete form of the Church as a social reality', and on the other, with sociology as his starting point, by seeking 'to show that the theology of the Church is the real, the only stable embodiment of the sociological doctrine of community'.[19]

Bonhoeffer had pointed out that crucial theological concepts are always social concepts as well. If human beings are social beings, then all the more so in the Church, where we recognize that it is Jesus Christ, the Son of God, who makes human beings capable of community and is, moreover, the ground of our community. Of course this immediately raises the question of how Jesus, who lived 2000 years ago, can be the ground of a community today. As 'teacher' and 'example', as liberal theologians say? As the Risen One, as Karl Barth and the Orthodox say? The Risen One is 'Christ existing as church-community' says Bonhoeffer, thereby adapting Hegel's dictum, 'God existing as church-community'.[20] In and through the church community we have the proof that Christ is the Risen One and that he is present there.

Anyone interested in the life of Bonhoeffer will be wondering how, at the age of 19, he came to choose this particular topic. Seeberg had suggested a different subject, and Harnack and Holl would certainly have done so. But to Bonhoeffer his own discovery was more important.

It is not only the 'communion of saints' which poses a problem; every human community has problems, even a privileged family with close ties among its members. The Bonhoeffers were such a family, and yet, as we have seen, both Dietrich and Susanne Bonhoeffer experienced loneliness within it. Bonhoeffer's older brothers teased him about his religious ideas, when he told them he was going to study theology. When they declared that the Church was old hat, he shot back, 'Well, then I'll reform the church!' What that meant at first was only, I'm not you, and what you're studying isn't for me! But underneath was his very early discovery of 'the gulf between his I and the Thou of other people' of which he was later to speak in his dissertation. Undoubtedly this gulf seemed threatening, first of all, because it seems to call the family community into question. That his father claimed, when matters of church and faith were raised, not to know anything about it, must have caused Bonhoeffer much more insecurity than the teasing of his brothers; at the age of 15, what could he say in reply? His father, who was both rather distant and an absolute authority to him, remained an example to Bonhoeffer all his life, and this also had an effect on his theology. Many years later he was to write to his fiancée:

[That element of severity] in the father–son relationship is a sign of great strength, and of an inner self-assurance that derives from an awareness of the sanctity of fatherhood. Most parents today are too spineless. For fear of losing their children, they devalue themselves into their friends and cronies, and end by rendering themselves superfluous to them. I abhor that type of upbringing, which is nothing of the kind. I believe our families think alike in that respect.[21]

His fiancée was to contradict him, for good reasons; to her, her father had been the best friend one could imagine.[22] That his father's feelings and thoughts were so different from his own, precisely in matters of religion, must have been quite a problem for Dietrich as a teenage boy, particularly because he couldn't talk about it with him, and presumably never did so, even later in their lives.

And then in Rome, in St Peter's on Palm Sunday 1924, he saw the *communio sanctorum* as a living reality before him: 'illustrating the univer-sality of the church in a marvellously effective manner: white, black, yellow, all ... united under the church'. So there was, after all, something that brings people together and makes them into a community, even when their differences far outweigh those typically found among family members. That this must have something to do with the communion between humans and God, that mass in St Peter's had shown him. But it became truly recognizable through the revelation of God in Christ, which for Bonhoeffer no one had so clearly described as Karl Barth. In the opinion of the young doctoral candidate, however, Barth did not tie this recognition clearly enough to the Church.[23] What actually happens in the Church, and how an individual becomes a member of a true community, therefore became the question on which everything depends.

We shall see how the early picture that Bonhoeffer had of the *Volkskirche* fell apart, when it did not measure up to reality from 1933 onward. Suddenly he found in his church an enormous lack of faith and too little 'loving community'. However, because very few theologians have 'lived' their theology to the extent that Bonhoeffer did – it was not just an intellectual matter for him – we shall find him discovering new, radical questions and trying to answer them. If his church is no longer the 'true Church', then where is the true Church? The church as community, with Christ as its centre, was to remain the defining issue in his 'journey to reality'.

3. Years Abroad (1929–1931)

As pastoral assistant in Barcelona

Bonhoeffer's next step was decided by a telephone call, and by much more than that. Here is what he wrote to the caller, Superintendent Max Diestel, in 1942 on the occasion of Diestel's 70th birthday:

I realize that I am indebted to you for the decisive initiatives in my external, professional and personal life ... It was perhaps one single telephone call – namely, in December 1927 – that set my entire thinking on a track from which it has not yet deviated and never will. At that time you asked me ... whether I would like to go to Barcelona as a vicar. Just a few weeks later, I had my first encounter with a foreign German congregation and with ecumenical Christianity. (DBWE 16, 367)

At the time there was no lack of advice to Bonhoeffer to turn down this proposal. The Catalan capital is a lovely and important city in Spain, but to those who expected this young German theologian to be preparing himself for an academic future, as a teacher, it looked like a sidetrack. If he really wanted to work in an expatriate German congregation, why not in London, Paris or Rome? It was certainly not by chance that the High Church Council of the Evangelical Church had had no luck, despite enquiries to all the regional consistories, in finding a candidate for ordination to send to Barcelona, until Diestel thought of asking Bonhoeffer. Diestel's idea was that this would be a completely different world from that of his home, which would do him good, 'high-flyer' that he was. Diestel himself had served as a pastor in Middlesbrough, in the north of England, when he was young. His proposal coincided with Bonhoeffer's own thoughts.

This offer seemed to bring to fruition a wish that had grown stronger and stronger over the past few years and months, namely to stand on my own two feet for a longer period completely outside my previous circle of acquaintances. I believe I was already certain of the matter right after the telephone conversation. (DBWE 10, 57)

In Barcelona, Bonhoeffer wrote in his travel diary that he had been thinking about the way he actually made personal decisions. Decisions on matters of faith he could make quickly and clearly – even before 1933 – but decisions which affected his personal life were usually entirely different for him.

I myself find the way such a decision comes about to be problematic. One thing is clear to me, however, that one personally – that is, consciously – has very little control over the ultimate yes or no, but rather that time decides everything. Maybe not with everybody, but in any event with me. Recently I have noticed again and again that all the decisions I had to make were not really my own decisions. Whenever there was a dilemma, I just left it in abeyance and – without being really conscious of dealing with it intensively – let it grow toward the clarity of a decision. But this clarity is not so much intellectual as it is instinctive. The decision is made; whether one can adequately justify it in retrospect is another question. (DBWE 10, 58)

Pastor Olbricht would have liked his new assistant to start at Christmas time, but in those days no consistory worked that fast. It was February 1928 by the time he received a copy of the order officially dispatching Bonhoeffer to Barcelona. A message particularly for Olbricht had been added: 'We shall expect, by 1st March 1929, two copies of a report from you, Reverend Sir, regarding the training of Dr Bonhoeffer as pastoral assistant and his performance.'

After a series of farewell parties, Bonhoeffer's whole family came to the railway station, on a cold, wet Berlin evening, to see him aboard the night train to Paris. He was leaving the family space for the first time, with its high expectations and its warm protection. His grandmother's house in Tübingen had been an extension of home; so had Italy, which had so deeply impressed him during his holiday stay there with his brother Klaus. When Klaus came to Spain later in the spring, Dietrich proved an able host, who not only already knew a great deal about the land and people, but had also learned Spanish astonishingly well.

It was typical of the Bonhoeffers for his parents, brothers and sisters to be on the platform to see him off, and also typical that he didn't miss the opportunity of a stopover in Paris. A former classmate arranged a hotel room for him, took him to the Louvre and twice to the opera, and showed him the famous Père Lachaise cemetery. What especially impressed Bonhoeffer, however, was a solemn high mass at Sacré Coeur, the basilica atop Montmartre.

The people in the church were almost exclusively from Montmartre, prostitutes and their men went to mass, submitted to all the ceremonies; it was an enormously impressive picture, and once again one could see quite clearly how close, precisely through their fate and guilt, these most heavily burdened people are to the heart of the Gospel. I have long thought that Tauentzien Street in Berlin[1] would be an extremely fruitful field for church work. It's much easier for me to imagine a praying murderer, a praying prostitute, than a vain person praying. Nothing is so at odds with prayer as vanity. (DBWE 10, 59)

Here we see, as in his description of his farewell to the Sunday school in the Grunewald Church, how much the issue of true community was still with him. In Grunewald the pastor had prayed for his journey to Spain and for his future work there. He wrote in his diary:

Pastor Meumann mentioned me in his general prayer and – the congregational prayer has long sent shivers down my spine, and it did so incomparably more when the group of children, with whom I had spent two years, prayed for me. Where a people prays, there is the church; and where the church is, there is never loneliness. (DBWE 10, 58)

In Paris, too, the weather was cold and damp. So he was amazed when he woke up the next morning somewhere near Narbonne and looked out the train window at a glorious spring landscape. Soon he could see the snowy summits of the Pyrenees, and from the border he took a 'luxury train' along the Mediterranean coast to Barcelona, a trip that didn't last a minute too long through the enchanting Catalan countryside with its almond trees in bloom. At the station his new mentor, Pastor Olbricht, was waiting for him.

The 'Evangelical Church' in Barcelona was in more ways than one typical of German expatriate congregations in large European cities. There are similar churches in northern, western and southern European countries to this day. The elders of the church were respectable businessmen, but that didn't necessarily mean that they came to church very often. 'A generally supportive disposition toward the church' went together with 'extremely poor church attendance', the new pastoral assistant concluded (DBWE 10, 77). However, it was a matter of pride to belong to the German club and the tennis club, to support the choral society and the German school. Barcelona's German colony numbered about 6000, which of course included many Catholics.

The congregation had 313 members. However, only those who paid contributions were counted, so if family members were included as well it amounted to quite a few more people. That did not include Germans living in smaller cities in the region, in Valencia and on the island of

Majorca. These people expected the pastor to visit now and then to conduct worship services. As in other port cities where there were German congregations, Pastor Olbricht was also pastor for the sailors' mission, and by agreement with the German consulate he also maintained a 'welfare office' where Germans could come if they were in trouble. So there was no lack of work, and one could see why Pastor Olbricht had asked for an assistant.

The Evangelical Church in Barcelona could hardly have been called a 'blooming' congregation at that time. About 40 people came to worship services on average, among them a few nationals of other countries. The simple name 'Evangelical Church' had been chosen on purpose, instead of 'German Evangelical Church', so that people from other countries could feel that they belonged there too. The Swedish and Swiss consuls were ex officio voting members of the presbytery. Bonhoeffer's mother wasn't familiar with the term 'presbytery', so he explained in a letter that this was the local church council.[2]

Bonhoeffer was shown the little church, which according to Spanish law was not allowed to have a steeple or a bell, the day of his arrival. He found it attractive in its simplicity, and looked forward to preaching there at least once a month.

His lodgings were in the home of three impoverished Spanish ladies, who rented rooms to Germans but did not speak a word of German themselves. This was fine with Bonhoeffer, since he wanted to learn Spanish as quickly as possible. He got along well with the two other Germans living in the house, and was soon going with them on his first outings in the beautiful countryside. Unfortunately the ladies didn't spend much time on their cooking, and that was how it tasted, according to Bonhoeffer. But the serious disadvantage of these lodgings was described to their grandmother by his brother Klaus: 'The only place for everyone in the house to wash is the lavatory, the toilet, which is hardly any different from a third-class lavatory on an express train except that it doesn't shake.'

Whether a pastoral assistant abroad can get his footing in an expatriate congregation, and also get to know the country and its people, depends on his enthusiasm and goodwill, but even more on the pastor who is supposed to be training him and assigning work to him. One could hardly say that this pastor in Barcelona and his assistant were 'made for each other'. 'We didn't become friends, but we liked each other well enough,' was the way Bonhoeffer expressed it privately. Olbricht was apt in his social relations with the business people in his congregation. Like them, and like most German pastors in those days, he was politically conservative. But he had a healthy understanding of human beings; his style was not emotive, nor his attitude superior. When he came to Berlin on a fundraising tour for the congregation's silver jubilee and called on the Bonhoeffers in Wangenheimstrasse, Dietrich described him as 'a man who preferred a good glass of wine and a good cigar to a bad sermon'. And he was 'not exactly a dynamic pulpit presence', Bonhoeffer adds elsewhere (DBWE 10, 77). Olbricht seems to have recognized quickly that it was best to let his assistant 'just do what he wanted', which testifies to his knowledge of people. Bonhoeffer, who always treated his elders with consummate politeness, behaved not only correctly but loyally towards him. He could have wished for many things to be different, but said to himself, 'It's only for one year.'

One of the first things Bonhoeffer was assigned to do was to start a Sunday school. As yet this was the only pastoral task with which he was familiar. Olbricht issued an invitation, but only one girl came. But she must have brought others along the next Sunday, so that there were already 15. The attendance soon grew to 40, and even in the summer months when many activities are in recess in Spain, the children wanted their Sunday school. Bonhoeffer reported to his brother-in-law, Walter Dreß: 'These children don't know anything; it's shocking, but also a good thing, since nothing about the church has yet been spoilt for them. They are very trusting and quite unrestrained in their relations with adults.'

Whenever new children joined the group, Bonhoeffer called on their parents, and found these visits much more meaningful than the introductory visits he had made during the first weeks. In such a small German colony people know how to size one another up. Nobody pretends to be anything he or she isn't, and people are pleasantly matter-of-fact in their conduct toward one another. However, in such a community gossip also flourishes, and this had disturbed Bonhoeffer very much during those introductory visits. Talking about the children, on the other hand, and how to help them grow, soon led to warmer relationships. Olbricht wrote, on 1 January 1929 when he sent the required report on his assistant to the High Church Council in Berlin and requested a successor:

He particularly devoted himself energetically and with kindness to the young people, who were enthusiastically devoted to him ... In a truly exemplary fashion, he produced a nativity play in the church with the children on the Sunday before Christmas, a project with endless rehearsals and practice that demanded a great deal of hard work. It was enormously well attended by the German colony, and the play was performed to great satisfaction. (DBWE 10, 172)

However, things probably didn't go quite that harmoniously. Bonhoeffer, who had been so pleased with the enthusiasm and abilities of the children, wrote about Olbricht: '... the success of the nativity play angered him so that we had a clash. Otherwise everything went smoothly' (DBWE 10, 175).

Bonhoeffer didn't have such an easy time with his proposal to introduce religious instruction into the upper classes at the German school. The teachers and Pastor Olbricht were immediately worried about what would happen to this when Bonhoeffer left. Olbricht didn't want to take on this instruction on top of his other duties. But as soon as he arrived with his fashionable round hat, the 'vicar' from Berlin had already created a sensation among the older pupils, and proved to be such a magnet that they took to visiting him at his *pension*. His room there was large enough to accommodate them, and weekly discussion evenings were soon under way. Bonhoeffer again began calling on the parents right away, and since he also helped to resolve difficulties at school, more than once putting in a good word with a teacher for one of his young visitors, he soon became very popular in the German colony. The parents of both children and youth began coming to Bonhoeffer's church services. He wrote to his own parents that the teenagers were very involved in the discussions, even though they were quite ignorant about religion, due to the lack of preparation at school.

Right now we are talking about the essence of Christianity and will then discuss individual problems, beginning with the problem of immortality. For this the seniors always have a reading assignment about which there is a report and then a discussion. The young people here of this age and younger are different from those in Germany; a peculiar mix of adulthood in terms of manners and career questions, and great naivety in other areas. There is not much intellectual arrogance or self-importance. In any event, intelligence is not overrated. One has the impression of greater honesty and clarity, which may derive from the Spanish influence. (DBWE 10, 154f)

A story that only became known in 1999 – when a cache of letters that Bonhoeffer had written in 1928 to Walter Dreß, his youngest sister's fiancé, was discovered – reveals just how unusual was Bonhoeffer's gift for dealing with children and young people.

At 11 in the morning there was a knock at my door, and in came a 10-year-old boy ... I soon noticed that there was something wrong ... then out it came. He broke into wild sobs, and I could only hear 'Mr Wolf is dead.' He wept and wept. 'So who is Mr Wolf?' It turned out it was a young German shepherd dog, which had been sick for a week and had just died half an hour ago. The boy was inconsolable, sat on my knee and could hardly compose himself again; but then he told me all about it, how the dog had died, so it was the end of every-thing ... So he talked for awhile, and then suddenly his heartrending sobbing stopped, he was very quiet, and then said, 'but of course I know he isn't really dead'. 'What do you mean?' 'Because now his spirit is in heaven, and he's happy

Bonhoeffer and the owner of Mr Wolf

there. At school one time, somebody asked the religion teacher what it's like in heaven, and she said she'd never been there. But now, you tell me: will I get to see Mr Wolf again? He is really and truly in heaven, isn't he?'

There I was and had to answer, yes or no. If I said 'We don't know', it would have meant 'no', and that's always a bad thing when someone wants to know. So on the spot I decided to say to him, 'Look, God made the animals, the same as people, and certainly loves the animals too. And I think God has arranged things so that everybody on earth who loved someone, really loved them, will get to be together with them in God's heaven, because loving is a part of God. Even though we don't know how it actually happens.' – You should have seen then, the happiness on that boy's face; he had stopped crying completely. 'So I'll see Mr Wolf again, when I'm dead too, and play with him' – he was transported with joy. I said to him a couple of times more that we don't know how that happens. But he knew ...

After a few minutes he said, 'I said such bad words about Adam and Eve today; if they hadn't eaten the apple, Mr Wolf wouldn't have died.' – The whole thing was as serious for this child as it is for us adults when something really tragic happens. But I was just astonished – gripped by that naive piety, suddenly appearing in a wild little boy at such a moment. As someone who is 'supposed to know', I felt very small compared with him, and I keep remembering his confident face when he left me. (DBW 17, 82–83)

Bonhoeffer asked his brother-in-law please not to read this letter aloud to the family at home. He knew how it would arouse the gibes of his brothers, and he felt that this story did not deserve that.

His brothers and sisters were amused that, in order to be seen as a proper member of the German colony, Dietrich had joined three clubs – the German club, the tennis club and the choral society. He accompanied the choral society on the piano, and did not disdain to play even the most sentimental songs they sang. He enjoyed tennis, and also wanted to stay fit. At the German club he was welcome as a chess player, among other things. He was sorry that he did not succeed in learning *Skat*, a popular German card game; it was a big favourite of Pastor Olbricht's. Small talk didn't bother Bonhoeffer, either at the club or during his pastoral visits. After all, here he wasn't in Berlin-Grunewald, and he consciously wanted to get to know a different world. 'When in Rome, do as the Romans do,' the English say; he made it his motto.

But in Barcelona a great deal was different from anything he had previously known, not least the crass difference between rich and poor. At that time the German businesses in Barcelona were having difficulties with competition from Western countries. It could happen that members of the church slid into complete poverty in a very short time. Bonhoeffer shared in the shock felt by the whole congregation when, in Pastor Olbricht's absence, he had to bury a respected businessman who had committed suicide out of despair over his sudden financial ruin. Several times Bonhoeffer asked his father for help for people in need. At Christmas he arranged an urgently needed loan for his three landladies.

In German expatriate churches, especially in port cities, people often turned up who needed help, or who perhaps were only pretending to be in need. Pastor Olbricht – who as treasurer of the German Welfare Society kept office hours for these persons, some of which he soon assigned to Bonhoeffer – was in the habit of treating the people asking for help rather roughly because so many of them were swindlers. This wasn't Bonhoeffer's manner at all, but he also could see that he shouldn't allow himself to be swayed by melodramatic stories. Whenever Pastor Olbricht was away, he had to take over this work, taking care not to waste the limited funds available; an experience – of which he gives a fascinating description in a letter to his eldest brother – that later had its effects on his social welfare activities in Berlin.

I get a look at the most varied ways of living, and have to deal with the strangest people, with whom I would otherwise scarcely have exchanged a word: globe-trotters, vagrants, escaped criminals, lots of foreign legionaries, lion tamers and other animal trainers who have run off from the Krone Circus during its Spanish tour, German dancers from the music halls here, German gangster murderers on the run, all of whom tell me their life stories in great detail. It's often very difficult in these cases to give or to refuse at one's own discretion. As it is impossible to establish any guidelines on principle, the decisive factor has to be my personal impression, and that can often and easily enough be mistaken. (DBW 10, 71)

Sermons and lectures at the church

The task to which Bonhoeffer had been looking forward most of all, perhaps not without a few jitters, was that of preaching. Pastor Olbricht had him give 19 sermons during his year in Spain; that was more than usual for a pastoral assistant at the time. Of these sermons, 14 manuscripts have been preserved and show that he invested a great deal of effort in each. 'I work on it the entire week, devoting some time to it every day', he wrote home, and after a time there was nothing he would rather that Pastor Olbricht asked him to do. Certain expressions he used, and at times whole paragraphs of these sermons, may have gone over the heads of the congregation. But for one thing, it is always better to expect too much of the listeners than to aim below their level, and for another, here in the pulpit was the man whom their children loved, who talked with the teenagers, visited people at home and did what he could to help at the welfare office.

Let us take a closer look at Bonhoeffer's sermon of 26 August 1928. He had chosen as his text, 'The world and its desires are passing away, but those who do the will of God live forever' (1 John 2:17). He brought in Faust and Prometheus, to show how the human soul longs and strives for immortality and that this is how great works of art are created. Bonhoeffer posed the question, 'but are these not all eternal? the works of a Beethoven, Bach, Goethe or Michelangelo?' and immediately answered No (DBWE 10, 517). Human beings are mortal, and everything they create also passes away. This is a passage from a typical beginner's sermon. One after another, Bonhoeffer called up other figures: Heraclitus, Buddha, the preacher Solomon, the novelist Fontane, Schiller and Nietzsche. But after evoking the end of the world, transience and death, the young preacher brought up, for the first time in his career, the distinction between the 'ultimate and penultimate things', and with this he succeeded in striking the balance and making God's eternity central to his interpretation.

This distinction was later to be one of the important categories of Bonhoeffer's *Ethics*. The 'ultimate' is God's Yes and No to humankind, in judgment and mercy. But no human being can live with reference only to this ultimate; instead, we must find our way in this world, learn an occupation, work, earn our living, find a partner, keep our house in order, bring up our children rightly if we have any, and so forth. These things, and everything else one might mention – Bonhoeffer later included working in the Resistance movement among them – are the 'penultimate things'. How to keep the two, penultimate and ultimate, in a proper relation to one another is one of the most important questions Bonhoeffer was to pose in his *Ethics*. That he was already speaking of it in Barcelona makes this sermon worth reading today, with its many literary quotations, even though he was still a long way from his great sermons of later years.

Apparently it did not suit Pastor Olbricht that church attendance had increased markedly during his summer vacation. In previous years no worship services had been held during that time. In any case, from then on he no longer announced who would be preaching the next Sunday. However, in the final report on his assistant, he was unstinting with his praise:

He ... was able to excite his listeners to such an extent that they came regularly. His sermons were well thought through and contained profound and rich ideas; in his presentation he developed a self-confidence remarkable for his young age and gave the impression of a pastor with many years of experience. (DBWE 10, 172)

A few years later Bonhoeffer was already an expert in homiletics. In Barcelona he was not at all concerned about standards or rules for preaching, although he later considered them quite important. But even then he warned his students against being tied down too slavishly by rules. For these early sermons, and also in his London pastorate, he chose the Bible texts himself rather than following those provided in the church lectionary for each Sunday. In Barcelona he usually chose a short Bible verse. Before 1933, he liked to use dramatic images and a style which we would find flowery today, and it is striking that he almost never mentioned political issues. Spain at that time was officially a monarchy, and its people had a relatively quiet life under the military dictatorship of Primo de Rivera. In Germany, the prudent policies of Stresemann seemed to be bearing some first fruits. Nobody had an inkling of the cruel civil war that lay ahead for the Spanish people, not to mention Hitler's dictatorship. Neither would the members of the German colony in Barcelona have believed the fate that awaited them. Under considerable pressure from the Nazi Party they were resettled in Germany, and church work among them was to be made well-nigh impossible by the Nazi authorities.[3]

One task which Bonhoeffer set himself in Barcelona was completely outside the usual parish parameters. During the winter he announced a series of lectures. Olbricht reported that four lectures were held and said they were very well attended, even by Catholics and people outside the church. 'He captivated people and offered them a great deal through his rich knowledge and excellent delivery, so that everyone parted from him with regret.' The texts of only three lectures have been preserved, entitled 'The Tragedy of the Prophetic and Its Lasting Meaning' (DBWE 10, 325ff), 'Jesus Christ and the Essence of Christianity' (DBWE 10, 342ff), and 'Basic Questions of a Christian Ethic' (DBWE 10, 359ff). These lectures are interesting especially because some ideas on which he lectured to the congregation were reworked by Bonhoeffer in his later theological writings.

He had decided deliberately to give the lecture on the Old Testament prophets first. It would allow him to speak about very ancient times and also bring in contemporary issues, without alarming his hearers. The prophets were people who lived in changing times, and Bonhoeffer was experiencing the period in which he was then living, following the First World War, as such a time. His audience's feelings would have been similar. He said of the prophets:

They had a covenant with God in which they were given two overwhelming experiences of God, namely as the world ruler who guides history according to his will, and as the Holy One. Whoever would be part of God's people should fall down in the dust before him. Although proclaiming this message cost the prophets their lives, the message itself became a permanent possession of humanity. We ourselves, through German philosophy, partake even now of the inheritance of the blood, the seed of the prophets ... All the blows of fate that come upon a people are both justified and merited, for it is God who has sent them. The point now is to draw the appropriate conclusions from such blows and to bear them as a burden that God lays upon us. Any people can go astray, can lapse. But they can then also find their way again by following God's path. (DBWE 10, 341)

In the second lecture, Bonhoeffer spoke much more directly and challengingly. Here the word 'decision', which was so important to him, appears right at the beginning.

The question before us today is whether in our own day Christ still stands in the place where decisions are made concerning the most profound matters we are facing, namely, concerning our own lives and the life of our people [*Volk*]. We want to talk about whether the spirit of Christ can still speak to us of the ultimate, final, decisive matters. (DBWE 10, 342)

Bonhoeffer described how, through the secularization of culture, Christ has become marginalized to the point of being considered a historical figure. Even among theological experts he is thought to be best understood and evaluated as such. But in truth, said Bonhoeffer, Christ represents an all-or-nothing decision. 'Either we accept him as our Lord, or we do not accept him.' This seems to leave us in an ice-cold, hard world, but the reality is God's love for humankind. Bonhoeffer showed how this is seen in the persons to whom Jesus' words and actions were especially directed. 'Jesus turns his attention to children, and to the morally and socially 'least of these', those viewed as less worthy. This is something totally unprecedented and new in world history, and in the person of Jesus it seems to constitute a break' (DBWE 10, 350). This requires us to rethink completely what we have always believed. For Jesus, Bonhoeffer declared, childhood is not just a phase on the way to adulthood, but rather something that has its own character, deserving of great respect from adults. 'God is closer to children than to adults. Thus Jesus becomes the discoverer of childhood.' We have seen what a joy it was to Bonhoeffer, both in Berlin and in Barcelona, to work with children and youth. Theological insights – and this is a theological insight, expressed here by Bonhoeffer – always carry something of the person who proclaims them.

The third lecture has always had a special interest for researchers in Bonhoeffer's thought, because it was the first time that he who today is considered an ethicist, among other things, spoke in detail about ethical issues. Not least of all, it shows how his thinking developed. That a 'historical regime' is something distinct from a 'regime of love', he had learned at university, and this was still the way he presented it in Spain. The commandment to love your neighbour he described to his hearers as incumbent on everyone, and then showed that Christians, when confronted by a war that threatens their own nation, must take up arms, out of love for their own people, against persons who belong to another nation. This 'nationalist theology' was to play a decisive role in Germany only a few years later; but by then, as we shall see, Bonhoeffer had left it far behind.

However, he retained some other ideas from this lecture in Barcelona, including the opposition between the will of God and worldly reality. Each must be taken with radical seriousness. Consequently, Christian ethics must be concrete, related to the present, and can never be about ethical and moral principles.

The significance of all of Jesus' ethical commandments is ... to say to people: You stand before the face of God, God's grace rules over you; but you are at the disposal of someone else in the world. You must act and believe in such a way that in each of your actions you are mindful also of acting under God's gaze, mindful that God has a certain will and wants to see that will done. Each particular moment will reveal the nature of that will. You must merely be perfectly clear that your own will must in every instance be accommodated to the divine will; your will must be surrendered if the divine will is to be realized. (DBWE 10, 365)

That sounds forceful, but here one must remember the idea of the 'ultimate and penultimate'. Bonhoeffer is by no means thinking of a Christian as someone who must continually practise self-violation, for 'Christ is the one who brings freedom'. It is always and only the decisive moment that matters, for 'I will do something again today not because it seemed the right thing to do yesterday, but because today, too, God's will has pointed me in that direction'. One wonders what the church members must have understood, when he said: 'There are no acts that are bad in and of themselves; even murder can be sanctified. There is only faithfulness to or deviation from God's will. There is no law with a specific content, but only the law of freedom, that is, bearing responsibility alone before God and oneself' (DBWE 10, 367). This sentence might make us think of his involvement in the conspiracy to assassinate Hitler, and at least be amazed that, in a lecture in a church in February 1929, Bonhoeffer already was not only thinking of such a thing as possible, but even saying it out loud – with, as yet, no idea of the weight such words could carry.

Don Quixote and bullfighting

Everyone who undertakes employment abroad probably hopes to see as much as possible of the foreign country and its scenery, and to learn about its culture and people. *Erfahren* means 'to learn' in German, and *fahren* means 'to travel'. While still in Berlin, Bonhoeffer had asked Olbricht whether he would have time for travel while in Spain, and Olbricht had assured him: 'Of course. We shall sort that out together, for you must certainly see something of Spain.' And in fact Bonhoeffer did see much of the country, between travel for work and for pleasure. He preached in Madrid and on Majorca, and took his first big trip as early as Easter 1928, when his brother Klaus came to join him. The two of them went as far as Andalusia, and even undertook a second African adventure, which went off this time without any unfortunate incidents. A major discovery for Bonhoeffer during this holiday in Spain was the paintings of El Greco, and from then on he went to see as many as possible, wherever he could find them.

From his first day in Barcelona, Bonhoeffer found it an unusually lively city, in the midst of a grand-scale economic upturn. He wrote home that there were good concerts, and the theatre was also good, though old-fashioned. What was unfortunately lacking was conversation, sharing of ideas at the academic level, 'even when one goes looking for Spanish academics'. He did find the old city 'even dirtier than Naples', but he was full of praise for the countryside round about, deeming it as among the most beautiful in Spain. He went on hikes and long excursions with the church youth. Alone, or with acquaintances, he often climbed the Tibidabo, the mountain that looms over Barcelona. There was a legend that this was the mountain from the top of which the devil showed Jesus all the kingdoms of the earth, saying 'Tibi dabo [I will give you] all these, if you will fall down and worship me' (Matthew 4:8–9).

Bonhoeffer was amazed by the Spaniards' manifest indifference towards striking contrasts in social status; this was a country where it was possible to see master and servant sitting at the same table in a café. 'None are so low that they believe they have to think even less of themselves than of others, and none – least of all the king, whom I have seen several times – think so highly of themselves that they permit themselves to look down upon others' (DBWE 10, 121).

However, Bonhoeffer's encounter with Spanish Catholicism was a bitter disappointment to him. He was fascinated, as is every tourist to this day, by the grand processions during Holy Week; but after his experiences in Italy, he had looked forward to conversations with members of the Spanish clergy, and found these people, on average, 'shockingly uncultivated'. So his 'longing to get to know them better' evaporated. Conversations with educated Spaniards were also hard to come by, and when he did have the opportunity, he found them vehemently opposed to the church. To his surprise, when he knew enough Spanish to read more difficult texts, he discovered this attitude also in modern Spanish literature. On later occasions when he was abroad, Bonhoeffer enjoyed evaluating each country and its people, and often did so in letters. Here is a typical passage from a letter to his parents:

In diametrical contrast to Italy, Spain is a country that ancient culture – in the preliterary period as well as the Renaissance – passed by without leaving a trace, and which instead existed for four hundred years under the rule of Eastern culture.[4] It is a country that, to one who has been educated in the humanities, initially seems totally alien; one lacks all clues, so to speak, for understanding it. This is true not only of the historical but just as much of contemporary Spain. But this alienation is joined by a certain element of sympathy, a feeling of kinship that one does not really sense, at least in this way, toward Italy. Again, I can only explain it by adducing the position regarding ancient and humanistic culture. For Italy humanism and the classical period represent the solution to all problems, whereas in Spain there is an element of resistance, which I think is also evident, to a certain degree, time and again among Germans. Spaniards and Germans, I think, are similar in that neither culture ever completely opened itself up to humanism; instead, a remnant of something else always persisted. (DBWE 10, 95)

Even in March 1928 Bonhoeffer was already aware that being in Spain was having an effect on his thinking, and a note in his diary says, 'My theology is taking a humanistic turn; what's that all about? I wonder whether Barth ever lived abroad.'[5]

In July he wrote to Harnack that the time he was spending in Spain, in retreat from academic influences and focusing instead on many new impressions in practical life, seemed to him to be quite fruitful in its way:

One gains distance from so many things about which one had become a bit obsessive, one acquires a measure of freedom from didactic doctrines and also learns to recognize much more precisely the limits of the value of pure scholarship; and in turn all that provides a point of departure from which one re-examines everything one has previously worked out. (DBWE 10, 116)

One of Bonhoeffer's great discoveries during his year in Spain came soon after his arrival in Barcelona: *Don Quixote*. An acquaintaince took him to the cinema, where a film version of the novel was being shown. He couldn't understand all of it, and not knowing whether this was due to his insufficient knowledge of Spanish or to the film itself, he bought Cervantes' book and was captivated by it for the rest of his life. Twelve years after his first encounter with this greatest work of Spanish literature, it had become for him a symbol of the present age:

The perennial figure of Don Quixote has become contemporary, the 'knight of the doleful countenance' who, with a shaving basin for a helmet and a miserable nag for a charger, rides into endless battle for the chosen lady of his heart, who doesn't even exist. This is the picture of the adventurous enterprise of an old world against a new one, of a past reality against a contemporary one, of a noble dreamer against the overpowering force of the commonplace ...

Whoever wants to fight against the injustice and the crimes of the Nazi state, but uses the weapons of a time that is past, will fail because these swords are rusty instead of being shiny and strong. On the other hand, it is also true that

It is too cheap to deride the weapons that we have inherited from our ancestors, with which they achieved great things, but that are not sufficient for the present struggle. Only the mean-spirited can read the fate of Don Quixote without sharing in and being moved by it. (DBWE 6, 80–81)

Many admirers of Bonhoeffer today are astonished that he was keen on watching bullfights. At the very beginning of his stay in Spain, a teacher at the German school took him to a *corrida*. He was immediately fascinated by the hair-raising drama being played out before him, and remained so all his life. His enthusiasm also infected his brother Klaus, and wherever they had the opportunity during their travels together in Spain, they went to see the local bullfights. His twin sister wrote to him that she wouldn't

'Greetings from a matador': postcard from Dietrich Bonhoeffer, from Barcelona, to Rüdiger Schleicher

'have such a spectacle on a silver platter'; it must make boxing seem totally benign. His students in Finkenwalde were also surprised at the seriousness with which Bonhoeffer described bullfighting to them, and demonstrated the steps and rapier thrusts of the *torero*, when they asked him to tell them something about Spain. Bonhoeffer also took his parents to a *corrida* when they came to visit him in Spain; but of course he knew how outlandish bullfighting would seem to his family and most people he knew.

I ... cannot really say that it shocked me all that much, that is, the way many people think they owe it to their central European civilization to be shocked. It is, after all, a great spectacle to see wild, unrestrained strength and blind rage fight against and ultimately succumb to disciplined courage, presence of mind and skill ... Overall, the people vent all these powerful emotions, and one gets drawn into it oneself. I think it's no accident that in the country with the gloomiest and most stark Catholicism the bullfight is ineradicably secure. Here is a remnant of unrestrained, passionate life, and perhaps it is the bullfight that, precisely by stirring up the entire soul of the people, indeed by fanning it to a frenzy, renders possible a relatively elevated morality in the other areas of life, since other passions are killed off by the bullfight – so that the Sunday *corrida* constitutes the necessary counterpart to Sunday mass. (DBWE 10, 83)

Back in Berlin: examinations, publications and a eulogy

The year in Spain was important to Bonhoeffer not only because he was moving out and trying his wings away from his family, but also because in Barcelona he became aware that he could not be tempted by a strictly academic career. His plan for the future was to combine teaching at university level with a pastorate. The congregation in Barcelona would have liked to keep him permanently, and had already offered him a position in November 1928. But he only considered it briefly. He wanted to return to Berlin, write his postdoctoral thesis, which was required for lecturing at a German university, and take the Second Theological Examination required by the consistory of his Protestant Church of Berlin and Brandenburg – then he would decide on his future course. But the letters he exchanged from Berlin with friends in Barcelona show that he left part of his heart in Spain and the congregation in Barcelona. When he went back there in 1930 for the wedding of one of the teachers, it seemed to him that he had never been away.

Superintendent Diestel, whose job it was to receive Bonhoeffer's registration for the Second Examination and curriculum vitae and pass them on to the appropriate church office, was delighted to read of all that Bonheoffer had learned in Barcelona, having recommended that he go there. In his strong handwriting, Diestel wrote in the margin of the c.v.:

I consider him to be a young man who is outstandingly gifted both in church praxis and in scholarly activities, a young man who can only broaden his experience through his anticipated activities in the United States. I recommend that things be made as easy for him as possible and that at the same time we keep him in mind for future *practical* work. (DBWE 10, 221 Note 11)

The word 'practical' was energetically underlined. Diestel had soon arranged the first alleviation himself. Bonhoeffer and his friends did not think it necessary to attend a preachers' seminary, as required of candidates for ordination in the Old Prussian church. For half a year they had to live in a dormitory, and instead of being prepared for the pastoral ministry in ways that had not been adequately covered by their studies to date, they often had to attend courses at a lower level than their university preparation. Those who could find a way – even Bonhoeffer, who was to become director of a preachers' seminary six years later – tried to avoid this requirement which they found nonsensical. Diestel helped him do so, thinking it made more sense for Bonhoeffer to concentrate on his postdoctoral thesis and then to have some additional experience abroad.

In Berlin, Bonhoeffer found that politics had changed. Those who, like Foreign Minister Stresemann of the Weimar Republic government, were concerned about reconciliation with the Western powers, were denounced by rapidly growing right-wing groups as 'too dutiful' in fulfilling the reparations and disarmament clauses of the Treaty of Versailles. Hitler's National Socialist German Workers' Party (NSDAP, the incipient Nazi Party) only controlled 12 votes in the Reichstag (parliament), but that didn't stop his SA (Storm Trooper militia) from even more raucous rampages in the streets. Together with the *Stahlhelm*[6] and German Nationalists, the NSDAP circulated a petition against the Young Plan to have Germany's war debts renegotiated. The proposal did not get enough votes in the Reichstag to succeed, but the shouting grew ever louder that the government was in the hands of 'defeatists' who were 'lackeys of the Western powers' in carrying out the Treaty. Even voices in the churches joined in these irresponsible claims.

On 3 October 1929, Gustav Stresemann died – one of the few political leaders who could be counted on by honest democrats in Germany. Not long afterward came the New York stock market crash of 29 October, triggering a worldwide economic crisis that had especially disastrous effects in Germany. From one day to the next, the 'golden twenties' were over. Banks closed. All short-term loans were called in. Thousands of businesses went bankrupt, and as each catastrophe brought on others, unemployment grew rapidly. This raised to a new pitch the government's conflicts with the Nazis and the communists. There was fighting in the streets of large German cities, especially Berlin. Bloodshed during police actions became frequent.

On 27 March 1930, the Social Democratic Party (SPD), which traditionally represents labour, decided to leave the governing coalition because the premiums for unemployment insurance had to be raised. 'Suicide out of the fear of death', one SPD deputy called it. By the end of the month, the centrist politician Brüning had become Reich Chancellor for the first time. Since he could now rule by means of emergency decrees, issued by the Reich President whenever the government couldn't get a majority for necessary measures, the Republic began to crumble. Brüning's cruelly tight economic regime contributed to making condi-tions unbearable as unemployment ballooned to over six million. In the election of 14 September 1930, Germany experienced the Nazi Party's first landslide victory; instead of 12 seats in the Reichstag, it now held 107. Even the communists gained some, although not nearly on the same scale. Germany was headed for chaos.

Sometime after his return from Spain, Bonhoeffer is supposed to have said that he wasn't especially interested in politics. Nevertheless, in a letter at Christmas 1932 to a friend from his student days, Helmut Rößler, he wrote: 'I hope you will not misunderstand the term "disinterestedness" that I let drop a long time ago (I can't even remember that any more); it now actually strikes me as frivolous' (DBWE 12, I/23). Whether he used the expression or not, the fact is that Bonhoeffer's brothers were much more involved in discussing politics than he was. He read the *Vossische Zeitung* newspaper and heard a lot of political discussion at home, especially since his sister Christine's husband, Hans von Dohnanyi, who lived next door, had become personal assistant to the Reich Minister of Justice.

But if Bonhoeffer wanted to pass his postdoctoral *Habilitation* requirement and take his Second Theological Examination, he had to concentrate first and foremost on his theology studies. In addition he was looking into having his doctoral thesis published, and above all looking for a position as a lecturer at the university. It did not help that Reinhold Seeberg, who had supervised his thesis, was now retired and could no longer offer him a position, and that Seeberg's successor, Wilhelm Lütgert, had reservations about Bonhoeffer's inclination toward 'dialectical theology'; nevertheless Bonhoeffer did obtain a position as a 'volunteer' assistant lecturer. As such he was expected to supervise the seminar library and card file, hand out keys to rooms and make sure they were returned; but not being keen on these tasks, he delegated them to students. Lütgert soon came to appreciate his new assistant, but said to Hans Christoph von Hase, who was the next to hold the job 'I really just took over your cousin, from Seeberg; otherwise I would have exercised rather more pressure on his philosophy.'

Getting the doctoral thesis published turned out to be a difficult business. The university's requirement would have been satisfied by simply having the text duplicated inexpensively, but Bonhoeffer wanted this chance to show Barth and his disciples that he had taken up their thinking and reworked it critically. In the meantime Barth, who had not read any of Bonhoeffer's work, had brought out the first half-volume of his *Christian Dogmatics*, and a book had appeared by Paul Althaus, the Luther specialist at the University of Erlangen, with the same title as Bonhoeffer's thesis. When a publisher was finally found that would print *Sanctorum Communio* if 1000 Reichsmarks were paid in advance for the printing costs – about three months' salary for a parish pastor in those days – three years had passed and Bonhoeffer was on his way to America. His postdoctoral thesis had been accepted in the meantime so he was looking for a publisher for his second book, and had lost his interest in the first. The publisher complained bitterly to Bonhoeffer's father about this lack of interest. That first book did not really become known until after Bonhoeffer's death. At the time it aroused scarcely any discussion, and was misunderstood for the most part.

Bonhoeffer's second book, *Act and Being*, also only began to interest people after his death in Flossenbürg and the publication of his *Letters and Papers from Prison* [*Widerstand und Ergebung*] had made him well known. In *Act and Being*, Bonhoeffer tried to enter into a dispute going on at the time between advocates of transcendental philosophy and supporters of ontology. Both these forms of knowledge, when taken as absolutes, seemed to him to be doomed to failure, and he tried, as he had done in his doctoral dissertation, to bring the two sides together in the concept of the church. '[With regard to] contents, both works are the kind of thing a man has to write while he is young and still has the courage to write it', said Carl Friedrich von Weizsäcker.[7] Both books, in contrast to all Bonhoeffer's subsequent writings, are composed in scholarly language which requires an effort from the reader to get used to it. So it is not surprising that they lay unnoticed for so long. For some years, however, renewed interest in them has been shown by younger theologians.[8]

For his postdoctoral thesis, Bonhoeffer – with Lütgert's help – quickly found a publisher. Bertelsmann took it on and asked for only 200 Reichsmarks in advance for printing costs, after Paul Althaus had recommended the book as a 'very important piece of work, which unquestionably must be printed as soon as possible'. Bonhoeffer thanked him for this with a polite letter, after returning from the USA, and also sent Althaus both his books. This is all the more interesting because at that time he and Althaus belonged to different camps, as we shall see. Althaus returned the favour by sending Bonhoeffer his book *Communio Sanctorum*, along with a warm letter.

Max Diestel, who wanted to groom Bonhoeffer for work in the ecumenical movement, had proposed in 1929 that after his Second Examination for the church, Bonhoeffer should go to England for a while, learn English and get to know what it was like to study there, and then apply for a grant to study in the USA. Bonhoeffer was attracted to this idea, but in order to carry it out he had to concentrate hard and prepare quickly for the Prussian church's Second Examination. His postdoctoral thesis was accepted in lieu of a 'theological essay' for this purpose. The time to accomplish the rest was shortened yet more because the grant for the USA was approved even sooner than he and Diestel had planned for it. He had to give up the plan for a study trip to England beforehand.

He took his oral examination at the Prussian church consistory from 5 to 8 July 1930, and received a very good mark for it. Amusingly, it was his written proposal for a Sunday school session which was found lacking (it was considered 'over the children's heads') and earned him only a passing mark. But Diestel, who was present when Bonhoeffer conducted the Sunday school session, judged it quite differently. His superintendent's evaluation sheet read, succinctly: '1. Catechist's bearing: serious and dignified. 2. Mastery of material: excellent. 3. Posing of questions: correct. 4. Ability to respond to the children's answers: excellent. 5. Class discipline: excellent' (DBWE 10, 230). Bonhoeffer had long since mastered this area of parish work and, in contrast to the expert who was evaluating his work, he did not hesitate to discuss even difficult questions with children and youth.

In the midst of preparing for his Second church Examination, Bonhoeffer found out that Adolf von Harnack had died unexpectedly in Heidelberg on 10 June 1930. This was a blow to him, for it marked the end of a chapter in his life. Harnack had been much more to Bonhoeffer than the teacher of six seminars he had attended in Berlin; he had also been a fatherly friend. On 15 June, following the funeral, the King Wilhelm Society, of which Harnack was still president at the time of his death, held a memorial (a secular event rather than a worship service) for him. Following speeches by three government ministers, the Dean of the Theological Faculty and the Director of the National Library, Dietrich Bonhoeffer spoke on behalf of Harnack's former students. His speech was published, and it made a wider public aware of him for the first time. He said:

Through him, it became clear to us that truth is born only of freedom. We saw in him the champion of the free expression of truth, once it was recognized, who formed his own free judgement afresh time and again and expressed it clearly, notwithstanding the anxious inhibitions of the crowd. This made him ... the friend of all young people who spoke their opinions freely, as he asked them to do. And if he sometimes expressed concern or warned us about recent developments in our field, it was motivated exclusively by his fear that the opinions of others might be in danger of confusing irrelevant issues with the pure search for the truth. Because we knew that with him we were in good and solicitous hands, we saw him as the bulwark against all superficiality and stagnation, against all fossilization of intellectual life. (DBWE 10, 380)

Bonhoeffer missed Harnack when he took up his duties as lecturer at the university in Berlin in 1931; there was no longer any mentor for him there.

Weddings and a new friend

In the meantime there had been noticeable changes in Bonhoeffer's family. The circle of siblings was gradually becoming a circle of sibling families, with Dietrich the only unmarried one. This caused his relationship with his mother to become even closer, and when his parents moved from the Wangenheimstrasse in Grunewald to a house of their own in the Heerstrasse neighbourhood, he was the only one who still had a room at home with them. This house, in Marienburger Allee, now belongs to the church and is kept as a Bonhoeffer memorial.

The first of his brothers and sisters to marry was Ursula; in 1923 she wedded Rüdiger Schleicher, a lawyer from Stuttgart, who had been introduced to the family as a 'fellow Hedgehog' of Dietrich's. An excellent violinist, he had soon become a regular visitor. In 1925, Christine married her schoolmate, Hans von Dohnanyi, two years older than she; he and his sister Grete had long been among the Bonhoeffer children's neighbourhood friends. A year later, Dietrich's twin sister Sabine became the wife of Gerhard Leibholz, also a lawyer, who at the age of only 28 was made full professor at the University of Greifswald, holding the chair of Public Law, in 1929. He was from a Jewish family but had been baptized a Christian as a child. In 1929 Susanne married Walter Dreß, a fellow theology student of Dietrich's whom he had introduced to the family. In 1930 they were followed by Karl Friedrich, who married Grete von Dohnanyi, and by Klaus, whose bride was Emmi Delbrück, daughter of Hans and sister of Justus, another of the Bonhoeffers' long-time neighbourhood friends.

Probably because he belonged to such a close-knit family, Dietrich had never had a really intimate friend during his childhood and youth. The playmate who came nearest to that status was his cousin Hans Christoph von Hase, with whom he had often spent vacations as a child and a teenager, and whose decision also to study theology enabled them to remain in close contact. But this cousin was almost like a brother to him, and in the friendships of youth one normally looks for kindred spirits outside the family. Bonhoeffer found such a friend in Franz Hildebrandt, a theology student three years younger than he, whose father was professor of Art History at the University of Berlin and whose mother came from a Jewish family. The two young men first became acquainted in Seeberg's seminar, shortly before Bonhoeffer received his doctoral degree. In 1929 they ran across each other again at a performance of J. S. Bach's *St Matthew Passion* at the Berlin Choral Academy; they then arranged to meet, and were soon the best of friends. Hildebrandt knew a great deal about Luther, and he not only made Luther's writings more familiar to Bonhoeffer, but also influenced his developing a much stronger relationship with the Bible in his theology. Hildebrandt was brilliant intellectually and extremely witty, and not least because of this was soon a welcome guest in the Bonhoeffer home. He and Dietrich often argued about theological and philosophical issues, on which they had some quite divergent opinions, and on 31 July Hildebrandt gave Bonhoeffer a little book of Luther's sayings, inscribed, in allusion to Luther's hymn 'A Mighty Fortress': 'To my ancient foe, on the occasion of the completion of your postdoctoral studies.'

As a scholarship student in the USA

Forward-looking German students were drawn to study in the USA in those days, not because it was made advantageous for them, as it was after the Second World War, but to get to know this rising world power with its great potential and perhaps even greater problems. The German Academic Exchange Service (DAAD) paid for their ship's passage, and there were study grants offered in the USA. Bonhoeffer's predecessor grantee, Johannes Schattenmann from Bavaria, had stayed on for a second year in order to learn more.

Certainly if Bonhoeffer had had the choice, in 1930, between a study grant in India and one in the USA, he would have chosen India without hesitation. It was his grandmother who had first suggested this idea to him. India was not a 'majority Christian' country; people there lived according to other laws and a completely different philosophy from that of Europe or America. Like Barth and his students, Bonhoeffer believed that religion was the way chosen by human beings to come to God, and therefore a futile way. To him, the Christian faith was therefore exactly the opposite of all other religions, since only through Christ can human beings encounter God. This could be considered a narrow-minded view, because it does not appear to take seriously the beliefs of followers of other religions. But Bonhoeffer was equally convinced that everything depended on learning from the others. He saw the errors of Western civilization and of the churches much too clearly to be able to speak in favour of fundamentalist Christianity. In any case he didn't want to talk about other religions like a blind person talking about colours.

Though he was now on his way to the USA, could he perhaps return to Germany by way of the Far East, and thus carry out his plan to visit India? The American with whom he was sharing a stateroom on the *Columbus* turned out to be the president of a college in Lahore, India (now in Pakistan), and immediately invited Bonhoeffer to visit him there. Bonhoeffer's brothers and sisters were full of enthusiasm for this idea, especially Christine von Dohnanyi, the liveliest of his four sisters. She wrote to him:

Perhaps gradual pressure on Papa and Mama will do the trick, possibly dressing it up as a big loan. If you accept a position here immediately afterward and promise not to marry soon, you can pay it back. Incidentally, I have the feeling that they would be quite sympathetic to such an idea, so that in the end you will manage it.

She was almost more disappointed than her brother when he had to postpone the scheme, because it turned out that crossing the Pacific would be far more expensive than travelling from Germany through the Suez Canal. 'The chance certainly won't come again', she wrote, and she turned out to be right in the end, even though six years later Bonhoeffer actually received an invitation from Gandhi to visit his ashram.

Bonhoeffer had never been so carefree, and never was to be so again, as during his year of study in the USA. He had taken the examinations to clear his way to both the pastorate and university teaching in Germany, and passed both with flying colours. While in the United States he could have done, or left undone, anything he pleased. But it would have been completely out of character for him not to make use of his year of study at Union Theological Seminary in New York to work as hard as everyone else there. As in Spain, he would still have enough time to learn about the country and its people, if he could find ways to see the 'New World' through the eyes of friends who belonged to it. His time in New York saw the beginning of four fast friendships, two with Americans and two with Europeans, and all four became so important in his future life that we shall have much more to say about them later.

New York City, of course, fascinated Bonhoeffer like everyone else seeing it for the first time. In those days it was the silhouette of Lower Manhattan that dominated the skyline. Rockefeller Center and all the other skyscrapers were yet to be built; even the Empire State Building was still under construction. Yet nobody landing in New York for the first time could ever have seen anything like it. For Bonhoeffer it was the beginning of 'an uninterrupted assault of new experiences' (DBWE 10, 261). 'If you really try to experience New York completely, it almost does you in' (DBWE 10, 296), he wrote to Diestel. A few of his impressions were rather distressing, for the unemployment rate in New York and throughout the country in 1930 was far higher even than in Germany, and 'Prohibition' led to unbridled alcohol smuggling which greatly increased organized crime. He wrote to his sister Sabine on their 25th birthday: 'Unfortunately I cannot even toast you with a glass of wine on this occasion, since it's forbidden by federal law; what a frightful bore, this Prohibition in which no one believes' (DBWE 10, 271).[9] As a budding ethicist, he was bemused to see the same churches which had used their influence to bring about Prohibition having to fight later to get it repealed.

In common with visitors arriving from other continents in the USA today, especially in church circles, Bonhoeffer – after a brief stay with relatives in Philadelphia – was expected to speak to groups of people and tell them about Germany and the German church. Even before he could speak English comfortably, he was also asked to preach in English. In one local church he arrived to find a thousand school children awaiting him. One would love to know more about all this, but unfortunately many letters he wrote to his parents during this time have been lost.

The environment which he was to share with 300 other people during an academic year took some getting used to for Bonhoeffer. Like many graduate schools in the USA, Union Seminary in New York was rather like an English university college in the nineteenth century, and for his taste there was too little privacy – it was hard to find any place to be alone. That the lecturers were dealing with more contemporary issues than their colleagues in Germany, and saw their students as persons with equal rights, pleased Bonhoeffer. But that doors were left open everywhere, on the assumption that others – even professors – would welcome a conversation, was hard on him – totally different from Germany. 'There's a lot of time-wasting chatter around here, but at least I'm learning English from it', he said in a letter.

Union Seminary had been founded as a college by the Presbyterian Church and was then about a hundred years old. Around 1900 it had been transformed into a graduate theological seminary for Protestants of all denominations. It had then become infused with a liberal mindset, and had an outstanding reputation in the USA as a place for modern and critical thinking. American fundamentalist groups were often scandalized by the political, social and ecclesiastical views of professors at 'Union'. Nevertheless, or perhaps precisely because of this, many students from these very conservative churches could be found there. At that time the Seminary already valued and sought out relationships with churches and theologians overseas, and had quite a few grants available for foreign students, like Bonhoeffer's Sloane Fellowship. In 1920 a Mrs Sloane had endowed a year-long study grant for a French student, which she later expanded so that three Europeans could be offered places each year. The two other Sloane Fellows, Erwin Sutz from Switzerland and Jean Lasserre from France, became Bonhoeffer's European friends in America.

Bonhoeffer's previous theological education had taken him far beyond that of the other students, so that he actually belonged on the faculty. The impression he made on his fellow students was described by one of his four friends, Paul Lehmann, in 1960 on British radio. Of course Lehmann told his British audience about Bonhoeffer as a Resistance fighter who had been murdered at Flossenbürg, and that probably overshadowed his

With professors and fellow students at Union Theological Seminary in New York. Identified by numbers: 1. Daniel J. Fleming, 2. Ernest F. Scott, 3. Harry F. Ward, 4. Reinhold Niebuhr, 5. Henry Sloane Coffin, 6. John Baillie, 7. Julius A. Bewer, 8. James Moffat, 9. Frank Fisher, 10. ??, 11. Erwin Sutz, 12. Dietrich Bonhoeffer

memories of Bonhoeffer from 1930. But he also told of other experiences shared with Bonhoeffer, repeatedly expressing how fascinating their time at Union together had been for him. In the radio programme he said of Bonhoeffer:

He was German in his passion for perfection, whether of manners, or of performance, or of all that is connoted by the word *Kultur*. Here, in short, was an aristocracy of the spirit at its best … His aristocracy was unmistakable, yet not obtrusive, chiefly I think owing to his boundless curiosity about every new environment in which he found himself and to his irresistible and unfailing sense of humour … the capacity to see oneself and the world from a perspective other than one's own. (DB-ER 155–56)

None of the other Americans at Union Seminary came to know Bonhoeffer as well as Lehmann, who came from a Russian-German family and spoke fluent German, or to understand so precisely what he wanted to contribute as a German theologian to the discussions there. He kept hoping for years that Bonhoeffer would become a professor in the USA and be able to influence theological developments there.

Bonhoeffer's other American friend was Frank Fisher, who was black. It was not easy to win him over, to gain his trust, but Bonhoeffer was genuinely interested in the life of the black community.

At that time, the term 'Negro' was not yet taboo.[10] Lehmann used it quite freely in 1960 in describing Bonhoeffer's interest in the situation of African-Americans:

What was so impressive was the way in which he pursued the understanding of the problem to its minutest detail through books and countless visits to Harlem, through participation in Negro youth work, but even more through a remarkable kind of identity with the Negro community, so that he was received there as if he had never been an outsider at all. (DB-ER 155)

It was Frank Fisher who made these experiences possible for Bonhoeffer, and they were among the most important of his year in America, perhaps the most important of all to him. Almost every Sunday, and also during the week, he could be found at the Abyssinian Baptist Church on West 138th Street in Harlem, where he taught a Sunday school class. He took part in countless discussions and in excursions with the church youth. Ruth Zerner, an American who worked at the same church in the 1960s, found that a number of the church members still remembered the blond pastor from Germany who had been part of their congregation 30 years earlier.

On a trip to Washington DC, Bonhoeffer was impressed by the monumental buildings of the capital, especially the Lincoln Memorial, which he found 'enormously imposing, portraying Lincoln himself ten or twenty times larger than life, brightly illuminated at night, in a mighty hall ... Moreover, the more I hear about Lincoln, the more he interests me. He must have been a tremendous man' (DBWE 10, 257). He was impressed also by the 'unbelievable' conditions under which black citizens had to live. Not only were there separate train and streetcar carriages and buses, but 'when I wanted to have dinner in a small restaurant with a Negro acquaintance, I was refused service there'.

He had been invited to take part in a conference in Washington of the Federal Council of Churches, the predecessor of the present National Council of Churches of Christ in the USA. He was not happy with its theological debates. 'They talked about everything, but not about theology', he wrote to Diestel. However, Bonhoeffer was impressed by a political resolution of which he witnessed the discussion and adoption. It was a 'Message to Our Christian Brothers in Germany' in which the 'theory of the sole guilt of Germany for the war' was rejected. Bonhoeffer had been speaking in New York churches about the First World War and the postwar situation in Germany. This resolution encouraged him, and after his return to Germany he was indignant that respected professors of theology there did not take it into account, but rather demanded that no German take part in theological discussions of the ecumenical movement without first denouncing the lies about guilt for the war and the continuing war of the Western powers against Germany.

On theology as it was taught at Union Seminary, Bonhoeffer's judgement was rather harsh. In the report he wrote after his return to Germany for the Church Federation Office in Berlin, he delivered his verdict with youthful insouciance:

The faculty at Union Theological Seminary represents what the enlightened American demands of theology and the church, from the most radical sociali-zation – Professors [Harry F.] Ward and [Reinhold] Niebuhr – and philosophical and organizational secularization of Christianity – Professor [Eugene W.] Lyman, Professor [H. S.] Elliott – to a liberal theology that takes its orientation from [Albrecht] Ritschl – Professor [John] Baillie. The students can be classified accordingly into three or four groups. Doubtless the most lively if not the most profound among them belong to the first group. Here they have turned their backs on any sort of proper theology; they study many economic and political problems, are actively engaged in all sorts of corresponding organizations, are conducting one of the endless 'surveys' of the sort commonly conducted by the more progressive elements in America, and all this within a so-called ethical inter-pretation. Here they sense the renewal of the Gospel for our age and develop a strong self-consciousness in which they believe it possible to pass over various 'theological' objections rather hastily. (DBWE 10, 307–8)

The report, which is 18 pages long, is regarded today as unjust by many who are in a position to know, but it is the result of keen observation. No one could have written such a report who did not have a thorough knowledge of the professors and the courses which they offered. And it should not be seen as motivated by condescension. Bonhoeffer was impressed by the experience of life which his fellow students at Union had, which he admitted was not the case among students of theology in Germany; he also admired the American students' readiness to get involved in social work. He not only joined them in these projects, but found them worth emulating in social welfare undertakings of his own, later on in Berlin. He was discovering the theological 'social gospel' movement, not only in this active way, but through the relevant literature.

With the horrific unemployment in New York during the past winter, it dawned on many Americans for the first time that the presupposition of their social thinking is antiquated. People no longer really have the status in the world that they have earned through their own work and competence. This situation now makes the principle of voluntary charity as a means of social aid immoral. That principle was based on a false valuation of the lives of others. Such notions predominate in the so-called social gospel, which has been overcome in name but is still powerfully present in substance. The right of other persons to exist must be respected. (DBWE 10, 318)

But he was very offended when, during a seminar, students laughed loudly at theological terms, such as a quotation from Luther about sin and grace, as if people in modern times could only regard such language as grotesque. What theology was for him was almost unknown to his American fellow students. But the teachings of the fundamentalist seminaries in the USA he found backward and unscholarly. In a seminar with Professor John Baillie from Scotland, a follower of German liberal theology, Bonhoeffer became the first person in the history of Union Seminary to put forward Barth's theology. He began his presentation with the words: 'I confess that I do not see any other possible way for you to get into real contact with his thinking than by forgetting, at least for this one hour, everything you have learned before' (DB-ER 159). And then he began to lecture on Barth's theology, including also some theological ideas of his own, as a doctoral student later discovered,[11] with such enthusiasm that even after the Second World War, Baillie still regarded him as a dyed-in-the-wool Barthian, not knowing that Bonhoeffer had just begun, in his postdoctoral thesis, to express some criticism of Barth. In the United States Bonhoeffer did not go into fine distinctions, however: here his purpose was to bring the ideas of dialectical theology into the debate for the first time. His effort was not in vain. The very next year a first doctoral thesis was published at Union which showed that the issues as formulated in European theology were beginning to receive consideration there.

One fellow student at Union not only understood Bonhoeffer's theological concerns there, but also shared them: Erwin Sutz, from Switzerland. His friendship was to endure into the war years and become very important to Bonhoeffer. As a student of Barth, Sutz thought along the same lines theologically, and they were both excellent pianists and helped one another scout out the houses around Union in which they were welcome to play music. Sutz believed that Bonhoeffer ought to find an opportunity as soon as possible to talk with Barth personally, and, before they both returned to Europe, Sutz wrote to Barth proposing that Bonhoeffer visit him in Bonn, where he was now teaching. The two friends also shared their astonishment, not to say horror, at what was considered preaching in New York. Bonhoeffer wrote to Diestel:

The sermon has been reduced to parenthetical church remarks about events in the newspaper. As long as I've been here, I have heard only *one* sermon in which you could hear something like a genuine proclamation of the Gospel, and that was delivered by a Negro (indeed, in general I'm increasingly discovering greater religious power and originality in Negroes). One big question that continually occupies me in view of these facts is whether one can really still speak of Christianity [*Christlichkeit*] here, and where the criterion might be found. There's no sense in expecting the fruits where the Word really is no longer being preached. But then what becomes of Christianity per se? Ultimately it can't really be the responsibility of theology, can it? Well, it's good that Christmas is coming again here as well. (DBWE 10, 266)

Bonhoeffer found the teaching at Union stimulating in important ways, especially during the second semester. The way that ethical issues – such as the problems with Prohibition and the deprivations of ordinary people ruined in the stock market crash – were analysed on the basis of articles in the press, he found exemplary. Since he felt that the American way of life was based on American philosophy, he made use of tutorial sessions in which a student could discuss problems individually with a professor, to work through a great deal of American philosophical literature with Eugene Lyman, Professor of Philosophy of Religion, especially the works of William James (1842–1910), the brother of the great novelist Henry James.

James was an exceptionally many-sided philosopher and psychologist who also had a degree in medicine. He was one of the founders of American pragmatism, which condemns mere verbal speculation as without consequences for the context of daily life. His main interests were in studying human actions and the results to which they led. In one of his best-known works, he also studied the 'varieties of religious experience'.[12] Bonhoeffer seems to have read this book of his first and strongly disagreed with it, but that did not stop him from continuing, with Lyman as tutor, to study James's other works. Pragmatic philosophy did indeed provide Bonhoeffer with explanations for what he had observed around the seminary.

That the professors there also had their students read works of fine literature and write papers on them not only fascinated Bonhoeffer, but gave him ideas later for his preachers' seminary in Finkenwalde. Like the other Union students, he wrote assessments of the books that were dealt with in seminars. In this connection, an odd coincidence arose. Bonhoeffer's judgement of George Bernard Shaw's *Androcles and the Lion* was negative, but he seems to have neglected to read the author's afterword. In it, Shaw attacks the Church of England bishops who, during the First World War, allowed a little German church in London to be closed because it was 'inadmissible for God to be worshipped in the German language'. If he was seeing truly, said Shaw, the only people to be dumbfounded by this argument were freethinkers, people who drew their own conclusions independently of religious authority. Bonhoeffer would certainly not have reproached someone who made this statement as being a 'shallow' and 'blasphemous' writer, as he had characterized Shaw.

But the story goes further. In 1933, the little German church to which Shaw was referring became the place where Bonhoeffer himself preached, when he went to London as a pastor. During the Second World War it was destroyed by German bombs, but after the war the congregation received money from the British War Damage Commission, with which, on the site of their ruined house of God, they were able to erect the Dietrich Bonhoeffer Church.

Trips to Cuba and Mexico

Bonhoeffer spent the Christmas holidays with Erwin Sutz in the blazing heat of Cuba. They had been invited there by a sister of his former governess Maria Horn, who was working in Havana as a teacher. Bonhoeffer was as yet unsatisfied with his knowledge of English and enjoyed being able to speak Spanish again in Cuba. He took over some class sessions from Miss Horn, and at the German church service on the Sunday before Christmas he gave a rather gloomy Advent sermon.

It is probably correct to say that each of us who has looked around a bit in the world perhaps finds it particularly strange to be celebrating Christmas this year. Before our eyes stand hordes of unemployed persons, millions of children throughout the world who are hungry and miserable, people starving in China, the oppressed in India and other unfortunate countries, and in everyone's eyes we see despair and perplexity. And despite all this, Christmas is coming. Whether we want to or not, whether we are in the mood for it or not, we must hear once again: Christ, the Saviour, is born ... (DBWE 10, 589)

It would be hard to decide which of Bonhoeffer's four friendships which began in the USA became most important to him later in his life. Each in its own way had a lasting influence on him. Paul Lehmann was the first to visit him in Berlin and experienced with him the first consequences of Hitler's seizure of power. Even then he became a close friend of the Bonhoeffer family, and remained so until his death. Through Frank Fisher, Bonhoeffer first learned to see the world 'from below, from the perspective of the outcasts, the suspects, the maltreated, the powerless, the oppressed and reviled, in short from the perspective of the suffering' (DBWE 8, Prologue). He wrote this on New Year's Eve, 1943, in his essay 'After Ten Years', and described it as 'an experience of incomparable value'. This practice, even before the Hitler era, in seeing the world from the underside was one of the learning experiences that made him a man for the Resistance.

After his return from the USA Erwin Sutz remained an important theological conversation partner. That they had to carry on their dialogue in written form, and that the letters still exist, gives us deep insights into Bonhoeffer's personal and theological development. From 1938 on Sutz became the link between Bonhoeffer and his twin sister Sabine, who had to flee with her family to England. Since Sutz was in Switzerland, a neutral country, they could send important family news back and forth through him.

The Frenchman Jean Lasserre was the first Christian minister with pacifist tendencies Bonhoeffer had met, and was the one who got him to read the peace commandment in the Sermon on the Mount (Matthew 5) as the commandment of Jesus to his disciples that they must follow until Judgement Day.

The passionate appeals for peace for which Bonhoeffer became known a few years later in the ecumenical movement had their origins in conversations in America with Jean Lasserre. Even when, speaking in American churches, Bonhoeffer was emphasizing that there was a peace movement in Germany, Lasserre's influence could already be felt. After describing the First World War and its horrors, Bonhoeffer said 'We will not reopen an old and painful wound.'

Let me tell you frankly that no German, and no stranger who knows well the history of the origin of the war, believes that Germany bears the sole guilt of the war, a sentence which we were compelled to sign in the treaty of Versailles.[13] I personally do not believe on the other hand that Germany was the only guiltless country, but I as a Christian see the main guilt of Germany in quite a different light. I see it in Germany's complacency, in her belief in her allmightiness, in the lack of humility and faith in God and fear of God. (DBWE 10, 579, original in English)

However, it was in Bonhoeffer's ecumenical work, which began right after his return to Germany, that Lasserre's influence was fully revealed. That he got along especially well with French conversation partners, with whom reconciliation was considered impossible because of their attitude toward Germany, was certainly not least of all the result of the generous amounts of time which he and Jean Lasserre had devoted to one another.

Since North America is not just the United States, but is much larger and more diverse, toward the end of their time there the two friends wanted to get acquainted with Mexico, the Spanish-speaking part. They had 'a tent and a little money', and the help of the Ern family – Americans who were ready without hesitation to lend Bonhoeffer an old car.

Travelling to Mexico: lots of time and little money

Their 10-year-old son Richard had met and become attached to Bonhoeffer during the Atlantic crossing on the *Columbus*, and had been writing to him since then.

Bonhoeffer had also been invited to visit the Erns at several weekends. On receiving their generous offer, Bonhoeffer took driving lessons. He failed the test for his driver's licence twice, as he laughingly told friends later, because he refused to pay the customary 20-dollar bribe.

Bonhoeffer with Richard Ern

Lehmann rode with them as far as Chicago and then decided that Bonhoeffer, after having reached that city, could drive reasonably well. In St Louis Sutz turned back. The car needed repairs a few times along the way, but Lasserre and Bonhoeffer managed to go nearly 4000 miles in it, and only took the train for the 1200 miles they travelled in Mexico. They were enchanted with the varied scenery they encountered, as can be gathered from brief postcards they sent; unfortunately there is no long letter telling us more about their Mexican adventure. But at last the two friends had unlimited time together. They must have had some intense discussions about the Sermon on the Mount and Jesus' peace commandment; of this we have one indication. At a teacher training college in Victoria, where Lasserre had acquaintances, they created a sensation by appearing on the same platform, a Frenchman and a German together, to speak on 'peace'. They spent a week in Mexico City, including excursions to see ancient Aztec pyramids and sacrificial sites. Again, Bonhoeffer enjoyed speaking Spanish with ordinary people whom they met.

Although the trip had gone well so far, despite a few breakdowns, they suddenly ran into trouble crossing the border back into the USA. The border officials suspected these two Europeans of being illegal immigrants, about to become a burden on the American labour market. Only with the help of telegrams sent by Paul Lehmann and the German ambassador in Mexico to the border station could they prove that they were scholarship students and that their ship's passage home had already been paid. They were allowed entry. With great relief they climbed into the Erns' ramshackle Oldsmobile and headed back to New York.

How important this trip was for Bonhoeffer we can see from a letter he later wrote to Erwin Sutz, in which the memory of Mexico became tied up with his dream of going to India:

A year ago I was with Lasserre in Mexico! I can hardly think of that without having an irresistible urge to go off again, but this time to the East. I don't know when, but I don't want to wait much longer. There must be more people on earth who are different from us, who know more and can do more than we can. And only a Philistine wouldn't go there too, and learn from them. *In any case they're not the Nazis, these people, and they're not our Communists, not as I got to know them a bit better last winter.* (DBW 11, 89–90)

A conversation between Bonhoeffer`and Lasserre in New York has become famous. Bonhoeffer mentions it in his letter of 21 July 1944 to Eberhard Bethge, just after the failure of the attempt on Hitler's life. This is, for many people, the deepest and most moving letter Bonhoeffer ever wrote. He tells Bethge about a conversation with a French friend in America, in which they talked about their life's aims. The Frenchman said that he wanted to become a saint. Bonhoeffer writes that he thinks possibly his friend did become one; for himself, he had answered that he wanted to learn to have faith (DBWE 8, IV/178). After the Second World War, Lasserre said that they had been speaking English, and not yet well enough to avoid misunderstanding one another. Rather than sainthood, he had meant simply the observance of a life sanctified by consistently following God's commandments. This is the very purpose which Bonhoeffer describes in his book, *Discipleship* [*Nachfolge*, better known in English as *The Cost of Discipleship*]. The letter of 21 July 1944 shows that, in speaking of religious matters, even misunderstandings can be fruitful.

Homecoming in troubled times

Professors Reinhold Niebuhr[14] and John Baillie have said in retrospect that during his study year in America Bonhoeffer was quite unpolitical. But can this be said of someone who in 1930, long before most white Christians in the USA, was disturbed to see that the African-American churches were losing the hearts of their younger generation? And all the more because the white American churches, much more than their sister churches in Europe, had no problems at all in feeling integrated into mainstream American society. Even then Bonhoeffer saw serious racial conflict in America's future. And his letters show that he indeed had a burning interest in political developments in Germany. He was so concerned about the votes gained by the Nazi Party in the spring of 1931 that each of his parents wrote to him separately, reassuring him that there was as yet no real danger from this party. But his brother Klaus was already thinking otherwise:

Since your departure the political situation has changed greatly. The success of Nazism has convinced the widest circles that the democratic regime has failed in the past ten years. The consequences of the world economic crisis are explained in purely domestic terms. People are flirting with fascism. If this radical wave captures the educated classes, I am afraid it will be all over for this nation of poets and thinkers. (DB-ER 166–67)

Likewise, from Helmut Rößler – a friend from student days and now pastor of a village church – came a disturbing description of the inroads the Nazis were making in the rural population.

In Berlin, Superintendent Diestel had long been thinking over the best future course for his protégé. He had been discussing Bonhoeffer's doctoral thesis with the other candidates for ordination under his care. With regard to the difficult terminology of the book, he said to Bonhoeffer's uncle, Karl Alfred von Hase, 'But your nephew still needs to learn German!' (DBWE 10, 255). However, since Bonhoeffer now spoke fluent English, as soon as he got back Diestel could introduce him into ecumenical work. This energetic and far-sighted man of the church was vice-president of the German section of the World Alliance for Promoting International Friendship through the Churches, and the actual president left all the work to him. For some time he had looked forward to Bonhoeffer's becoming his new comrade-in-arms. When Bonhoeffer wrote that he would like some time off in Berlin at first, to reflect on his experiences in America, Diestel took his part. The consistory rejected this proposal immediately, but Diestel found a way to let Bonhoeffer avoid any new assignment until the beginning of October.

Reinhold Seeberg also wrote to Bonhoeffer to congratulate him on having learned English, and confessed that in recent years he himself had hardly felt any gap in his education so keenly as the inability to speak 'with the tongues of angels' (10, 291).[15] Indeed, the languages that Bonhoeffer had learned put him ahead of most Germans in theological fields at that time.

That Diestel was not the only one awaiting his return to Berlin, he found out from his mother:

At the Diestels' recently I saw Dibelius;[16] he spoke *very kindly* of you and asked when you would be back, and said he hoped to see you as chaplain to students at the Technical College, and thus won over entirely for a career as a pastor. Schreiber also sang your praises.

August Wilhelm Schreiber was the church official responsible for ecumenical work. At the end of June or the beginning of July 1931, Bonhoeffer was back in Berlin.

Hans Pfeifer, a German scholar who has made an in-depth study of Bonhoeffer's time in the USA, has come to the conclusion that 'Bonhoeffer's study year at Union Theological Seminary in 1930/31 enabled him to find his own way to learn faith, leaving behind everything that might be in his way, however precious and impressive it might be.' He refers here to Bonhoeffer's strong ties with his family and goes on:

It is not far-fetched to say that, for Bonhoeffer's theology, discipleship began to become the centre of Christian life right then and there, when he befriended Jean Lasserre and matured as a member of a small group of similarly minded friends. By their mutual encouragement, this friendship paved the way to find life directly in the Gospel. He learned that as an individual, all by himself, he could never be strong enough to go this way. *Sanctorum communio* (the fellowship of saints) was not only a theological concept but had of necessity to become a real social community of disciples.[17]

4. Before the Storm (1931–1932)

A visit to Karl Barth

Bonhoeffer was hardly back from the USA when he turned down an offer from his parents to take some time in Friedrichsbrunn to rest after his travels. Instead, he took the train to Frankfurt to visit his brother Karl-Friedrich and family, then journeyed on to Mainz where he boarded a steamer down the Rhine River. A postcard to his parents shows his elation and how much he was looking forward to Bonn: 'Karl-Friedrich and Grete were very glad to see me, and so is the Rhine.'

He was on his way to see Karl Barth, whom he wanted at last to meet in person. He had given up his holiday time in order to arrive before the end of the summer semester and hear a few of Barth's lectures. Sutz, who had arranged the contact, soon received three letters from Bonn in which Bonhoeffer described not only the impression Barth made on him, but also his impression of Barth's eager students, which was that they did not give much credit to views other than those of their great master.

I'm sitting here in the park in front of the University. Barth lectured this morning at 7 a.m., and I spoke briefly with him afterwards. This evening there is a discussion group at his house with people from Maria Laach.[1] I'm looking forward to it very much. In spite of all you did to prepare me, there were a number of surprises in his lecture. (DBW 11, 16)

You can imagine yourself that I have often wished you were here, especially at times, in the company of his anointed initiates, when there would have been chances (at least for the not yet initiated) to laugh out loud. But I daren't do that here, only a quiet little snicker (doesn't sound likely, does it?) But there's not much opportunity for me as a *theological illegitimate*, as I see here all too clearly. They have a sharp scent for thoroughbreds here. No *Negro* passes for white; they even examine his fingernails and the soles of his feet. Until now they are still showing me hospitality as the unknown stranger. (DBW 11, 18)[2]

Bonhoeffer experienced Barth differently from the way Barth's students did; that is, he saw him as a theologian who had 'gone beyond his own books' and was hungry to hear from others who were grappling with the same problems. 'I'm even more impressed with him in a discussion than in his writings and lectures. In a discussion he's really all there.' We have an account of one of the 'open evenings' at Barth's home which Bonhoeffer attended, by Winfried Maechler, who was not long afterwards to become one of the most enthusiastic of Bonhoeffer's own students. He described his first encounter with his future teacher:

As usual [at Barth's evenings] we were discussing the content of his lecture on dogmatics. Then a blond Teuton stood up and quoted Luther: 'For God, the cursing of a godless person can be more agreeable than the hallelujahs of the pious!' Barth jumped up from his chair: 'That's magnificent. Where does it come from, and who are you anyway?' (DBW 11, 19)

Others who remember this incident say that Bonhoeffer did not stand up to speak, and that Barth didn't know at first who had tossed in the quote from Luther, but they do remember his delight. So it was not long until Bonhoeffer received a personal invitation from Barth, and they had a lengthy conversation on the problem of ethics. Bonhoeffer's burning interest at the time was the question of how the Church could proclaim God's commandments, including of course the peace commandment in the Sermon on the Mount, in such a way as to make them ethically concrete and obligatory. In his view, the Church was not supposed to proclaim ethical principles, but only God's commandments for here and now. Barth did not want to take on this question with such intensity, and Bonhoeffer reported to his friend in Switzerland:

He wouldn't concede to me what I expected he would have to concede. For him, besides the one great light in the night, there are also a lot of smaller lights, so-called 'relative ethical criteria', the nature of which, and the meaning and the right, he nonetheless couldn't make sense of for me; he could only point to the Bible. In the end he said I was making a principle out of grace and using it to strike everything else dead. Of course I contested the first point, though I still wanted to know why all the rest shouldn't be struck dead ... Finally I had to tear myself away. This is really someone who has something to offer, and there we sit moping in poor old Berlin because there is no one there who can teach us theology. (DBW 11, 20)

It was precisely the dispute they had that won Bonhoeffer over definitively for the professor in Bonn.

Anyone beginning a new career should have some time to go slowly and find his way in his chosen work, but this was denied Bonhoeffer. His visit to Karl Barth in Bonn was an important epilogue to his studies, but the 25-year-old was hardly back in Berlin when demands began to be made of him as if he had already been practising a profession for years. His life for the next year and a half called for him to be many things at once, as never before. This was indeed strenuous, but it could not have prepared him better for the years of struggle that lay ahead. Eberhard Bethge speaks of Bonhoeffer's return from the USA as marking a sharp break in his life.

He now began to teach on a faculty whose theology he did not share, and to preach in a church whose self-confidence he regarded as unfounded. More aware than before, he now became part of a society that was moving toward political, social and economic chaos. (DB-ER 173)

On 21 July 1931 the 13th German Student Assembly in Graz, Austria,[3] had unanimously elected a Nazi as chair of the German student organization. He and his helpers decided that in place of the building of a democratic state, which until now had been the watchword of Germany's students, they should introduce the 'leader principle [*Führerprinzip*]' of Hitler's National Socialist (Nazi) Party. Even though this young man was soon forced to resign his position for lack of competence, from then on it was difficult for democratically minded students to make their voices heard. A fight over issues of 'German racial origin' and 'being *Volk*-minded'[4] had already taken place. Jews were to be excluded, and the 'German race', for which the soldiers who fell in the First World War had made a 'holy sacrifice in their blood', was to be honoured. The religious language was unmistakable. 'Germany, O sacred word' was not sung in those days only by students with Nazi leanings, and in poetry Germany was even described as 'blessed', in the sense in which canonized saints are blessed.[5] A carefully planned infiltration of the German student organization had begun, and it increasingly became a brown-shirted unit of shock troops in universities and graduate schools.[6]

Pompous poetry was also written by the man whom Hitler named as *Reich* (national) youth leader of his Nazi Party, Baldur Benedikt von Schirach. One of his 'poems' bore the title, 'Repentance':

Lightly we bear heavy sins
happy despite every crime,

Allied only with the best
such as our souls seek always.
When, our colours flying brave
Nor foe nor scaffold frightened us
Did our penance without prayer
And yet God forgave our debt.[7]

As a student, Schirach threw himself so totally into working for the Party that he could no longer keep up with his studies. When he confessed this to Hitler, the Führer said to him, 'Schirach, you're studying with me!' The newly appointed Reich youth leader had come into Hitler's inner circle because, from 1925 on, whenever Hitler went to Weimar he was invited to the Schirachs' home. The father had been fired as director of the theatre there in 1918 and was bitter about it. The Schirach home had a certain international flair since the mother was an American. The son, thrilled by Hitler's first visit there, had joined the Party at the age of 18. The 'old warriors' didn't think he was tough enough, but he enjoyed Hitler's protection, who was well aware of how much he owed to Schirach's agitation at German universities. 'If anything keeps me believing in the victory of our movement,' said Hitler in July 1931, 'it is the progress we are making among German students.'[8]

Bonhoeffer was soon to have plenty to do with the Nazi Student Federation, but first he had to concentrate on preparing his lectures for the winter semester. Even before that, however, Franz Hildebrandt requested his help as a friend. Hildebrandt had become pastoral assistant in Dobrilugk, in the rural Mark Brandenburg, the province surrounding Berlin, and was grappling with the problem of how to make the Christian faith relevant to youth preparing for confirmation. At that time, confirmation classes were taught using Luther's *Shorter Catechism*, a series of questions and answers to be learned by heart, explaining the Ten Commandments, the creed and the Lord's Prayer. Pupils also had to memorize many hymns from the church's hymnal. This way of teaching youngsters was being increasingly criticized; so Hildebrandt suddenly descended on his friend with a plan to develop a new catechism, containing the 'Lutheran faith for today'. Bonhoeffer, with his wealth of experience with youth, was immediately captivated by the idea. His rather difficult book *Act and Being* had just been published, so Hildebrandt received a copy with the ironic inscription, 'And this is going to become a catechism?'

Even today the catechetical text they produced glows with the joy the two friends had in working on it together. 'What you believe, you have' was their title. They used the traditional format of questions and answers, but these were not to be learned by heart, becoming instead a stimulus for discussion with the young people. One of the first questions was 'Who is a Protestant?' The answer begins with a formulation by the two friends, and then leads into a confession of faith that Hildebrandt had found in Luther's writings. Bonhoeffer put a copy of this into his own hymnal and later used it in many worship services.

[A Protestant is] anyone who rejoices in the grace of God, acknowledges the name of Christ, and prays for the Holy Spirit. Anyone who is ready for the lordship of God, who is not afraid of alien powers and knows of the final consummation. Anyone who hears the Word of God in preaching, who loves his[/her] community and lives from forgiveness. The faith of the Gospel acknowledges that God has given himself completely to us with all that he is and has, in these words:

'I believe in God, that he is my Creator, in Jesus Christ, that he is my Lord, in the Holy Spirit, that he is my Justifier. God has made me and given me life, soul, body and all good things, Christ has brought me under his dominion through his body, and the Holy Spirit justifies me through his word and the sacraments which are in the church, and will justify us completely at the Last Day. That is the Christian faith; know what you must do and what you have been given.'[9]

For the answer to what a Christian should do in the world, the catechism follows the Lutheran tradition by pointing to one's work, one's occupation, but in the awareness of how much injustice there is in this area of life. 'Those who are earning their living today are taking bread out of the mouths of others.' At the time, six million Germans were unemployed. In some of the other questions, too, the friends adopted a new-sounding tone. 'The church prays to God for peace, and does not consider any war a holy war.' And the question, 'Why are there so many churches?' is also answered in this catechism:

We are really supposed to be *one* church. In the midst of our incredible divisions we urgently seek communion among all Christians. It will only be possible for us humans ever to have it if we keep waiting and believing [in him] who is faithful to his church. (DBW 11, 235)

Bonhoeffer and Hildebrandt may have been the first to ask and answer a question on the ecumenical issue in a catechism. Their joint effort was published in the *Monatschrift für Pastoraltheologie* (Pastoral Theology Monthly), but what response there was, or whether others besides themselves used it, is not known.

Looking at Bonhoeffer's calendar for the period that followed, one finds not only the obligations he had to fulfil as a lecturer, but also dates for his work as student chaplain at the Technical College and as an assistant in parish work on the east side of Berlin. He once said in a letter to his parents that he could only work with concentration at night or very early in the morning, and this must often have been the case in the year-and-a-half before 1933. As we shall see, he had taken on additional responsibilities in both teaching and parish work, far beyond what was normally expected. In addition, there were tasks for the Protestant ecumenical movement which Diestel was planning for him, never suspecting how time-consuming these were to become for Bonhoeffer.

To get a picture of this period in Bonhoeffer's life, we must consider each area separately; otherwise we will become too confused by his rushing back and forth between lectures, seminars, evenings with students, meetings in Berlin or elsewhere, confirmation classes, worship services, desk work and trips abroad. Let us begin with the ecumenical work.

Ecumenical work

In Germany today, the 'ecumenical' sphere usually means cooperation between the two major churches, Catholic and Protestant. This was not true in Bonhoeffer's day because the Catholic Church did not then want any contact with others. On the other hand, there was a desire among many other Christian confessions, on every continent, for conversation and cooperation.

Young people had been pressing for such contact since the first half of the nineteenth century, and had preceded their elders by founding the worldwide YWCA in 1844, YMCA in 1855 and World Student Christian Association in 1895. The church mission societies and associations agreed in 1910 to cooperate among themselves, because there had long been the feeling that it was a scandal for the churches overseas to preach the 'one Lord Jesus Christ' while at the same time competing or even fighting with one another. Shortly before the First World War, most Protestant churches, along with the Anglican and Greek Orthodox Churches, were ready to negotiate on ways of cooperation. The war postponed this somewhat. But by the time Bonhoeffer began to participate in it, the ecumenical movement had for years consisted of three independent organizations: the World Alliance for Promoting International Friendship through the Churches, founded in Konstanz, Germany in 1914; the Life and Work [of the Church] movement, founded in 1925 in Stockholm, and the Faith and Order movement, begun in Lausanne, Switzerland in 1927. These three had set up a joint office in Geneva, Switzerland, which maintained contacts and organized meetings and conferences.[10]

On the basis of his interests, Bonhoeffer would have belonged in the theological area, the Commission on Faith and Order, where issues defined as theological were discussed. But he never warmed to this branch of the work, and his one encounter with it came through a dispute. The World Alliance into which Diestel brought him was, at the time Bonhoeffer joined, the one least concerned with theology as such; but it was concerned about the peace issue, which provided the starting point for his work with the organization.

When he left Bonn, Bonhoeffer would have liked to visit his friend Sutz in Switzerland, but he had already promised to go to an ecumenical conference in England. Diestel had obtained permission from the consistory for his ecumenical helper to attend 'because he speaks several languages and can move in the intellectual sphere with enough freedom' (DB-ER 198). With this assignment to travel to England, Diestel had put Bonhoeffer's life 'on a track' that it never left, as Bonhoeffer said in 1942 (DBWE 16, 367). On 14 August 1931 he went to Cambridge as a German delegate to a conference of the World Alliance for Promoting International Friendship through the Churches. On 6 September he came back as one of its three International Youth Secretaries, and from then on he was responsible for the youth work of the World Alliance in the Scandinavian countries and central Europe, including Austria and Hungary.[11] The other two Youth Secretaries were Tom Craske in England and Pierre Toureille in France.

It didn't take long for Bonhoeffer to discover that he had allowed himself to be elected to a highly labour-intensive volunteer job. Another consequence was that it made him a member of the German section of the World Alliance, in which Diestel had the say. In Berlin, Bonhoeffer became secretary of the Central Office for Ecumenical Youth Work, from which all ecumenical activities for Protestant youth in Germany were to be coordinated.

This first ecumenical meeting in which Bonhoeffer took part was concerned, among other things, with disarmament. It had been preceded by a drum roll in Germany. In June 1931, during a preparatory meeting in Hamburg of the German section of the World Alliance, Professors

Paul Althaus and Emanuel Hirsch published an article in the *Hamburger Nachrichten* newspaper in which they said:

In this situation, in our judgement, there can be no understanding between us Germans and the victorious nations in the world war; we can only show them that as long as they continue the war against us, understanding is impossible ... Thus we give full weight to the demand that we break through all artificial semblance of commonality with them, and unreservedly profess our conviction that Christian understanding and cooperation among churches on issues of rapprochement among peoples is impossible as long as the others pursue a policy against our people which we find murderous. Those who believe that such understanding can be better served otherwise at this time are denying the fate which Germany has suffered and confounding consciences here at home and abroad, because such a view fails to honour the truth.[12]

The right-wing newspapers carried the article on their front pages, and thus began an anti-ecumenical campaign that lasted a year. Among those who tried to inject some reason into the situation was Bonhoeffer, who had seen in Washington that the attitude toward Germany was beginning to change. He felt that everything depended on German forbearance and consistent participation instead of self-pitying, nationalistic pronouncements. The French delegation in Cambridge had said:

After the war mania had disappeared, our churches expected some gesture of regret from the German churches about what had happened, and a desire to lead their people along the path of justice and fellowship. No act of penance was expected from them, only a word of sympathy for our plundered and destroyed churches. But nothing came. The German churches bewailed only the suffering of their own people, whose complete innocence they proclaimed. (DB-ER 198–99)

With his report on the meeting in Cambridge, Bonhoeffer intervened in the debate going on in Germany. He said that people who weren't interested in the work of the World Alliance, or felt resentful towards it, should allow their judgement to be either confirmed or revised by this meeting. For the churches, the question on disarmament was whether the nations which had committed themselves to disarm under the treaty would keep their word or not. In Cambridge the churches had called for truth-telling and good faith, for honouring promises made by carrying them out. The youth conference, however, had not adopted a similar resolution, not least because Bonhoeffer had urged it not to do so.

There was too strong a feeling that we must first learn to see new situations in a new way, and not wade in right away with big declarations ... Nowhere was criticism of the entire undertaking heard more loudly, from more different viewpoints, than in the youth conference. Moreover, it was here that, once again, the intellectual division into two groups, the continental [European] group, especially the Germans and French (also the Danes) on one side, and the British and American group on the other, emerged clearly. The French youth saw many essential things very much the way we did, especially theologically. (See Bonhoeffer's report in DBWE 11)

Here we hear for the first time Bonhoeffer's two demands of the ecumenical movement, on which he stubbornly insisted, time and again: ecumenical statements should only be made when participants really had something to say, that is, they must learn to guard against empty words; secondly, they must be clear about what theology they wanted to stand for. His report ended with the thought that the churches almost never spoke their words at the appropriate moment. 'When will the time come when Christianity speaks the right word at the right time?' Behind this statement we hear once again the question of concrete commandments.

The Geneva office, with the ecumenical movement's few full-time employees, was not at all pleased that the conference in Cambridge had appointed three youth secretaries, who of course were supposed to work with the Geneva office but were not subject to its directives. The research department especially, headed by the German economist and pastor Hans Schönfeld, thought it ought to have a say in all work projects initiated by the youth secretaries; instead, it wasn't even consulted. When Bonhoeffer began talking about 'unemployment' as the theme for upcoming youth conferences, Schönfeld saw it as proof that the work of the youth secretaries wouldn't accomplish anything, since they weren't qualified to deal with such a topic. In this way Hans Schönfeld became one of Bonhoeffer's earliest opponents.

Among the experienced ecumenical leaders as well, a number were discontented that, through the youth conferences and appointment of youth secretaries, younger leaders were gaining influence in the movement. From this time on World Alliance work became much more explosive theologically, because these younger persons were not afraid of any controversy. But the Danish bishop Valdemar Ammundsen, as chairman, had insisted that the World Alliance needed to be rejuvenated so that it wouldn't become 'too respectable'.

Schönfeld's criticism of the conference proceedings was not entirely unjustified, since the structures of the ecumenical movement had already been quite complicated. His own department was a case in point. Though it belonged to the Geneva office, Schönfeld's position was paid for by the German churches, so he was personally dependent on the goodwill of Germans towards the work of his department. Unlike the youth secretaries, he was not independent.

Moreover, during this time the World Alliance's sources of income were drying up, due to the world economic crisis. The German office was only saved from being closed because Diestel incorporated it into his Superintendent's office. Bonhoeffer received polite instructions from Geneva asking him to ensure that 'a maximum of activities and effectiveness' was achieved 'with a minimum of resources' (DBW 11, 36). However, recognizing that in the long run, such a directive tends to be little more than a pious hope, the World Alliance and the Life and Work movement were already making overtures to one another and beginning to plan and carry out much of their work together.

The conference in Cambridge convinced Bonhoeffer that he needed to know the economic context in order to understand worldly reality. He therefore joined a Theological Working Group on Questions of National Economy and began to study relevant literature on the subject.

Ecumenical work in Germany differed from that of other European countries and the USA in that it was carried out notably by members of university faculties of theology, especially so within the Faith and Order movement. Among these ecumenical academics, those at the University of Berlin played a leading role. Church officials preferred to be involved in the Life and Work movement, or Practical Christianity as it was called in German. The World Alliance was never especially popular in Germany, because it was considered to be 'Western-dominated'. It was a less regimented organization, meaning that committed individuals were still playing the decisive roles. Bureaucracies of every kind, even church bureaucracies, do not particularly care for this style. The World Alliance's most prominent representative in Berlin was Professor Friedrich Siegmund-Schulze. As a student, Bonhoeffer had not been interested in meeting him, but now this had changed, since Siegmund-Schulze was not only a co-founder of the World Alliance but also well known for his social work on the east side of Berlin. In addition, Siegmund-Schulze made no secret of his opposition to the Nazi regime, to the point that he became one of the first German academics forced to emigrate. Bonhoeffer, however, did not lose contact with him.[13]

The letters Bonhoeffer had to write as secretary for the Central Office for Youth Work give evidence of many quarrels over who was responsible for what. So he soon had plenty to do with everyday details of church business.

The ecumenical circle was trying hard to come up with a theological basis for its work, but the appeal by Professors Hirsch and Althaus had involved the Central Office, too, in the dispute between supporters and opponents of international ecumenical cooperation. Before 1933 there was still hope of settling it through theological discussions. Bonhoeffer participated energetically in these as well as taking the minutes. Two extended sessions were held in Berlin on 'The Church and the Churches' and 'The Church and the Nations'. The first was intended to tackle the confessional problem; the second, the question of peace. The sessions were chaired by Professor Wilhelm Stählin from the University of Münster, who was anxious to mediate between the two sides (DB-ER 241–42).

These discussions at the Central Office, to judge by the minutes, give the impression of a preliminary skirmish to the fierce disputes of 1933. For example, one of the participants, Revd Friedrich Peter, strongly objected to Bonhoeffer's view that the ecumenical movement had a mission to work for peace. Peter had fought in the volunteer corps and felt that after experiencing a great war, people were entitled to think war might come again and to maintain defence forces and an army. A strong person, called by God through Christ, could have the right to do things that were not the business of the Christian community. The other participants found this statement so inept that they urged the Revd Peter be replaced in the group by another clergyman. But only a year later the 'strong person called by God' of whom Revd Peter was thinking became German Reich Chancellor, and he himself became the new Bishop of Magdeburg.

That Bonhoeffer himself spoke out strongly against these nationalistic tendencies hardly needs to be mentioned. Bethge says:

His interest in the ecumenical movement was at first incidental, but it took such a hold on him that it became an integral part of his being. He was soon furiously involved in the internal battles about its orientation, while at the same time defending it enthusiastically in public. (DB-ER 189–90)

In March 1933 a last attempt was made to keep ecumenically minded German theologians together, at a conference in Dassel on 'Common Perspectives for Ecumenical Work in Germany'. But the political conflicts, in which church circles were also involved, had become so strong that it was no longer possible to accomplish much. It is interesting that, in Dassel, Bonhoeffer was already pointing out that ecumenical study must bring back the concept of heresy, of false doctrine. 'The loss of this concept means a heavy sacrifice of confessional substance' (cf. DBW 11,

260–63). A few months later he was to enter into a long struggle on this question with ecumenical partners in Geneva and in England.

As disappointing as these early ecumenical experiences in Germany were for Bonhoeffer, he was gaining an acquaintance with influential ecumenists, which was to prove very useful to him in the years to come. With most of his conversation partners he was to cross paths again later. The former General Superintendent of Westphalia, Wilhelm Zoellner, and the foreign affairs expert in the Church Federation Office, Theodor Heckel – both participants in the Central Youth Work Office discussions – were to become opponents of his, while others became friends or remained conversation partners.

Ecumenical journeys

Bonhoeffer was determinedly opposed to holding too many meetings. His report on a British–French youth conference in April 1932 at Epsom, near London, shows what he regarded as being relatively unproductive. For three days, three main themes relating to Christian faith were discussed: whether it should be practised (1) in politics, (2) in economic life or (3) in society. He reported that lively discussions had taken place in the groups as long as they consisted in sharing information. As soon as they tried to go further, however, they got stuck right on the threshold of the main issue, because they couldn't agree on what 'Christianity' was (DBW 11, 315). Although his official report on the main conference was politely positive, Bonhoeffer wrote to Sutz: 'In the meantime I've been in England again, at a very superfluous meeting.' (DBW 11, 88)

Bonhoeffer found a German–French conference held in July 1932, at Westerburg Castle in the Westerwald, much more successful, because participants weren't afraid to tackle concrete political issues. Papers had been exchanged beforehand so that the conference could begin right away with discussion. A great deal of time was spent on the rise of Nazism in Germany; this allowed Bonhoeffer to point out that in Hitler's successes, the policies of other countries were also playing a role, since they had turned down every request made by the democratic government in Germany for an easing of the peace terms of 1919. During the Second World War, he continued to represent this viewpoint when he came to Geneva on behalf of the German Resistance.

The German and French conference participants at Westerburg Castle, coming from two nations that were usually arch enemies, experienced their being together at that time as a gift, and looked forward to another conference in 1933. But after Hitler had seized power no further meetings could be held.

Probably the most important ecumenical conference for Bonhoeffer during these years was a youth peace conference hosted by a Czechoslovakian church from 20 to 30 July 1932 in Ciernohorské Kúpele. Bonhoeffer was substituting at this conference for Diestel, who was ill, doing so somewhat reluctantly as he had to be in Geneva three weeks later. Again he wrote to Sutz that the conference had been 'rather mediocre'; today it is seen as a small but important milestone in ecumenical history, because it was in Ciernohorské Kúpele that Bonhoeffer explained what he meant by a 'theology of the ecumenical movement'.

He had prepared in advance theses for his audience summarizing his lecture and making clear what the issues were for him at that time (DBW 11, 344ff.). A young Czech was to give proof many years later that Bonhoeffer's presentation influenced his own Czech church's resistance to the German conquerors. The first thesis made clear straightaway that the ecumenical movement was not united and therefore was letting itself be defined from outside.

The ecumenical movement does not have a theology. If this movement is a new form of self-understanding for the church, then it must put forward a theology. If it does not do so, it reveals that it exists only to achieve certain goals. The ecumenical idea becomes dependent on the political ups and downs (nationalism – internationalism) unless it has its own theological foundation. In many countries this has become a highly sensitive issue. We must have an end to disregard for theology on the part of 'practical' people. (DBW 11, 344)

Because Jesus Christ is Lord of the whole world, Bonhoeffer said, the Church must carry his word to all the world. But by what authority does the Church speak? His answer was that because it is the Church of Jesus Christ, it is by Christ's authority that it proclaims the gospel and commandments. But Christ is *present*, insisted Bonhoeffer, and therefore the gospel and commandments of Christ must address the concrete situation today, or else we are speaking of something other than Christ's message. The preaching of the commandments can only be made concrete when the person preaching them has a profound understanding of present reality. The word of God in this concrete sense, which Bonhoeffer repeated with penetrating force, was part of his struggle against the amiable, uncommitted discourse he found at such meetings. For him, the Church was not there to establish lofty principles; it either had to keep quiet or to give concrete commands. He granted that it might make mistakes in doing so, but each of its commands was based solely on the Church's belief in the forgiveness of sins. The fourth thesis says:

How does the church know what God's command is for the present hour? Neither the biblical law, nor any sort of established orders of creation, can be sources of such knowledge; either would simply be conformity to a natural law. Only from Christ, from whom we have the Gospel, can we also know God's command. From Christ comes, necessarily, our recognition of the whole world as a fallen world; we no longer recognize its original orders. We know only orders that keep us holding onto Christ, and whenever we have to judge that an order is no longer open to Christ, this order must be broken. There are no orders that are sacred in themselves. Only through its openness to Christ and for the new creation can an order be 'good'. The church must dare, through faith, to decide for or against such an order. Its goodness is not assured in any other way. (DBW 11, 345–6)

Bonhoeffer said that in Anglo-Saxon theological thinking, peace was understood as 'a piece of the kingdom of God on earth'; but that meant making it an absolute ideal, and this must be rejected. In this fallen world, the right to struggle exists; but, Bonhoeffer contended, this does not mean the right to wage war. War is a means of struggle which today is forbidden by God, because its consequence is to destroy human beings both outwardly and inwardly and thus to rob them of their chance to see Christ.

Socialism, he continued, has shown that a movement that has a message can establish itself on an international basis. The Church, with its message of an entirely different sort – that is, alone by means of Christian preaching and theology which keeps close to the present – must now create an all-embracing, supranational basis for its work. The churches of the World Alliance should tell Christendom to listen to the commandments of God, and should tell the world, the states that govern it, that they must change the present state of affairs and should listen to the words of criticism from the Church.

What church can speak in such a way? Only a church which proclaims the pure truth of the Gospel. But this truth has been torn apart; for the churches of the World Alliance, there is no longer *one* truth. It is this that is most deeply lacking in the ecumenical situation, and the peril it represents must never be disguised. But wherever the church recognizes its guilt with regard to the truth, and wherever the church is nevertheless called by God's command to speak, there the church must dare to speak, solely in faith that its sins are forgiven. (DBW 11, 347)

We wouldn't know today why this speech made such a deep impression on those who heard it, but for the Czech participant who wrote down Bonhoeffer's welcoming speech to the conference as international youth secretary, in which Bonhoeffer made clear what he meant by speaking concretely. This speech had the effect of translating his theological theses into political demands.

Peace work runs into a whole series of internal and external problems. In Germany there is a general feeling of having been treated unjustly by the one-sided declaration, in the Treaty of Versailles, that the German people are to blame for the World War. The League of Nations is not completely trusted here either. The feeling of injustice and our self-awareness as a people are being exploited by extreme elements. Our ecumenical forces, both inside and outside the World Alliance, have a lot of well-meant but theologically problematic statements to overcome, attempts to solve the problem of nationhood, the war and so forth …

The Hitler-nationalist party is misusing democratic means in its striving to set up a dictatorship. These next few days will decide to what extent the parties opposed to Hitler are capable of preventing the Nazis from taking over the government. Nazism is also penetrating into the church. Responsible theologians are faced, with the support of the ecumenical world, with the task of strengthening those Germans and Christians in Germany who are struggling against Hitler. A victory for Hitler's party will have consequences that cannot be foreseen, not only for Germany but for the whole world. Christians must unite in combatting the forces which are tempting peoples to follow false nationalisms, promoting militarism and threatening the world with an unrest that can lead to war. (DBW 11, 347–48)

That the Church only has the right to speak when it speaks in concrete terms was well-nigh hammered into the conference participants by Bonhoeffer:

The word the church speaks to the world must … from a profound knowledge of the world, be relevant to its very present reality, if it would resound with full authority … otherwise it will be saying something else, a human word, a powerless word. Thus the church must not proclaim principles which are true for all time, but only commands which are true for today. For whatever is 'always' true, is just what 'today' is not true: God is 'always', for us, the One who is God 'today'. (DBW 11, 332)

Bonhoeffer left the conference early, despite being begged to stay, in order to vote in the parliamentary (Reichstag) elections of 31 July 1932 against the Nazi Party and the German National People's Party (DNVP).

As a youth secretary, Bonhoeffer was also a member of the executive committee of the World Alliance. Its meeting in Geneva, 19–22 August 1932, was immediately preceded by a meeting of the Ecumenical Council of Life and Work. This body, to Bonhoeffer's joy, had elected Karl Barth to its theological committee; and it had also chosen the Bishop of Chichester in England, George Bell, to replace its president, who had died. Hermann Kapler, the ecumenically experienced President of the Old Prussian Union's High Church Council in Berlin, had declared that Bell should not only serve out the unfinished term of his predecessor, but be elected right away for two additional years, because the decisions that were expected to be made called for the greatest possible continuity. As a result of this being affirmed, Bishop Bell, as president of the Life and Work Council, was able during the following year to intervene in the German church struggle, being kept informed by Bonhoeffer of every detail of developments in Germany.

The disarmament conference which had just been taking place in Geneva had ended in failure. William Temple, the Archbishop of York in England, had preached a sermon at the time of its opening, in which he said:

One clause there is in the existing treaties which offends in principle the Christian conscience and for the deletion of which by proper authority the voice of Christendom must be raised. This is the clause which affixes to one group of belligerents in the Great War the whole guilt for its occurrence ... We have to ask not only who dropped the match but who strewed the ground with gunpowder.[14]

In Germany, where a nationalistic mood was heating up at that time, such voices were simply going unheard.

At the executive committee meeting of the World Alliance, to Bonhoeffer's astonishment Professor Wilfred Monod, head of the French branch of the World Alliance and considered a hardliner against Germany, argued for the World Alliance to reflect on its theological basis. This was completely along the lines of what Bonhoeffer wanted. In the executive it led to an impassioned dispute with the old pioneers of the movement, who urged that they not get involved in 'theological quarrels'. The 'younger generation' took the opposing view and, although no agreement was reached at that time, the signs were that the ecumenical movement was turning a page. Bonhoeffer was asked to draft a response to Monod's theses, but by the time of the next meeting the church struggle had begun and he had no time.

The youth conference of the World Alliance and Life and Work, which followed immediately in Gland, Switzerland, on Lake Geneva, under the leadership of the Bishop of Ripon, was also not very satisfying to Bonhoeffer, who had to preside in the German-language section. Even so, he invited Sutz to participate, saying he was only partly responsible for the leadership. 'In all events I already feel I am not responsible for its course. The British have now put their fingers in the pie too much for that ... though in spite of everything it will perhaps be quite interesting.'

This conference was substantially bigger than the preceding one, since there were representatives from almost all European countries. There were even a few individual delegates from Asian countries, including C. F. Andrews, Gandhi's friend and co-worker. They discussed the effects of capitalism and the machine age and, for the first time at such a conference, also India's situation. Then came, once again, the battle over whether the conference should adopt a resolution. Bonhoeffer pleaded successfully for 'qualified silence'. The extent to which his authority had grown in the course of the conference was shown when he was asked to give the closing address, the 'summing-up', in place of the respected Danish Bishop Ammundsen who had had to decline. Bonhoeffer reiterated much of what he had already said in Ciernohorské Kúpele, but he took a different tone:

Isn't it also especially in the spirit of these conferences that, whenever we find ourselves face to face with someone who seems completely strange to us, whose concerns we cannot understand yet who surely has a right to be heard, we hear in the voice of this brother the very voice of Christ, and thus do not refuse to listen, but rather take this voice completely seriously, hear it, and love this other person just because of his or her strangeness to us? (DBW 11, 352–53)

It could be, he continued, that some would have to say they had heard nothing at the conference, while others would say they had heard an enormous amount. But in this regard he had a great concern:

Hasn't it become shockingly clear, in everything we have talked about with one another here, that we are no longer obedient to the Bible? We like our own ideas better than those of the Bible. We are no longer reading the Bible seriously; we are no longer reading it against ourselves, but only in our own favour. If this whole conference were to have a great significance, perhaps this would be that we read the Bible in an entirely different way until we meet again. (DBW 11, 353)

Then, speaking of the situation in the world, Bonhoeffer asked: 'Why is the ... Church of Christ, as it appears in the World Alliance, afraid?'

Because it knows there is a commandment to peace, and yet with the clear vision that is given to the church, sees the reality that is full of hate, enmity, violence. It is as if all the powers on earth had conspired together against peace; as if money, the economy, the drive to power, even the love of one's fatherland have been dragged into the service of hate ...

How could it be anything but blasphemous mindlessness, if we were to declare 'No more war!' and think that with that, and a new organization – even a Christian one – we could exorcize the devil? Such organizations are nothing, no more than a house of cards that the whirlwind blows away ... Even our well-meaning good will amounts to nothing ...

Christ must be present among us in preaching and sacrament, the Crucified One who made peace between God and humankind. The Crucified One is our peace. (DBW 11, 354–55)

This trip to Switzerland had a prologue and an epilogue for Bonhoeffer. Both were of a private nature, but no less important to him than taking part in the conference. He spent 16–17 August as the guest of Jean Lasserre and Jean's parents, who had a holiday chalet near Chamonix. Unfortunately Lasserre was far too modest to come forward, after the Second World War, and speak of his relationship to Bonhoeffer. After their time together in the USA they were able to meet again several times; if only we knew more about these visits. In August 1932 especially, they must have had a lot to tell one another. In signing the Lasserres' guest book, Bonhoeffer thanked them 'for two fine and unforgettable days, during which I was privileged to feel cared for as if I were a member of your family' (DBW 11, 104).

About a visit to Sutz later that summer we do know more. The two went together to visit Karl Barth, on his invitation, at the chalet of his friend Rudolf Pestalozzi, a manufacturer from Zürich. However, since this was already after a visit with Barth in Berlin which had rather preoccupied Bonhoeffer, we shall first turn to his work in Berlin in his two callings as university lecturer and assistant pastor.

'Christianity entails a decision'

In Bonhoeffer's ecumenical work, echoed soon afterwards in his lectures as well, he had begun taking a tone that was not yet being heard in Barcelona. It came out most clearly in Gland when he said that we must read the Bible 'against ourselves as well'. A fundamental change of direction, a complete reorientation, must have taken place within him. This transition had been induced by Bonhoeffer's experience in the USA, particularly his conversations with Jean Lasserre. Bethge calls it 'the transition from theologian to Christian'. Bonhoeffer does not seem to have talked about it with anyone at the time, but Paul Lehmann saw the effects of this decision when he visited Bonhoeffer in Berlin in 1933. In New York he had felt that his friend had quite an easygoing attitude toward church and attending worship. Now he was struck by how deeply serious these matters had become for him.

There are three testimonies from later years from which one may deduce what must have taken place in Bonhoeffer's mind and heart. The first is in a letter he wrote in 1935 from London to his brother Karl Friedrich. To this eldest of his brothers, with whom he had a warm, close relationship, he was quite prepared to give an account of himself. Karl Friedrich had asked him if he really must take such an exposed position in the church struggle, as it was worrying their mother. Bonhoeffer replied:

Perhaps I seem to you rather fanatical and mad about a number of things. I myself am sometimes afraid of that. But I know that the day I become more 'reasonable', to be honest I should have to chuck my entire theology. When I first started in theology, my idea of it was quite different – rather more academic, probably. Now it has turned into something else altogether. But I do believe that at last I am on the right track, for the first time in my life. I often feel quite happy about it. I only worry about being so afraid of what other people will think as to get bogged down instead of going forward. I think I am right in saying that I would only achieve true inner clarity and honesty by really starting to take the Sermon on the Mount seriously. Here alone lies the force that can blow all this hocus-pocus [of Nazism] sky-high – like fireworks, leaving only a few burnt-out shells behind ... Things do exist that are worth standing up for without compromise. To me it seems that peace and social justice are such things, as is Christ himself. (DBWE 13, 284–85)

The second testimony is found in quite a long letter to his brother-in-law Rüdiger Schleicher, 11 years older than he. Bonhoeffer liked to discuss things with him, appreciating his humanistic, cultured mind and his gentle humour. In matters of church and Christianity, Rüdiger Schleicher thought along Harnack's lines and, when he had a chance to hear Bonhoeffer preach or give a lecture, usually had a lot of questions for him. On 8 April 1936, Bonhoeffer wrote to him from the Harz Mountains:

We have had a number of feuds with one another, and always been able to resolve them ... It is good always to be reminded that a pastor can never make it all seem right to a good 'lay' person. If I preach about faith and grace alone (Trinity

Church!) you ask, what about the Christian life? If I lecture about the Sermon on the Mount, you ask, what about *real* life? If I give you an interpretation of the very real and sinful life of a man from the Bible, then you ask, what about eternal truth? And all that is intended only to make one concern heard: how do I live a Christian life in the real world, and where are the ultimate authorities for such a life, the only life worth living?

At this point I simply want to confess that I believe the Bible alone is the answer to all our questions, and that all we need do is keep on asking, rather humbly, to get the answers from it. You can't just *read* the Bible like any other book. You have to be prepared really to ask it something. Only then will it open up to you. Only when we expect ultimate answers from it, will it give itself to us ... Of course we can *also* read the Bible like any other book, for example in doing text criticism. There's nothing wrong with that, only it's superficial; it's not the way that will open the essence of the Bible to us. We don't take apart the words of someone we love, and analyse them; we simply take in such words and let them go on echoing in our minds for days afterward ... that is the way we should treat the words of the Bible. (DBW 14, 144–45)

With even less reserve than in these two letters, Bonhoeffer expressed his thoughts to Elizabeth Zinn, a distant relative who also studied theology, with whom he had an especially close relationship. He told her quite openly how he had become a Christian:

I plunged into my work in a very unchristian way, quite lacking in humility. I was terribly ambitious, as many people noticed, and that made my life difficult and kept from me the love and trust of people around me. I was very much alone and left to my own devices; it was a bad time. Then something happened which has tossed about and changed my life to this day. For the first time I discovered the Bible. Again, that's a bad thing to have to say. I had often preached, I had seen a great deal of the church, spoken and written about it – but I had not yet become a Christian. Instead, I had been my own master, wild and undisciplined. I know that what I was doing then was using the cause of Jesus Christ for my own advantage, and being terribly vain about it. I pray God that it never happens again. Also I had never prayed, or only very little. For all my loneliness I was rather pleased with myself. Then the Bible freed me from that, in particular the Sermon on the Mount. Since then everything has changed. I have felt this plainly, and so have other people around me. (DBW 14, 112–13)[15]

Was this really Bonhoeffer's decision, or was his life 'tossed about and changed' by a higher authority, by God? Even in that first sermon he had said that the two belong together. 'To fight for God's honour, to work, but always to see clearly that only God can do the ultimate thing – that is what it means to be a Christian' (DBWE 9, 455).

Bonhoeffer was interested in literature throughout his life, and in 1931 he composed two literary texts that look as though they were intended for a novel. It seems he did indeed have something of the sort in mind, but he had to keep putting it off until, in the military prison in Tegel, he finally found time. In 1931 he only got as far as two short attempts. The style as well as the content of these texts reminds one of the French novelist Georges Bernanos, whose radical self-honesty had impressed Bonhoeffer deeply. In one of the two, Bonhoeffer as author tells us about a secondary school student; here we have the young theologian trying to see into himself. This portrayal must have been closely connected with the experience of liberation which the Bible had meant for Bonhoeffer. He shows us the 17-year-old answering his teacher's question about what he wants to be: he wants to study theology. The teacher, dismayed, answers quietly 'You are going to be amazed.' This causes a rush of thoughts through the student's mind. He is proud of having stood by his own intention, then is overcome by holy feelings, and at the same time wonders whether the expression on his face is serious and resolute enough, now that the whole class is looking at him:

O, he knew himself well, unusually well for age 17; he knew about himself and his weaknesses, and he also knew just that: that he knew himself well. This dizzying knowledge only succeeded, again and again, in letting his profound vanity descend on the house of his soul and frighten him. It had made an incomparable impression on him to read in Schiller that a human being only needed a few slight weaknesses to die out in order to be godlike. Since then he had been on the lookout. There was no doubt that he would emerge from this battle as the hero, was the thought that came to him; he had just solemnly sworn to do so. Now his path lay clear before him, the path he had known since the age of 14 that he would certainly follow. (DBW 11, 371)

That is only a part of this long, rather wild text in which Bonhoeffer struggles, in fear and trembling, with the vanity he described in his letter to Elisabeth Zinn. In this first year of professional work, one of the decisions to which the Bible led him, once he began reading it 'against as well as for himself', was one that lasted until his years in prison – a determination to give up this sort of self-analysis.

In one of his best-known poems, as a prisoner, he was once again to ask himself, 'Who am I?' The poem describes how he felt himself to be entirely different from the way people around him saw him. They said of him that he bore days of calamity serenely, smiling and proud, like one accustomed to victory', although he really felt 'restless, yearning, sick, like a caged bird'. And once again, he gave up making a decision about it himself:

> Who am I? This one or the other?
> Am I this one today and tomorrow another?
> Am I both at once? Before others a hypocrite
> and in my own eyes a pitiful, whimpering weakling?
> Or is what remains in me like a defeated army,
> Fleeing in disarray from victory already won?
> Who am I? They mock me, these lonely questions of mine.
> Whoever I am, thou knowest me; O God, I am thine!
> (DBWE 8, III/173)[16]

As an outsider at the University of Berlin

Wilhelm Lütgert, Seeberg's successor as Professor of Systematic Theology, took Bonhoeffer on as 'extraordinary assistant' in his seminar. Otherwise, as an assistant lecturer, he was only entitled to the meagre fees paid by students who registered for his courses. But the seminar post guaranteed him 214 Reichmarks a month, even though it was only paid retroactively after the end of each semester. Now the question was how many students would come to hear him.

There have always been, and still are today, two types of students: the goal-oriented, those who are studying for a profession, and the intellectually curious. The former are utilitarian, looking for the lectures one must absolutely attend because they are delivered by the professors who give the examinations; the latter are looking to hear something new and exciting. There were then around a thousand students at the Faculty of Theology in Berlin, including a group of such curious ones, who had passed the word around about Dietrich Bonhoeffer, even though he neither had assistant-ships to offer nor was in a position to give examinations. In 2003, Bishop Albrecht Schönherr recalled how, arriving from Tübingen in 1931, he met his friend Winfried Maechler and asked him, 'Who's the one to hear, here in Berlin?' and Maechler replied, 'Bonhoeffer, absolutely!'

To the 'Bonhoeffer circle' which gathered together in this way in 1931, and initially consisted of only 15 students, both women and men, we owe a great deal. Bonhoeffer's manuscripts of his lectures from that time were lost in Pomerania in the chaos at the end of the Second World War. From his students' notes we know at least how he went about his work, and we also have students' descriptions of the impression he made. For example, Otto Dudzus wrote:

He looked like a student himself when he mounted the platform. But then what he had to say gripped us all so greatly that we no longer came because of this very young man, but because of what he was saying – even though it was dreadfully early in the morning. I have never heard lectures that impressed me nearly so much as these. (DB-ER 219)

And Albrecht Schönherr described him thus:

His appearance was imposing, but not elegant; his voice was high, but not resonant; his formulations were laborious, not brilliant … Never did I discern anything low-minded, undisciplined or mean from him. He could be relaxed, but he never let himself go …

Bonhoeffer possessed what our church as a whole, and we Christians in particular, are so sorely lacking. He willed what he thought. And he thought sharply, logically.[17]

Of course this goes far beyond a first impression, but Bonhoeffer was a lecturer whom his students could soon get to know personally. He went hiking with his students, took them on weekend retreats, and before long there was also a weekly discussion evening in Wolf-Dieter Zimmermann's room, where any and all topics were discussed amid clouds of cigarette smoke. In those days nobody worried about the comfort of non-smokers. Bonhoeffer was never hasty in dropping his reserve. It took awhile to be invited to visit him in Wangenheim Street, but in time all members of the Bonhoeffer circle came to know his parents' upper middle-class home. Hungarian theologian Ferenc Lehel tells us:

What the Bonhoeffer family offered for the enjoyment of the mind as well as the body was on the same high level. When we felt we should refuse an invitation to a meal, he assured us: 'That is not just my bread, it is our bread, and when it is jointly consumed there will still be twelve baskets left over.' Such was his humour.[18]

For his part, Bonhoeffer gave his estimation of his first students, in describing to Sutz the participants in his seminar: 'I think I really have an elite group of interested people here, some of whom are astonishingly knowledgeable and good' (DBW 11, 50). In the winter semester 1931–1932 he was giving weekly two-hour lectures on the 'History of Twentieth-Century Systematic Theology' and holding a seminar on 'The Concept of Philosophy and Protestant Theology'. In his lectures, of course, he made plenty of room for Barthian theology – in it, the whole of the preceding reached its climax. But he himself had been a student of Harnack's and had no intention of denying it. Like Barth, he considered nineteenth-century theology so important that he required his hearers to 'get a picture' of the era of their fathers and grandfathers in general, besides the Church and theology of that time. Bonhoeffer wanted to show his students why they must distance themselves from the theology of the nineteenth century, but one cannot do this without knowing from what one is distancing oneself, and especially, why. Bonhoeffer's problem with Barth's students had to do, among other things, with the tendency among many to think that as long as they knew their master's teachings, they didn't need to know anything about what had been taught before him.

The loss of Bonhoeffer's manuscript for his first lecture is especially hard because he began with a portrayal of bourgeois society towards the end of the nineteenth century. Bethge says of the student notes available:

The key words suggest that he reviewed the lines of his own background with a critical love: the sober, tolerant bourgeois world of his father; the aristocratic church world from which his mother came; the empirical art of Leopold von Kalckreuth. It was a world that was disappearing, which he, like his parents, nonetheless loved with every fibre of his being. It was the world which he would acknowledge with gratitude from his prison cell in 1944. (DB-ER 212)

As a novice lecturer, Bonhoeffer did not have previous lecture manuscripts or seminar texts to give him a leg up. So he built on his preparations for his doctoral and postdoctoral dissertations. In the seminar he was able to speak of the philosophers whom he had dealt with in *Act and Being*, and he knew the nineteenth-century theologians because he had studied their concepts of the Church for *Sanctorum Communio*. But of course the lectures still cost him great efforts to prepare, as he wrote to his brother Karl-Friedrich:

The semester has begun again, and preparations for lectures and the seminar are again taking up most of my time. I often have the feeling that housewives must have when they have put a lot of effort into cooking something special, and then see it just gobbled up along with the rest. But I simply couldn't see myself giving a poorly prepared lecture; I'd get hopelessly bogged down. (DBWE 12, I/27)

When Bonhoeffer had been teaching at the university for half a year, his salary was finally paid him retroactively. With the money he bought a wooden cabin and had it put up in Biesenthal, near a small lake on the northern outskirts of Berlin. These were Spartan weekend quarters indeed, a single room used in the daytime for meals and discussions and at night as a dormitory; but it was here that, in the spring of 1932, the 'Bonhoeffer circle' experienced for the first time their teacher's idea of community. The days included devotions, Bible studies and singing, besides discussions on political, social and church issues, and also sharing meals, sports and games.[19] In a letter to Erwin Sutz, Bonhoeffer wrote that theologically he felt lonely in Berlin:

My theological background is gradually becoming suspect here; people must have the feeling that they have been nourishing a viper in their bosom. I hardly ever see any of the professors, which doesn't leave me inconsolable. Since coming back from Bonn, I've been much more aware of the poverty of the situation here. I recently had the other private lecturers here at my house, and then the next day my students, and I must say that the students are much more interested in theology than are the lecturers. (DBW 11, 50)

In large part, Bonhoeffer's feeling of loneliness was due to his colleagues' not sharing in his discovery of the Bible, while the majority of his students were willing to go with him on this new path, on which one could connect one's knowledge and one's commitment to the Church entirely differently from before. Other contacts too pointed to the conclusion that he would not find his spiritual home in the university, but rather in the Church. So at last he made his way to the Student Christian Movement group in Berlin, whose secretary, Martin Fischer, invited him several times as a speaker. Here too, Bonhoeffer spoke urgently on the issue of peace. Hans Brandenburg, a staff member at the Berlin City Mission, invited him to lead a Bible study and later gave him practical advice.

The 'Dehn case' was one of the scandalous situations in which the Nazi Party's student organization was able to exercise power even before 1933.[20] Günther Dehn was a pastor in Berlin whose parish was in the working-class district of Moabit. Dehn had been a member of the Social Democratic Party (SPD), but had resigned from it because he felt he was being unfairly 'put on show' as a pastor. His unusual success with prole-tarian youth had attracted attention. Moreover, on 6 November 1928 he had given a speech in Magdeburg on 'The Church and International Understanding', a topic close to his heart as a pacifist, in which he spoke against placing war monuments and commemorative plaques in Protestant churches, saying it was wrong to make heroes of soldiers who had died in wars, or to describe their deaths as a 'holy sacrifice'. A lady in the audience had said during the discussion that if soldiers who had died were no longer honoured with commemorative plaques, it would be the same as calling them murderers. The press had seized on this and reported that Dehn had called the soldiers who died in the World War murderers. A storm of indignation had blown up, but died down again when the church authorities issued a clarification.

But in 1931 when Dehn was offered a chair in Practical Theology by the theological faculties of the Universities of Heidelberg and Halle, a former pastor apparently had nothing better to do than to revive the old libel against him.[21] This time the Nazi student organization took up the matter, and made such a racket about it that the Heidelberg faculty immediately withdrew its offer. Dehn accepted the offer from Halle, but was unable to give his inaugural lecture there in the face of hordes of shouting students. The Nazi student organization threatened that all the students in Halle would leave, and instead of firmly rejecting this, the university authorities put Dehn on leave for two semesters.

At this time a social worker named Gertrud Staewen was attending Bonhoeffer's lectures. She was a friend of Dehn's and through him had come to know Karl Barth and his personal assistant, Charlotte von Kirschbaum, who in turn had arranged for her to meet Bonhoeffer. Since both Mrs Staewen and Bonhoeffer found the reaction of the theology professors in Halle to the 'Dehn case' to be entirely incorrect, Bonhoeffer drafted an open letter in which he challenged the professors in Halle to make their theological position clear on this matter. Gertrud Staewen copied out the letter and sent it to Barth, who made a few changes and then sent it to a number of colleagues, requesting their signatures. Since only a few wanted to join the appeal, he advised that the matter be dropped. However, from then on Gertrud Staewen could count on Dietrich Bonhoeffer as a dependable friend. This became important to both of them during the Second World War, when she risked her life to help Jews who were being deported to Theresienstadt and Auschwitz, some of whom were actually saved with the help of audacious Berliners.[22]

There was no theologian in whom Bonhoeffer was more interested than in Karl Barth. He was not much bothered by the fact that Barth had several times expressed strong reservations about his view of ethics. In April 1932 Barth was to address the Brandenburg Mission Conference on 'Theology and Contemporary Mission'; Bonhoeffer was not the only one who was looking forward to this. The evening before, Professor Julius Richter invited the members of the Berlin theological faculty and General Superintendents to meet the famous, or notorious, dogmatician from

Bonn. Bonhoeffer described the evening in a letter to his friend Sutz the next day:

Barth's meeting with the princes of the church here was in every way typical and, as expected, depressing. These people still harbour an inquisitorial spirit which is satisfied with symptoms and doesn't bother to pursue a matter to its roots, or even to ask daring questions – just disgustingly stuffy. It made quite a picture ... Barth sitting like a defendant on a little chair opposite the church dignitaries and having to explain himself; then when they were invited to ask questions, nothing ensued but a long, embarrassing silence, because nobody wanted to be the first to make a fool of himself ...

So after hours of agony, Barth somewhat shaken, the church dignitaries here quite pleased to have found him such a charming person after all, we all went home. (DBW 11, 88)

Rudolf Pestalozzi, the industrialist from Zürich who was a friend and promoter of Karl Barth and had come with him into the 'lions' den', had already heard about Bonhoeffer and brought him greetings from Sutz. It was in Pestalozzi's chalet above the Lake of Zürich, Bergli, that Barth used to spend the summers working and having friends visit. Probably Gertrud Staewen had suggested that Bonhoeffer be invited there after his ecumenical conferences in Geneva and Gland, Switzerland, for which he was already preparing. In any case, Bonhoeffer asked Sutz in another letter:

What do you think about this? I must admit that it seems a little pushy for me to go there, since I hardly know any of these people. On the other hand, of course I should like it very much ... Do you think it would be all right, or would I only be disturbing these folks during their holiday? (DBW 11, 101–2)

A letter Bonhoeffer wrote to Barth on Christmas Eve 1932 shows not only that he went to Bergli, but that Barth must have spent a substantial amount of time with him.

Before this year closes, I would like to thank you once again for all that I have received from you in the course of the year. The evening here in Berlin, and then the incomparably splendid hours spent with you on the Bergli, belong to the moments of this year that will remain with me. Please forgive me if I was a burden to you in August with my perhaps too obstinate, and – as you once said – 'godless' questions. (DBWE 12, I/21)

But, he said further, he did not know anyone who could steer him away so thoroughly from asking the wrong questions as could Barth. He felt that Barth could bring him right up to the real issue which he had previously only been circling around at a distance. The few hours they had had together during that year, he said, had been enough to direct his thoughts, which otherwise had a tendency to get bogged down in 'godless' questions, and to keep them focused on the issue at hand.

Student chaplain and pastor to youth

On 10 July 1931, General Superintendent Emil Karow wrote to his new 'synod pastoral assistant', Dietrich Bonhoeffer, that he was planning to appoint him chaplain to students at the Technical College, and asked him to work in cooperation with the Revd Ernst Bronisch-Holtze, the chaplain at the University of Berlin. This job did not actually begin until October, so until then Bonhoeffer was on leave – the leave that had been requested for him by Diestel before Bonhoeffer's return from America. At the same time he received a notice from the consistory of the Old Prussian Church, in best German officialese:

You are assigned to absolve your duties as assistant within our regional church. Your ordination will therefore take place on Sunday, 15 November 1931 at 10 a.m. in St. Matthew's Church. General Superintendent Vits will preside ... A fee of 5 Reichmarks is to be paid to the sexton before the ordination to cover its costs (compensation for church officials etc.). pp. etc. (DBW 11, 39)

It has been a long time since church authorities used such prosaic wording in regard to an ordination, and this attitude is also shown by the fact that we know nothing about Bonhoeffer's ordination service itself.

Robert Frick, a church historian whom Bonhoeffer later met at Bethel, was also ordained by General Superintendent Vits around that time. When Frick was asked rather emotionally, on the fiftieth anniversary of his ordination, about 'what must be the greatest day in the life of a pastor', he said that was not the way he experienced it. 'If you wanted to be a pastor, you had to get ordained, that was all.'[23] This only changed during the church struggle, when the Confessing Church, under persecution by the state, was ordaining its candidates for a service that was considered illegal. It not only promised them God's blessing and a brotherly community of fellow pastors, but also undertook to care for them and their families in case of need.

The main assignment for which General Superintendent Otto Dibelius had recommended Bonhoeffer, the office of chaplain to students at the Technical College, turned out to be extremely difficult. First of all, Bonhoeffer had to inform the students, two-thirds of whom already belonged to the Nazi student organization, that he was available to them as pastor. A notice he put on the bulletin board was removed several times by unknown hands. Finally Bonhoeffer replaced it with a note attached: 'Dear fellow student ... Why always the same joke ...? Why not come round to see me some time? We might not do so badly talking with one another' (DBWE 12, I/10).

The programme events he offered were poorly attended; often no one came at all. But it was different at his Sunday worship services in Trinity Church, where conspicuous numbers of students were present. Bonhoeffer suspected that even those who were interested had so much studying to do during the week that they had no time for anything else. He consulted one of the professors about this, who confirmed it. Bonhoeffer wrote to the student fraternities asking them to give him some publicity, and offering to speak at their meetings. When this actually took place, his talks were followed by lively discussions, since he chose topics which the students found interesting; but overall he had little success with these enquiries. Some fraternities didn't bother to reply, others only briefly acknowledged his letters, and the rest invited him to evening drinking parties at which he did not care to speak as pastor.

At that time there was already a conference of student chaplains in Germany. Bonhoeffer went to a meeting at Friedrichroda, near Gotha in Thuringia, having been especially asked to bring up for discussion the spread of the Nazi student organization. This was being talked of in many church circles, but nobody knew what to do about it. In 1933 Bonhoeffer submitted a report to the Old Prussian Church consistory, in which he described the attempt to establish a student chaplaincy at the Technical College as a failure. However, he ended his report with a suggestion as to what might be done instead.

I am becoming increasingly convinced that an attempt should be made to establish a professor's chair in Christian Thought at the Technical College, so as to gain influence from the inside in shaping student life. Only when the ground has first been prepared in this way does it seem to me that the work of a student chaplain, who really has to concentrate on the Gospel and not get sidetracked from it, can be spared from appearing to fail. (12, I/54)[24]

General Superintendent Karow wrote in the margin 'This report is not encouraging. But no tree is felled by the first blow. Let's wait and see how it goes.' But by the time he wrote that, Hitler was already in power and the time for Christian professorships and chaplains at technical colleges was as good as over.

Since Bonhoeffer was not only a student chaplain, but was also available to Berlin General Superintendent Karow as 'synod pastoral assistant', he was asked to take over the boys' confirmation class at Zion Church in the Prenzlauer Berg district of east Berlin. The old pastor, Johannes Müller, could no longer manage the group. Bethge writes of Bonhoeffer's first day there, as he described it:

The elderly minister and Bonhoeffer slowly walked up the stairs of the school building, which was several stories high. The children were leaning over the bannisters, making an indescribable din and dropping rubbish on the two men ascending the stairs. When they reached the top, the minister tried to force the throng back into the classroom by shouting and using physical force. He tried to announce that he had brought them a new minister who was going to teach them in future and that his name was Bonhoeffer. When they heard the name they started shouting 'Bon! Bon! Bon!' louder and louder. The old man left the scene in despair, leaving Bonhoeffer standing silently against the wall with his hands in his pockets. Minutes passed. His failure to react made the noise gradually less enjoyable. He began speaking quietly, so that only the boys in the front row could catch a few words of what he said. Suddenly all were silent. Bonhoeffer merely remarked that they had put up a remarkable initial performance, and went on to tell them a story about Harlem. If they listened, he told them, he would tell them more next time. Then he told them they could go. After that, he never had reason to complain about their lack of attentiveness. (DB-ER 226)

In 1985 a pensioner from Berlin made the 75-kilometre journey eastward to the holiday resort of Hirschluch, because he had read in the newsletter of the East German Christian Democratic Union that an international Bonhoeffer Congress was being held there. He told them that he had been confirmed by Bonhoeffer in 1932. More than 50 years later, his encounter with Bonhoeffer remained one of the unforgettable experiences of his life.

The young pastor who confirmed him, too, never forgot as long as he lived these working-class boys with whom he had gone hiking and on weekend excursions. The old pastor whom they had literally annoyed to death was carried to his grave not long after he had handed over the class to its new teacher. Bonhoeffer cancelled an important meeting in order to take all the boys to the funeral. He wrote to Sutz about this unaccustomed task:

This is just about the wildest district in Berlin, with the most difficult social and political conditions. At first the boys behaved as though they were crazy, so that for the first time I had real difficulties with discipline. But what helped the most was that I simply told them stories from the Bible, with great emphasis, particularly eschatological passages. And by the way, I also told some stories about Negroes. Now there is absolute quiet, the boys see to that themselves. (DBW 11, 50)

By 'eschatological passages' he meant the New Testament reports about the coming end of the world, about the Last Judgement and God's eternity. Probably the expert who gave Bonhoeffer such a low grade in the First Examination for his catechetical work would have said one couldn't talk about such things with youth, especially youth of this sort from east Berlin. But the young pastor was of an entirely different opinion.

Of course Bonhoeffer also wanted to get to know the parents of his confirmation pupils, but that turned out to be much harder. Even though, as he had done in Barcelona, he could visit them as the teacher working with their sons, it was seldom that a real conversation got started. He shared with Sutz:

To think of those excruciating hours or minutes when I or the other person try to begin a pastoral conversation, and how haltingly and lamely it goes on ... I sometimes try to console myself by thinking that this kind of pastoral work is something that just did not exist in earlier times and is quite unchristian. But perhaps it really means the end of our Christianity, that we fail here. We have learned to preach again, at any rate a little, but the care of souls? (DBW 11, 65)

As difficult as all this was, Bonhoeffer found here a mission that being a student chaplain could not offer him. With the help of Bertha Schulze, an acquaintance from Harnack's seminar, he rented a room on Oderberger Street so that he could live near his boys. Those who knew the area advised him against it; this was the 'darkest east side' of the city, not without its dangers for a minister. The hosts of unemployed workers there had mostly been organized into communist groups, which engaged the Nazi SA militia in street battles in which people were killed. The old master baker into whose house Bonhoeffer moved, for his part, had first enquired of another minister whether a 'synod pastoral assistant' might possibly be 'a Catholic', as he wanted no such person in his house. On his free evenings, Bonhoeffer invited the boys to his room one or two at a time, shared a meal and played games with them. A few became enthusiastic chess players. After some time, the baker's wife came to see Bertha

Dietrich Bonhoeffer as a young pastor with some of his 42 confirmation pupils in the Harz Mountains, 1932

Schulze, to thank her. Bonhoeffer had indeed brought a commotion into her home, his confirmands were always around and he was constantly asking her to prepare meals, but he had put new heart into her and her elderly husband.[25]

Whenever he possibly could, Bonhoeffer took his confirmands to Biesenthal for weekends, and after their confirmation he took them to Friedrichsbrunn in the Harz Mountains for 10 days, where they romped in the snow and behaved themselves especially well. Mrs S., who looked after the elder Bonhoeffers' vacation house there, turned up her nose at these 'proles' that young Mr Bonhoeffer had brought in. She was used to more genteel guests. But, except for one window, nothing got broken.

Fritz Figur, the pastor of the neighbouring parish in Berlin, met Bonhoeffer one day in late February with a huge bolt of black cloth, which he was dividing up so that each of his Zion's boys could have a proper suit for confirmation. Once again, it was his parents who paid for the fabric and the tailoring. The actual confirmation day, 13 March 1932, was dominated by election fever. Hitler, Thälmann and Duesterberg were candidates for the office of Reich President, but Hindenburg defeated all three of them by gaining 49 per cent, and later also won the runoff vote against Hitler. In Bonhoeffer's sermon to the boys being confirmed, taking Genesis 32:22–31 as his text, he said:

No one shall ever deprive you of the faith that God has prepared, for you too, a day and a sun and a dawn; that he guides us to this sun that is called Jesus Christ, that he wishes us to see the promised land in which justice and peace and love prevail, because Christ prevails; now we see it only from afar, but some day, in eternity. (DBW 11, 414)

In the autumn of 1932, Anneliese Schnurmann, a schoolfriend of Bonhoeffer's sister Susanne who had heard about his work on the east side of Berlin, asked him about the possibility of starting an inter-confessional youth group, unaffiliated with any political party. She was convinced of the need and was prepared to make a monthly income available from money inherited from her parents. Bonhoeffer, who was already open to the idea, if only because of his contacts with Gertrud Staewen and Günther Dehn, discussed it with Hans Brandenburg, at whose request he had once led a Bible study at the City Mission. Brandenburg was a sophisticated gentleman from Riga in the Baltic region[26] who was passionately interested in bringing people distant from the Church to faith in Jesus Christ. He had experience with many kinds of groups, including communists, and was able to introduce Bonhoeffer in the city social work offices. There it was recommended that he consult Anna von Gierke, a social worker with a wealth of experience with youth groups. Anneliese Schnurmann and Bonhoeffer went to see her, and she recommended two suitable social workers who were available as staff. So by winter the Charlottenburg Youth Club had been set up in Charlottenburg Castle Street on the west side of Berlin, offering job training courses for young people. Bonhoeffer got one of his students, Karl-Heinz Corbach, to give an English course.

The Youth Club was such a success that by November 1932 they had to move it to larger quarters. There were a few problems, but more encouraging successes, until the end of January 1933 when Hitler came to power. Then Mrs Gierke was ousted from her job and Anneliese Schnurmann, who was Jewish, had to emigrate. She became a psychoanalyst in London, where she worked with Anna Freud. The communist young people who had participated in the Youth Club began to be harassed on the street. Bonhoeffer let them use his Biesenthal cabin as a refuge until they found places to go in other parts of the city. But when the Nazi SA militia began trying to get hold of the Youth Club's card file, the Club had to be closed without further ado.

Bonhoeffer's year as a 'church assistant' was coming to an end at this point. It did not take him long to evaluate which had been more important to him, the student chaplaincy or the confirmation class. He accordingly sought out the father of his student Wolf-Dieter Zimmermann; the elder Zimmermann was superintendent of the eastern Berlin I district of the Protestant Church in the city, and Bonhoeffer asked him about the possibility of a permanent ministry on the east side. At the time, Zimmermann was looking for candidates for a pastorate that was open at St Bartholomew's Church, near Alexander Square in central east Berlin, and the two agreed that this might be the right place for Bonhoeffer. He then preached there as a candidate, but lost out to a much older candidate with a more 'folksy' style, by 25 votes to 47. His 42 Zion's boys would not have been entitled to vote even had they belonged to St Bartholomew's. The girls' group of Zion Church, who knew Bonhoeffer only from his sermons, had said right away that they didn't want him as pastor. 'He keeps stopping to think, as though he doesn't know what he wants to say.'[27]

Sermons in the 'year of decision'

'We have to read the Bible against ourselves [and not just in our favour]', Bonhoeffer had said in Gland, and had also called for a precise knowledge of reality. His own attitude in this regard had to be apparent in his preaching, and more than once he was near despair over the preparation of sermons. He had written to his classmate Rößler that, from outside of Germany, the situation there seemed such a local affair.

How do you think Christianity can carry on in view of the situation in the world and our own lifestyle? It is becoming less and less imaginable that, for the sake of *one* righteous person, God said 'I will not destroy the city.' [Genesis 18:22–33] I am now student chaplain at the T.H. How can one preach such things to these people? Who believes in them anymore? They're invisible, that's what ruins our efforts. (DBW 11, 33)

We can take as an example here one of these sermons in which Bonhoeffer really had to struggle for the right interpretation.[28] Gerhard Jacobi, pastor of the King Wilhelm Memorial Church, had asked Bonhoeffer to take a service for him, and Bonhoeffer chose as his text Colossians 3:1–4:

So if you have been raised with Christ, seek the things that are above, where Christ is, seated at the right hand of God. Set your minds on things that are above, not on things that are on earth, for you have died, and your life is hidden with Christ in God. When Christ who is your life is revealed, then you also will be revealed with him in glory.

'How can one preach such things?' he had asked Rößler. Within the church space one could read such a text aloud, but only imagine saying such words to someone or other in daily life and the strangeness of the Bible becomes shockingly clear. It was true, Bonhoeffer wrote, that politicians such as Papen and Hindenburg publicly proclaimed that they were speaking 'In the name of God, Amen', but that was only giving worldly business a bit of a religious sheen. It had nothing whatever to do with the message of the Bible. Bonhoeffer made such a thorough analysis of the situation and of people's thinking in modern times that he only got a few steps beyond this introductory idea, and had to ask Jacobi to let him preach again on the same text the following Sunday. He said that in these modern times people were concerned about ideal forms or techniques for trading goods, for hygiene, for education, for psychoanalysis, even for philosophy, art and religion; and the more acute the crisis, the louder the calls for experts to bring some order into the chaos.

How much more trust we have in this feverish striving for knowledge in all areas of human life; how much better prospects it seems to have than the sober 'In the name of God, Amen', which doesn't say anything. And that goes even more for that dusty old saying we have long since forgotten, 'So if you have been raised with Christ ...' (DBW 11, 439)

At this point, many preachers would have raised an admonishing forefinger and said: all we need to do is go back to the Bible and its truth. But that was exactly what Bonhoeffer did not do; instead he quoted, not from the Bible, but from a work of literature. Half a year earlier he had heard Otto Klemperer direct the Berlin Philharmonic in an oratorio by Paul Hindemith. The oratorio, instead of being based on a biblical text, used as its text a poem by Gottfried Benn, 'The Unceasing'. Instead of asking, like Bonhoeffer in his sermon, whether the modern world towards which we are rushing can arrive at a meaningful goal, Benn describes the never-ending journey into nothingness. Bonhoeffer quotes in his sermon the words which the poem repeats several times: 'Taste you the cup of nothingness, that dark draught?' In his painstaking analysis of the sermon, Jürgen Henkys also considers the text of the oratorio. At the end the men's choir sings: 'In every age has human flesh proclaimed / What is existence, but to be content!' and is contradicted by a boys' choir:

> But no, another word must follow us
> For in creation, struggle has its place.
> In struggle, our contentments fade away,
> in pain, in which the shadows hover round,
> in thirst that drinks from both the cups at once,
> both cups that with destruction overflow.
> In suffering the combat will continue,
> in loneliness, in silence, which alone
> can sense those ancient powers, ever with us – :
> and thus we know: unceasing human life.[29]

Then, instead of setting the Epistle to the Colossians beside the quotation from Benn, Bonhoeffer takes up the image of the two cups about which the boys' choir sang, and transforms it:

But now we are overcome by a terrible certainty, that we are fleeing from God. Whether we dare to drink 'the cup of nothingness, that dark draught' – or whether we avoid it and turn to religious busyness and blather – we are fleeing from that other cup of which the Bible has tasted and which it proclaims to the world in a mighty voice. The cup of God's anger ... To drink from this cup of God, if we really know what we are doing, is to be serious. And to drink that cup of nothingness, that dark draught, is also to be serious. And to those who do so, the eternal God is infinitely nearer, with the shining promise of God, than they can realize from afar. (DBW 11, 441–2)

By taking Benn's poem seriously as a description of reality, as he himself also felt and thought about it, Bonhoeffer was able to read the biblical text, Colossians 3:1–4, as aimed at himself, that is, against him. Christians live, as he said in the second sermon on the text, in a world which turns the Bible's words around and says 'Set your minds on things that are on earth.' Here again, Bonhoeffer does not offer a polemic against this, but instead says:

This is where a tremendous decision takes place: whether we Christians have enough strength to witness before the world that we are not dreamers with our heads in the clouds ... that our faith really is not opium that keeps us content within an unjust world. Instead, and precisely because our minds are set on things above, we are that much more stubborn and purposeful in protesting here on earth ... Does it have to be so that Christianity, which began as immensely revolutionary, now has to remain conservative for all time? That every new movement has to blaze its path without the church, and that the church always takes twenty years to see what has actually happened? If it really must be so, then we must not be surprised when, for our church as well, times come when the blood of martyrs will be demanded. But this blood, if we truly have the courage and honour and loyalty to shed it, will not be so innocent and shining as that of the first witnesses. Our blood will be overlaid with our own great guilt. (DBW 11, 446)

To be faithful to the earth for the sake of 'things above', to let one's earthly hopes be renewed by eternal hope, dashes any hope for a comfortable life. That certainly goes against the grain, particularly for devout church folk; but only by reading the Bible against ourselves, no less than in our favour, do we read it rightly.

To learn to read the Bible in this way, one needs to do 'spiritual exercises' like those of St Ignatius of Loyola, the founder of the Jesuit order, to whom the Protestant Dietrich Bonhoeffer is said to have referred on several occasions. For the winter semester 1932–1933 he announced a theological exegesis of the first three chapters of the Bible, which was to be such an exercise for himself and his students. The word had been passed around in the meantime that exciting new things were to be heard from Bonhoeffer, and for the first time some three hundred students turned up for his lectures. At their urging, his text was later published, entitled *Creation and Fall*. This third book of Bonhoeffer's reads differently from the first two. He had found a new style to go with his new thinking. We have enthusiastic descriptions by those who heard the lectures at the time, but also the somewhat ill-humoured opinion of Hilde Enterlein, the philosophically inclined future wife of Albrecht Schönherr, that Bonhoeffer was 'telling fairy tales' (DBWE 3, 3).

Nevertheless, in these lectures as well we hear in the background Bonhoeffer's dispute with contemporary criticism of the theory of knowledge. Taking his stand on a biblically based anthropology, Bonhoeffer questions the usual way of talking about ethics, and especially attacks the pseudo-Lutheran doctrine of the orders of creation. At meetings of the Central Office for Youth Work, which we have mentioned, Wilhelm Stählin had tried to justify the 'duty of peoples [Völker] to fight' on the basis that God had created the different peoples and therefore had given them the right to defend themselves. Bonhoeffer had argued that anything could be justified in some way by referring back to the creation, even the exploitation of the weak by the strong and economic competition unto life and death. The creation, however, had been corrupted by the fall, by human sin. He had proposed speaking instead of 'orders of preservation', because God had preserved the world until Christ came, so that through him the world might be reconciled with its Creator. Thus Bonhoeffer began with the Christ event in interpreting the stories of the creation and the fall, leading to new insights.

Let us look at one such insight. That human beings are in the image of God (Genesis 1:26–27), Bonhoeffer sees in God's creation of humankind, 'male and female', dependent on one another and at the same time as free for one another as God is free for God's creatures. Thus being made in God's image means that God created us to be capable of relationship and commitment. It was not least because of Bonhoeffer's thinking about the Old Testament that the Jewish theologian Pinchas Lapide called Bonhoeffer's theology 'primally Jewish'.[29] When *Creation and Fall* first appeared in 1933, there were already vehement attacks being made on the Old Testament, and one reviewer said, 'Anyone who is inclined to take cheap shots at the Old Testament today should first get hold of this book ...' (DBWE 3, 172).

On 31 January 1933, the day after Hitler came to power, Bonhoeffer came, in his lecture course, to Genesis 3:4, the promise made by the serpent in Eden: 'You will be like God' (if you eat the fruit of the tree which God has forbidden you to eat). And the students, who had passed through a forest of swastika flags in order to enter the university building in Unter den Linden Boulevard, heard his exegesis of the serpent's promise:

Sicut deus [to be like God] – for Adam that can only be a new, deeper kind of creaturely being. This is how he is bound to understand the serpent. To be sure, Adam sees that the new, deeper kind of creatureliness must be won at the cost of transgressing the commandment. And this very fact must focus his attention. Adam is in fact *between* God and God, or better, between God and a false god [*Götze*], in a situation in which the false god portrays itself as a true God ... (DBWE 3, 113f)

5. The Year 1933

The 'new age' and the German Christians

The year 1933 was the most hectic Bonhoeffer ever experienced, either before or afterwards. From 30 January, the day on which Reich President Hindenburg named Adolf Hitler as Reich Chancellor (Prime Minister), 27-year-old Pastor Bonhoeffer was caught up in a whirlwind of events which at times called upon him to make new decisions from one day to the next.

Hitler did not become Reich Chancellor through a victory by his party or by the will of the people, as the term 'taking power [*Machtergreifung*]' might suggest. In the election of 6 November 1932, two-thirds of the voters did not vote for him. It was some influential conservative leaders – including former Chancellors Papen and Schleicher, and Oskar von Hindenburg, son of the Reich President – who thought it would be a clever tactical move to bring Hitler into the coalition in power and thus exercise some restraint over him. Then the parliamentary parties could no longer block one another in the Reichstag, and in the cabinet the conservatives would still have a majority and therefore hold onto power, even with Hitler as Reich Chancellor. This upstart from Austria would soon prove himself unfit to govern, they thought, and would thus have to give up what power he held. In Hitler's new government his Nazi Party was a minority – besides his own position, it held only two cabinet posts – so it could be outvoted.[1]

But even after these conservatives who had pulled the strings saw how greatly they had been deceived in this new Reich Chancellor and his party, they did not so much as attempt to turn the wheel back again. The people, including the millions-strong army of the unemployed, reacted with a mixture of apprehension and dim hope. Perhaps at last their fortunes were about to take a turn for the better.

From 30 January 1933 onward Hitler was on parade as a statesman aware of his responsibilities, but inwardly he remained the leader of a criminal organization whose functionaries were required to swear absolute loyalty to him, to join with him in bending the whole of Germany to his will. Even then he already wanted to make Eastern Europe the 'living space for the Nordic [Aryan] race', which meant that in 1933 he was already planning war. However, he was filled above all with an out-and-out hatred of Jews. He saw 'worldwide Jewry' as the embodiment of evil. To him, Jews had been the driving force behind the German defeat in 1918 and the 'shameful Treaty of Versailles', and he also saw Jews as the leaders of Bolshevism, the Russian communist movement which would soon be flooding all of Europe unless Germany succeeded in putting up 'a dam against the Red tide from the east'.[2]

Anyone in Germany could have known long before 1933 what Hitler was thinking, for he had described his ideas in great detail, so that their consequences in war, oppression and murder were unmistakable, in his book *Mein Kampf* (My Struggle). But very few Germans had read the book, and even in 1933 the great majority of the people considered it unnecessary to concern themselves with it. Hitler had long since settled on his plan for making Germany into a dictatorship, after taking over its government. His aim as newly appointed Reich Chancellor was to conceal his intentions behind statesmanlike speeches and symbolic actions, through which he would show that, though violence had been done – 'you cannot make an omelette without breaking eggs' – as soon as the 'national revolution' had banished the Bolshevist threat, law and order would return, and the fate of the German people was in good hands.

He encountered scarcely any resistance as he proceeded to carry this out. The judiciary made no protest against his violations of laws. Civil servants, the majority of whom had been against Hitler until 1932, adapted themselves surprisingly quickly to the new power structures. The great majority of university professors kept themselves in waiting, as the Nazi Federation of Students was strongly represented at all institutions of learning, always ready to kick up a row. Even the military saw no reason to intervene, although the generals had misgivings as they watched the growth of the SA militia.[3]

Roland Freisler, Hitler's judge who had so much blood on his hands, said in 1944, before sentencing the young Resistance leader, Count Helmuth James von Moltke, to death: 'We National Socialists [Nazis] and Christianity resemble each other in only one respect: we claim the whole man!'[4] This was Hitler's thinking from the beginning, and therefore he saw the two main churches as the two significant groups that could seriously threaten his cause. He had to treat the Catholic Church differently from the Protestants, since he had no influence over the pope and the Vatican, and he knew that though the Catholic bishops negotiated with him they would never give up their tie to Rome. What he wanted from the Catholic Church was a concordat, a treaty between state and church, which the Vatican had been trying for a number of years to obtain, but without success.

The situation of German Protestants was entirely different: their churches did not extend beyond Germany's borders. There were 28 provincial churches, all of which had for centuries lived, as a rule, in close partnerships with their respective states.[5] Hitler wanted to make use of this for his purposes. The 'church struggle [*Kirchenkampf*]', as the years of fierce disputes over the Protestant churches were rightly known, began soon after 30 January 1933. In this struggle, Hitler and his henchmen were the churches' real opponents throughout, but hardly a member of the church opposition realized it at the time. Many would probably not have admitted it if they had; instead, they declared loudly and repeatedly that the dispute was only going on within the Protestant church, and that they were not at all opposed to 'Adolf Hitler's new Germany'.[6] So the battlefronts were never clear.

Since Bonhoeffer was striving from the beginning, as scarcely anyone else was doing, to make the situation clear and to show what decisions needed to be made, the only way to portray his life in the year 1933 is to tell of the many fronts on which he was fighting and the many groups of people with whom he wrestled. This means speaking of a bewildering abundance of events. Eberhard Bethge devotes almost a hundred pages of his great biography[7] to the life of his friend during this one year, in the course of which he mentions the names of more than 200 persons. Even a shorter portrayal will have to capture some of that bewildering diversity, for it was during the chaotic, fateful year, 1933, that the course was set for the 12 years of Hitler's dictatorship, and thus for everything that was to follow in Bonhoeffer's life.

The year had begun for Bonhoeffer with ecumenical work. The Universal Council for Life and Work and the World Alliance for Promoting International Friendship through the Churches were holding meetings of their governing bodies in Berlin, and Bonhoeffer's collaboration was essential because preparations were being made for the youth committees of the two organizations to merge.

So it was together with delegates from around the world that, in a sea of flags, Bonhoeffer lived through the turbulent days of Hitler's 'coming to power', as it was called in the propaganda around 30 January. This term was intended not only to conceal the lack of a victory in the election, but also to give the impression that Hitler had been granted, right from the moment of taking over the government, the dictatorial powers which he was to create for himself in the coming weeks and months through a carefully calculated mixture of terrorist acts, law breaking and statesmanlike speeches.

But he was still far from having the trust of all the German people. The public mood was rather reserved during the first days of the 'Third Reich'. Even today, when this moment in history is portrayed, we are still shown scenes of an enthusiastic crowd in Berlin paying homage to Hitler, on the evening of 30 January, with a 'spontaneous torchlight procession' of the SA, SS and 'Steel Helmet' militias. But this footage comes from a film made later by Propaganda Minister Joseph Goebbels, because on the day itself no one had thought to bring out movie cameras. However, Hitler and Goebbels did not usually fail to make use of the new information media, which had been invented just in time for them.

Even in the parliamentary elections on 5 March, despite its clever and aggressive election propaganda, the Nazi Party only gained 44 per cent of the vote and had to continue depending on support from the German National People's Party. Protestant pastor Dietrich Bonhoeffer voted for the Catholic Centre Party, because he expected it to offer the necessary resistance to Hitler's policies.

Bonhoeffer had come, only hours after its beginning, into direct contact with the 'new age' in Germany's history. On 1 February he had to give a talk on the radio – the only time in his life that he ever did so. He had received the invitation weeks earlier, but the chosen theme, 'The Younger Generation's Altered View of the Concept of *Führer*',[8] was almost too good a fit with the drastically changed situation in Germany. In the frenzy of political transformation Bonhoeffer must have sounded like the voice of reason, when towards the end he said:

If the leader tries to become the idol the led are looking for – something the led always hope from their leader – then the image of the leader shifts to one of a mis-leader,[9] then the leader is acting improperly toward the led as well as toward himself. The true leader must always be able to disappoint. This, especially, is part of the leader's responsibility and objectivity. (DBWE 12, II/9)

However, his listeners no longer heard these words since, to his great annoyance, someone at the radio station had switched off the microphone. But he was able to have his lecture printed and circulated it to friends and acquaintances (DB-ER 260).

Eberhard Bethge described the well-planned proceedings of Germany's new ruler in his first weeks in power as 'controlled chaos'. The SA militia carried on its terrorism in the streets unhindered. Prominent opponents who hadn't fled the country quickly enough, Hitler had arrested and maltreated. On the other hand, in his speeches broadcast on the radio, he paid court to conservative elements in the population; in particular, he explained to the two main churches that their participation was indispensable in building the new Germany. In doing so, beginning with his own radio speech on 1 February, he knew how to 'make it sound religious':

Now, German *Volk*, give us four years and then pass judgment upon us! True to the order of the Field Marshal [Hindenburg], we shall begin. May God Almighty look mercifully upon our work, lead our will on the right path, bless our wisdom and reward us with the confidence of our *Volk*. We are not fighting for ourselves but for Germany![10]

Far too many people were gripped by such language and didn't hear its false overtones. 'Give us four years' time' meant, of course, that on the third day of his chancellorship, Hitler was already thinking he could avoid being judged by the governed for years to come. On 10 February at the Sports Palace in Berlin, he began his campaign for the parliamentary elections by portraying his office as Reich Chancellor as a divine mission, concluding his speech in the style of the Lord's Prayer:

For I cannot divest myself of my faith in my *Volk*, cannot dissociate myself from the conviction that this nation will one day rise again, cannot divorce myself from my love for this my *Volk*, and I cherish the firm conviction that the hour will come at last in which the millions who despise us today will stand by us and with us will hail the new, hard-won and painfully acquired German Reich we have created together, the new German kingdom of greatness and honour and power and glory and justice. Amen![11]

During the night of 27 February, the Reichstag building was burned down. Hitler made such immediate and clever use of this happening that rumours, both at home and abroad, claimed that the Nazis themselves had been the arsonists. This supposition was supported by the fact that the very morning after the fire, they were already accusing the communists of having set it; they immediately produced a well-prepared emergency decree and had it signed by President Hindenburg, the 'Reich President's Edict for the Protection of People and State'. After the Second World War, the theory that Hitler's closest associates must have set the fire was contested for decades. It seemed to have been finally laid to rest, but recently it has again been defended with cogent arguments.[12]

His 'Reichstag Fire Edict' enabled Hitler to abolish some of the most important articles of the Reich constitution. Even more than the famous 'Enabling Act' in which, four weeks later, the newly elected parliament yielded up its own rights, the 'Reichstag Fire Edict' made Germany a state without justice. Beginning even on 28 February, the right to privacy of communication by mail or telephone no longer existed. Anything that the government, the Party or the secret police found inconvenient could now be forbidden on the spot. Even the most crassly unjust actions taken on the basis of this edict were no longer subject to any appeal. Bonhoeffer later found this out personally when the police closed the preachers' seminary of which he was director.

But the powers which Hitler had created for himself went much further. Himmler was able to set up his concentration camps and send there anyone who had become *persona non grata*, to be held or executed without a court judgment. In one of these camps, shortly before Germany's surrender ended the validity of the edict in 1945, Dietrich Bonhoeffer was put to death. Of course, in the spring of 1933, the first persons to be affected by the new law, besides Jewish intellectuals, were mainly Communist Party functionaries and influential pundits such as Carl von Ossietzky, who were hunted down and arrested by Hitler's henchmen.

By such means as these Hitler could expand his power, but they were not yet sufficient for him to make it stick. Instead he had to demonstrate, after the first few weeks of his government, that he intended to have an orderly state system. This was the purpose of the 'Potsdam Day' ceremony on 21 March, which began with parades and worship services and reached its climax in the Garrison Church of Potsdam, the imperial city just south of Berlin, broadcast by every radio station in the country. Here, at the tomb of the earlier Prussian King Frederick the Great, Hitler bowed before Hindenburg – 'the World War I lance-corporal before his grey-haired field marshal'. The Crown Prince, who would have been the King's successor, sat in the first pew. This state spectacle, which historian Friedrich Meinecke called 'the Potsdam heartstring theatrical', was staged in its every detail with all Joseph Goebbels' ingenuity. He even had an empty throne set up for the absent King. It was all intended to look like the renewal of Prussian tradition, and especially to throw sand in the eyes of the military and conservative circles. Thus it was hardly noticed that on the same day, Hitler had issued the Malicious Practices Act, which in effect made punishable any criticism of Nazi policies and especially any communication with the outside world about what was going on in Germany. Indeed, large parts of the population began to hope that they were seeing the 'renewal' of Germany.

During this political storm, in April 1933, Paul Lehmann and his wife were guests in the Bonhoeffer home in Wangenheim Street (DB-ER 268–69). They were surprised to find how serious their friend Dietrich had become – they remembered him as always ready to enjoy a joke. Bonhoeffer took time whenever he could to show them around Berlin. They marvelled at the forest of swastika flags in the city centre, visited the Wedding district,[13] and went to the opera. But what most interested the Lehmanns was what they saw of their friend's parental home, with its upper middle-class atmosphere and the many servants responding to almost imperceptible signals from their mistress.

Even that soon after the Malicious Practices Act had been promulgated, frank conversations no longer took place without precautions being taken. The Lehmanns found it irresistibly funny when, in the middle of a conversation, Klaus Bonhoeffer would quietly get up, steal over to the door and fling it open suddenly to see if anyone was secretly listening outside. The conversations were indeed of a sort that no enthusiastic servant of the new regime ought to be hearing. Klaus and Dietrich Bonhoeffer discussed with Paul Lehmann, among other things, how it would be possible to keep people outside Germany quickly and reliably informed about developments inside the country, since Hitler had made such an undertaking a punishable offence.

During this period Hitler was careful not to speak openly about his war plans. With regard to his hatred of the Jews, he did not have to restrain himself. There were plenty of Germans who not only were afraid of Russian Bolshevism, but made no secret of their aversion to Jews, including many Christians, both Protestant and Catholic. So there were no protests against the arrests of communists, nor was there resistance to the Nazi Party's declaration calling for a boycott of Jewish businesses on 1 April, instructing the party members:

The action committees are further responsible ... to explain and disseminate the truth – that peace and order reign in Germany, that the German *Volk* desires wholeheartedly to pursue its work in peace and to live at peace with the rest of the world, that its fight against the Jewish conspiracy is only conducted in self-defence ... On Saturday, at the stroke of 10, Jews will know whom they are fighting. (DB-ER 267)

The photos of SA militiamen holding up their signs in front of Jewish stores: 'Germans! defend yourselves, don't buy from Jews!', were sent around the world. We have already told how Bonhoeffer's 91-year-old grandmother was among the few Berliners who pointedly went shopping in these stores on 1 April. Most people preferred to let this event pass. Church leaders such as Otto Dibelius were writing to their partners abroad not to believe the 'propaganda against Germany'. In doing so they did not mention that, on that same day, Hitler's compliant parliament had passed the Law on the Reconstruction of the Professional Civil Service, of which the third clause, the infamous Aryan paragraph, provided for all those not of the Aryan race, i.e. Jews, to be dismissed from the civil service.[14]

There are indications that men like Dibelius at that time were not acting of their own free will. In her spirited biography of Bonhoeffer, Renate Wind said that at the time 'almost all the Protestant church was prostrate before Hitler'.[15] But, vivid as this description is, one need only have met Otto Dibelius to know that such an attitude must be foreign to his nature. At the time, the President of the Evangelical High Church Council in Berlin, Hermann Kapler, informed it and the General Superintendents that he had sent telegrams of protest to several government ministries. But the first protests had already arrived from churches abroad. On 4 March 1933, the Executive Committee of the Federal Council of Churches in the USA, whose meeting in 1930 in Washington Bonhoeffer had attended, issued a statement 'condemning persecution of the Jews in Germany'; it was mentioned in an article in the *Frankfurter Zeitung*, a widely read national newspaper, on 23 March. It was clear to everyone involved that such protests would soon swell to an angry flood. The result might be that the new rulers of Germany would become unwilling to negotiate.[16]

When Bonhoeffer wrote on 14 April 1933 to his friend Erwin Sutz that, on the Jewish question, 'here the most intelligent people have totally lost both their heads and their Bible' (DBWE 12 I/38), the reason was not to be found in total blindness, nor in the national mood of exuberance, but rather in the hope that through clever diplomacy one could still avoid the worst outcome and stay in dialogue with the new regime. This view was shared by the Catholic bishops and the leaders of the Catholic Centre Party, who could not be suspected either of harbouring any enthusiasm for Hitler. Like the overwhelming majority of the people, the leaders of both churches were fatally deceived by Hitler, with the fear of a communist revolution playing the decisive role in their thinking.

While 'Potsdam Day' had been put on for the benefit of the general public, Hitler's plan to get the majority of the people behind him had to include bringing a positive image of the 'new age' to small towns and even to villages. From Ilsenburg in the Harz Mountains, Friedrich Busch – a 24-year-old lecturer in a seminary there that prepared pastors for German congregations in South America – wrote to his fiancée:

On the first of May there was a big commotion here. It was only with sharp pricks of conscience that I declined to join the insubordinates [the insufficiently submissive], and instead went along with the seminary to the big procession. Led by the brown-shirted Nazi student group, which until now has existed secretly at the seminary and was coming out in uniform for the first time, we closed ranks with the trade associations directly behind the schoolteachers ... Not a house to be seen that wasn't decked out with evergreens, fir trees set up in front, colourful flags, pictures of Hitler or Goebbels, or banners ... You can imagine how it irked me to be forced to march with the hallelujah-shouting rabble in Mr Goebbels' propaganda procession.[17]

At the May Day celebrations, the processions ended with entertainment and free beer. That probably pleased a lot of people; but Hitler also wanted to win over those who weren't so easily tempted, including both the main churches. So in his May Day speech, in which he promised to end unemployment, the greatest social problem of the day, by building the *Autobahn* (national highway) system, he again finished with a prayer: 'Lord, we are with you! Now bless our fight for our freedom and our German fatherland!' For those who didn't think much of theatrical religious declarations, he found other phrasing. On 23 May, in his speech announcing the Enabling Act, which was given the high-sounding name 'The Law to Relieve the Emergency of the People and the State', he included a passage intended to reassure the church leaders in Germany: 'The National Government perceives in the two Christian confessions the most important factors for the preservation of our national heritage [*Volkstum*] ... It will respect any contracts concluded between these Churches and the provincial governments [*Länder*].'[18]

Hitler knew that words alone would not be sufficient. How much the Third Reich needed the churches' support should be made plain in the sight of all, so it sent its 'movement fighting troops' in uniform to attend Sunday worship services. Many local church members, but also pastors and professors of theology, let themselves be bedazzled by this; in fact, the idea soon spread among church circles that the Nazis were bringing about a new era of a 'people's mission', to make Germany a Christian country again. Friedrich Busch described to his fiancée how this was happening in Ilsenburg:

Today was the installation of the new representatives to the synods from local churches, a big fuss, most of them in uniform, the rest in top hats. The storm troopers and the Hitler youth came marching in. Such things are too grotesque to have any kind of reality, except an extremely dangerous reality. All day I've kept seeing these uniformed men before me, as they sang 'Let us all set our faces / and our entire being / straight towards Jerusalem!' Some were so totally inattentive that surely they didn't hear themselves singing about Jerusalem. But others' faces looked as though they thought it was about a battle against Jerusalem.[19]

This was written on 30 July 1933, when the struggle for the Protestant church was already in full swing, and when Bonhoeffer and everyone who thought as he did had already lost the church elections and thus the first battle with those who followed Hitler.

Long before 1933 there had already been Nazi Party members in the Protestant church. In 1932 most of them banded together in the German Christian Faith Movement. Now that Hitler was in power, they concluded that it was their duty to transform the Protestant provincial churches into a 'German Reich Church in the national socialist [Nazi] spirit'.[20] Until then, the 28 provincial Protestant churches had been loosely gathered together in the German Protestant Church Federation, founded in 1922, but by now all the provincial churches wanted closer ties than that.

Of the 28 independent churches in the Federation, the Church of the Old Prussian Union (APU) had by far the most members. It was called Old Prussian because the 'new Prussian' provinces incorporated by Bismarck into the Prussian state following the war of 1866 – Schleswig-Holstein, Hanover, Hessen-Kassel and Nassau, along with the city of Frankfurt – had kept their independent provincial churches. 'Union' indicated the APU's continuity with the united Prussian Church created by King Friedrich Wilhelm in 1817, bringing together Lutheran and Reformed churches, though most of the local congregations remained either Lutheran or Reformed.

Besides the APU, the Federation included such large provincial churches as the Evangelical Lutheran Churches in Bavaria, Württemberg and Hanover, but there were also some very small ones, in small German provinces that had previously been independent states. The APU, to which Bonhoeffer belonged, reached from East Prussia (including Königsberg, now part of Russia) to Aachen in the west, near the Belgian border; as the largest Protestant church, it carried a disproportionate weight in the

Church Federation. The call to unite the Protestant churches had been popular long before the German Christians made it their cause. Now it was raised even more loudly, as Protestants saw their government treating the Catholic Church as a partner and negotiating a treaty of state, the so-called Concordat, with the Vatican.

But the German Christians, unlike Hitler and his propagandist Goebbels, were not very clever at public relations. They organized a 'Reich Conference' on 3–4 April in Berlin, at which they shouted for all to hear that the Church must now 'synchronize' (gleichschalten) with the new Germany;[21] it must adopt the Führer principle, and alien (artfremdes) blood did not belong in the pulpit, therefore the Church must adopt the Aryan paragraph and dismiss its Christian pastors of Jewish heritage. It is important to appreciate the extent to which, before Hitler, German Jews had been integrated in German society. There were no ghettos, and no one gave any thought to the fact that, for instance, Bonhoeffer's friend Franz Hildebrandt, who was preparing for ordination as a Lutheran pastor, had a Jewish mother.

Two of Hitler's cabinet ministers, Göring and Frick, appeared at the Reich Conference, thus giving it an official whitewash. The Berlin Party Secretary, Wilhelm Kube,[22] made a long speech in which he rudely insulted church leaders such as Dibelius. All this went too far even for many supporters of the German Christians. The signs were that the convictions on various sides were irreconcilable, and thus there would be a fight over the Protestant church in Germany (DB-ER 269–71).

'The Church and the Jewish Question'

The Bonhoeffers, like the middle- and upper-class majority in the country, were under no immediate threat from this political upheaval, but they soon began to feel the effects of the new laws. Gerhard Leibholz, Sabine's husband, a professor of law at Göttingen University, was threatened with the loss of his position due to his Jewish ancestry. Karl Bonhoeffer and his eldest son Karl Friedrich, also as professors, had to resist pressure from the new regime within their respective institutions. Dietrich Bonhoeffer could easily become a victim of the Malicious Practices Act merely by keeping in touch with his friends abroad.[23]

Through the Reichstag fire, Karl Bonhoeffer became the first family member to come into direct contact with the new government. His services were requested as consulting psychiatrist in the highly publicized trial of the lone suspect, the Dutchman van der Lubbe, who was supposed to have started the fire. Dr Bonhoeffer accepted this task and carried it out as he saw it his duty to do. It would not have occurred to him, at the time, to act otherwise. But even at this early stage, the Bonhoeffers were among the best-informed families in the country, having more specific experience than most people of the criminal methods being employed by the new government. Bonhoeffer's brother-in-law, Hans von Dohnanyi, was chief of staff for the Minister of Justice, Franz Gürtner, whom Hitler had inherited from the previous government, intentionally in order to show that 'justice is independent in the National Socialist [Nazi] state'. Gürtner knew that Dohnanyi was secretly keeping a chronological list of the legal offences committed by the Nazi regime. In the years to come, Hans von Dohnanyi and Dietrich Bonhoeffer were to be drawn into an ever closer partnership in their struggle against the terrorism of the Nazi dictatorship.

Dietrich Bonhoeffer was one of the first theologians, after 30 January 1933, to recognize Hitler's policy against the Jews as a problem for the Church. There were never to be many who agreed with him. He had very soon realized that this was not just a church problem, but also an eminently political one. Having been warned by Dohnanyi, he was already writing his essay on 'The Church and the Jewish Question' even before the law on the civil service containing the Aryan paragraph was issued. He had first presented his theses on this topic to a group of pastors invited by Revd Gerhard Jacobi in the parish house of the Kaiser Wilhelm Memorial Church, some of whom left the room in protest because they, like most Germans at the time, were of a different opinion.

The essay, which he was still able to have printed in the June issue of *Vormarsch*, a Protestant 'monthly magazine for politics and culture' (DB-ER 240), shows how hard it was at the time, even for such an independent-minded theologian as Bonhoeffer, to subject the government and its legal conduct to theologically based criticism. A long tradition stood against it. During the Counter-Reformation, when the Lutheran provincial churches in Germany were in great danger, they had been protected by the Protestant German princes. This was the beginning of more than four hundred years of a close relationship between church and state in Germany, and a sharing of responsibilities between them based on Luther's 'doctrine of the two kingdoms'. According to traditional Lutheran thinking, it was the state's responsibility to uphold law and order in the 'kingdom of this world'. It exercised its power as the authority established by God, and the Church had no right to interfere here. The Church was responsible 'to proclaim the kingdom of God', and the state was not allowed to meddle in the spiritual mission of the Church. However, it was supposed to provide the legal framework within which the Church could carry out its mission unhindered, and could watch over the conduct of church office-bearers in legal matters, to see that they obeyed the law of the land.

This is what Bonhoeffer had been taught at university. This theology did not even allow for the theoretical possibility that the state could itself become unjust. Because he was the first Lutheran theologian to think this particular matter through, Bonhoeffer in 1933 saw the Church's situation more clearly and drew more radical conclusions from it than most of his teachers and friends, even Karl Barth whom he so admired. Bonhoeffer wrote in his essay:

There are thus three possibilities for action that the church can take vis-à-vis the state: *first* (as we have said), questioning the state as to the legitimate state character of its actions, that is, making the state responsible for what it does. *Second* is service to the victims of the state's actions. The church has an unconditional obligation towards the victims of any societal order, even if they do not belong to the Christian community. 'Let us work for the good of all.' These are both ways in which the church, in its freedom, conducts itself in the interest of a free state. In times when the laws are changing, the church may under no circumstances neglect either of these duties. The *third* possibility is not just to bind up the wounds of the victims beneath the wheel, but to seize the wheel itself. Such an action would be direct political action on the part of the church. This is only possible and called for if the church sees the state to be failing in its function of creating law and order ... The necessity for immediate political action by the church must, however, be decided by an 'evangelical council' as and when the occasion arises. (DBWE 12, II/13)

Here Bonhoeffer was far-sightedly addressing the question that was to decide whether Germany under Hitler would remain a civilized nation or slide into barbarism. He was standing before his church and demanding that it develop a political conscience and take determined action. If it had done so, there might have been a 'timely resistance movement', but the response at that point was only a very limited one, carried out by a small number of Christians. In such a situation there are a thousand reasons to say it would be better to wait and see. Resistance might look unpatriotic, other people are in a better position to undertake it, we aren't yet dealing with the really important issues, and whatever else one might consider as reasons to put off action. Resistance is almost always avoided because those who must offer it say that the time has not yet come.

Bonhoeffer's early rejection of Nazism had much to do with the Jewish question. Again, this was not an isolated decision, but rather, like so much else in his life, one that was influenced by family and friends. Even before 1933, all the members of his family had disapproved of Hitler. Moreover, his twin sister was married to a Jewish Christian, and his friend and theological dialogue partner Franz Hildebrandt was, according to Nazi terminology, a 'half-Jew'. But in April 1933, even though the whole family agreed on this matter, only the youngest son, the one who had become a pastor, had, with his essay 'The Church and the Jewish Question', already put these thoughts into a call to action.[24] At the same time, his brother-in-law Hans von Dohnanyi had initiated a sustained struggle behind the scenes in the Ministry of Justice. In the spring of 1933, Bonhoeffer understood right away that the persecution of the Jews, then just getting under way, was to be the state's decisive challenge to the Church; thus he was already ahead of the church struggle before it began. From our point of view today, this gives him a particular status within it; but at the time, his clear-sightedness about the political consequences of theological statements made him, even for his friends in what was to be the Confessing Church, an inconvenient Cassandra.

The church struggle begins

Towards the end of April, the Church's situation became considerably more acute. The German Christians took for granted that, since Hitler's victory, they were in charge of the Church. But the picture they painted of the coming 'Reich Church' was anything but attractive to the great majority of practising Protestant Christians. In this way the German Christians themselves brought about the development of an opposition against them: the Young Reformation Movement for the Renewal of the Church. True to the above-mentioned 'doctrine of the two kingdoms', the Young Reformation declared: We say yes to the new government under Adolf Hitler, but no to the German Christians. The Church must remain the Church, and the state may not be allowed to interfere in its affairs. The only sources for the concerns of the Church are the Bible and the confessional writings of the Reformation. The German Christian attempt to change that is unacceptable. The Young Reformation was saying No specifically to the German Christians, not to the government; on the contrary, it was second to no one in its political loyalty.

Looking back decades later at the religious groupings confronting one another at that time, one finds not only contradictions, but also some surprising areas of agreement. This explains why, for many people, it was so hard to see what Hitler's intentions really were. For example, the Young Reformation declared its 'wish [for the Church] to reverse the aging trend among office-holders and in the membership of governing bodies, through more efforts to bring in younger persons, especially from those who served in the first world war (DBWE 12, I/44)'. They spoke of 'alliances in the struggle', and were in favour of 'setting up a practical training year' which was to bring future pastors together 'in genuine companionship and service with people from all walks of life'.

Today it is not enough to declare in a general and uncommitted way that the church must continue in future to take up the cause of the poor and those in need; instead it must help to bear the severe hardships of people who have been traumatized socially and emotionally by the political fate that has inevitably been the outcome of struggle for them.[25]

It was thoughts like these that persuaded a naval officer named Martin Niemöller to make the move 'From the U-Boat to the Pulpit'. This was the title under which the feisty pastor from Dahlem had published his widely read memoir; and years later, when colleagues from southern Germany heard the tone of voice of the former submarine commander at meetings in his parish house, they could have sworn they were sitting in the officers' mess. It didn't make any difference to the Nazis, however. All they heard was what the Young Reformation was saying: 'We confess our faith in the Holy Spirit, and therefore reject, as a matter of principle, the exclusion of non-Aryans from the Church, because it is based on confusion between State and Church. The State is supposed to judge; the Church is supposed to save' (DBWE 12, I/44). How strong was the hope of being able to curb the excesses of the Nazis and, in view of 'what all German people have in common', to work amicably with them, is shown by the efforts of Hans Joachim Schoeps. After Easter 1933 he founded a new Jewish youth organization which he called the German Advance Guard, German Jewish Followers, to gather up the Jewish members of youth groups which had been dissolved or 'synchronized' with the Nazis. Schoeps, who was also a public speaker for the Reich Association of Jewish Front-Line Soldiers, was at the same time trying to get an audience with Hitler to persuade him that the old liberal leading class needed to be replaced by 'veterans' association forces'. He thought that in this way he would get the Nazis to be more willing to negotiate. In 1956 he reported:

I was working with some friends on a memorandum about the legal situation and the condition of German Jews, showing how they could be included as an incorporation among others in building the new Reich ... The Jews who have immigrated from the east since 1918, and the Zionists, to the extent that they didn't, as they said themselves, already consider themselves a Palestinian diaspora rather than Germans, I wanted to put under the protection of the minority laws until they emigrated; for the old-established Jews, however, I wanted a firm guarantee of their full rights and duties as citizens by the Reich leadership.[26]

When the leaders of the Church Federation proposed to write a consti-tution for the newly uniting German Evangelical Church, the member churches agreed that there was no question of allowing the German Christians to be involved in this. On 25 April a 'triumvirate' met to begin work on the draft. Hermann Kapler, President of the Evangelical High Church Council, represented the Old Prussian Union Church. The Lutheran churches were represented by Bishop August Marahrens from Hanover, the Reformed churches by Pastor Hermann Albert Hesse, a well-known Reformed leader from Wuppertal.

But Hitler had no intention of respecting Luther's doctrine of the 'two kingdoms'; he saw any opposition, even by the Church, as directed against himself, and he very cleverly found a way to meddle in the work of the new drafting committee. He appointed Ludwig Müller, a military chaplain from Königsberg, East Prussia, who had long been a Nazi Party member, as his Authorized Representative for Protestant Church Affairs, and assigned him to 'promote all efforts in the creation of an Evangelical German Reich Church'. The triumvirate had to take him on board right away in order not to offend Hitler, and the German Christians also had to react to Hitler's surprise move. On no account did they want to make Müller the head of their movement – their Reich leader was a pastor named Joachim Hossenfelder – but they named Müller as their patron and as candidate for the office of Reich Bishop. The Young Reformation countered that it was the triumvirate which must nominate a candidate for bishop, and it named Pastor Friedrich von Bodelschwingh, the highly respected director of a church community for the disabled at Bethel in Westphalia.

The draft constitution for the new German Evangelical Church was published on 25 May. During the following two days, representatives of the 28 provincial churches hastened to hold their deliberations on it, and also to elect Friedrich von Bodelschwingh as Reich Bishop. But neither Hitler nor Hindenburg was prepared to accept Bodelschwingh in this capacity. Ludwig Müller and the German Christians unleashed a ruthless campaign against him, saying that the constitution was not yet in force and therefore the churches' representatives were not authorized to elect a bishop.

In the midst of this crisis, Hermann Kapler retired as President of the High Church Council, and General Superintendent Ernst Stoltenhoff from the Rhineland was appointed as an acting successor. This could be interpreted as a procedural error, since according to a state agreement the provincial government of Prussia was entitled to be consulted in appointments to this office. It was indeed only a provisional appointment, but the Prussian Minister of Culture and Religious Affairs, Bernhard Rust, immediately declared that the Church had transgressed its legal limits and therefore lost its entitlement to conduct its own legal affairs.

Anyone who could read the signs of the times had to be deeply alarmed, in 1933, by the appointment of Rust to his own job. His enmity towards the Church and his hatred of Jews were as well known as the fact that his sole qualification for office was being an 'old guard' Nazi Party member. This man was now in charge of Prussia's schools and universities, as well as the Religious Affairs department. After the war, Karl Bonhoeffer wrote of him:

Of the official ceremonies at the university, the only one I attended was the inaugural speech of Rust, the Minister for Cultural Affairs. Unfortunately neither I nor any of the other professors had the courage on this occasion to get up and walk out in protest against the Minister's insulting position toward the professors. (DB-ER 279)

Rust named August Jäger, an anti-church lawyer on his ministry staff, as state commissioner for Prussia's provincial churches. Jäger began 'restoring order' by suspending all clergymen in positions of leadership from their offices, allowing the SA militia to take over church office buildings, and filling all key positions in church structures with German Christians. This, now, really had the look of a battle by the Hitler state against the Protestant church. But Jäger's arbitrary actions aroused such a storm of protest all over Germany, as well as an appeal from Hindenburg, that Hitler called them off.

To this day it is often overlooked that the Protestant church never fought against Hitler's policies, or even posed objections to them; instead, Hitler, by ingenious means, conducted a fight against the Protestant church, for of course Rust had acted in consultation with him. However, since Hitler had not appeared in person on behalf of any of these measures, he could say they were departmental errors. Orders that turned out to be false moves could be taken back without being blamed on Hitler or damaging him. The truth was that at this stage of his takeover of power, nothing that was happening in the Protestant church was a matter of indifference to him. So, immediately upon reversing Rust's move, he undertook another.

Hitler was not a Protestant church member – he was nominally a Catholic, and never officially left the Church of Rome – but on 14 July he personally ordered elections to be held for the leadership of the new Protestant church, and set the date as 23 July. This meant there were only nine days to prepare, following his announcement. The German Christians were not nearly well enough organized, but Hitler made it the duty of all local Nazi Party secretaries to support their cause enthusiastically. This led to a frenzy of activity on behalf of the German Christians all over the country. Among other things, rallies were held at universities appealing to students to demonstrate 'spontaneously' on behalf of Ludwig Müller. 'Spontaneous' was one of the Nazis' favourite words for actions planned by the Party. Years later, boys coming home from dutiful participation in Hitler Youth meetings, on being asked what they did there, might say, 'We practised spontaneous applause.'[27]

As a pastor in a university setting, Bonhoeffer, together with his students, had thoroughly prepared for the German Christian rally that was held at the university in Berlin. The Tägliche Rundschau (*Daily Review*), a Protestant newspaper, said that 'when the resolution supporting Chaplain Müller's candidacy for bishop was read out, nine-tenths of the audience left the auditorium'. Three days later, there was a debate organized by Bonhoeffer and a colleague in the university building in Unter den Linden Boulevard. The report on it was entitled 'The Struggle for the Church'. In those days, heavy with religious tension, 2000 students are said to have turned up. Can we imagine that today? The speakers included German Christian professors, representatives of the neutral group of theology students and teachers who could not or did not want to take sides, and as sole representative of the Young Reformation, Dietrich Bonhoeffer. According to the reports in the church press, his words must have profoundly impressed his audience. Here the work he had put into the essay on 'The Church and the Jewish Question' had its first public effect, since he was able to express in simple words why a church which adopted the Aryan paragraph, or which put up with the state's deposing church leaders and appointing others, was giving itself up for lost.

Hectic days were ahead for Bonhoeffer's students during this summer semester, since besides their own work they organized a news service for the suspended church General Superintendents and were drafting and distributing their own protest statements. Bonhoeffer himself participated in many pastors' conferences in Berlin, and was shocked to see how hesitant the pastors were about active struggle. After the war, Gerhard Jacobi reported that on two occasions, when the pastors were discussing only the possibility that protests might bring further harm to the Church, Bonhoeffer stood up and merely quoted a brief couplet from Theodor Storm: 'One man asks: What is to come? / The other, What is right? / And that is the difference / Between the free man and the slave.'[28] If the state has driven its leaders from office, and arrogated to itself the decision as to who may be a member of the Church and who may not, shouldn't the Church's ministers feel free to launch their sharpest counterattack?

Bonhoeffer and Franz Hildebrandt then proposed an interdict, a sort of strike by pastors. There would be no more church funerals in Germany until the state restored the Church's rights under law. A better moment could not have been chosen to take such a decision. Hitler wanted to show the world that he had brought his German revolution to a successful conclusion; so alongside the solemn signing on 20 July of the Concordat between the Reich government and the Vatican, an uproar in the Protestant church was really not what he wanted. If such pressure had been applied right at that moment, Hitler would have had to yield. But everyone to whom Bonhoeffer and Hildebrandt turned with the idea was shocked and wouldn't even consider it. So then the two friends wondered together whether the time had not come for them to leave the church which had ordained them as pastors.

During these tempestuous days in which one piece of news was swept away by the next, Church Councillor Heckel, who was in charge of German expatriate congregations for the Church Federation, asked Bonhoeffer to come and see him. They knew each other from ecumenical discussion meetings and had met more recently several times at Young Reformation events. Heckel asked Bonhoeffer if he would be willing to take a German pastorate in London. Was this the solution? Hildebrandt had already been thinking of looking for a pastorate abroad. But first they had to wait and see how the church elections turned out.

Hitler had purposefully allowed only nine days for the church election campaign. He had named Hans Pfundtner, a leading government official, as his Authorized Representative to ensure that the character of 'free elections' was preserved. But the opposition's campaign rallies were broken up by SA commandos and their flyers and lists of candidates confiscated by the secret police, the Gestapo. The one and only daily church newspaper had to cease publication. The German Christians obtained a court injunction against the name the Young Reformation had chosen for its list of candidates, 'Evangelical Church List'. Together with Gerhard Jacobi, Bonhoeffer managed to get in to see Rudolf Diels, the head of the Gestapo, to register their protest, pointing out that Hitler had guaranteed free elections. They were told that the Young Reformation could continue to campaign if it changed the name of its list: the name Gospel and Church was agreed upon. The police even gave back some of the flyers.

Then, on the eve of the election, Hitler made a speech on the radio, during an intermission at the Wagner Festival in Bayreuth, in which he said he was expecting a vote in favour of 'the forces that are exemplified by the German Christians who stand firmly upon the foundation of the National Socialist State' (DB-ER 296). He also made it the duty of all good Nazis who were not Catholics and had not left the Church to cast their votes. The result could not have been worse. The German Christians got 70 per cent of all votes, in some areas even more, and in the majority of the provincial churches they filled all the key positions. Ludwig Müller, Hitler's man, became president of the High Church Council in Berlin, and also bishop of the Old Prussian Church, in which he had dictatorial powers. Hermann Göring, Prime Minister of Prussia, bestowed on him the honorary title of State Councillor.

In Hanover, but especially in the southern German provincial churches of Bavaria and Württemberg, where there had already been German Christians in office before the election, things looked a little better. Since Bishops Meiser, Wurm and Marahrens and their staffs could stay in office, these three churches were henceforth referred to as the 'intact' churches, while those now dominated by German Christians were regarded as 'destroyed'. The latter included all the Prussian provincial churches except that of Westphalia, where the election results had not been sufficient to allow the German Christians to take over completely.

On the Sunday of the election, Bonhoeffer preached in Trinity Church in Berlin, on Matthew 16:13–18, about the rock on which Jesus wants to build his Church:

If we had our way, we would prefer to keep detouring around the decisions confronting us. If we had our way, we would prefer not to be dragged into this fight over the church … But – God be thanked – it is not up to us. With God, we get just what we don't want … We will not be spared any of this – making a decision means that we differ with others … In the midst of the creaking and groaning of the church structures, which have been profoundly shaken and are collapsing and crumbling away here and there, we can still hear the promise of the eternal church, against which the gates of hell shall not prevail, the church on the rock, which Christ has built and continues to build through all the ages. Where is this church? … Come, all of you who are asking this seriously, you who are left alone and lonely, who have lost your church. Let us go back to the Holy Scriptures, let us look together for the eternal church. Let anyone with ears to hear listen. (DBWE 12, III/8)

The question of power had been decided in Hitler's favour; but, as Bonhoeffer made clear to his hearers, this had been the very means of posing the question of truth in such a way that it could not be ignored. After this heavy election defeat, the Young Reformation withdrew from politics and announced that from then on it would concentrate on missions, which meant 'home missions': evangelizing its own compatriots. Bishop Dibelius and several others resigned from their offices.

From the Pastors' Emergency League to the Bethel Confession

Groups of pastors were now gathering all over Germany to formulate confessions of faith intended to correct the false teachings of the German Christians. What they wanted to accomplish was formulated by Martin Niemöller on 2 August at a Young Reformation meeting:

Theologically, is there a fundamental difference between the teachings of the Reformation and the ones the German Christians are proclaiming? Yes! is our fear, though No! is what they say. We must do away with this lack of clarity, by means of a confession of faith for our time. If this doesn't come from the other side – and there's no sign of it coming soon – then it has to come from us! and it must come in such a way that the others must answer Yes or No to it …[29]

Dietrich Bonhoeffer and Hermann Sasse, another Lutheran theologian who in 1932 was already criticizing the Nazi statements on church policy, had accordingly been charged with writing a confession of faith appropriate to the time for the Protestant church. They were to work at Bethel, where Bodelschwingh made some of his staff available to support them. Bodelschwingh had given up his candidacy for Reich Bishop after four nerve-wracking weeks, but he was still the church leader around whom the opposition could gather. Georg Merz, a lecturer in the Church College at Bethel, was to moderate the discussion meetings.

Bonhoeffer did not go directly to Bethel, but travelled by way of London, where he preached as a candidate in the two German-speaking local churches which were seeking a shared pastor. Both congregations wanted to call him, but he did not immediately accept. He was tormented by the decision, whether to leave Germany and his church, which was just getting its opposition together again. Didn't it really mean running away?

Bodelschwingh personally took his guests on a tour of the Bethel community for the disabled. Bonhoeffer wrote to his grandmother about a church service there:

It is said of Buddha that he was converted by an encounter with a seriously ill person. What utter madness, that some people today think that the sick can or ought to be legally eliminated. It is almost like building a Tower of Babel and must bring vengeance on us. Anyhow, our concept of sickness and health is pretty ambiguous. What we see as 'sick' is actually healthier, in essential aspects of life and of insight, than health is. And that the two conditions depend on one another is surely an essential part of the plan and the laws of life, which can't simply be changed to suit people's impertinence and lack of understanding. (DBWE 12, I/86)

Only a few years later, Hitler commanded that just this be done, and had sick and disabled people removed from the population by murder. His 'euthanasia doctors' were only too willing to help.

About the theological task which occupied him in Bethel, Bonhoeffer wrote to his grandmother:

Our work here is very enjoyable, and also very demanding. We want to try to make the German Christians declare their intentions. I rather doubt we shall succeed ... It is becoming increasingly clear to me that what we are going to get is a big, *völkisch* national church that in its essence can no longer be reconciled with Christianity, and that we must make up our minds to take entirely new paths and to follow where they lead. The issue is really Germanism or Christianity, and the sooner the conflict comes out in the open, the better. The greatest danger of all would be in trying to conceal this. (DBWE 12, I/86)

The theologians helping to draft the Bethel Confession stayed close to Luther and the confessional writings of the Reformation. In each of six articles they stated first what the Church believes, and in a second paragraph rejected as false doctrine what the German Christians had made of that article of faith. In the article on the people Israel, contributed by Wilhelm Vischer, a Swiss who taught Old Testament at Bethel, it says:

The fellowship of those belonging to the church is not determined by blood nor, therefore, by race, but by the Holy Spirit and baptism. We reject any attempt to compare or confuse the mission of any other nation with that of Israel, which is part of salvation history. It can never in any case be the mission of any nation to take revenge on the Jews for the murder committed at Golgotha ... We object to the attempt to make the German Protestant church into a Reich church for Christians of the Aryan race, thus robbing it of its promise. This would set up a racial law at the entrance to the church ... (DBWE 12, II/15)

For Bonhoeffer the article on the Jews was the most important part of the confession, because it was here that concrete decisions had to be made. He found Vischer's text particularly well done. But when the draft text was sent to 20 theologians in Germany – including Althaus and Schlatter – for their expert opinions, he already suspected no good would come of it. Not only were the drafters overwhelmed with proposed corrections; it was above all Vischer's text which was so watered down that Bonhoeffer no longer wanted to own the confession and withdrew his signature from it. His disappointment in the outcome of this work on the Bethel Confession was a significant reason why he sent his acceptance to the two congregations in London. A year later he gave a copy of the final version of the confession to his colleague in England, Julius Rieger, inscribed: 'Too many cooks spoil the broth – from an anonymous collaborator D.B.'

What turned out to be more important than the confession for Bonhoeffer was that in Bethel he met Georg Merz, a theologian from Bavaria who had an unusual feeling for excellence and for contemporary cultural developments. He was an early admirer of the great German writer Thomas Mann and had baptized Mann's daughter Elisabeth. A consultant to the publisher Kaiser in Munich since the late 1920s, Merz in 1933 arranged for Bonhoeffer to become one of its regular authors, among whom it already counted Karl Barth. The first of Bonhoeffer's books to be published there, in 1933, was *Creation and Fall*.[30]

A General Synod of the Old Prussian Union Church had been called for 5 September. It was to meet in the *Herrenhaus*, where the Bundesrat, the upper chamber of the German parliament, sits today. Since the question was still open of what decisions the synod would make with regard to the Aryan paragraph, Bonhoeffer had composed a pamphlet entitled 'The Aryan Paragraph in the Church'. It was widely distributed and particularly annoyed those who did not want to see any quarrel with the government over this issue. These included the Church Federation and Councillor Heckel, who was in charge of expatriate congregations. After reading the pamphlet, Heckel decided that Bonhoeffer, whom he had recommended for the pastorate in London, was actually unsuited for the post and resolved to keep him from being sent there. Bonhoeffer had portrayed the Aryan paragraph as adopted by the church as blatantly false doctrine:

The German Christians say: We are not so much concerned with these thousand Jewish Christians as with the millions of our fellow citizens who are estranged from God. For their sake, these others might in certain cases have to be sacrificed. We answer: We too are concerned for those outside the church, but the church does not sacrifice a single one of its members. It may even be that the church, for the sake of a thousand believing Jewish Christians that it is not allowed to sacrifice, might fail to win over those millions. But what good would it do to gain millions of people at the price of the truth and of love for even a single one? (DBWE 12, II/16)

The General Synod turned into a spectacle in brown. Many of the delegates appeared in uniform. Those presiding were Party comrades such as Joachim Hossenfelder, August Jäger and Kapler's successor, Friedrich Werner. They quickly ruled out any discussion as to whether the question of a confession of faith should be debated. Next, the church constitution was thrown out; the provincial church structures were replaced with ten bishoprics, whose bishops were under the authority of Ludwig Müller as head bishop. Finally, the Church Law on the Legal Position of Clergy and Church Officials was adopted. Besides containing the Aryan paragraph, it demanded 'unconditional support for the National Socialist State and the German Protestant Church' from all clergy and office-holders. The small group of those who objected was shouted down and left the room. This disgraceful assembly was soon known throughout Germany as the Brown Synod. However, by refusing to tolerate a small opposition in its midst, it unintentionally created an extra-Synodal opposition which was that much more powerful.

Martin Niemöller, together with 20 other pastors including Bonhoeffer and Hildebrandt, called for the creation of a Pastors' Emergency League. The suggestion had come from two pastors in the countryside, Eugen Weschke and Günter Jacob. Thus the Confessing Church was built from the beginning on cooperation among many pastors and members of local churches. The members of the Emergency League were, first of all, to commit themselves anew to the Scriptures and Confessions; secondly, to

Ludwig Müller's formal installation as Reich Bishop at a national meeting of the German Christians, Berlin Cathedral, 23 September 1934

resist any violation of these; third, to give financial help to those affected by Nazi laws or by violence; and fourth, to reject the Aryan paragraph. In a very short time as many as 2000 pastors signed up to the commitments of the Emergency League. By the end of the year their number had grown to 6000, and was still to grow by a further thousand. Kurt Scharf, a 32-year-old pastor who was to be elected the following year as president of the Confessing Church in Brandenburg, wrote at the time to his fellow pastors in his district:

We commended to one another to take upon ourselves, in the struggle for our confession as a church of the Reformation, everything possible including the ultimate commitment, and to stand by one another unconditionally. We believe that only our willingness to do so will compel the people now in power in the church offices to take notice, and that in our church's present situation we owe it our profession of faith.[31]

In October, a Council of Brethren was elected to lead the Pastors' Emergency League, the first democratically elected governing body in the history of German Protestant churches. There was now a church opposition which could fight the arbitrary decisions of the German Christians as the Young Reformation had not been able to do. Klaus Scholder, in his book *The Churches and the Third Reich*, describes it thus:

The strict limitation to church and confession and along with it the deliberate openness of its approach also made the League politically almost impregnable. Thus the organization of the Pastors' Emergency League became the core of the Confessing Church and remained so until the collapse of the Third Reich.[32]

But before the opposition had thus established itself, those who initiated the Emergency League had to take action against the forthcoming National Synod in Wittenberg. Here they were not dealing just with the Prussian Church, but with the new German Evangelical Church. This synod was to meet soon after the Prussian Brown Synod, and now it was time to tell the Church publicly, and inform the whole ecumenical community, about what was going on in Germany.

In Kurhessen, where, despite a German Christian majority, August Jäger's attempt to synchronize the provincial church with the Nazis had foundered, the provincial synod decided on 11 September to request from the theological faculties in Marburg and Erlangen 'a solemn and responsible instruction to German Evangelical Christianity' as to whether the law adopted by the Old Prussian Church and intended for the entire Reich Church on the conditions of employment for clergy 'is in conformity with or contradicts the teaching of Holy Scripture, the Gospel of Jesus Christ and the teaching of the apostles ...'[33] The reply from Marburg, signed by the Dean of the Faculty, church historian Hans von Soden, was unambiguous. It declared the Aryan paragraph to be irreconcilable with the essence of the Christian Church, and this statement was supported, within a few weeks, by 21 New Testament professors from all over Germany.

Lutheran dogmatists Paul Althaus and Werner Elert from Erlangen came to a different conclusion. They declared that the *'völkisch* diversity of external church organization' expressed 'a necessary consequence of the divisions of the peoples which are to be affirmed in terms of destiny as well as ethics' and thus had to be taken into account 'in admission to the ministry of the church'. For the Church's new task 'of being a *Volkskirche* of the Germans', in the present situation, 'the occupation of its ministry by persons of Jewish origin generally would be a severe burden and a hindrance'. Therefore the Church must 'require the withholding of its Jewish Christians from office'.[34] That with these words the two professors were, retrospectively, calling for Jesus, the Apostles and many New Testament authors to be 'withheld' from the German Evangelical Church, does not seem to have entered their minds. Quarrels over the Aryan paragraph continued well into 1934 and flared up again afterwards from time to time.

'Break with our theologically grounded reserve'

Bonhoeffer had been cancelling his participation in all ecumenical meetings since February, for lack of time; but he wanted to make use of the World Alliance conference in Sofia, Bulgaria, 15–20 September 1933, to inform his friends abroad fully about the situation in Germany. The opposite was the intention of Theodor Heckel, who went to a concurrent meeting in Novi Sad, Yugoslavia, to reassure ecumenical circles about developments in Germany. He was about to be named as bishop in charge of the church Foreign Office and, although he was not a German Christian, had made up his mind to go along with the Nazi government. Until the outbreak of the Second World War, the Geneva office, the nerve centre of the ecumenical movement, was more accommodating towards him than towards his sparring partner Bonhoeffer. But at that time there were still more ecumenical partners who agreed with Bonhoeffer, and it was he who was invited to give one of the keynote speeches on 'The Churches and the Peace Question' at the World Conference to be held in 1934 on the Danish island of Fanø.

In Sofia, behind the scenes, Bonhoeffer was able to inform influential men in the ecumenical movement about political developments in Germany and the church struggle, while Heckel was soothing the participants in the Novi Sad meeting. Heckel could not yet manage to block Bonhoeffer's call as pastor to the two German churches in London, but from this point on the two of them realized that they were on opposite sides. Heckel's role in Bonhoeffer's life was henceforth to be that of an adversary. A Bavarian pastor who knew Heckel well, confirmed that he had a nose for politics; he was a seeker after influence and power.

The National Synod, which included all the German provincial churches, met at Wittenberg on 27 September and elected Ludwig Müller Reich Bishop by acclamation. Over Luther's tomb in the castle church, the German Christian leader Hossenfelder extolled him: 'I greet thee, my Reich Bishop!' Hildebrandt whispered to Bonhoeffer that now Luther 'really would turn over in his grave' (DB-ER 320). From then on the people called Müller the 'Reibi'.

Karl Bonhoeffer's chauffeur had driven Bonhoeffer, Hildebrandt and Gertrud Staewen to Wittenberg with flyers making known the protest of the Pastors' Emergency League, which were then distributed there. When the new Reich Bishop made no mention in his report to the synod of the resistance within the Church, the three sent him a telegram asking him to redress this that afternoon. But instead, Müller proclaimed in his speech that the church struggle was over. At this point, it is said, a snort of laughter was heard from the castle church gallery where Bonhoeffer was standing discreetly.[35]

There was public astonishment that the synod did not adopt the Aryan paragraph for the new Reich Church. Hitler had flatly forbidden it to do so, at the urgent request of the Foreign Office. Bonhoeffer considered the synod a disaster precisely for this reason, since the 'intact churches' and their Lutheran bishops were thereby spared the necessity of protesting against the Aryan paragraph. The Archbishop of Sweden, Erling Eidem, known to be a friend of Germany, had come to Germany especially to implore the leaders of the Protestant church to prevent the Aryan paragraph from being adopted at Wittenberg. If only because of his involvement, the bishops of Hanover, Bavaria and Württemberg would have had to follow suit. Precisely because 'nothing happened' at Wittenberg, the new German Reich church had, in effect, confirmed the Old Prussian Union's Brown Synod.

With hindsight, this would have been the moment for a successful protest against Hitler by Protestant Christians in Germany. Against the 2000 pastors in the Emergency League, whose ranks were swelling from day to day, he would not have been able to act at that point, with the nations outside Germany watching attentively and the international newspapers carrying full reports. If the churches had followed Bonhoeffer and cried 'Schism', charged Hitler's obedient Reich Church with heresy and renounced all fellowship with it, Hitler would probably have backed off again. Above all it had become clear that the issues were political, that the real opponent of the church opposition was the government. But on all sides, Bonhoeffer's and Hildebrandt's radical proposals fell on deaf ears.

The German Christians had indeed triumphed in Hitler's church elections and been able to profit from their victory until the National Synod; but it was a Pyrrhic victory, for two reasons. On one hand, it was the Nazi Party which, at Hitler's command, had brought about their victory, while they themselves had scarcely any competent staff and no national-level organization at all. Among the many indications of this is that there was no interference with the enquiry to theological faculties from the Kurhessian provincial church synod. Any competent organization would have been able to hinder such an undertaking through negotiations behind the scenes.

On the other hand, and this was the decisive fact, the great majority of Hitler's followers in the Nazi Party, beginning with the local Party secretaries, were in no way friends of the Church. The dream of a strong Nazi church was not that of the Party, and was certainly not Hitler's dream. The only thing that interested the dictator, and even fascinated him, about the Church was that the Catholic Church as an institution had survived for 19 centuries; only in this sense did it serve as a model for his 'Thousand-Year Reich'. Thus the German Christians found themselves in a very unclear and confusing situation, which soon led to sharp internal quarrels. Their unity fell apart, leaving various groups fighting among themselves.

At this point, if not before, the church opposition should have perceived that it was confronted with a government that would be happy to get rid of Christianity in any form. Hitler's solemn speeches indeed painted a different picture, but these could have been recognized as tactical manoeuvres intended to deceive. The struggle of the Confessing Church against the German Christians was from the beginning a struggle against the wrong opponent. Bonhoeffer, who had never seen it in any other light, wrote to Sutz in 1934:

It is [also] time for a final break with our theologically grounded reserve about whatever is being done by the state – which really only comes down to fear. 'Speak out for those who cannot speak' [Prov. 31:8] – who in the church today still remembers that this is the very least the Bible asks of us in such times as these? (DBWE 13, 217)

Heckel put Bonhoeffer under pressure to withdraw his acceptance of his call to the London churches himself. Bonhoeffer not only resisted this, but demanded an appointment with Ludwig Müller, at which he told him quite plainly that he had no intention of speaking or acting on behalf of the Reich Church while in London. When the Reich Bishop tried to argue with him, Bonhoeffer commenced quoting an article from the *Confessio Augustana* in Latin. As the Swedish mission chaplain in Berlin wrote to his Archbishop, at that point 'M. got a bit hot under the collar and suggested postponing the conversation until later' (DB-ER 322). Müller was not a very clever man, and certainly not much of a theologian. It did not take long until nobody took him seriously any more, beginning with his protector, Hitler.[36]

6. London (1933–1935)

As a German pastor in London

When Bonhoeffer moved into the parsonage of the German congregation in south London, on 17 October 1933, it meant a radical change in his life. Until that day he had lived in his parents' home, except for brief periods, and had not had to keep house for himself in either Barcelona or New York. Now he had to learn, and his new surroundings could hardly have been less suited to that purpose.

The main rooms of the parsonage were being rented by a private German school, leaving the new pastor with just two, quite large rooms upstairs, which were cold and damp. An addition had been built onto the house years before and had now settled, so that stepping from one room into the other felt like being on board ship in heavy seas. The windows would not close properly and the wooden doors were warped. There was neither central heating nor warm water. There was a gas fire in the

Bonhoeffer's vicarage in the 1950s

fireplace, but when turned on it made no difference unless one sat directly in front of it, and mice could not be deterred from scurrying around everywhere.

Except for the plague of mice, most of this was fairly normal for an old house in London. Until long after the Second World War, hardly any English private homes had central heating, but for someone coming from Berlin this was an unaccustomed hardship. In his first months in London Bonhoeffer was often ill with colds and fever. From November he had the help of Franz Hildebrandt, who stayed for three months. He also had other visitors, to whom he offered meals and lodging without a great deal of bother. All those who were guests in this household gave glowing reports. Among them was the physicist Herbert Jehle, who had attended Bonhoeffer's lectures on 'Creation and Fall'; he came over often from Oxford and later also turned up in Finkenwalde.

Bonhoeffer had some fine old furniture from his parents' home sent to London, along with his Bechstein grand piano. When spring came he could see that this house in Forest Hill was in an especially attractive part of London. There was a large garden with old trees, and only a short walk away was a famous park on a hill with splendid views, reaching far into the Kentish countryside in the south and to the north offering the world-renowned skyline of London.

However, Bonhoeffer must not have had much time to enjoy all this. 'His year and a half in London was the only time in his life when Bonhoeffer worked as a parish minister in a full-time pastorate.'[1] Every Sunday he had to conduct two worship services, and even though he preached the same sermon in both churches, this was new for him. He was not the sort of preacher who stood up in the pulpit with just a few notes; every sermon was written out word for word. Sixteen of his sermons in London have been preserved.[2]

In Barcelona, Bonhoeffer had already found out how many small tasks there are to do each day in an expatriate congregation, but now, in a much bigger city, he had to take care of them all, for two congregations, without an assistant. 'It is really hard to understand how so much can be going on in such a small congregation', he wrote home. His colleague Julius Rieger reported:

Towards the end of the week I quite often had a telephone call from Bonhoeffer, for the sole purpose of asking, What are you preaching about next Sunday? Then we would exchange some ideas, either critical or in support of one another, which were always of great benefit, at least to me. Occasionally he would say, 'I wrote something about that once,' and the next morning's post would bring some essay of his; on one of these he wrote, 'Don't let this get in the way of preparing your sermon.'

Bonhoeffer expected a great deal of congregations who listened to his sermons; even so, once again he demonstrated how easy it was for him to win people over. The church in south London consisted of well-off business people and German diplomats, in contrast to 200-year-old St Paul's Church in the East End, which consisted of small businessmen, bakers, butchers, tailors and other artisans, many of whose families had been there since the late nineteenth century. During the First World War these people had been treated badly because of their German origins, even though they had long been British subjects. This had traumatized their children, none of whom spoke German anymore or had any contact with the Church. However, there were also more recent immigrants with children, so that Bonhoeffer started a Sunday school as he had done in Barcelona, and it soon began to flourish. They also had a nativity play at Christmas 1934, and like the one in Barcelona it made a great impression. The choir, too, acquired new energy, to the extent that it performed Johannes Brahms' *German Requiem*.

Bonhoeffer made regular pastoral visits to his parishioners, and since the distances he had to travel in London took a lot of his time, he liked to use the lunch hour to meet with colleagues. Rieger describes with what aplomb Bonhoeffer could order a meal in a foreign restaurant. Sometimes after lunch they would go to the cinema, and Bonhoeffer was not averse to taking in a crime thriller. So one day Rieger and his wife found themselves with Bonhoeffer at *The Mystery of Mr X*. Mr X was an enemy of all policemen, droves of whom were soon breathing their last on the screen. Mrs Rieger found this perfectly dreadful, so they simply stuck a hat in front of her face whenever another doughty guardian of the law fell to the enemy. Rieger wrote that it was one of the most amusing times he ever had at the cinema.

From reading Bonhoeffer's writings one has almost solely an impression of great seriousness, but his friends report plenty of laughter shared with him, too, even at the most difficult times. In particular there was merriment over the lively theological arguments between him and Hildebrandt. One such debate was brought to an end by Hildebrandt, to roars of laughter from those listening, by using his sparring partner's own favourite expressions; he characterized Bonhoeffer's arguments as 'doctrinaire, affected, formalistic and cheap'.

They usually went to bed very late, because the parish work took up so much afternoon and evening time and there was still much to do afterwards. Franz Hildebrandt also played the piano very well and loved to do so. When the two friends played four-hands piano pieces late at night there was no one else in the big house to be disturbed. In the mornings, breakfast was late in the bachelor pad in Forest Hill, with the latest news in *The Times* and the mail from Germany providing the main themes.

Carrying on the struggle by other means

At the beginning Bonhoeffer may still have wondered whether his move to London really meant running away, but it soon became clear to him that here he would be carrying on with the struggle by other means: '... one is close enough to want to take part in everything and too far away for really active participation' (DBWE 13, 81), he wrote to his brother Karl Friedrich in January 1934. But he never stopped thinking about what was going on in Germany. It kept him on the telephone almost daily with friends, and especially with his mother, who had become a member and great supporter of Niemöller's church in Dahlem. The post office responsible for Bonhoeffer's telephone bills is said to have voluntarily reduced the amount by more than half, since a parish minister could not possibly pay such monumental sums. Every six to eight weeks, whenever he felt that he needed to do something, Bonhoeffer flew to Berlin to help his friends there or to plead with them not to back down. Comrades-in-arms such as Niemöller were not always enchanted when Hildebrandt and Bonhoeffer wrote to 'embrace you in fellowship ... with all the force of our youth'.

Now is the time when we must be radical on all points, including the *Aryan paragraph*, without fear of the possible disagreeable consequences for ourselves. If we are untrue to ourselves in any way at this point, we shall *discredit* the entire struggle of last summer. Please, please, *you* be the one who makes sure that everything is kept clear, courageous and untainted. (DBWE 13, 56)

Niemöller replied that the two friends had added stress to his life when it was already stressful enough. The issue at this point was a new scandal unleashed by the German Christians. On 13 November they had put on a big rally in the Berlin Sports Palace, with all the leaders of the Reich Church on hand. The keynote speech was given by the Berlin Nazi Party leader Reinhard Krause, a secondary school teacher, who called on the Church to 'liberate itself' finally, in Adolf Hitler's new Germany, 'from the Old Testament with its Jewish money morality and from these stories of cattle dealers and pimps'; all offices in the church must be taken over by 'men of the movement', and the Aryan paragraph must be implemented everywhere without exception.

The press carried full reports, and the news spread like the wind through Germany that none of the Ministry of Church Affairs officials and bishops of the Reich Church who had been present had raised a word of protest against Krause's speech. Outraged letters and telegrams were received from individuals and groups, including many rank-and-file German Christians. For the first time people resigned in large numbers from the German Christian Faith Movement.

Bonhoeffer and Hildebrandt were reading about all this in *The Times*, which was outstandingly well informed and could count on great public interest in stories such as these. In the same paper they also read that, because of this scandal, Ludwig Müller had to rescind the Reich Church adoption of the Aryan paragraph and dismiss Hossenfelder's Church Ministry Council. Meanwhile, a position paper by the Pastors' Emergency League on the Sports Palace scandal was immediately confiscated, and some members of the League were suspended from their pastorates; but, once again, Hitler knew exactly how he should react. This time he presented himself as being 'above church party politics', and had his Interior Minister announce that he had no intention either of intervening in the church dispute or of using police measures. So the seas continued to rise. Müller was drenched with telegrams and had to postpone indefinitely his solemn installation as Reich Bishop, which had been scheduled for 3 December. He began to look unsure of himself; we now know that Hitler had sent for him and told him that he had to sort this matter out by himself, and that he could not afford to make any more mistakes.

Müller also had influential enemies in the government itself. If his arbitrary action in handing over the Protestant youth groups to be absorbed by the Hitler Youth was taken in order to shore up his relationship with Hitler, it was a smart move. Like all ideological dictators, Hitler wanted to cut the youth off from all influences outside the Party. He is supposed on one occasion to have formulated his idea of this as follows:

These young people are learning nothing other than to think as Germans and act as Germans, and when these boys come into our organization at the age of ten ... then, four years later, come from the boys' groups into the Hitler Youth, and we keep them there another four years, then we are certainly not going to let them go ... instead, we take them directly into the Party, into the Storm Troops, into the SS ... and so on, and they never get away for the rest of their lives, and are quite content so.[3]

Hitler, for whom 'youth' apparently consisted of boys only, was never really able to carry out this totalitarian idea, but it was clear what he wanted. Baldur von Schirach was determined from the beginning to bind German youth exclusively to Hitler. In a speech on 5 October 1933 in Frankfurt on the Oder,[4] having mentioned the national church which was being established, he declared to great applause: 'I belong to no confession. I am neither Protestant nor Catholic. I believe only in Germany.'[5] The leaders of the church youth groups, however much the majority of them supported 'German *Volk*-ish' thinking, were not inclined to hand over their big youth organizations to this man. In Berlin in 1933 there were about a thousand boys in the Hitler Youth, but 2500 secondary school pupils in Protestant Bible study groups alone and many more in the YMCA, the Boy Scouts and various other groups.[6]

The leaders of the Evangelical Church Youth had declared several times to the Reich Bishop that there was no question of annexation of their groups by the Hitler Youth, and he had promised them not to take any action without consulting them. He had solemnly made the same promise to the south German bishops. But the last time he promised not to do anything without consultation, he had already made his deal with Schirach. The latter had invited him to dinner at the Hotel Esplanade, because he knew the Reich Bishop was a fan of the violinist Barnabas von Géczy who was appearing there with his orchestra, and in this pleasant atmosphere the two were soon of one mind. The next day Müller didn't want to confess this to the Protestant youth leaders. When finally confronted with his betrayal, he lied his way out of it. Probably his claim that Hitler had described the incorporation of the Evangelical Church Youth into the Hitler Youth as 'his best Christmas present' was also a lie.[7]

Müller's opponents in the government did not at all approve of his over-hasty agreement with Schirach. The Foreign Minister, Konstantin von Neurath, found the Reich Bishop's stupid mistakes and mendacity to be disturbing for foreign relations. Being a diplomat, he expressed this a bit more formally, saying the Reich Bishop must be lacking in 'intelligence and character'. Wilhelm Frick, the Interior Minister and his staff also wanted to get rid of Müller. He had even forfeited much of the respect of his own followers; but Hitler still kept him on. Karl Barth told an American church representative, Charles MacFarland, who was visiting Germany on his own initiative and had been invited to meet Hitler, to give the Reich Chancellor the message that 'putting the German church into the hands of Ludwig Müller is like turning the army over to the

Captain from Köpenick'.[8] Hitler simply didn't want to admit that he had made a completely incompetent one of his plenipotentiaries. Men like Göring and Rust supported Müller for other reasons. They wanted a Nazi church or no church at all.

Nevertheless it looked as though the Reich Church, and with it the German Christians, had their backs to the wall, and that Müller would soon fall. The church opposition was growing from day to day. The Pastors' Emergency League now had 7000 members. In this situation, Bonhoeffer in London urged a new course for the Emergency League. He had heard that the bishops of the 'intact' churches were already negotiating with Müller again instead of fighting against him. Bonhoeffer implored his friends to have the Emergency League press for the election of new synods to replace the ones in which German Christians were in charge, and that the Emergency League itself must stop taking in new members, lest the opposition be infiltrated by its enemies. These were by no means illusory proposals. A councillor of the Reich Court in Leipzig, Dr Wilhelm Flor, had been studying the issues in the church struggle and had proved that the entire church constitutional structure which the German Christians had erected with the help of the Party was contrary to the law of the land. As became clear later on, it could have been knocked down by a lawsuit.

The Bishop of Magdeburg Friedrich Peter, Reich Bishop Ludwig Müller, and Bishop Heinrich Oberheid

Finding himself in such difficulty, Müller sought out two protectors who were cleverer than he and who considered him useful as a puppet. One was August Jäger, who was glad of another chance to get the Church under the Nazis' thumb and thereby to become an important official in the Third Reich; the other was Heinrich Oberheid, whom Müller had made Bishop of the Köln-Aachen region (Cologne and Aix-la-Chapelle). Oberheid was only too happy to come to Berlin and leave the work in the Rhineland to a deputy. He was one of the most ambivalent figures in the church struggle. A theology student in 1914, he had gone to war and come back as a lieutenant, then worked his way up in the management of the Stinnes conglomerate, where he had made many contacts. He also earned a doctorate in economics before returning to his theological studies. In 1930 he joined the Nazi Party and in 1932, the German Christians. For a few months in 1933 he was assistant pastor in a little town in the Westerwald, before being made a bishop.[9]

He now took over the office of the Reich Bishop and from day one never let his 'boss' out of his sight. He decided who might speak with Müller, went with him to all his engagements, intervened whenever Müller put a foot wrong and probably also wrote his speeches. It was Oberheid who gave Jäger his second chance. The latter became – while keeping his post at the Prussian Ministry of Culture – legal administrator for Müller's office, and Oberheid showed him how the Reich Church could still gain acceptance despite the Sports Palace fiasco.

Oberheid introduced Jäger to the new jurisprudence being taught by Carl Schmitt and his students. During his theological studies, Oberheid had come to know Schmitt personally and was very impressed with him. Schmitt's school promoted the view that the Nazi revolution had created a new order, quite the opposite of the Weimar Republic's constitution: that of the 'total' state, not a balance of different forces as in a democracy, but instead characterized and 'completely penetrated by one all-embracing idea'. Such an idea could not be used to transform the Catholic Church, since its centre was in Rome; but, according to Carl Schmitt and his school, the power of the state could help in founding a Protestant Reich Church. As yet, however, this new church policy existed only in the heads of a few men.

Meanwhile, the Pastors' Emergency League, headed by Niemöller, was working to bring Müller down, knowing that they could count on support not only from the Interior Minister and the Foreign Minister, but also from Reich President Hindenburg.

The goal of getting Hindenburg's support for the removal of the Reich Bishop was being promoted fervently by Bonhoeffer from London. He tried to support the church opposition by informing his fellow pastors and the German congregations in Great Britain as thoroughly as possible about the situation, then working with them to formulate letters of protest. He also wanted to persuade the Church of England to intervene strongly in the German church struggle. He succeeded on both counts, which brought him into conflict with the church authorities back home. The German pastors in England, in their conference at Bradford, Yorkshire, protested unanimously against the scandal of the Sports Palace rally, declaring that the 'close relationship' of the German Protestant churches with the home church would be dissolved if members of the church government failed to uphold the 'belief in justification by grace alone through Jesus Christ' as 'the sole basis of Reformation thought' and 'the Holy Scriptures of the New and Old Testaments' as 'the sole standard for the faith' (DBWE 13, 50). The president of the Association of German Evangelical Congregations in Great Britain, the banker Baron Bruno von Schröder, accentuated this by pointing out that the congregations in England enjoyed 'full liberty to resign from the Church Federation should we so desire' (DBWE 13, 51).

Heckel, as foreign officer for the German Evangelical Church, immediately sent a letter to reassure the German clergy in England that the Reich Bishop himself wanted to uphold the full authority of the Bible and the Church's confession. However, his letter arrived simultaneously with the news that Müller had handed the Protestant youth associations over to the Hitler Youth without consulting anyone. Furthermore, there was no sign of the efforts to 'bring peace to the church' which Heckel's letter promised. Instead, Müller reinstated the Aryan paragraph and, on 4 January 1934, enacted the notorious 'muzzling decree', which forbade the Protestant pastors in Germany any public discussion of the church struggle, and threatened to dismiss anyone who disregarded the ban. In other words, the Oberheid and Jäger regime was now in place: the two of them were dictating to the Reich Bishop what he was to do.

The Pastors' Emergency League declared that it would not respect this decree, and called for a protest worship service in Berlin Cathedral. Müller ordered this prohibited by the police, which resulted in a large crowd singing Luther's hymn 'A Mighty Fortress Is Our God' in front of the cathedral. Thus the foreign press again had something to report about the church struggle. The German pastors in London reacted to every step taken by the Reich Bishop with another protest by telegram.

When they heard that Hitler was planning to hold a reception at his Chancellery for the leaders of the Protestant church, they wrote to Reich President Hindenburg, with copies to Hitler and several of his ministers: 'We implore you, Mr President, to avert the terrible danger that threatens the unity of the Church and the Third Reich now, at the eleventh hour. As long as Reich Bishop Müller remains in office, the danger of secession remains imminent' (DB-ER 344).

George Bell, Bishop of Chichester, also wrote to Hindenburg, which was then something completely unheard of. Here, Bonhoeffer was also at work behind the scenes, since in a very short time he had become this unusual bishop's adviser on the German church struggle. Bonhoeffer had seen Bell, who was exactly 23 years older than he – they were both born on 4 February – at ecumenical conferences, but had never spoken with him. Now, in a very few weeks, a relationship developed which Bell described after the death of Bonhoeffer:

I knew him in London in the early days of the evil regime; and from him, more than from any other German, I learned the true character of the conflict, in an intimate friendship. I have no doubt that he did fine work with his German congregation: but he taught many besides his fellow countrymen while a pastor in England. He was crystal clear in his convictions; and young as he was, and humble-minded as he was, he saw the truth, and spoke it with a complete absence of fear. (DB-ER 362)

Anglican bishops are, to this day, generally friendly and kind in relating to Christians from abroad, but they are unusually cautious. Yet Bell seems not to have spent much time enquiring as to who this 27-year-old German might be, and whether he could be trusted. In a very short time the two had such confidence in one another that the English bishop began getting

George Bell, Bishop of Chichester, with Franz Hildebrandt on the steps of the Church of St Martin in the Fields, London, on 1 July 1941 after a service of intercessory prayer for Martin Niemöller

involved, vigorously and quite undiplomatically, in the affairs of the German church. Few of Bonhoeffer's other relationships illustrate so clearly his effect as a person upon other human beings. It did not take long to recognize that he had an excellent education; more unusual was the perfection of his conduct towards others. He was both self-confident and modest. Through Bonhoeffer, first in Germany and later in Britain, Bell became so much the 'spokesman for the other Germany' that the British Foreign Ministry called him 'our good German bishop'.[10]

Hindenburg sent the letters he had received from London to Hitler, expressing also his own deep concern about what was happening in the Protestant church. It seemed as though Müller's days in office were numbered. However, thinking of the church leaders gathering at Hitler's Chancellery reception on 25 January made Bonhoeffer extremely uneasy.[11] Four days before that, he preached on the prophet Jeremiah's plaintive cry: 'O Lord, you have enticed me, and I was enticed; you have overpowered me, and you have prevailed' (Jeremiah 20:7). After just the first few words of this sermon, it was hard for the church members to tell anymore whether their pastor was speaking of Jeremiah or of himself.

Jeremiah was not eager to become a prophet of God ... he resisted, he tried to get away. But as he was running away, he was seized by the word, by the call. Now he cannot get away anymore ...

He was accused of fantasizing, being stubborn, disturbing the peace and being an enemy of the people, as have those in every age even up to the present day who were seized and possessed by God – for whom God had become too strong ... O Lord, you have enticed me, and I was enticed ... I had no idea what was coming when you seized me – and now I cannot get away from you anymore; you have carried me off as your booty. You tie us to your victory chariot and pull us along behind you, so that we have to march, chastened and enslaved, in your victory procession. How could we know that your love hurts so much, that your grace is so stern? ... You have bound me to you for better or worse. God, why are you so terrifyingly near us? (DBWE 13, 347ff.)[12]

Bonhoeffer seldom spoke words so full of feeling; he was a very self-contained person. At the same time, he was unusually well informed. This is what made him so credible when he analysed the political situation in the presence of others. There are very few texts which reveal the burning passion concealed behind his reserve. One such is this 1934 sermon on Jeremiah.

The anxiety which is visible here was only too well justified. The chancellery reception with the Führer did turn out to be a defeat for the church opposition, even beyond Bonhoeffer's worst fears. Shortly after the church leaders presented themselves, Prussian prime minister Hermann Göring appeared with a transcript, made by wiretapping, of a telephone call in which Niemöller had expressed himself very colloquially about the preparations for the chancellery reception: that the old gentleman (Hindenburg) had received 'extreme unction' etc. Hitler, who had of course been informed in advance, acted outraged. This was 'backstairs politics' and he was not prepared to put up with it. The bishops of the Lutheran provincial churches immediately distanced themselves from Niemöller, and two days later, 'under the influence of that great hour when the heads of the German Evangelical Church met the Reich Chancellor', joined with the German Christians in issuing a declaration that they 'took a united stand behind the Reich Bishop'.

... and declare themselves willing to enforce his policies and decrees in the sense desired by him, to hinder church-political opposition to them, and to consolidate the authority of the Reich Bishop by all available constitutional means ...

[The church leaders] condemn most strongly any intrigue involving criticism of the state, *Volk* or movement, because such criticism is calculated to imperil the Third Reich. In particular they condemn the use of the foreign press to present the false view that the controversy within the church is a struggle against the state. (DBWE 13, 91)

The opposition found itself divided and confused. Hitler had succeeded in isolating Niemöller completely, and with him the Pastors' Emergency League. After keeping himself out of the disputes among the church groups, the Führer could now stand there, shaking hands and taking leave of his guests, as the great mediator, and Müller had some new people for his bandwagon. None of those who were present at this reception could ever forget it, not even Hitler. In 1942, at table in his Führer's Headquarters, he told how the church leaders 'were terrified, cowered down so that they almost weren't there any more'.[13]

Heckel, who had to cooperate with Oberheid and Jäger if he wanted to keep his position, was charged with getting the pastors in London to concede and if possible also to stop up *The Times'* source of information. This was anything but easy. He first sent a letter to all the German expatriate pastors:

In particular I must urgently impress upon the clergy abroad the necessity for the greatest possible discretion in regard to church politics. Just as the soldier at the front is not in a position to assess the overall plan, but must carry out the duties that immediately concern him, so I expect the clergy abroad to distinguish between their own particular task and the task of the church authorities in shaping the German Evangelical Church at home. (DBWE 13, 85)

At that time Heckel believed that he could keep his area of responsibility, namely the congregations abroad and ecumenical relationships with partner churches, out of the church struggle. After Müller named him a bishop he let himself be forced into one compromise after another, and thus became mired deeper and deeper in dependence on the Nazi regime. After the war, almost all those who had trod this path tried to excuse themselves by explaining that they had hoped, by so doing, to avoid even worse outcomes. Heckel's path to becoming an accomplice began with this letter with its odd military simile and with his visit to London in February 1934, during which he and Bonhoeffer found themselves at loggerheads.

Heckel arrived with two colleagues, and began by describing the events in Berlin to the German pastors in England in such a way as to show the Reich government correcting the faux pas of the German Christians and supporting the orientation of church work towards its confessional responsibility. Thus he claimed that the protests he had received from London were signs of a detrimental radicalization and had only hindered things. This led to a fierce dispute, since the pastors saw such claims as a grotesque playing down of the issue.

At the end of his second session with them, Heckel demanded baldly that they sign a declaration that his report of the meeting was 'unanimously agreed to by all the German Evangelical clergy in England'. Bonhoeffer protested vehemently, since the visitors from Berlin had not responded to any of the pastors' actual questions and arguments. Heckel replied with the threat that 'those in opposition must realize, in their own interest, that if they did not yield they would be aligning themselves inevitably with the Prague emigrants' (DBWE 13, 111). 'Prague emigrants' meant opponents of the Third Reich who had fled when the Nazis took power, including especially members of the Social Democratic Party, many of whom had found refuge in Czechoslovakia. When Heckel began, in this connection, to give examples of 'treasonous activities', Bonhoeffer and two of his friends got up and left the room in protest.

His meeting with Bishop Bell did not go any better for Heckel. Bell had invited him and his colleagues to the Athenaeum Club, which today is still the place in London where Anglican bishops invite important guests for a conversation or a meal. Bonhoeffer himself met with Bell there several times while he was in London. He had prepared the bishop well for these three visitors. When Heckel tried to broach basic theological issues, and suggested to the bishop that he should stay out of German church conflicts, Bell asked him a series of very concrete questions about the conduct of the Reich Bishop and how the Reich Church was handling the church opposition. Heckel did not have much to answer, and when he later described this conversation as though all differences between the Reich Church and Bishop Bell – as the representative of the ecumenical community – had been cleared up, Bell responded with a sharply worded letter in *The Times*.

Thus Heckel went home empty-handed, and he knew very well whom he had to thank for the twofold failure of his mission in London. He sent for Bonhoeffer to come to Berlin, where he categorically ordered him to refrain from all further ecumenical contacts. Bonhoeffer pointed out to him that, as a youth secretary of the World Alliance, providing information to ecumenical partners was part of his job.

This trip to Berlin unexpectedly brought Bonhoeffer a sign of hope. On 7 March 1934 he was able to participate as a guest in the first synod of the Confessing Church in Berlin-Brandenburg. Such synods had already taken place in the Rhineland and in several other German provinces. Bonhoeffer had never seen the Reich Church as anything other than a church that had fallen away from God. Now, out of the ruins of the destroyed church, in several places at once, a new Confessing Church was beginning to grow. He returned to London full of hope.

In a contemporary report on the Confessing Church synod in Berlin-Brandenburg, Kurt Scharf wrote:

Their unanimity, which was evident not only in the agreement they expressed outwardly, but also in a close, warmhearted fellowship among all the participants, is the mark of spiritual legitimacy. Last Wednesday I was at the German Christians' rally at the Sports Palace. The difference in tone and content between our synod and that mass event put on by those who claim to represent the official church exemplified the most extreme contrast between 'spiritual' and 'secular'. The sneers and slanders over there were unbelievable, whereas our meeting expressed an earnest resolve to fight for the basic articles of the Reformation church, all the way and with all our might, and the strength of this resolve was at least as notable among the lay members of the Free Synod as among the pastors who were speaking and voting.[14]

Two developments in Germany kept Bonhoeffer in suspense following his return from Berlin, and Oberheid and Jäger were involved, in one way or another, in each of them. One was their attempt to build on the advantage gained from Hitler's chancellery reception of the church leaders to obtain quick general acceptance of the Reich Church, by force if necessary. On the other hand, it was precisely the use of force by both Oberheid and Jäger that made them, against their will, midwives of the Confessing Church. The shared need to resist brought the 'intact' and 'destroyed' churches back together, and at the famous Confessing Church synod in Barmen they solemnly adopted a common confession opposing the false teachings of the Reich Church and the German Christians.

An important word in the language of the Third Reich was *Gleichschaltung* ('synchronization', i.e. Nazification). For example, through a law of 30 January 1934 the governments of the German provinces lost all their particular rights and became mere rubber stamps, instruments of the Reich government; they were 'synchronized' with it. The goal was as always to design a state in which, according to the so-called 'Führer principle', everything was subject to one single will.

This measure was the example Oberheid and Jäger were following when they first took away the autonomy of the church governments in the Prussian provinces, and shortly thereafter incorporated 11 other provincial churches into the Reich Church. The bishops of these churches were placed under the authority of the Reich Bishop and of the provincial church offices within the Reich Church government, and henceforth were bound to follow their instructions. Jäger also made two attempts to bring this about in Württemberg province. The first time, he tried to exploit a row that had suddenly broken out in the city of Stuttgart, in which the German Christians were demanding the resignation of Bishop Wurm. Jäger hurried there with the Reich Bishop, intending to establish in Württemberg, by force, his idea of order in the Church. But the only result was great agitation among the clergy and congregations, which stood by their bishop.

This unrest alarmed the Bavarian church, because they assumed they would be next in line. Now the experiences of the destroyed churches got serious attention from the south German churches. The Evangelical Church in Westphalia had tried standing up to Jäger and had succeeded. Its provincial synod was the only one in Prussia where the German Christians had not gained a majority in the 1933 church election; it had refused to recognize Jäger's measures, and when he ordered its synod dissolved by the police, the thing for which Bonhoeffer had been waiting so ardently for a year finally happened. A rally with 20,000 church members was held in Westphalia Hall in Dortmund, with more people in two neighbouring churches. Paul Humburg, President of the Evangelical Church in the Rhineland, spoke again of gratitude to the Reich Chancellor and confidence in him, but he also said:

What do people care whether Jesus was *perhaps an Aryan?* Behind this in turn there is the idea that Aryan blood is better than Jewish blood ... But Scripture says: he died *for all!* It is said that for Germany there is 'only one authority, the authority of the Führer'. That applies only to the Germany of the Third Reich, but not to the community of the Son of God.[15]

It must have been very impressive to hear 20,000 people sing their hymns and say the Lord's Prayer together.

After this Confessing assembly, the Westphalian synod, which had been dissolved, reconstituted itself, and within a short time over half of all local churches in Westphalia had joined it. Later when the Confessing Church distributed membership cards, 90 per cent of the practising Christians in Westphalia became 'red card' carriers.[16] Representatives of the West German (i.e. Westphalian and Rhineland) church opposition met on 19 March in Frankfurt on the Main with representatives of the south German churches and decided to call Confessing assemblies like the one in Dortmund; these were to be held in the Bavarian cities of Munich, Nuremberg and Augsburg (Evangelical Church in Bavaria) and Stuttgart (Evangelical Church of Württemberg).

At this point, in Bonhoeffer's view, it became crucial for the ecumenical community to make very clear, for all to see, on which side it stood. On 7 April, the day when the Reich Bishop made Oberheid his chief of staff and placed the 'synchronized' churches under his authority, Bonhoeffer wrote a letter to Geneva. This letter again reminds us of the beginning of his first sermon, 'Christianity entails decision'.

My dear Henriod ... I would very much have liked to discuss the situation with you again; the slowness of ecumenical procedure is beginning to look to me like irresponsibility. A decision has got to be made some time, and it's no good waiting indefinitely for a sign from heaven, for the solution to the difficulty to fall into one's lap. Even the ecumenical movement has to make up its mind and is therefore subject to error, like everything human. But to put off acting and taking a position simply because you are afraid of erring, while others – I mean our brethren in Germany – have to reach infinitely difficult decisions daily, seems to me almost to go against love. To delay or fail to make decisions may be more sinful than to make wrong decisions out of faith and love ... and in this case it is really now or never. 'Too late' means 'Never'. Should the ecumenical movement fail to realize this ... then the ecumenical movement is no longer church, but a useless association for making fine speeches. 'If you do not stand firm in faith, you shall not stand at all' [Isaiah 7:9]. But to believe, to stand firm, means to decide. And can there still be any doubt as to which way that decision should go? For Germany today the confession is the way, as the confession is the way for the ecumenical movement today. Let us shake off our fear of this word – the cause of Christ is at stake; are we to be found sleeping? (DBWE 13, 126–27)

If at this moment there was one thing that could have helped the two church opposition groups – that of the Pastors' Emergency League and that of the 'intact churches' – really to come together in one Confessing Church, it would have been strong support from the ecumenical movement. But Bonhoeffer found no ears to hear him in Geneva. The office there kept to its statutes, according to which the Reich Church could not be denied its membership in the ecumenical community. If a Confessing Church were constituted alongside it, then this new church must apply for membership as a second German church. One can well imagine how horrified Bonhoeffer was by such formalism. But he had the trust of the Bishop of Chichester, who had a great deal of influence in the ecumenical movement and who *did* have ears to hear him.

As President of the Universal Christian Council for Life and Work, Bishop Bell sent a pastoral letter on Ascension Day, in May 1934, to the member churches of the Council, in which he expressed his deep concern about the situation in Germany.

The chief cause of anxiety is the assumption by the Reichbishop, in the name of the principle of leadership, of autocratic powers unqualified by constitutional or traditional restraints, which are without precedent in the history of the Church. The exercise of these autocratic powers by the Church Government appears incompatible with the Christian principle of seeking in brotherly fellowship to receive the guidance of the Holy Spirit. It has had disastrous results on the internal unity of the Church; and the disciplinary measures which have been taken by the Church government against Ministers of the Gospel on account of their loyalty to the fundamental principles of Christian truth have made a painful impression on Christian opinion abroad, already disturbed by the introduction of racial distinctions in the universal fellowship of the Christian Church. No wonder that voices should be raised in Germany itself, making a solemn pronouncement before the whole Christian world on the dangers to which the spiritual life of the Evangelical Church is exposed. (DBWE 13, 144–45; see also 139 and 179–80)

Other questions of fundamental significance would, in view of the situation in Germany,, also have to be discussed at the upcoming meeting of the Universal Council in Denmark. Bell's pastoral letter was a definite encouragement to the 'Confessing front', as it was still being called at that point, just before it held its first big assembly. Bonhoeffer immediately sent a letter of thanks to Chichester.

Representatives of all the opposition groups had met on 17 April in Nuremberg, and there a reconciliation had taken place between Niemöller and Meiser, who had been at odds since Hitler's chancellery reception. And when it turned out that Bishop Wurm had already issued a call to rally again in Ulm on 23 April, it was decided to make this Confessing worship service the founding act of the Confessing Church. Five thousand worshippers came streaming into Ulm Minster. In the choir pews sat emissaries from all the provincial churches in Germany. Following the sermon by Bishop Wurm, Bishop Meiser mounted the pulpit and read out, 'in the name of the Father, the Son and the Holy Spirit, before this congregation and all Christendom', a document in which the provincial and local churches of Germany which remained faithful to the confession declared themselves to be the rightful church.

This was the schism, the break with the Reich Church which had become godless, towards which Bonhoeffer had been working for more than a year. Müller immediately characterized the declaration as a 'declaration of war', but at this point his own troops were again in disarray. A few days before the Confessing assembly in Ulm, Jäger had succeeded in pushing Oberheid out of power and making the Reich Bishop, whom he despised, dependent on him alone. He wanted to achieve his goal of bringing the Church into subjection to the Party as quickly as possible, and carried on with the synchronization of the provincial churches which were still independent.

The Confessing Synod of Barmen

What the Reich Bishop and his legal administrator must have totally failed to grasp during those confusing days was that their behaviour was actually bringing the opposition together within the German Evangelical Church. They thus helped to make possible the Confessing Synod of Barmen, the most important event in the entire church struggle.

From 29 to 31 May, 139 delegates – including one woman and one blue-collar worker – from 18 Lutheran, United and Reformed churches in Germany, gathered in Barmen, on the east side of the city of Wuppertal in the Rhineland. They were to discuss a 'Theological Declaration', the essential points of which had been contributed by Karl Barth. Hans

Asmussen, whom the German Christians had forced out of his pastorate in Altona near Hamburg, and Church Councillor Thomas Breit from Munich had worked with Barth to prepare from his draft a proposed resolution for the Synod. In Barmen, Asmussen introduced the proposed resolution 'with a captivating speech', assuring that, after a very thorough discussion, the resolution was unanimously adopted on its second reading. It is not saying too much to call this confessional statement the most significant church document of the first half of the twentieth century.[17]

From our viewpoint today, there is surely more to say about Asmussen's speech than that it captivated his audience. Although in Barmen there was no longer any emotional affirmation of Hitler's government, it is striking that the synod, as did Asmussen in his speech, made sure it avoided any confrontation with the Nazi state, and did not risk even a mention of the Aryan paragraph. People felt at the time that they could leave out all the political problems; even Karl Barth, the Swiss, was of this opinion. Hermann Sasse, with whom Bonhoeffer had worked in Bethel to draft a more political confession, left Barmen before the Theological Declaration was adopted, because he could not vote for it but did not want to be the only one to vote against it. He was convinced that the Lutheran Church was being violated by joining the Reformed Church in adopting a common confession. Thus in 1934 a fissure was already appearing within the Confessing Church, which was to have disastrous effects on it in the years to come. However, as Klaus Scholder rightly says:

The first Barmen thesis was soon attacked by some Lutheran theologians as a Reformed error, indeed as heresy. Here, however, no one could have overlooked the fact that the Barmen Declaration was more Lutheran than anything that the Lutherans objected to.[18]

The synod was 'Lutheran' in agreeing with Asmussen that the falling away from God then taking place in Germany was not to be ascribed to Nazism alone, but had already been among the effects of the Enlightenment. Without even a glance at the 'thinking believers [Denkgläubigen]'[19] – from Lessing and Kant to Goethe, then to Harnack, or any contemporary philosophers and authors – the Synod declared its loyalty to the fundamental teachings of Martin Luther, with his threefold 'solus': *solus Christus, sola scriptura* and *sola fide*. That meant that human beings are saved through Christ alone, the Scriptures alone can tell us this, and by faith alone can we be justified before God.

While the church struggle lasted, these were the statements which, again and again, gave the Confessing Church its foothold. Inevitably, however, after the Second World War the questions of the 'thinking believers' came back onto the agenda, and it speaks for Bonhoeffer's rank as a theologian that he had already faced these questions before that, in the Tegel military prison. For him it was a matter of intellectual honesty in doing theology (DBWE 8, III/177).

Since Bonhoeffer counted the Barmen Synod, in which he did not take part, as one of the most important events in his life, and it became the reason for his to return to Germany, we quote here from the Preamble and the first of its six theses:

In view of the errors of the German Christians of the present Reich Church government which are devastating the Church and also therefore breaking up the unity of the German Evangelical Church, we confess the following evangelical truths:

[Jesus Christ says:] 'I am the way, and the truth, and the life; no one comes to the Father, but by me' (John 14:6). 'Truly, truly, I say to you, he who does not enter the sheepfold by the door, but climbs in by another way, that man is a thief and a robber ... I am the door; if anyone enters by me, he will be saved' (John 10:1, 9).

Jesus Christ, as he is attested for us in Holy Scripture, is the one Word of God which we have to hear and which we have to trust and obey in life and in death.

We reject the false doctrine, as though the church could and would have to acknowledge as a source of its proclamation, apart from and besides this one Word of God, still other events and powers, figures and truths, as God's revelation.[20]

Each of the six theses follows this pattern: after quoting words from the Bible, it states what the Confessing Church believes, then the false teaching of the German Christians which is solemnly rejected. For us today it is painfully obvious that this confession does not include the statement on the Jewish question which was so important to Bonhoeffer in working on the Bethel Confession. But at the time, this and other utterances against Adolf Hitler's government would have been asking too much of the majority of synod members. Even so, there were plenty of objections afterwards from the ranks of Lutherans. To a considerable degree, it was Jäger's violent actions that caused the unanimous declaration of Barmen to enter into history at all. And there was great relief and joy over its unanimity. Kurt Scharf communicated something of the exalted mood of those days when he wrote to the Confessing Church pastors in Brandenburg:

What had been promised in Ulm on 24 April was fulfilled in Barmen on 30–31 May. There, church groups faithful to the confession had gathered for a particular reason; as if there, beams and stones, mortar and bricks lay in disorder, waiting to be sawn, hewn, fired and fitted together. Here then, in Barmen, through the goodness of God the hard work was done in a few days; the great Evangelical Confessing Church of Germany was built out of all these diverse materials. Not a board or brick was left unused.[21]

From the Röhm Coup to the Confessing Synod of Dahlem

August Jäger was involved in bringing about the second Confessing Synod of the German Evangelical Church – that of Dahlem on 19–20 October 1934 – just as he had been involved in the first. A man such as he could only be spurred on by such events as the 'Röhm affair' in the summer of 1934, in which the SS, the elite Nazi paramilitary, massacred not only the leaders of the SA militia, who were suspected of preparing a coup, but also people who had nothing to do with the SA and were merely considered opponents of Hitler.[22] In this connection, Hitler had set himself up as the highest judicial authority, and without further ado declared the murders just. On 13 July 1934, he spoke of 77 deaths in his most bloodthirsty speech to the parliament, declaring: 'If anyone reproaches me and asks why we did not call upon the regular courts for sentencing, my only answer is this: in that hour I was responsible for the fate of the German nation and was thus the Supreme Justice of the German *Volk!*'[23]

Hitler wanted to be informed about everything, yet there were things he was far from wanting to know. Fritz Günther von Tschirschky, a close colleague of Vice-Chancellor Franz von Papen, belonged to a group of opponents of the regime who were the first, in those days, to try to oust Hitler from office. After 30 June 1934, Tschirschky had fallen into the clutches of the SS and had witnessed how Gregor Straßer, one of Hitler's early comrades-in-arms and his Party organizer, was butchered in the prison in Prince Albert Street. Tschirschky himself was not only released, but shortly thereafter was invited by Hitler, along with Papen, to the Obersalzberg resort. When he hinted that he had been present at Straßer's death, Hitler took him into the next room and demanded a full report; he had been told that Straßer committed suicide. Hitler's sister in the dining room heard every word and said later that her brother had been beside himself that day, and for a long time afterwards had screamed and struggled in nightmares every night.[24]

Bonhoeffer told his London friends that he knew through the Ministry of Justice that there had been many more than 77 murders. There are supposed to have been at least a hundred victims of the massacres. With these deeds, the SS began its rise; as its reward, Hitler made it a separate organization, independent of the SA militia. That there was no protest at the time, from anyone whatsoever, shows how far Germany had already travelled toward accepting a government without justice.

Jäger must have concluded during this critical phase that after so much violence done at the behest of the state, he would have no problem incorporating the Evangelical Churches of Bavaria and Württemberg into the Reich Church by force. But he was to be disappointed. In Württemberg, and more so in Bavaria, the response to his placing Bishops Wurm and Meiser under house arrest was mass protests. Those who, up to that point, had felt that the Lutheran churches should keep to their own path and not join a combined Lutheran and Reformed church, put aside their reservations. So the Confessing Church was able to take a second step, no less crucial than the first. On 19–20 October it held another Synod, in Berlin-Dahlem, at which it provided itself with a new, united church administration, by adopting the following resolution:

1. The constitution of the German Evangelical Church has been destroyed. Its lawful organs no longer exist. By their actions, the men who have taken over the leadership of the church in the Reich [Müller and Jäger] and in the provinces have separated themselves from the Christian Church.
2. On the basis of the emergency law of the churches, congregations and bearers of spiritual office bound by Scripture and confession, the Confessing Synod of the German Evangelical Church creates new organs of leadership.[25]

The main decision-making body for this administration became the Council of Brethren. So the democratic structure that had been introduced by the Pastors' Emergency League now entered into the Confessing Church.

The Dahlem Synod had been arranged at very short notice, so that many of its members had to leave before it was over. This made it possible for the Lutheran churches to argue that they had strong reservations about the resolutions which had been adopted there. For many Lutherans, the decisions taken in Dahlem seemed too radical, while for Bonhoeffer and all those who thought as he did, the decisions of Dahlem were just the necessary 'form', the ordering of the Church required by the 'content' of the Theological Declaration of Barmen.[26]

Following the example of the Emergency League, the new church administration consisted of a 22-person Council of Brethren and within it a 6-person executive council. Both the 'destroyed' and the 'intact' churches were represented in each, but the members who had come from the Old Prussian Union were in the majority by far since it had contained such large provincial churches. It was important to find the right balance. After lengthy discussion, the 'first Provisional Church Administration of the Confessing German Evangelical Church' was constituted in November, with Bishop Marahrens from Hanover as its President.

In his fight with the southern German churches, Jäger turned out to be at cross-purposes with Hitler. The Treaty of Versailles had provided for a plebiscite in January 1935 for the Saar region, to determine whether this small southwestern province should be returned to Germany or remain French. Warnings had come to Hitler from several different sources that if further measures were taken against the Church, the Saar vote would go against Germany. He therefore had August Jäger immediately dismissed from all the offices he held. Thus Jäger came to a miserable end, which was to be followed by a far more dreadful one. He left the Church in 1938, and during the war was involved in serious war crimes in Poland; after the war he was condemned to death, and was hanged on 17 June 1949.

Bonhoeffer was crucially involved in Jäger's ousting. The latter's heavy-handed measures had caused outrage even in England, so that Bonhoeffer, with his precise information from Berlin, was able to persuade Bishop Bell to visit the German embassy in London, and through him also the Archbishop of Canterbury, who asked the German Ambassador to come to Lambeth Palace. They both threatened to take public positions on the matter. In Berlin, Foreign Minister Neurath had already summoned the Reich Bishop to his office and read him the riot act, but the news from London was far more disturbing for the Reich government. The German ambassador, Prince Bismarck, sent telegrams:

[Bishop Bell assumes] that the Reich Chancellor is insufficiently informed about actual events and their repercussions abroad ...

[I attempted] to mollify his deep concerns that there has been a conscious turning away from Christianity in Germany, but I fear that all my counter-arguments made little impression upon this bishop, who is so well informed about every detail of these events.[27]

In this conversation, Bell gave most of the blame for the persecution of the churches to August Jäger, and the Archbishop of Canterbury went a step further and politely asked for nothing less than Jäger's dismissal. He said that he would soon have to take a public position on the church struggle in Germany, and that the churches in France and Sweden were thinking of following suit.

The telegrams from the German embassy in London were brought immediately to Hitler. In reply, the English bishops were requested by the embassy please to be patient a bit longer, since an announcement by the German government was expected shortly. In any case, Jäger was dismissed immediately from all his posts.

The ecumenical conference on Fanø

Even more than the Röhm affair, and the assassination by Nazis of Austria's Federal Chancellor Engelbert Dollfuß, public sentiment in Germany was preoccupied by the death of President Hindenburg on 2 August 1934. He was buried in Prussian military style in the Tannenberg Mausoleum. Hitler's farewell cry, 'Departed Chief, now enter into Valhalla!' was regarded by many as being in bad taste.

As he had done on 'Potsdam Day', Hitler presented himself as a loyal follower and now the successor of Hindenburg. He assumed the office of President, but took care never to be addressed by the title 'Reich President', only as 'Führer and Reich Chancellor', schoolchildren being taught at the time that this was out of respect for Field Marshal Hindenburg. In reality, this new title was intended to make clear that, with Hindenburg, the last relic of the republic had gone, and from now on the country was governed by a single will.

It was a fateful moment in German history, the last day in the Third Reich on which civil resistance might still have been possible. But even in the churches – the only organizations, once the political parties and the trade unions had been crushed, in which Hitler still had a substantial number of critics – too few people were aware of this at the time. Bonhoeffer, who knew that the events of the summer of 1934 had brought the threat of war much closer, was regarded by most church people who knew him as a pessimist. In April he had already written to Erwin Sutz: 'Naive, starry-eyed idealists like Niemöller can still think they are the real National Socialists – and perhaps it's a benevolent Providence that keeps them under the spell of this delusion; maybe it is even in the interest of the church struggle' (DBWE 13, 135).

This was the critical situation in which the joint conference of the World Alliance for Promoting International Friendship through the Churches and the Universal Christian Council for Life and Work on the Danish island of Fanø had to be prepared. Bonhoeffer had agreed to give one of the main speeches and to direct the international Youth Conference. More important to him than his own contribution, however, was the position the ecumenical movement would take toward the church struggle in Germany. The Geneva office was demanding anew that the Confessing Church agree to participate in ecumenical bodies as a sort of German 'free church',[28] despite its claim to be the true, constitutionally grounded Evangelical Church in Germany.

Heckel had managed to get the ecumenical Faith and Order movement, which studied theological issues, largely on his side in 1933, since no Germans belonged to it who could present the situation from the viewpoint of the Confessing Church. So the people in Faith and Order, whether British, Swiss or Americans, always objected when the Confessing Church protested against the German Christians and the Reich Church. Bonhoeffer meanwhile fought for a decision to have only delegates who stood on the ground of the Barmen Confession take part in the Fanø Conference; otherwise he could not participate himself.

For the Youth Conference he succeeded. He could not hope for support from Geneva, but he could count on the energetic Bishop Bell and the Danish Bishop Valdemar Ammundsen. The latter proposed that, as President of the Council, Bell could make use of his right to co-opt advisers to the conference; thus he could invite Karl Koch, president of the Westphalian church and of the Confessing Church Synod, and if possible also Friedrich von Bodelschwingh. In any case, neither of the two bishops wanted to do without Bonhoeffer's participation and his speech at the conference.

Bonhoeffer travelled back and forth between London and Berlin, carrying news and counselling his friends in the Confessing Church, who were rather inexperienced in international affairs. It looked for awhile as though he were going to cancel his participation in Fanø, especially when the Confessing Church representatives decided not to go because of the political situation in Germany; but they, like the two bishops, were convinced that Bonhoeffer must be there. So he was destined to face there, once again, his opponent Theodor Heckel, who had just been named *Auslandsbischof* [bishop for the German congregations abroad] and who therefore headed the Reich Church delegation.

In proposing his theses for his keynote speech (DBWE 13, 304ff), Bonhoeffer had concentrated wholly on the danger of war, and once again had not consulted the Research Department in Geneva. Hans Schönfeld was decidedly annoyed. He found the theses one-sided and radical and asked Bonhoeffer to change them, but Bonhoeffer would not budge. This showed how dependent Schönfeld was on Heckel, although at the time he would not yet have considered this a problem. He was a conservative Lutheran and believed that, on 'order of creation' questions such as national character and race, the other churches should learn from the German ones (DB-ER 385–87).

The Youth Conference remained a lifelong memory for many of Bonhoeffer's students, for in order to avoid having any German Christian supporters smuggled into the delegation, he had mobilized conference participants largely from among his students in Berlin. The Youth Conference adopted two resolutions, after intense discussion of each. The first declared:

The [conference] members ... agree that the rights of conscience, undertaken in obedience to God's Word, exceed in importance those of any State whatever. They believe that the attacks upon these rights made in various countries justly provoke an ever-growing condemnation by general public opinion. They notice however that even those States which have inscribed in their law liberty of conscience violate this law by severely punishing, in one way or another, conscientious objectors [to military service]. (DBWE 13, 205–6)

The second resolution spoke out even more plainly against the Nazi state:

Recent years have witnessed a strengthening of the sovereignty of the State and the attempt on the part of the State to become the only centre and source of spiritual life. Most of the Churches have replied by mere academic protests, or they have shirked their responsibilities ... As the Church has for its essential task the preaching of the Word of God this can never be a function (not even the highest function) of the nation. The Church works within the nation, but it is not 'of the nation'. (DBWE 13, 207)

A Swedish youth delegate asked Bonhoeffer, as they sat together among the sand dunes, what he would do if he were drafted into military service. He replied that he hoped God would give him the strength to refuse to serve.

The main ecumenical conference on Fanø had to respond to the Ascension Day pastoral letter which Bishop Bell had sent to all World Alliance and Universal Council member churches. They had to approve it or reject it, and that brought the German question squarely into the centre of their deliberations. It was discussed in an animated plenary session. An envoy from the Reich Bishop, Church Councillor Walter Birnbaum, came swooping in to the island by specially chartered seaplane, so that Heckel was already afraid he was being replaced. But after this man had taken up 15 minutes with an 'absurd rigmarole' of a speech, as Julius Rieger noted in his diary, Heckel resumed his attempts to have Bell's pastoral letter rejected. The resolution in favour of the letter passed nevertheless. It condemned the use of force by Müller and Jäger, their autocratic government, the ban on free discussion and the loyalty oath, instituted by Müller, which German pastors had to swear to Hitler after Hindenburg's death. It also said: 'The Council [on Life and Work] desires to assure its brethren in the Confessional Synod of the German Evangelical Church of its prayers and heartfelt sympathy in their witness to the principles of the Gospel, and of its resolve to maintain close fellowship with them' (DB-ER 383).

That same day, President Karl Koch (of the Confessing Synod) and Dietrich Bonhoeffer were both co-opted as Council members of the Life and Work movement. Heckel protested against this one-sided privileging of the Confessing Church, but had no more success there than he had had in protesting the resolution. He could only record a protest in the minutes:

The German delegation repudiates the allegation that in the German Reich the free proclamation of the spoken and written Gospel is imperilled ... On the contrary, it holds that the prevalent conditions in Germany today provide a more favourable opportunity for proclaiming the Gospel than ever before. (DB-ER 384)

The fact that the church press in Germany had just been synchronized, he preferred not to mention. However, he had managed after all to have a small note inserted in the resolution, to the effect that the Council wished 'to remain in friendly contact with all groups in the German Evangelical Church'.

Such amiable formulations meet with success at most conferences; the one in Fanø was no exception. But it was just this sentence which made the Confessing Church's relations with the ecumenical movement so difficult later on, because Heckel was usually the only one deciding what contacts there would be. Even the staff in Geneva came to regret that the Fanø Conference had not made a clean break with him. Despite such limitations, Bonhoeffer was well satisfied with the outcome. He considered it a good beginning; yet in reality, the ecumenical community was never again to side with the Confessing Church to such an extent.

Today, Fanø is known as the conference at which Dietrich Bonhoeffer, who is now admired and revered by all churches, gave two prophetic speeches. Both were about 'The Churches and Peace'. At the time they certainly still provoked head-shaking and strong criticism behind the scenes. In his speech to the conference he said:

The destiny of the [World] Alliance is determined by the following: whether it regards itself as church or as a society with a definite purpose. The World Alliance is church as long as its fundamental principles lie in obediently listening to and preaching the Word of God. It is a society, if its essential object is to realise aims and conditions of whatever kind they may be. It is only as church that the World Alliance can preach the Word of Christ in full authority to the Churches and nations... The work of the World Alliance means work of the Churches for peace amongst the nations. Its aim is the end of war and the victory over war. (DBWE 13, 304f)

He expressed this even more urgently, and much more directly, in a sermon on the morning of 28 August 1934:

'Let me hear what God the Lord will speak: for he will speak peace to his people, and to his faithful' (Psalm 85:8). Between the twin crags of nationalism and internationalism, ecumenical Christendom calls upon its Lord and asks for guidance. Nationalism and internationalism have to do with political necessities and possibilities. The ecumenical church movement, however, does not concern itself with these things, but with the commandments of God, and regardless of consequences it transmits these commandments to the world[29] ... Peace on earth is not a problem, but a commandment given at Christ's coming. There are two ways of reacting to this command from God: the unconditional, blind obedience of action, or the hypocritical question of the Serpent: 'Did God say ...?' This question is the mortal enemy of obedience, and therefore the mortal enemy of all real peace ... Has God not understood human nature well enough to know that wars must occur in this world, like laws of nature? Must God not have meant that we should talk about peace, to be sure, but that it is not to be literally translated into action? Must God not really have said that we should work for peace, of course, but also make ready tanks and poison gas for security? And then perhaps the most serious question: Did God say you should not protect your own people? Did God say you should leave your own a prey to the enemy?

No, God did not say all that. What God has said is that there shall be peace among all people – that we shall obey God without further question, that is what God means. Anyone who questions the commandment of God before obeying has already denied God ...

Why do we fear the fury of the world powers? Why don't we take the power from them and give it back to Christ? We can still do it today. The Ecumenical Council is in session; it can send out to all believers this radical call to peace. The nations are waiting for it in the East and in the West. Must we be put to shame by non-Christian peoples in the East? ... We want to give the world a whole word, not half a word – a courageous word, a Christian word. We want to pray that this word may be given us, today. Who knows if we shall see each other again another year? (DBWE 13, 307ff)

In Fanø at that time Bonhoeffer encountered more agreement than criticism. Several of those who were present have spoken of the silence in the hall from the moment he began to speak, as if the audience were holding its breath. 'Non-Christian peoples in the East' referred to Mahatma Gandhi and his life of passive resistance. Bonhoeffer so admired him that twice already he had made plans to go to India to learn more. He had written to his grandmother in May 1934 that, before undertaking a new assignment in Germany, he definitely wanted to get to know India. It sometimes seemed to him that there was more Christianity in their 'heathenism than in the whole of our Reich Church'. In fact, he pointed out, Christianity did 'come from the East originally', but 'it has become so westernized and so permeated by purely civilized thought that, as we can now see, it is almost lost to us' (DBWE 13, 152).

So for the third time he made plans to travel eastward, to become a pupil of Gandhi's, and through Bishop Bell as intermediary he received a kind invitation from Gandhi himself. Julius Rieger wanted to come with him, and the two friends pored over prospectuses, looked for the cheapest routes and means of travel, and read whatever they could find about India and its culture. But once again the plan fell through, first because of considerable follow-up work after the Fanø Conference, and later because Bonhoeffer was urgently needed in Germany for the work of the Confessing Church. After the war Gerhard Jacobi said with some pride that he was the one who had thwarted this intention of Bonhoeffer's. Jacobi had indeed never had much understanding of Bonhoeffer's ideas:[30] 'At my instigation, the Confessing Church called Bonhoeffer to a preachers' seminary which was to be set up ... I also wanted to keep Bonhoeffer away from India by directing him towards a serious task to be done with young Germans.'[31]

There was no one in the Confessing Church who took the decisions of the Confessing Synod of Dahlem more seriously than did Bonhoeffer. He urgently advised the Council of Brethren of the Confessing Church not to leave ecumenical relations to Heckel, but rather to take them in hand itself. He assured his friends that, after Fanø, no representatives of churches in other countries would come to Müller's installation as Reich Bishop, and his prediction proved correct. The only bishop at the ceremony in Berlin Cathedral who did not belong to the German Christians was Theodor Heckel who, at the laying on of hands, quoted Psalm 144: 'Happy are the people to whom such blessings fall.' One wonders whether it was clear to him that this was a verse from the Hebrew Bible, from the Jewish tradition. In Fanø, when asked about the Aryan paragraph, his answer had been: 'That is not my province.'

To get the German congregations abroad to secede from the Foreign Office of the Reich Church, Bonhoeffer proposed, at a London meeting of the congregations in England, that they place themselves under the authority of the Confessing Church. Though Heckel managed to drive a wedge between the German pastors in England, the majority of their congregations declared their independence from his Foreign Office.[32] At the same time the Overseas Seminary of the Church at Ilsenburg in the Harz Mountains declared itself to be under the auspices of the Confessing Church, thus earning the enmity of Bishop Heckel. It was in fact a friend of Bonhoeffer's from student days, Helmut Rößler, serving a congregation in Holland, who wrote at Heckel's behest to all the German pastors abroad that the only right thing to do was to stay out of the church dispute in Germany. This meant the end of his and Bonhoeffer's friendship.[33] At that time the Confessing Church did have an 'ecumenical advisory board', but, despite Bonhoeffer's urging, it never set up an office for ecumenical affairs and work abroad. Probably it didn't have enough money to do so.

Plans for the future

The Youth Conference on Fanø brought Bonhoeffer a chance to see Jean Lasserre again, the friend with whom he had had the conversation in New York about what it means, according to the Sermon on the Mount, to be a Christian. Soon after the conference, he visited Lasserre at his mining village church in the north of France. Like other guests there, Bonhoeffer took part in street preaching as part of an evangelization drive. He was deeply impressed by Lasserre's solidarity with the poor folk in his congregation. Lasserre's idea that one should live according to the

Dietrich Bonhoeffer with Jean Lasserre during the Fanø Conference, August 1934

Sermon on the Mount was looming larger than ever in Bonhoeffer's thoughts.

When Bonhoeffer went to England, he must have known that he would be returning to Germany in the not too distant future. But he wanted to return under conditions in which he had a say. The concept taking shape in his mind was that of an action group of young, unattached persons committed to theology; the sort of actions they should undertake was what he had wanted to study at Gandhi's ashram. Some time earlier he had asked Professor Stählin what he would think of a community of Protestants living together, upon which Stählin expressed the desire to enlist him for the 'Berneuchener' liturgical movement of which he himself was the president. The Berneuchener aimed to revitalize the church through renewal of its worship, taking many of their ideas from monasticism.

In the meantime, however, Stählin had opposed the resolutions of the Dahlem Synod, so he was no longer the partner Bonhoeffer was seeking. Instead, at Niemöller's suggestion, he turned to the Bruderhof movement founded by Eberhard Arnold. Arnold's son was studying in Birmingham and met with Bonhoeffer in London. He reported to his father that Bonhoeffer wanted to found a sort of Protestant monastery, with 'spiritual exercises, confessional etc.' and was planning to study with Gandhi.

The assumption is that though they do not know the will of God for our time, they want to try to live exactly according to Jesus' words and by thorough study of the Bible to discern God's will. Unfortunately Bonhoeffer makes a distinction between theology students and lay persons ... The *essential* seems to me the fact that behind Bonhoeffer stands a group of sixty to seventy[34] young persons who are seriously struggling to recognize and to do God's will ... and are prepared to do *everything* to further this cause ... It would be wonderful if we could make common cause with this group. (DBWE 13, 158–60)

It is fascinating to see Bonhoeffer in London, already describing to young Hardy Arnold what he was to make come true, over a year later in Finkenwalde: a House of Brethren, where six other pastors (though not fifty or more) joined with him in training pastors-to-be, and were available for a diversity of other services, for the Confessing Church.

Hardy Arnold had not fully understood the points that Bonhoeffer made. For example, Bonhoeffer must have talked about the necessity of intensive Bible study in order to know God's concrete commandments for the present time. The Bruderhof Community believed instead in the 'outpouring of the Spirit' that took place if only a group of people agreed unanimously to live together in Christian faith. However, in the end Bonhoeffer apparently did not have time to meet with Eberhard Arnold at his Rhönhof community.

Bonhoeffer and Rieger did not get to India either. But Bishop Bell had written not only to Gandhi about them, but also to three monastic communities belonging to the Church of England; Bonhoeffer also wanted to see how a 'life together' would look in the context of the Anglican Church. He had written to his brother Karl Friedrich in January 1935:

The restoration of the church must surely depend on a new kind of monasticism, which has nothing in common with the old but a life of uncompromising discipleship, following Christ according to the Sermon on the Mount. I believe the time has come to gather people together and do this. (DBWE 13, 285)

To receive inspiration for developing such an effort, Bonhoeffer and Rieger paid visits to the Society of St John the Evangelist in Oxford (founded 1865), the Society of the Resurrection in Mirfield (1892) and the Society of the Sacred Mission in Kelham (1893). These were the first communities in the restoration of the monastic movement in the Anglican Church. All three have made great contributions to the educational work of the Church, and in training a new generation of priests, but as with all monasteries there are certain differences among them. With British humour, these were described as follows: in Oxford the use of tobacco is strictly forbidden, while in Mirfield smoking is allowed and in Kelham one is expected to smoke.

This trip became Bonhoeffer's preparation for his work as director of a preachers' seminary. The Anglican monks made a deep impression on him. The set times for prayer observed by monks seem restrictive to the individual; but even for Protestant Christians, they can create a space for community life to develop. They establish a predetermined spiritual order, in which private thoughts – even pious private thoughts – are excluded for a short while. In this an outstanding role is played by the Psalms of the Old Testament. The visitors also found that during leisure time in English monasteries – which is as much a part of their day as prayer – monks could play football (soccer to Americans) and tennis. We shall meet all of this again at Bonhoeffer's seminary.

During this period, in the interests of the church struggle, Dietrich Bonhoeffer apparently decided to put aside thoughts of marriage. Members of the House of Brethren, which he wanted to found, should be

As newly appointed director of the Church seminary in Zingst

available to serve the Church wherever they might be needed, without consideration for the needs of a wife or children. The director of the House must of course take the lead in this renunciation.

Bonhoeffer had indicated to Bishop Bell even before the Saar plebiscite that if the Saarland were annexed by Germany, there would be a considerable surge of refugees reaching Britain. He was able to make the first preparations for aiding them himself, with Bell's help, before he left London. He found lodgings for refugees, raised money and gave pastoral care himself to many of the new arrivals. Among the people whom Bonhoeffer aided during the first weeks of this migration was Armin T. Wegner, the German author who, as a war reporter, had witnessed the Armenian genocide. Wegner had protested to Hitler against the way Jews were being treated, and escaped to England after being tortured by the Nazis.[35] Former Transport Minister Treviranus was also compelled to flee, and his son was confirmed by Bonhoeffer at Sydenham Church in London.

The work with refugees was greatly expanded later on. In 1935, after Bonhoeffer had returned to Germany, Rieger followed Bonhoeffer in coordinating the work for refugees with Bishop Bell. In 1938 Bonhoeffer's twin sister Sabine and her family were also to seek asylum in England. Her husband, Professor Gerhard Leibholz, was to succeed his brother-in-law as adviser to the Bishop of Chichester on all matters having to do with church and politics in Germany.

7. Finkenwalde (1935–1937)

A preachers' seminary in Pomerania

When he said goodbye in London, Bonhoeffer had said that he was going to become the director of a Confessing Church preachers' seminary in Düsseldorf. In Germany at that time the Reich Church had its preachers' seminaries, which were recognized by the state;[1] beginning in 1935 there were also seminaries of the Confessing Church which, however, were considered 'illegal' before they even started their work. This is why, before Bonhoeffer arrived from London, a wise lawyer had advised the Council of Brethren to find a less conspicuous location than the large city of Düsseldorf in west Germany, in a densely populated industrial area well provided with 'security' by the Gestapo. So a suitable site was being sought in the Province of Brandenburg, in the countryside around Berlin and beyond, but by the time the seminarians arrived nothing had yet been found. However, the Westphalian School Bible Club had a youth holiday camp at Zingst on the Baltic Sea, which it made available for the first two months; there the seminary could at least get started, though under rather primitive conditions. After that, they were able to move to a country estate near the Baltic seaport of Stettin in Pomerania, where a house stood empty.

We have enthusiastic accounts of the beginnings of this seminary given by the first group that began their work with Bonhoeffer in Zingst. Many of these candidates for ordination had attended Bonhoeffer's lectures in Berlin and had taken part in his retreats in Biesenthal, or in the Fanø Conference. They were happy to be back with this teacher who was scarcely any older than they were and who had impressed them so strongly from the first time they heard him. Though the accommodation at Zingst was very basic, the nearness of the Baltic shore made up for this. Bonhoeffer often held sessions among the sand dunes, and on especially warm afternoons was known to call off work altogether in favour of a swim in the sea and community sports. The more ambitious sportsmen among the ordinands were not too happy to discover that their director could run faster than they could and was almost unbeatable at table tennis.

Those new to the group, who came from the Rhineland and the provinces of Saxony and East Pomerania, soon felt at home in this atmosphere. It was a time when the Confessing Church was apparently becoming well established, and victory over the German Christians seemed within reach. So the first seminary course took place amid generally high spirits and in confidence that director and candidates for ordination were on the right side.

The main house on the Finkenwalde estate had most recently served as a boarding school and therefore had a gymnasium which could serve as a chapel. But some necessary furniture and furnishings were lacking. Seminarian Winfried Maechler wrote a plea in verse:

> We want to move everything
> to Finkenwalde near Stettin.
> There stands an empty old estate
> for which we do not have to wait.
> It is in utter disrepair
> with a few beds and cupboards there
> standing in the house's hall ...

The appeal was not without success. Local congregations of the Confessing Church sent everything that was needed. Then, however, the seminary began to run out of food, so the next poem was sent out, with the moving verse: '... This poem then is admonition / Even theologians need nutrition' (DB-ER, 426–27). The Pomeranian country estate owners did themselves proud. A telephone call came one day: 'This is the railroad freight yard. A live pig has just arrived for Pastor Bonhoeffer.'

The boarding school gymnasium became a simple but beautiful chapel for the seminary. The music room soon had two Bechstein grand pianos, one of which had recently arrived from London. The library's basic inventory consisted of Bonhoeffer's personal stock of books. The pictures on the wall were also his, and so were some of the comfortable armchairs and the large collection of phonograph records, including black American spirituals, which were almost unknown in Germany at the time.

Any account of Finkenwalde written today must not fail to mention especially one of the candidates for ordination who became Bonhoeffer's students at that time. Eberhard Bethge was a pastor's son from a village east of Magdeburg in central Germany; together with a few friends, he had been expelled from the preachers' seminary in Wittenberg.

The chapel of the seminary and the Confessing Church congregation at Finkenwalde

These young men had protested against the Reich Bishop, had placed themselves under the care of the Confessing Church and were referred to Bonhoeffer's seminary to complete their preparation for the parish ministry.

Eberhard Bethge soon became Bonhoeffer's closest friend.[2] This could have had a negative effect on the sense of community in Finkenwalde, especially since there was a group from Berlin who could have asserted their entitlement to a special relationship with their revered teacher, having known him longer. But no one could resist the charm of this 'country boy'. Bonhoeffer once wrote to Bethge, years later:

I don't know a single person who can't stand you, whereas I know quite a few who can't stand me. I don't have a hard time with that; wherever I find opponents, I also find friends, and that's enough for me. But it's due to your being open and modest by nature, whereas I'm reserved and more demanding. (DBWE 8, II/101)

Eberhard Bethge had a capacity to enter into Bonhoeffer's thinking, and to draw him out by means of questions, which Bonhoeffer found extraordinarily stimulating and which had a generally positive effect on the studies at Finkenwalde. Bethge was also a competent organizer and could take over many of the director's tasks, so that a seminarian from the Rhineland said with a grin, 'Eberhard is the "Führer's deputy"'. Bethge started a choir, and through it introduced into the seminary the principles of a movement in the teaching of singing which, in the 1930s, was leading to a renewal in music education, music in the home and not least of all church music in Germany. Until then, apart from Johann Sebastian Bach, Bonhoeffer had been familiar mainly with the classical and romantic composers, from Mozart to Hugo Wolf and Richard Strauß, and had played much of their music. There were great moments when he and one of the ordinands sat down at the two pianos and gave a Bach or Beethoven concert. But Eberhard Bethge got the listeners to start making music too, and Bonhoeffer learned from him to appreciate older masters such as Heinrich Schütz, Johann Hermann Schein and Samuel Scheidt.

At the beginning of his time in Finkenwalde, Bonhoeffer became acquainted with the widow of a Pomeranian nobleman, Ruth von Kleist-Retzow, who in due course became a motherly friend to him. She had a lively interest in theology and a hearty loathing for Hitler and his cronies. Bonhoeffer had seen to it that a Confessing Church congregation was started at Finkenwalde, and Ruth von Kleist heard about it. She lived on her estate at Klein-Krössin, but kept a city apartment in Stettin so that her grandchildren could go to school there. Before long she was attending worship regularly at Finkenwalde and became a benefactress of the seminary.[3] Her grandchildren came to church with her, and Bonhoeffer later confirmed some of them. He soon became a welcome guest on their parents' estates, and friends of theirs also took an interest in him.

The old manor house at Finkenwalde was not actually very well suited for concentrated study. The seminary had to improvise in many ways, beginning with obtaining food for its dining hall. All the ordinands had to share one large dormitory, which certainly could have been a disturbing factor. But, as Bethge writes in his biography of Bonhoeffer, this was prevented by two things: the daily routine promoted by Bonhoeffer, and 'the inspiration offered by his own way of working'. Every morning and evening there was a long prayer service. As in the English monasteries, the Psalms were said in rotation. The Psalm was followed by a hymn, a chapter from the Old Testament, a set verse from a hymn – the same one was used over several weeks – and a chapter from the New Testament. Then Bonhoeffer offered a long prayer in his own words, followed by the Lord's Prayer. The service ended with another verse from a hymn, which stayed the same for several weeks. In this way the future pastors learned many hymns by heart. Only on Sundays did Bonhoeffer offer a brief homily.

This order of worship had a great influence on all Finkenwaldians, even though at first some of them would gladly have stayed away. What became almost more important to them, however, was a rule instituted by their director – never to talk about another member of the group in that person's absence, or if such a thing did happen, to tell the person about it afterwards. 'The participants learned almost as much from their failures to observe this simple rule, and from their renewed resolution to keep it, as they did from the sermons and exegeses', said Bethge.

Sermons and exegeses were, however, the focus of the hours that followed each day. In half a year each ordinand was supposed to learn how to prepare a sermon, to teach religion, to give pastoral care, and to baptize, marry and bury. This was a considerable assignment. Of course the ordinands already had the knowledge acquired from their university courses. But many things were completely new to them, for example the daily practice of meditation. Every morning after breakfast they were asked to think reflectively, alone for half an hour, on a text from Luther's Bible. Each text was set for a whole week of daily meditation. Most of the ordinands had trouble getting used to this practice. Wolf-Dieter Zimmermann wrote:

Half an hour of concentration: it is amazing what comes into your head during that time. The mind moves around, memories arise, dreams awaken. Suddenly anger flares up. When we told Bonhoeffer of this, he said that was all right, things have to come into the open; but they must also be tamed in and through prayer.[4]

In a letter to his brother-in-law, Rüdiger Schleicher, Bonhoeffer described how to meditate. When reading the Bible, he said, he didn't want to decide according to his own notions what was of God and what was of human origin. If one did that, one might encounter only a 'divine double' of one's own self.

I read [the Bible] every morning and evening, and often during the day. Every day I take a text – the same one for a whole week at a time – and try to immerse myself completely in it, truly hear it. I know that without this I couldn't live right anymore, and certainly couldn't believe. Every day there are also more things that puzzle me; these are still the completely superficial things that we just hang onto. In Hildesheim the other day I saw some medieval art again, and it struck me how much more they understood about the Bible in those days ... Maybe this is a very primitive thing. But you wouldn't believe what a joy it is to find one's way back from the wrong tracks where so much theology leads one, to these primitive things again. And I think in matters of faith we are all equally primitive, in every age. (DBW 14, 147–48)

Bonhoeffer saw very quickly that his intention for the preachers' seminary to constitute a community living and learning together could not be carried out if all members of this community except the director and his assistant left Finkenwalde at the end of half a year and were replaced by a new group of ordinands. He therefore reminded the Confessing Church's Council of Brethren that it had consented, after he returned from England, to allow him to found a House of Brethren as a spiritual centre. Of his first group of students, six wanted to stay and were allowed to do so, and with them Bonhoeffer was able to pursue the ideas inspired by his visits to the Anglican monasteries.

Each member of the House of Brethren received a particular assignment. One became pastor of the Confessing Church congregation at Finkenwalde; another became chaplain to the students at the nearby University of Greifswald, where the faculty of theology was determined to keep itself and its students out of the church struggle. This faculty accordingly had a rather strained relationship with Bonhoeffer and his ordinands, which made things especially hard for the one assigned as chaplain. Eberhard Bethge worked on theology with the group at Finkenwalde. The chief task for all members of the House of Brethren, however, was to maintain their 'life together' with its firm rules. Thus, as each new group of ordinands arrived, they found a monastic community life already established and did not have to be persuaded to adapt themselves to it.

In 1937, when Finkenwalde had been closed on the orders of Himmler's deputy, Reinhard Heydrich, Bonhoeffer wrote a little book entitled *Life Together (Gemeinsames Leben)*. Its five chapters, Community [*Gemeinschaft*], The Day Together, The Day Alone, Service and Confession [*Beichte*] and the Lord's Supper, describe his experience in the preachers' seminary and the House of Brethren. He was able to have it printed at the time, and it has been reprinted many times since, both in German and translated into other languages, including English.[5]

There was no lack of criticism and suspicion of the work going on at Finkenwalde. Bonhoeffer's ideas were not everyone's cup of tea. Many of his colleagues considered them 'monkish', and there were some strange rumours in circulation about the seminary. Not least among those who expressed astonishment was Karl Barth (DBW 14, 253). But more and more candidates for ordination were asking to be assigned to Bonhoeffer's seminary.

Bonhoeffer kept to his once-weekly lectures at the University of Berlin with an iron will. If he were to be ousted from the state faculty of theology, then his opponents would have to push for it actively; he had no intention whatsoever of withdrawing voluntarily. His regular trips to Berlin, however, were even more important for another reason: they enabled him to visit his friends who were leaders of the Confessing Church, and to speak with his very well-informed relatives about current developments. When he got back to Finkenwalde, and after the midday meal, he could usually be found sitting together with his assistant, Wilhelm Rott.

The picture is unforgettable: the small wooden staircase, Dietrich sitting on it with his legs crossed, reaching now and then for a cigarette, or accepting a cup of coffee from the only coffee machine in the house. He had been in Berlin yesterday; he told us about it. When he came home late in the evening, he gave those waiting up for him one of his exciting reports on the deviations and embroilments of that time of church committees, about spiritual and worldly affairs, politics of the church and of the state, about those who were standing firm, those who were wavering and those who fell. But there was more: characteristic details which did not escape his sharp observation and could not be told to a larger audience.[6]

The Reich Ministry for Church Affairs fights against the Church

Hitler and his followers did not fail to notice that the Confessing Church had not only gained respect and influence, but that in court it was almost always found to be in the right. This they were not willing to tolerate any longer. So from March to July 1935 three new laws appeared, designed to look like the state's care for the Church's welfare but actually intended to shackle it. The first was signed by Hermann Göring as prime minister of Prussia and provided 'finance' departments' for the Prussian provincial churches, which were to 'guarantee' local church assets and contributions; in reality, however, this meant that local Confessing pastors in the Old Prussian Union could no longer take up their usual collections without risking prison. The other two laws were signed by Hitler himself, because they applied to the entire nation. One created a 'Legislative Authority for [the administration of] Legal Matters in the German Evangelical Church'.

Thus it denied the Confessing Church access to the regular public courts. It was one of Hitler's countless violations of German law.

The other of Hitler's decrees, one which was to prove particularly drastic, created a Ministry for Church Affairs headed by Hanns Kerrl, who was one of Hitler's old comrades-in-arms and had his confidence. Kerrl had lost his position as Prussian Minister of Justice due to synchronization, and was to be compensated for it. It was said of him that he was the only Nazi leader who knew the sayings of the Bible, but he was noted particularly for having described the Party's policies toward the Church as blunders on several occasions. Along with regional Party leader Wilhelm Kube, he was one of the few highly placed Nazi functionaries who wanted to see the nineteenth-century dream of a 'national church for all Germans' realized.[7]

Hitler may have thought that the appointment of Kerrl, who had sharply criticized August Jäger and his methods, would serve as a cooperative gesture towards the Protestant churches. He charged Kerrl with 'pacifying' the Protestant church. The new Reich Church Minister attempted to do so by issuing a Law for the Protection of the German Evangelical Church. Its 17 Decrees on Implementation, which were published gradually one after the other, had the effect of tying the hands of the Confessing Church almost completely. They also made cooperation between the 'destroyed' and 'intact' provincial churches increasingly difficult.

This new law nullified the authority of all church governing bodies, whether of the Reich Church, the German Christians or the Provisional Church Administration of the Confessing Church, including the authority of the Reich Bishop. These were replaced by committees which were now recognized as being in charge, one for the German Evangelical Church as a whole and one for each of the provincial churches. As president of the Reich Church Committee, Kerrl recalled General Superintendent Wilhelm Zoellner from retirement; Zoellner was a church leader who thought in terms of the whole nation, and had never belonged to the German Christian movement. As committee members Kerrl chose people representing all different points of view, for the committees of the provincial churches as well as at the national level. The 'intact' churches were subject to the Reich Church Committee, but did not have to form their own committees. Otto Dibelius protested by means of a pamphlet, The State Church is Here; among those who helped distribute it were the ordinands of Finkenwalde. Before the printed copies could be confiscated, thousands were already in circulation.

This measure of Kerrl's was a serious attack, for the state did not have the legal right to set up church governing bodies. From this point on, the opposition was no longer within the Church, but was now a political opposition. Anyone who resisted the Church Ministry's decrees was refusing to obey Hitler's government. No one felt the effects of this second phase of the church struggle more keenly than did the church colleges in Wuppertal, Berlin and Bethel, the Overseas Seminary in Ilsenburg and the five preachers' seminaries which the Confessing Church had established to keep its younger generation out of the Reich Church. All those studying at these institutions or preparing for the parish ministry – and there may have been well over a thousand such young people – along with their teachers, had placed themselves, for good or ill, under the care of the Confessing Church, which now had to look after them financially as well as spiritually. They were known as 'illegals', because this kind of education was now forbidden by law for both teachers and students.

Like Finkenwalde, all these institutions had begun their work with enthusiasm and readiness to sacrifice. The question now was how long they could go on. The 'intact' churches did not have this problem. For them everything, including the education of their next generation of pastors, was the same as ever. They only stood to gain by distancing themselves gradually from the resolutions made at the Dahlem Synod, since the new Church Ministry left them alone. Soon after the Barmen Synod they had formed the Lutheran Council, which represented their concerns. The Councils of Brethren of the 'destroyed' churches, however, from which this Lutheran Council was increasingly keeping its distance, had to defend their own work and pastoral training. The state was not immediately able to track down all of this, but combated whatever it did find with great severity.

From our viewpoint today it is hard to understand the attitude of the 'intact' churches. At that time the reasons for it were taken very seriously, in particular by committed Christians. The Old Prussian Union was a church in which Lutheran, Reformed and United Churches had been bound together by royal decree since 1817, and that included fellowship at the communion table, although local congregations kept their confessional identity. When this was introduced, however, force had been used, especially in Silesia. During the nineteenth century more than 200,000 Lutherans emigrated from Prussia, mostly to the USA, in order to remain loyal to their Lutheran faith. For the churches outside Prussia, there was a stigma attached to the union church. They claimed that in Prussia even the Lutheran local churches no longer followed pure Lutheran doctrine. This was combined with the old prejudice of southern Germans against Prussia, a 'non-theological factor' that was still playing a significant role during Hitler's time.

By setting up its Ministry of Church Affairs in 1935, Hitler's state caused the Confessing Church to fall apart into two groups that engaged in a bitter feud with one another. Now every member was either a 'Lutheran' or a Dahlemite, and among the most resolute Dahlemites was Bonhoeffer. We have already spoken of Luther's doctrine of the 'two kingdoms' (see Chapter 5, 'The Church and the Jewish Question'). Bonhoeffer could be quite vehement on this subject; as a Lutheran theologian, he accused the Lutheran Council and its followers of being, with their willingness to adapt to the state, the ones who were turning Luther's original idea into a heresy.

And indeed, until 1945 the Lutheran bishops issued decrees and signed statements of which, after the Third Reich ended, they could only be ashamed. For example, after the failed coup of 20 July 1944 they ordered prayers of thanksgiving said that the life of the Führer had been saved, with a text that, even at the time, outraged many worshippers in their churches. The division also had the effect that the Confessing Church's ecumenical friends no longer knew which way to turn. So Bonhoeffer continued the struggle on two fronts: with the Councils of Brethren on behalf of the Dahlem resolutions, and within the ecumenical community against the policies of Heckel's Foreign Office and for better information sharing. It is amazing how much energy and time he was able to invest in this in addition to his work in Finkenwalde. What helped was that, in his lectures at the seminary and in the weekly major discussion evenings at Finkenwalde, he was able to develop many of the theological ideas he needed in order to achieve clarity on both fronts.

Ecumenical tasks and theological essays

As an expert in ecumenical matters, Bonhoeffer had more interruptions than he liked in his ongoing work in Finkenwalde, but he saw that the Confessing Church urgently needed him to stay active ecumenically. During the first semester at Finkenwalde he was sent twice to see Bishop Bell, and in Germany he had to attend several meetings on ecumenical issues. This brought the conflict between Bonhoeffer and the Geneva staff out into the open. He was demanding of them the courage to stand up for the Confessing Church and thus for the truth of the gospel, whereas they were increasingly inclined to listen to Heckel. This was why Bonhoeffer cancelled his attendance at the youth conference in Chamby, which he was supposed to direct. His adversary Schönfeld very quickly found someone to take his place, and wrote to Eugen Gerstenmaier in the Church Foreign Office, before the new youth conference director, an American, made his introductory visit there:

You know yourself, of course, how important it is ... especially in ecumenical work, to have a man who is really well-suited for this task. If we had not found this solution, we in the Research Department would have tried every means to bring to an end this work as it has been carried out until now. (DBW 14, 164)

Bonhoeffer had not actually wanted to attend the main 1936 ecumenical conference at Chamby either, because Zoellner, as President of the Reich Church Committee, was claiming the sole right to represent the German church, and Heckel, pleased to be rid of the Reich Bishop, was supporting him with all his might. But neither had reckoned with Bishop Bell's tenacity. Bell declared that President Koch and Dietrich Bonhoeffer were nevertheless members of the Council on Life and Work, and two further representatives of the Confessing Church were to be invited as guests. Of course Bonhoeffer found this unsatisfactory, but since the Provisional Church Administration of the Confessing Church said that he must go, he and Eberhard Bethge set off for Switzerland together. It was the first and last time that a delegation from the Confessing Church appeared in an official capacity at an ecumenical conference. They were not even mentioned as such in the minutes. Bonhoeffer did not ask to speak at any time, and he avoided the Reich Church delegation with Zoellner and Heckel.

Thus he was able to make full use of the days in Chamby to inform Bishop Bell and Bishop Ammundsen about the new situation with the Ministry of Church Affairs and the committees. Meanwhile, Zoellner gave a major speech at the conference about the situation of the German church, and even the Confessing Church representatives were so impressed that they asked him why he didn't come over to their side. Bishop Ammundsen later recalled that Zoellner said goodbye to one of the Confessing Church representatives with the words, 'See you in concentration camp.' Within a year, Zoellner had recognized what he had become involved in as head of the Reich committee, and resigned.

By the time of the Oxford World Conference on Life and Work in 1937, no representatives of the German Evangelical Church were allowed to participate anymore, on Hitler's orders – not even Heckel, although he made great efforts to be allowed to go. Still later, in 1939, Dietrich Bonhoeffer and W. A. Visser 't Hooft of the Netherlands, the new ecumenical General Secretary, were able to turn over a new leaf in the work of the ecumenical movement with the church in Germany.

Because Bonhoeffer felt that the theological decisions being made at the time by the ecumenical movement were unclear and wrong, and because he also found that his own church must to some extent share the blame for this, in 1935 he undertook to write an essay on 'The Confessing Church and the Ecumenical Movement', which was published in the journal *Evangelische Theologie*. It analyses the unequal relations between the two partners and draws conclusions from them.

Under the onslaught of new nationalism, the fact that Christ's Church does not stop at national and racial boundaries, but reaches beyond them, so powerfully attested in the New Testament and in the confessional writings, has been far too easily forgotten and denied. Even where it was found impossible to make a theoretical refutation, voices have never ceased to declare emphatically that of course a conversation with foreign Christians about so-called internal German church matters was unthinkable, and that any judgement or public position on these things from outside would be impossible and reprehensible.[8]

Bonhoeffer praised the ecumenical movement's willingness, despite this defensiveness, on a number of occasions to raise its voice on behalf of the Confessing Church in Germany, and the ecumenical recognition that the German church struggle was about the proclamation of the gospel and needed to be fought on behalf of all Christendom. He said that the Confessing Church had brought the ecumenical movement face to face with the issue of confessing the faith.

To this confession as it has been *authoritatively* expounded in the decisions of the Synods of Barmen and Dahlem, there is only a Yes or No ... This is an unheard-of claim. But this is the only way in which the Confessing Church can enter into ecumenical conversations.[9]

The ecumenical movement, Bonhoeffer wrote, must answer the question: upon what authority does it speak? It must not allow the necessary theological dialogues on this topic to be misused to cover up the true situation.

Theological conversation [between churches of different confessions] will become a bad joke by concealing the fact that it is properly concerned not with unauthoritative discussion, but with responsible, legitimate decisions of the church ... The Confessing Church knows of the fatal ambivalence of any theological conversation and presses for a clear church decision.[10]

The simplest way to deal with such clear criticism is not to take any notice of it, and this was the attitude adopted by the Geneva office towards Bonhoeffer's essay.

A second essay, however, which he published a year later in the same journal, could not be hushed up so completely. The measures taken by Kerrl, the Minister for Church Affairs, were tightening their grip. Besides German Christians and the Reich Church, there were now also those who followed the 'committees', as well as the Dahlemites, the Lutheran Council people and the 'neutrals'. How was one supposed to find one's way through all of that, and how was a Christian plain and simple supposed to know where he or she belonged, when even pastors of churches disagreed to such an extent?

Bonhoeffer wrote a 29-page essay, 'On the Church Community', in which the words *Scheidung* (distinction), *Entscheidung* (decision) and *entscheiden* (decide) occur 53 times. This essay made him known overnight in all the provincial churches and provoked a fierce discussion. One sentence in particular so outraged the critics that they declared that anyone who wrote such a thing must be dismissed by the leadership of the Confessing Church from the job of training its pastors. This sentence, which could still raise indignation among older theologians long after the Second World War, said: 'Whoever knowingly separates himself from the Confessing Church separates himself from salvation' (DBW 14, 676). This borrows from the centuries-old phrase *extra ecclesiam nulla salus* – outside the Church there is no salvation – which Bonhoeffer also, purposefully, cites in this connection. A corrupted version was very soon in circulation, to wit: 'If you haven't got a red card you're not going to heaven.' This referred to the membership cards distributed earlier by the Confessing Church.

Bonhoeffer had touched a sensitive nerve when he said that for pious and right-believing people, such as General Superintendent Zoellner, to work with the committees still didn't make the committee work any better, since church leadership imposed by the state is not church leadership, and a church that allows pure and false doctrines to be preached together is not a church. He also refused to admit the possibility for anyone to be 'neutral'.

In the first place, it has to be said that in reality there are no 'neutrals'. They actually belong to the other side ... It is not possible to take a clear position in regard to them, because their own position is not unambiguous, because the boundary they draw between themselves and the true Church is not clear. (DBW 14, 678–89)

The word 'boundary' was important to Bonhoeffer. It was the German Christians with their Aryan paragraph and other heresies who had set up a boundary over against the Church of the gospel, a boundary which was a barrier to fellowship. The Church itself does not create any boundaries, but through its confession of faith makes clear that those who teach heresy have shut themselves out. The Church takes cognizance – and it can only do so through decisions made by synods – that it has encountered here an insurmountable boundary (DBW 14, 678–89).

Bonhoeffer's essay appeared at a time when many Confessing Church pastors had just made the decision to work with the committees or to submit to them. Having Zoellner in charge of the committee work seemed to them a guarantee that German Christian rule was at an end. They felt that in Bonhoeffer's essay they were being treated as though they had fallen away from the faith, which was indeed the way he viewed them. On page after page of the essay he insisted that a decision was called for; that the cause was that of every individual believer but above all a cause of the Church.

In early 1936 Bonhoeffer held a Bible study on King David, which he subsequently published in the journal *Junge Kirche* (DBW 14, 878ff.). The professional theologians paid no attention to it, but it was reviled in the Nazi press. Bonhoeffer had had the audacity to speak of Judah, the worldwide enemy, as the 'eternal people', the 'true nobility', and 'the people of God'. The reaction was different to a Bible study on Ezra and Nehemiah, in which he did not even mention the time and place in which these two books of the Bible were written (DBW 14, 930ff.). It was printed in the same journal and unleashed an intense debate. Friedrich Baumgärtel, Professor of Old Testament at Greifswald, wrote that Bonhoeffer was leading his ordinands astray with unscholarly thinking. He was able to prove that Bonhoeffer had treated the text in an arbitrary fashion by simply ignoring the content of verses which spoke of state assistance in rebuilding the temple in Jerusalem and of the protection of a state commissar, because this did not fit with his argumentation (DB-ER 528). The faculty in which Baumgärtel taught had stood up for the committees and against the Confessing Church, and was annoyed by the fact that when Bonhoeffer preached in a Greifswald church almost 500 people attended worship, especially students.

The Old Testament was the one theological discipline that Bonhoeffer had neglected somewhat during his own studies. Thus it was no wonder that his Bible study was rejected even by Old Testament scholars in the Confessing Church. His friend Gerhard von Rad, with whom he had often played music when they were schoolboys, wrote in his diary that he ought to 'take Bonhoeffer by the collar' here. Rad had shown, as no one else had done, that there was no need to bend Old Testament texts out of shape in order to interpret them in the spirit of the Confessing Church.[11] So during a visit of Bonhoeffer's to the University of Jena, the two theologians, friends since their youth, had a lively but very friendly dispute over the interpretation of the Old Testament for the present time.[12]

Enthusiasm and tribulation

Through these personal attacks on Bonhoeffer, 'decision' had also become a key word for every individual Finkenwaldian. So we must now look back again and see how the seminary experienced the measures taken by the Ministry of Church Affairs.

Minister Kerrl may have raised hopes when he invited each of the different Protestant church groups to send representatives to a meeting with him. He began with Committee President Zoellner and his colleagues, including a few men who until then had been working within the Confessing Church. When this group proposed that some especially radical German Christian members be dismissed from the Reich committee, he left the room instead of replying. This did not bode well for the future. His second meeting was with the Provisional Church Administration of the Confessing Church chaired by Bishop Marahrens. To its representatives, he proposed that the Councils of Brethren should dissolve themselves, before he compelled them by force to do so. To his third meeting he invited representatives of the Dahlemites, and towards them the Minister was harsh and uninterested in any compromise. He said he 'didn't want to hear anything more about heresy'. He announced that now he would put everything to rights, so that 'no loose end is left for a mouse to chew'. This sentence, alien in a theological context, made the rounds of the Confessing Church; in particular it was reported that when the speaker of the group tried to explain what the Confessing Church was about, Kerrl said to him, 'Why talk so much? As far as I'm concerned it's quite pointless.' The speaker replied, 'I note that the Reich Minister considers what we have to say pointless. Then we will end the negotiations.' (DB-ER 495)

Bonhoeffer's conclusion, on hearing the report of this meeting, was that the Confessing Church was very close to being banned altogether. He wrote to his former ordinands:

We write to let you know that you will not be left on your own in the days to come. After recent events we must now reckon seriously with the possibility of the Confessing Church being banned ... Even a forbidden Church Administration will remain irrevocably ours ... No directive that invalidates or goes against our Church Administration may be complied with, unless on explicit instructions from the church leadership ... (DB-ER 496)

This was exactly what it meant to be a Dahlemite, and the ordinands at Finkenwalde saw this no differently from the way their director saw it.

One of the most difficult but important decisions that should have been made was missed, to Bonhoeffer's deep disappointment. From 23 to 26 September 1935, the synod of the Old Prussian Confessing Church met in Steglitz in west Berlin. Franz Hildebrandt telephoned to Bonhoeffer from Dahlem, saying there was a danger that the synod, while still condemning the Aryan paragraph for use by the Church, would explicitly accept it for use by the state. After giving his morning lecture at the University in Berlin, Bonhoeffer went to Steglitz and met there the entire Finkenwalde seminary, which had come to act as a 'pressure group'. The synod meeting showed that there really was no longer firm unity, now that Kerrl was making enticing peace offers. Shouldn't the Church make concessions to the state, in its own interest? The discussion went back and forth, any move towards weakening greeted by heckling from the Finkenwaldians.

In the end, by dint of great effort, a collapse of the Confessing Church front was averted. The synod stood by its earlier decisions, including the rejection of the Aryan paragraph. Bonhoeffer nevertheless considered it a fatefully missed opportunity, since the synod had allowed its agenda for discussion to be dictated by the government rather than setting its own priorities. He had wanted to see it finally take a stand on behalf of the Jews who were being persecuted. On 15 September, at the national Party Rally, Hitler had announced the anti-Jewish Nuremberg Laws; Bonhoeffer felt that the Old Prussian Confessing Synod should not fail to state its position against these.

On 2 December 1935, the Reich Minister of Church Affairs declared the Confessing Church to be illegal by forbidding it to hire employees, issue proclamations and circular letters, or raise funds through collections and subscriptions except as authorized by the committees – pastors who were being paid salaries previously still received them, but otherwise taking up any offerings for one's church was punishable by prison – and, especially, holding examinations and ordinations of candidates for the church's ministry.[13] This meant the end of Finkenwalde and the other Confessing seminaries unless they were prepared to disobey the government (DB-ER 496–97).

In the evening of 2 December, Bonhoeffer called all the Finkenwaldians together, explained the new situation to them and gave his reasons for his decision to continue the work of the seminary. He left the seminarians free to decide individually whether they wanted to leave or stay. What should become of the seminary's work was for the leadership of the Confessing Church to decide, but the Councils of Brethren were dependent on the individual willingness to carry on of the ordinands under their care. It must have been an impressive evening at Finkenwalde. All those present declared that they wanted to continue their studies and their life with the House of Brethren, despite the government prohibition upon them. Bonhoeffer then wrote to Niemöller:

Despite the seriousness of the situation we are very happy and confident. For the rest we act in accordance with Matthias Claudius's wonderful hymn ...
  I pray that God may grant / the little that I want;
  For if he doth the sparrows feed / will he not fill my daily need? (DB-ER 497)

Which is right: 'Let every person be subject to the governing authorities' (Romans 13:1) or 'We must obey God rather than any human authority' (Acts 5:29)? Both are in the Bible. For the Finkenwaldians during the years of the church struggle, it was not even worth discussing, since the government was already in the wrong according to the laws of the land.

The first great debate after the synod of Steglitz took place very near Finkenwalde, in Bredow, a district of the city of Stettin. The day after Christmas, a holiday, found 200 pastors there, wrestling all day long about which way the Confessing Church should go in Pomerania. Now that the German Christians no longer held power, and Zoellner, a highly respected Protestant church leader was the head of the new church government, was it really necessary to go on fighting? Wasn't it finally time to settle down to the real work of the Church, in well-deserved peace? This was the view of many who had stood up loyally for the Confessing Church. Bonhoeffer tried to present his radical understanding of the situation as persuasively as possible.

Instead of going forward, we are standing still and asking who are we really – a church, a movement or a group? ... But we must not been seen like that! By standing still we lose everything; the church can exist only by going forward. The way ahead is shown us by the beacons of the synods: Barmen as a tower against the subversion of church doctrine, Dahlem the tower against the subversion of the ecclesiastical order. Barmen holds the sword forged by the Word. Without Dahlem, however, Barmen would be like a weapon carelessly left in the hands of a foreign power's general staff. A third synod (Oeynhausen) must now provide our defence against the subversion of the church by the world as, in the shape of the Nazi state, it intervenes through its finance departments, Legislative Authority and committees, and is now tearing into separate groups the church of those who confess our faith. Here we cannot and must not give in one single time! (DB-ER 499)

Although there had been an agreement not to indulge in applause or disapproval, the atmosphere in the hall became quite stormy, and the Finkenwaldians did not remain on the sidelines either. They were criticized for this by a well-respected Stettin pastor, and Bonhoeffer defended them: 'I do not enter such meetings as would a Quaker who on principle must await the directions of the Holy Spirit, but rather as one who arrives on a battlefield where God's Word is in conflict with all manner of human opinions ...' (DB-ER 500). And with regard to a judgement expressed by his student, Winfried Krause, Bonhoeffer asserted that Krause had not called Bishop Marahrens 'a traitor', but had said that he had betrayed the church – an essential distinction. It was a judgement about an objective decision and action, not about a person. The theological justice of this statement could be disputed. 'And my only factual objection to it would be that Marahrens could not possibly betray the Confessing Church, since he had never belonged to it' (DB-ER 500).

While it was said of Martin Niemöller that he was best suited for an open field of battle, the Bishop of Hanover was precisely unsuited for such conflict. Some Confessing Church people were apt to relate with a smirk that the bishop's children had sung at his silver wedding anniversary, 'He doesn't say yes, he doesn't say no, he says let's wait and see!' because this was exactly his attitude toward conflicts in the Church.[14] When August Jäger tried to take the Hanover provincial church into the Reich Church by force, the bishop could neither sign the agreement nor break off the negotiations. The matter was finally resolved by his withdrawing for a while. Then he was said to be 'detained', because if the bishop were detained, his deputy could sign on behalf of the provincial church. In the same half-hearted way as he had done with legal administrator Jäger, Marahrens yielded to the new Minister of Church affairs on every disputed point. No battles could be won with such an ally at one's side. This is why Bonhoeffer said that Marahrens had never belonged to the Confessing Church.

In the studies undertaken by Bonhoeffer and his students, significant portions were defined by the church struggle. Nevertheless, in their half-year in the seminary, the ordinands had to cover an impressive syllabus. There was much to learn about the parish ministry: about pastoral visits and pastoral conversations, teaching religion, Sunday school, baptizing children, conducting weddings and funerals. At the university there was no opportunity, or only insufficient ones, to work on all this.

Bonhoeffer and his assistant, Wilhelm Rott, held daily practice sessions in preaching and teaching; each ordinand had to prepare and deliver sermons and class sessions for discussion by the whole group. However, an ordinand's sermon was not criticized as such, so as not to 'talk it to death'. On all the above-mentioned practical areas of parish work, Bonhoeffer also gave lectures; but more important was his aim to focus on the strengths and weaknesses of every individual candidate. How well he knew each of his students by the end of their training is shown by the assessments he wrote for the Confessing Church authorities. Bonhoeffer had reservations about psychological probing, but he described his students with sensitivity, and made suggestions not only concerning their placement but about what should be especially kept in mind for each (for an example, see DBW 14, 288–89).

With groups of students, even during the first Finkenwalde course, Bonhoeffer made trips by bicycle to two church districts to support lonely Confessing Church pastors, to make pastoral visits in their villages, and to lecture and hold services. This strengthened the host pastors as well as preparing Bonhoeffer's ordinands for the work they would soon be doing. The only way they would have of obtaining a pastorate, since the normal procedure was controlled by the 'committees', was through owners of estates who were patrons of village churches and had the right to choose their pastors. A few could be taken on at a pittance as assistants to Confessing Church pastors who were already serving in parishes by 1933.

In 1936 the entire seminary went to the Belgard church district in East Pomerania, now northwest Poland. In each village, four of the brethren spent a week visiting church members and leading children's groups and Bible studies. On four of the days, evening worship was held in the village church, at which one of the four ordinands gave a 10-minute homily. With hymns and prayers, each service lasted about an hour. In all the villages the response was stronger than expected. In other areas the seminary visited later, however, they met with rejection and enmity. It was no wonder that how to deal with 'dead congregations' later became a topic of lively discussions in the seminary.

As soon as former Finkenwaldians had their pastoral assignments, they found themselves rather isolated and keenly missed the 'life together' at the seminary. Bonhoeffer informed and supported them through a pastoral newsletter. It was now forbidden for the Confessing Church to circulate newsletters, but if they were in envelopes addressed by hand and put into different post-boxes they didn't arouse any suspicions. Former ordinands were also invited to retreats at Finkenwalde. Most of Bonhoeffer's students were later called up for military service and lost their lives in the war, but the small group that survived had a sense of belonging together which lasted all their lives and was evident to everyone who came into contact with them.

On 4 February 1936, the second Finkenwalde course celebrated Bonhoeffer's thirtieth birthday with him. He told stories about Barcelona, Mexico and London. Suddenly, one of the ordinands asked whether they, too, might express a wish for Bonhoeffer's birthday. Could he, with the help of his ecumenical contacts, arrange a seminary trip to Sweden? Bonhoeffer – with characteristic spontaneity – promised that same evening he would do so.

Before the Church Foreign Office of the Reich Church or the secret police (Gestapo) got wind of these plans, Bonhoeffer had obtained an official invitation from the Church of Sweden, free board and lodgings had been promised the seminarians, and they had left by boat from Stettin. He had the advice of Birger Forell, the chaplain at the Swedish embassy in Berlin, who was a great friend and helper of the Confessing Church. The seminarians were warmly welcomed everywhere in Sweden; their hosts even made a celebration of their visit. The Archbishop and the widow of his predecessor, the great ecumenicist Nathan Söderblum, at whose grave an impressive memorial service was held, invited ordinands to stay in their homes, as did many other members of local churches. The main Swedish newspapers carried the event on their front pages.

Delighted though the ordinands were with their journey, and cordially received as they had been, the repercussions afterwards were not so pleasant, and once again Theodor Heckel was involved. He drafted a letter for Zoellner to send to Archbishop Eidem in Uppsala, asking whether his invitation to the Finkenwaldians should be understood as a statement by the Church of Sweden against the leadership of the German Evangelical Church. The Archbishop hastened to reply that it was a purely private invitation, but after his secretary corrected him he was obliged to admit that it had taken place through official channels in Sweden. In short, there were a number of embarrassing consequences. Heckel, having once again been outmanoeuvred by Bonhoeffer through his ecumenical contacts, wanted finally to get revenge on this opponent who since 1933 had called him an accomplice in heresy. He wrote to the Prussian church committee:

Lecturer and Pastor Bonhoeffer, director of a confessional seminary in Finkenwalde near Stettin, has received an invitation from the Ecumenical Committee of the Church of Sweden to visit Sweden with the confessional seminary. The ramifications of this action for foreign policy are being dealt with by the appropriate authorities. I feel impelled, however, to draw the attention of the provincial church committee to the fact that this incident has brought Dr Bonhoeffer very much into the public eye. Since he can be accused of being a pacifist and an enemy of the state, it might well be advisable for the provincial church committee to dissociate itself from him and take steps to assure that he will no longer train German theology students. (DB-ER 511–12)

As dangerous as it could be for Bonhoeffer to be so denounced, another consequence of the trip to Sweden was more drastic for him. He lost his *venia legendi*, his right to lecture at the University of Berlin. He had not noticed that, since June 1935, university lecturers were not allowed to travel abroad without official permission. The Minister of Education wrote to him that he had not only failed to obtain permission to travel abroad, but had also continued to direct a seminary which, under the Fifth Decree on the Implementation of the Law for the Protection of the German Evangelical Church, no longer had the right to exist. He was therefore permanently excluded from the university lecturing staff (DBW 14, 213). Furthermore, Finkenwalde, in its remote corner of the country, was now in the authorities' field of vision.

The Memorandum to Hitler from the Confessing Church

Bonhoeffer often made his comrades-in-arms uncomfortable because he felt the Confessing Church was too timid in its resistance. In 1934 he had written from London to his friend Sutz:

And while I'm working with the church opposition with all my might, it's perfectly clear to me that *this* opposition is only a very temporary transitional phase on the way to an opposition of a very different kind, and that very few of those involved in this preliminary skirmish are going to be there for that second struggle. I believe that all of Christendom should be praying with us for the coming of resistance 'to the point of shedding blood' [Hebrews 12:4] and for the finding of people who can suffer it through. Simply suffering is what it will be about, not parries, blows or thrusts such as may still be allowed and possible in the preliminary battles; the real struggle that perhaps lies ahead must be one of simply suffering through in faith. Then, perhaps then God will acknowledge his church again with his word, but until then a great deal must be believed, and prayed, and suffered. (DBWE 13, 135)

For him, the Steglitz synod had been far too much about self-defence, about preserving the existence of the Confessing Church. Then he heard that the new Provisional Administration and the Reich Council of Brethren of his church were writing a memorandum that was to be presented to Hitler. One of the members of the three committees preparing the draft was Franz Hildebrandt, who also worked on the final version and asked Bonhoeffer for advice several times during the process. The memorandum was a clear statement of position against the policies of the Third Reich. It was not intended to be published, since the aim was to offer Hitler a possibility for discussion of the facts. It was handed in to the Reich Chancellory on 4 June 1936. The issues were addressed in seven main sections:

1. It had been said that the victory over Bolshevism represented the defeat of the enemy which had also been fighting against Christianity and the Church. 'What we are experiencing is that the fight against the Christian church has never, since 1918, been so alive and effective in the German nation.' This was a danger to the people, especially to youth.

2. It must be asked what the formulation in the Party programme which claimed that it stood on the ground of 'positive Christianity' actually meant.

3. The recent 'pacification work' of Kerrl through the Ministry of Church Affairs may have cleared up some shortcomings, but it was muzzling the churches.

4. In breach of existing agreements, young people, schools, universities and the press were being forcibly de-Christianized under the slogan 'deconfessionalization'.

5. The fifth point, since it most clearly concerns the conflict with the state, is quoted here verbatim:

Protestant members of National Socialist organizations are being required to commit themselves without reservation to the [Nazi] world view. This world view is very frequently proposed as a positive replacement for Christianity, which has to be given up. But while blood, race, national heritage and honour are elevated to the status of eternal values, a Protestant Christian, according to the First Commandment, cannot accept this. While people of the Aryan race are glorified, God's Word testifies that all human beings are sinful. While the [Nazi] view imposes on Christians an anti-Semitism which commits them to *hatred of the Jews*, Christians are commanded to love our neighbours. This lays an especially heavy burden on the conscience of our Protestant church members, since it is their duty as Christian parents to combat this anti-Christian thinking in their children.

6. There was also anxiety about the moral precepts, essentially alien to Christianity, which were being propagated by elements within the Party. 'By and large, anything is considered good nowadays, if it benefits our *Volk*.'

7. In many ways the Führer was the object of a veneration that belonged to God alone. 'We, however, ask that the people of our nation be free to go forward into the future following the cross of Christ as their standard, that their grandchildren may not curse them some day ...'[15]

Hitler had no intention whatever of replying; he did not even acknowledge receipt of the memorandum. It is possible that he never even saw it, since the Reich Chancellery office sent it to the Ministry of Church Affairs, as the 'appropriate' destination, and the Ministry forwarded it on to the Evangelical High Church Council in Berlin. After six weeks had passed, the *Morning Post* in England reported the existence of such a document, and on 23 July the entire text, word for word, appeared in the Swiss paper *Basler Nachrichten*. For those who had sent it to Hitler, who had wanted to avoid this very outcome, this was a heavy blow. The Provisional Administration of the Confessing Church now sought to prove that the memorandum was intended as an act of genuine loyalty and not as an attack. Letters were sent to the administrations and Councils of Brethren of the provincial Confessing churches to say that the publication had occurred without the knowledge or assistance of the church leaders. They even went to the presidential office of the Reich Chancellery and asked for an investigation, since it was suspected that the leak must be on the side of the government.

The memorandum made a deep impression abroad, as a sign of courageous resistance. What it did in Germany was to increase the gulf between the Dahlemites and the members of the Lutheran Council, since the latter immediately distanced themselves in every way from the authors of the memorandum, whom the press was decrying as guilty of high treason. When it was suggested that the memorandum be made the basis of a pulpit proclamation, the representatives of the 'intact' churches stayed away from the Reich Council of Brethren meeting, thus depriving it of a quorum needed to take action. Bonhoeffer wrote at the time to the former Finkenwaldians:

Dear Brothers, we can all tell that things have started moving once more in our church. We do not know where they will go. What makes me most anxious of all is the Lutheran Council. We are faced with the announcement of a Lutheran Reich church. Then we shall have the Confessing Church for which many yearn. And the incomprehensible thing is that we shall not be able to participate. Then our conscience will be racked with fear and anguish ... may God build a wall around us so that we can keep together. (DB-ER 534)

While the writers of the memorandum still had no idea who had leaked it to the foreign press, Bonhoeffer had managed to find out. Two of his former students, Werner Koch and Ernst Tillich, had both had a hand in it. Tillich had been one of Bonhoeffer's students in Berlin before 1933, but had ended all contact with him since then. Werner Koch had taken part in the second course at Finkenwalde and in the trip to Sweden. He was a gifted journalist and, on Karl Barth's recommendation, had provided several important foreign news organizations with information and articles. Several Confessing Church staff members knew about this and were troubled, so Koch was sent as a pastoral assistant to Wuppertal in order to separate him from his sources of information in Berlin. Friedrich Weißler, the Jewish Christian head of the Provisional Administration office, had one of the only three copies of the memorandum in his safe, and Ernst Tillich had been able to borrow it overnight. Without Weißler's knowledge he had not only made some notes, but had copied out the text word for word. He had made contact with the *Basler Nachrichten* through Koch.

The secret could not be kept very long. Tillich and Weißler were arrested on 6 October, Koch on 13 November 1936. On 13 February 1937 all three of them were sent to the concentration camp at Sachsenhausen, where Weißler died six days later after being tortured as a Jew. Koch was released in December 1938, Tillich in 1939.

Emil Fackenheim, a Jewish fellow prisoner in Sachsenhausen who survived, found out long after the war from Bethge's biography of Bonhoeffer why Ernst Tillich had been sent to the camp. Tillich had told his fellow prisoners only that he had circulated an anti-Nazi pamphlet. Fackenheim is exactly right in remarking that the authors of the memorandum – 'naively, to say the least' – had expected an answer from Hitler.

And then two of these people, Werner Koch and Ernst Tillich, leaked the memorandum to the foreign press, thereby transforming a heroic, but certainly futile gesture into a tremendous political act ... The Nazis would certainly have murdered Tillich if he had talked around about what he had done. So, well over thirty years later, I understood that I had been that close to a historical event.[16]

In case Hitler did not reply, the authors of the memorandum had planned to demonstrate, through a proclamation from the Church's pulpits, that the Church was not completely silent. That the authors pursued this intent, after being labelled as 'traitors to the Fatherland', was certainly courageous; they had just seen for the first time, through the consequences of the leak to the press, what the Nazi state did to people who spoke the truth openly. During that time, Bonhoeffer came across a placard in a bookshop in Berlin:

> After the end of the Olympiade
> we'll beat the CC to marmalade,
> Then we'll chuck out the Jew,
> the CC will end too.
> (DB-ER 536: 'CC' = Confessing Church)

The memorandum was edited into a – rather less radical – proclamation, and thousands of copies of a flyer were also printed. Since severe reprisals were expected, the Provisional Administration of the Confessing Church had ordered Bonhoeffer to go to the ecumenical conference at Chamby, despite his decision not to attend. He was charged with giving bishops Bell and Ammundsen precise information in case a dramatic conflict with the government should ensue.

A large number of Confessing Church pastors read out the proclamation, including former Finkenwalde seminarians in their lonely villages. Nothing happened to any of them. We know today that the Gestapo had received orders not to interfere. The Olympic Games were about to be held in Berlin, so that Germany was more than ever in the spotlight of the whole world. But the police did register the names of those pastors who read the proclamation. Since no heavy strife had resulted, Bonhoeffer and Bethge took a few days after the conference in Switzerland for a brief trip to Rome, the city Bonhoeffer had loved best since his stay there at the age of 18.

The Cost of Discipleship and the end of Finkenwalde

Bonhoeffer could still, even now, take time off from the work of the seminary on hot days and head for the beach with his students; there were games and laughter. For the keen sports fans among his students, he bought tickets to Olympic events, and for two ordinands whose dream was to fly, a trip to Berlin by plane. It was only lack of discipline that he couldn't stand, due to his somewhat 'tyrannical nature' (DBWE 8, II/79).

For the winter semester 1936–1937 there was an especially gifted group of ordinands at Finkenwalde, and theology was pursued there even more passionately than before.[17] Sometimes it even seemed as though the heated battles on the outside no longer existed. During this high point in the seminary's work, suddenly there was word that the Finkenwalde estate was to be sold. To avert such a catastrophe, Friedrich Justus Perels, the legal adviser to the Confessing Church, came from Berlin and solved the problems involved so cleverly that the seminary was able to carry on. In the process, a close and trusting friendship developed between Perels and Bonhoeffer, which was to be important to both of them when they became members of the inner circle of the Resistance movement.

It was at this time that a sharp dispute broke out in Pomerania – somewhat later than in the other church provinces – as to whether to go over to Zoellner's committee system after all. Reinhold von Thadden, who after the war was to be the initiator of the Protestant church conventions (Kirchentage) in Germany, organized a large assembly to discuss the matter in October 1936 in Stettin. Bonhoeffer, who had turned up with all his ordinands from Finkenwalde, was strongly attacked. When someone quoted him as having said that anyone who didn't have a 'red card' could not be saved, he jumped up and called out, 'Bonhoeffer here. You're misquoting!' When it was said further that Pastors Pecina and Brandenburg, who had refused to leave their pastorates on orders from the government, were 'needlessly and purposelessly fanatical', the Finkenwaldians could only be restrained with difficulty, since Willi Brandenburg was a former Finkenwalde seminarian who had been imprisoned for his resistance, and was sitting in their midst.

At the end of this vehement dispute it was decided that all participants should submit written statements as to whether the provincial Council of Brethren should continue to govern the Confessing Church in Pomerania, or should yield its responsibility to the provincial church committee. The vote turned out better than expected: the assembly of Confessing Church pastors decided 181 to 58 in favour of the Council of Brethren. But the phalanx of the Confessing Church was beginning to crumble on all sides. A month later, Zoellner was able to announce that the Lutheran Council had declared its willingness to work with the committees. It was not long until one or another of Bonhoeffer's former students was having himself 'legalized'. The consistories of the provincial churches were making it easy for ordinands of the Confessing Church. An ordinand had only to come over to them and say he wanted to be assigned to a pastorate, and he would receive a job, a parsonage and a salary. Many of the Finkenwalde graduates were under pressure from their parents or fiancées not to be more courageous than necessary. Bonhoeffer and the members of the House of Brethren struggled to keep each one, and it was a heavy blow to all concerned every time the fellowship suffered a break. In the Rhineland during that time, 200 Confessing ordinands had themselves 'legalized', while 200 remained 'illegal'; in Bonhoeffer's sphere, only a few took the step of going over to the consistories.

Zoellner, who as committee president was the leading clergyman of the state-dependent German Evangelical Church, was in no way willing to tolerate German Christian excesses in a few of the smaller provincial churches. In the northern city of Lübeck, the German Christians had attempted to have all pastors belonging to the Confessing Church dismissed. They persisted in this cause even when courts declared it to be contrary to the law. Zoellner thereupon arranged to preach in Lübeck on 4 February 1937. When the police prevented him from entering the pulpit there, he submitted his resignation, on 12 February, along with the other members of the Reich Church Committee. Since not all of the provincial church committees followed them in doing so, Kerrl as Minister for Church Affairs was able to give a speech to a remnant of committee people, in which he called for bringing 'the preaching of the church into the correct relationship with National Socialism'.

Some of his statements in that speech were so unfounded that Otto Dibelius was moved to write another of his letters of protest.

According to the report I have here, the Catholic bishop Count Galen and the Protestant General Superintendent Zoellner tried to tell you what Christianity is about, namely the recognition that Jesus is the Son of God. This, you claim, is ridiculous and merely a side issue. You say all that is needed is to be influenced by the figure of Jesus, and to live by a Christianity of good deeds ... The New Testament says nothing about the will of God being given to us in our blood. It says only that everything human is cursed with selfishness, and that the will of God is proclaimed to humankind through Jesus Christ, the Living Word ... You said the priests are claiming that Jesus was a Jew; they speak of St Paul as a Jew, and say that salvation is from the Jews. This, you say, will not do! As far as I can remember, the church never used to emphasize this in earlier times. But now that it is being denied, the church has to say, 'Yes indeed, Jesus of Nazareth is a Jew! and that salvation is from the Jews is written in the 4th chapter of the Gospel of John.' You may certainly not forbid pastors to say what is in the Bible.[18]

Such open speaking made Dibelius popular with the Finkenwaldians. Like so many others, he had been wrong about Hitler in 1933; but after that he didn't keep still or keep his distance, but rather protested strongly against Nazism. So it is unjust to call him, as does Hans-Ulrich Wehler, 'one of the most disastrous figures in twentieth-century German Protestantism'.[19]

During the confused situation after Zoellner's resignation, Hitler again made a surprise announcement, ordering that church elections be held. The Church, 'in full freedom, may now provide itself with a new constitution and thereby a new order as determined by its members'. But these elections were never held. Announcing them was just part of the game of hopes, disappointments and renewed hopes through which church groups were kept in suspense through the years.

In place of the committees, there now appeared Dr Friedrich Werner, who on 20 March 1937 became director of the state-dependent German Evangelical Church's chancellery and president of the Evangelical High Church Council in Berlin. He was a lawyer, totally uninterested in issues of Christian confession, and a high-ranking Nazi Party member. In 1933 he had been on the presidium of the Brown Synod. Now Kerrl conferred on him full authority to govern the Church. Werner appointed Albert Freitag, a notorious representative of the German Christians, as head of personnel. From 10 December 1937 until the end of the war these two 'governed' the German Evangelical Church, trying to suffocate whatever was left of the Confessing Church through decrees and orders. For example, they banned worship services from being held in 'unconsecrated buildings'. This affected all the Confessing congregations that were obliged to meet in homes or in public meeting halls because German Christians were in control of the local churches. Anyone who resisted could be arrested, and from now on the number of pastors being sent to prison rose steadily.

Since 1933, worship services in the Confessing Church had included praying for those who had been arrested, by name; this too was now forbidden. Confessing congregations also were forbidden to take up collections, since this was an offence against the state's law on collections. The main point of attack, however, was the training of the next generation of pastors. Lecturers at the church colleges were forbidden to exercise their profession. Anyone who tried to get around this ban was arrested. Thus the end of Finkenwalde and the four other Confessing preachers' seminaries could be foreseen. These and many other such measures were being steered from behind the scenes by the former district president in Hildesheim, Dr Hermann Muhs, whom Kerrl had made head administrator in the Ministry for Church Affairs. In all the provincial church offices and consistories there were still properly appointed officials from the time before 1933, but they no longer had any authority. The power exercised by Werner and Freitag was unlimited.[20]

The cynicism evident in the way these two operated had the good effect of bringing the estranged wings of the Confessing Church together again. In March 1937 the Reich Council of Brethren held a full meeting, as it had not done for a long time. But this spurred on people like Werner to intensify their persecution. In June, a meeting of the Reich Council of Brethren in Berlin was broken up and eight of its members were arrested. When such things happened, Bonhoeffer immediately went to Berlin to see if he could help. In this way, when on 2 July 1937 he went to discuss the situation with Niemöller and Hildebrandt, he fell into the clutches of the Gestapo.

Niemöller had been arrested that morning. He was not to return until after the war; although he was acquitted in the forced trial held against him, Hitler made him his 'personal prisoner' and had him sent to the Sachsenhausen concentration camp. In his parsonage that day, Bonhoeffer found several men of the Confessing Church trying to deal with the new situation, when suddenly the Gestapo appeared with orders to search the house. The visitors watched as Niemöller's study was turned upside down. Behind a picture on the wall, a safe was found, containing 30,000 Reichsmarks belonging to the Pastors' Emergency League, of which the police took possession. The visitors were released by evening, after having to give their particulars, and allowed to go home.

All this had seemed to take place without any grave danger, but for Bonhoeffer the day brought a decided break in his life. His friend Franz Hildebrandt, who had been among those present, and preached in Niemöller's pulpit at the Dahlem church on 12 and 18 July, was arrested for announcing the collections for the Confessing Church and reading the list of names for intercessory prayer. As a 'non-Aryan' his situation was precarious, but Bonhoeffer's parents and many other friends exerted every possible influence, so that after four weeks he was released. Since the police had not found his passport, he was able to emigrate to England, where Julius Rieger took him on as assistant preacher in his congregation.

Before we come to the end of the work at Finkenwalde, we must speak of the book that grew out of Bonhoeffer's lectures there and his discussions with those who heard them. The preparations for this book go back to Bonhoeffer's time in London, and even before that. The first inspiration had been his conversations with Jean Lasserre in New York. Bonhoeffer's stirring phrase, 'Christianity entails decision', was now sharpened to the more precise point that faith means making a decision, for there is no faith without obedience. For several semesters at Finkenwalde Bonhoeffer lectured to his ordinands on being disciples of Christ, and in so doing he placed the Gospels, especially the Sermon on the Mount, at the centre of the Christian life.

At all Nazi public events there were speeches about 'Führer and followers'. During the war these were made into a song with the refrain, 'Führer, command, we'll follow you [wir folgen dir]'. When Bonhoeffer called his lecture course Nachfolge (following, or discipleship), he was not only using a New Testament concept, but also contrasting it expressly to a term widely used by the Nazis.

During the political dispute, which was discussed almost daily in Finkenwalde, he developed the idea that, contrary to the usual Lutheran interpretation, the Sermon on the Mount was intended not only to lead human beings to the conviction that they are sinners who can be saved only through faith in the grace of God; even more, Jesus required consistent obedience from his followers. Anyone who claimed otherwise was preaching 'cheap grace'. 'Only the believers obey, and only the obedient believe. It is really unfaithfulness to the Bible to have the first statement without the second' (DBWE 4, 63). This statement had the effect of a 'thunderbolt of insight' on Bonhoeffer's students, according to a description at the time in Finkenwalde (DBW 14, 989).

The book *Discipleship* (first published in English as *The Cost of Discipleship*[21]), completed in 1937, grew out of these lectures of Bonhoeffer's. It caused a stir, especially because this interpretation of the Sermon on the Mount was new for Protestant churches. This caused the shorter second part, which interpreted the apostolic letters – notably the theology of the apostle Paul – to receive less attention. Of course Eberhard Bethge had a point when, in his discussion of the book in his Bonhoeffer biography, he called the chapter 'Discipleship and the Cross' (DBWE 4, 84ff) a 'cornerstone of the work from the beginning' (DB-ER 450).

The second part makes no bones about the fact that Christians are persecuted in this world and are therefore lonely, and that they must spare no effort in remaining faithful. 'The church-community moves through the world like a sealed train passing through foreign territory' (DBWE 4, 260). This image of a 'sealed train' neatly reflects the situation of the Confessing Church, the influence of which was being combated and increasingly pushed back by the Nazi authorities and the Reich Church, which followed Hitler's lead.[22]

On thorough examination, it is striking that the last chapter of the book, entitled 'The Image of Christ', takes up the theme of 'Discipleship and the Cross' in another way, which one might call 'mystical'; and it is not by chance that this theme is the result of a decision that Bonhoeffer had to make, almost completely alone, at that time. It includes a passage that, while much gentler than his sermon in London on Jeremiah, reflects again moments of the absolute presence of God.

To those who have heard the call to be disciples of Jesus Christ is given the incomprehensible great promise that they are to become like Christ ... All those who submit themselves completely to Jesus Christ will, indeed must, bear his image. They become sons and daughters of God; they stand next to Christ, their invisible brother, who bears the same form as they do, the image of God. (DBWE 4, 281)

The form of Christ on earth is the *form of death* [*Todesgestalt*] of the Crucified One ... It is into this image that the disciple's life must be transformed. It is a life in the image and likeness of Christ's death (Philippians 3:10; Romans 6:4–5). (DBWE 4, 285)

Christ honours only a few of his followers with being in the most intimate community with his suffering, that is, with martyrdom. It is here that the life of the disciple is most profoundly identical with the likeness of Jesus Christ's form of death. It is by Christians' being publicly disgraced, having to suffer and be put to death for the sake of Christ, that Christ himself attains visible form within his community. However, from baptism all the way to martyrdom, it is the same suffering and the same death. It is the new creation of the image of God through the Crucified One. All those who remain in community with the Incarnate and Crucified One and in whom he gained his form will also become like the *Glorified and Risen One*. 'We will bear the image of the heavenly human being' (1 Corinthians 15:49). 'We will be like him, for we will behold him as he is' (1 John 3:2). The image of the Risen One will transform those who look at it in the same way as the image of the Crucified One. (DBWE 4, 285f)

Bonhoeffer is speaking here not only of the communion of suffering, which the ordinands were ready to take upon themselves together with their director, and did take upon themselves; he is also speaking explicitly of martyrdom, in which there can no longer be any communion of sufferers. There were reasons why Bonhoeffer came to speak of this. He felt personally obligated by Jesus' commandment to peace to refuse military service whenever war broke out, and he was certain that it would. But he wanted neither to discuss this idea with his ordinands nor to challenge them to follow him on a course which would end in a death sentence.

The few leaders in the Confessing Church who had any idea that Bonhoeffer was contemplating such a thing were horrified. The Protestant church had neither theological concepts, nor yet any examples, of conscientious objection to military service. That Luther had expressly forbidden the participation of any Christian in an unjust war had long been forgotten, and if Bonhoeffer, one of the best-known theologians in the Confessing Church, should declare Hitler's war to be an unjust war, there was no doubt that the whole Church would be endangered. The German secretary of the Fellowship of Reconciliation, Dr Hermann Stöhr, took this stance at the beginning of the Second World War and was executed.[23] There had been attempts to save him, but the Confessing Church did not stand up for him or for the step he had taken. Some friends in the Confessing Church were happy when Bonhoeffer was invited to the USA in the spring of 1939, hoping that war might break out while he was there, catching him by surprise and preventing his return.

That the Finkenwalde seminary was able to continue its work undisturbed, after the new church administration imposed by Kerrl's ministry had begun its attacks, amazed many people. Were the authorities

Dietrich Bonhoeffer on the shore of the Baltic Sea. Photo taken by Helmut Morlinhaus in 1937

purposely looking the other way? There had been cases in which members of the Gestapo had protected Confessing Church pastors and their work. Even the Finkenwaldians' mission trips were not disturbed. The fifth seminary course finished up with a few sunny days on the Baltic shore. The evening farewell celebration was held on 8 September, and everyone left on vacation.

Bonhoeffer and Bethge took a holiday in Bavaria. On the way back at the end of September, they were at Bonhoeffer's twin sister's home in Göttingen when they received a telephone call from Stettin. The Gestapo had arrived at Finkenwalde, served orders to quit on the housekeeper, Erna Struwe and the inspector of studies, Fritz Onnasch, the successor of Wilhelm Rott, and then sealed the doors of the seminary rooms. There were many appeals. The old Field Marshal August von Mackensen sent a handwritten letter of protest to Minister Kerrl; but the order was not rescinded. 'We must obey God rather than any human authority,' says the New Testament. On this basis, despite the ban by the government, Bonhoeffer did not consider his mission to train pastors for the Confessing Church to be at an end.

8.   In the Woods of East Pomerania (1938–1940)

The collective pastorates

Bonhoeffer's superiors and colleagues in the Confessing Church were as convinced as he was that the training of pastors must continue; the question was only how to go about this. The East Prussian seminary under Hans Iwand had been hastily moved to Dortmund in the western Ruhr district, but once there had soon been broken up; Iwand and a number of others were now in prison. A more effective solution was found to replace Finkenwalde. The towns of Köslin and Schlawe in east Pomerania, about 100 and 125 miles east of Stettin respectively, each had a church district superintendent who not only belonged to the Confessing Church but also had managed to keep his pastorates largely free of German Christians.

Superintendent Onnasch in Köslin had a very large parsonage, in which he could offer lodgings to as many as ten ordinands. He assigned these ordinands pro forma to Confessing Church pastors in his district as apprentice pastoral assistants. His son Fritz, who had already been inspector of studies in Finkenwalde, continued in that role at Köslin, while Eberhard Bethge assumed it for Schlawe. In Schlawe, Superintendent Block also arranged for the ordinands to be assigned, on paper, to dependable Confessing Church pastors, and to be registered with the police as residents of the town in that capacity.[1] However, rather than actually living scattered in these various parishes, they and Eberhard Bethge all lived together still further east in the village of Groß Schlönwitz, in a little parsonage with crooked walls, bent by the strong winds of the north German plain. Here the group could live only if it had its own transport, so besides Bonhoeffer's car they obtained another one and also a motorcycle. Bonhoeffer spent half of each week in Köslin and the other half in Groß Schlönwitz, as well as alternating weekends with each group. His residence was registered in Schlawe at the home of Superintendent Block, who was especially adroit at dealing with police enquiries.

In Finkenwalde Bonhoeffer had been able to lead five seminary courses, for five groups of ordinands; in Köslin and Schlawe, he

Eberhard Bethge and Dietrich Bonhoeffer in Groß Schlönwitz

was able to offer five more. It was no longer possible to maintain the House of Brethren, but community life was carried on in the form developed at Finkenwalde. Especially because life in the new locations was more primitive and in many ways harder than it had been near Stettin, Bonhoeffer insisted on leisure time, relaxing on the Baltic shore and games in the evening. One ordinand, who like so many of Bonhoeffer's students was later killed in the war, wrote to him after participating in the 'collective pastorate':

I did not come to Schlönwitz eagerly or hopefully ... I thought of it as a necessary evil that one had to bear with a good grace and go through for the sake of self-discipline ... It all turned out differently from the way I had feared. Instead of the stuffy atmosphere of theological cant, I found a world that embraced a good deal of what I love and need; straightforward theological work in a friendly community ... brotherhood under the Word irrespective of the person, and with it all, open-mindedness and creativity that still makes this fallen creation lovable – music, literature, sport and the beauty of the earth – a grand way of life ... When I look back today, I have a fine clear picture before me: the brothers sitting down to their afternoon coffee with bread and jam. The chief has come back after being away rather a long time ... Now we get the latest news, and the world breaks into the peacefulness and simplicity of life on a Pomeranian estate. (DB-ER 592–3)

After a time the community life became even more primitive, when the parsonage in Schlönwitz was needed by its pastor, and Bethge and his group had to move to a small, quite isolated house, Sigurdshof. Water had to be fetched from a pump at the edge of the deep Pomerian forest; food, and coal for heating, had to be brought from far away, and in winter everything was buried under deep snow.

At the end of June 1938, Bonhoeffer invited all the former seminarians to a retreat at Zingst, back where it all started. Forty-five young pastors came, and Bonhoeffer was especially happy that some had even made the long journey from the Rhineland, or from East Prussia (today divided between Russia and Poland). It was the time when the Confessing Church was truly at its lowest ebb, and Bonhoeffer made passionate efforts to ensure that his former students remained loyal to it.

The collective pastorates, in turn, lasted until after Hitler's invasion of Poland. This final period of Bonhoeffer's work as a teacher of theology took place during one of the most depressing times of his life.

'They belong to the other side'

In early 1938, official church president Werner gave orders that on Hitler's 49th birthday in April, all Protestant pastors must swear an 'oath of allegiance to the Führer and Reich Chancellor' (Hitler's two titles). Werner's decree included the words, 'Anyone who refuses to take the oath is to be dismissed.' It was the time just following the annexation of Austria, which had been greeted with a wave of enthusiasm nationwide, so that any pastor who expressed reservations about Werner's order came under a cloud; 'the nation could not depend on him'. German Christians took the oath immediately, 'with joyful hearts and in obedience to an inner command'. Confessing Church pastors, however, felt that they had been ordered to to break their ordination vow, for the text that accompanied this oath described it as more than the recognition of the duty, according to the New Testament, to 'be subject to the governing authorities'. It meant being in 'the most intimate solidarity with the Third Reich ... and with the man who created that community and embodies it'.[2]

No explanation is needed as to why Bonhoeffer found this loyalty oath reprehensible; however, like all the 'illegal pastors', he was not on any list of Werner's, so he was not being asked to take the oath. For the many Confessing Church pastors who had taken up their pastorates before 1933, however, it was another matter. Though they didn't acknowlege the Old Prussion Union represented by Werner as their legitimate Church, they still received their monthly salaries from it. (This was just one of the many confusing situations in the church struggle in Germany.) Before any synod of the Confessing Church could even discuss the matter, many of them had already taken the oath, and then, on 31 July 1938, the Old Prussian Confessing Synod – after agonizing deliberations in pastoral conferences and among friends – made it a matter which each clergyman was free to decide for himself. Bonhoeffer and his ordinands travelled from one pastors' meeting to another, trying to prevent the clergy from taking the oath, but since they themselves were not affected, they had no success with their arguments. The whole matter became one of the most shameful defeats of the Confessing Church, for, after the great majority of pastors had taken the oath, Reich Party chief Bormann wrote to the local party chiefs that it was the churches themselves which had prescribed the oath; it only had significance within the churches. For the state and the Party, it was irrelevant whether a pastor had taken the oath or not.[3]

At that time, Karl Barth asked the leadership of the Confessing Church, 'Was there and is there really no one among you who can lead you back to the simplicity of the straight and narrow way?' (DB-ER 602) And Bonhoeffer wrote to the Council of Brethren:

It is a hard step for a Confessing pastor to be compelled to oppose the decision of an Old Prussian Confessing synod, particularly when he can look back with nothing but great thankfulness and respect on the service that synod has rendered until now. (DB-ER 602)

The Confessing Church has never left its younger clergy so alone as it has in the case of this irrevocable decision ... Will the Confessing Church be willing to confess publicly its guilt and the rupture within its ranks? Will it find the room it now needs for prayer for forgiveness and a fresh start? (DB-ER 603)

One of the patterns of the church struggle was that, after every disaster which pushed the Dahlemites and the southern German bishops apart, a few men wrestled to restore the unity of the Confessing front. They were able to get conversations going, but these conversations were snuffed out very quickly by increased pressure from the government. Each of these attempts to restore unity worried Bonhoeffer, since he expected that they could only result in shabby compromises. The negotiations toward reconciliation in the summer of 1938 were begun, not least, at the urging of Hans Joachim Iwand who, after his preachers' seminary had been closed and after serving a jail sentence, had become pastor of a large church in Dortmund. Iwand had never stopped trying to win over his Lutheran friends in Bavaria, especially Bishop Meiser.[4] So it was that, at this time, provincial 'intact churches', members of the Confessing Church who had cooperated with the committees, and Dahlemites together with neutrals, negotiated a reconciliation, in the city of Essen in the Ruhr valley. They had decided to give the decisive weight to the first thesis of the Barmen confession. Bonhoeffer was horrified. He wrote to one of his students:

Here we are being haunted by the ghost of Essen, which is turning the heads of the best people we have. I can see only confusion and apostasy to come. The planned agreement on the Barmen 1st thesis (without even mentioning the name Barmen, of which we are almost obliged to be ashamed these days in the Confessing Church!) ... is simply untruthfulness and abandonment of God's grace revealed to us in Barmen and Dahlem. (DBW 15, 42–43)

Let us keep in mind that in Bonhoeffer's estimation, there could not be any 'neutrals': 'they belong to the other side'. After writing a letter of protest to the whole Council of Brethren, Bonhoeffer wrote to Wilhelm Niesel, the Council member responsible for the 'illegals', that is, for the preachers' seminaries and ordinands who wanted nothing to do with the consistories of the official church: 'The new draft is the most disastrous document in the history of the Confessing Church. Even when we cannot expect it ever to be put into practice, it must be rejected' (DBW 15, 42). He asked that the younger brethren be heard on the subject, and Niesel would be the only one in a position to arrange that. The most original comment that was made on this episode came from Bonhoeffer's old friend Ruth von Kleist-Retzow, who wrote to Bethge at the time:

I don't know anything about legal matters, but it looks to me like the founding of a 'cattle-raisers' association', as though the church has sold itself away ... The Essen draft seems to me nothing but plain unvarnished unbelief; all I have to do is look at the potpourri of signatures. (DB-ER 604)

These negotiations in Essen ended in failure, in a way that was particularly humiliating for the Confessing Church. In September 1938 it looked as though Hitler had decided to attack Czechoslovakia. As tanks were already parading through Berlin, members of the Confessing Church drew up a liturgy for a prayer service which included a daring confession of guilt and a prayer for peace. A wild cry of hatred was raised against it in the newspapers, which were all synchronized and under Goebbels' control. Almost at the same time as the prayer liturgy, a letter was made known which Karl Barth had written to the Czech professor of theology Josef Hromádka, including these words about the imminent war:

Every Czech soldier who fights and suffers will be doing so for us too, and – I say this without reservation – he will also be doing it for the church of Jesus, which in the atmosphere of Hitler and Mussolini must become the victim either of ridicule or of extermination. (DB-ER 606)

The SS newspaper *Das Schwarze Korps* (the Black Corps) claimed that they now had sufficient proof that the prayer liturgy was 'treasonable action in clerical garb'. Suddenly the men of the Dahlem wing found themselves standing alone, for their negotiating partners in the Essen conversations were distancing themselves from them in open declarations. It did no good for the authors of the prayer liturgy to assert that they had nothing to do with Barth's letter. They were put on unpaid leave until the disciplinary process that was to result in their removal from office, and this measure was extended to all those who had supported them. Bishop Wurm of Stuttgart, who as much as anyone had left the authors of the prayer liturgy in the lurch, confessed after the war that the 'power of darkness' over him had been 'greater than the power of light' (DB-ER 606). Bishop Meiser never uttered a word to show that he regretted what he had done in this and many similar situations.

The war did not begin after all at that time, because the Western powers and Mussolini reached the famous agreement with Hitler at Munich. Czechoslovakia had to cede to the German Reich those of its territories in which the Sudeten Germans lived, and Hitler declared that with this all the German territorial claims had finally been fulfilled.

On 9 November 1938, synagogues were ablaze all over Germany. A young Jew whose parents had been expelled from Germany to Poland had shot the German diplomat Ernst von Rath in Paris, seriously wounding him. When Rath died a few days later, Goebbels had already organized the 'spontaneous' revenge of the German people, carried out not by them but by SS and SA militia, dressed as civilians. The synagogues were set on fire and Jewish homes and businesses devastated; the streets full of broken glass caused that night to be known in German as the *Kristallnacht*. Many Jews were tortured, around 100 were murdered and 30,000 were deported to concentration camps. The Confessing Church no longer had the strength to protest. It had been thrown completely off balance by Werner's decrees. Only isolated individuals still felt able to speak out. In a repentant sermon the following Sunday, Pastor Julius von Jan in Oberlenningen, Württemberg said:

Who would have thought that this single crime in Paris could result in so many crimes committed here in Germany? Now we are facing the consequences of our great apostasy, our falling away from God and Christ, of organized anti-Christianity. Passions are being unleashed and the commandments of God ignored. Houses of God which were sacred for others are being burnt down, the property of others is being plundered or destroyed. Men who have served our nation loyally and conscientiously fulfilled their duties have been thrown into concentration camps, merely because they belong to another race. Those in authority may not admit to any injustice, but to the healthy good sense of our people it is quite clear, even though no one dares speak of it.[5]

Pastor von Jan was hauled out of his parsonage by 500 demonstrators from outside his village and beaten to a pulp. He was dragged through a raging crowd to the town hall, where he was interrogated and thrown into prison, and remained there until the US Army freed him in 1945.

In Bonn, the wife and sons of the internationally known expert in ancient Near Eastern studies, Paul Kahle, had been aiding Jewish business people; on the morning after this pogrom, she and her eldest son were surprised by a policemen while helping to clean up the shop where she had always bought her household linens. The son had to appear before the university's court, where he was expelled from university study 'because of the seriousness of his offence'. Furious hate articles appeared in the press, and the family received massive threats. They were able to flee the country just in time.

How degraded the moral values of large parts of the population had become at that early date is shown by a letter to Kahle from one of his former students, who at that time held the chair in Oriental Studies at the University of Göttingen, addressing him as 'My dear and honoured colleague':

You surely remember the case of a former rector of Bonn University, who got into bad trouble because his wife shopped at a Jewish butcher shop; that could actually have been a warning ... We younger colleagues regret that, due to the insensitive behaviour of Mrs Kahle, it has been made impossible for you to conclude your university career with due honour.[6]

Bonhoeffer was with his group of ordinands in the woods of Groß Schlönwitz when the synagogue in Köslin was set afire, and only found out later what had happened. His thoughts were the same as those of Pastor von Jan and of Helmut Gollwitzer, who had made a public protest in a worship service in Dahlem.[7] That Bonhoeffer did not react in the same way as these brave colleagues does not indicate a lack of courage, but rather that in 1938 he already felt that a fundamentally different form of resistance against Nazism was necessary. He had been initiated into the plans for a coup. In his Bible, during those days, he underlined the sentence in Psalm 74 that says, 'they burned all the meeting-places of God in the land'. Next to it he wrote the date: 9 Nov. 1938.

There were still Confessing Church pastors, but almost anything they did could be declared illegal and could lead to their salaries being stopped or to a prison sentence. Any of them could be dismissed from his ministry without any reason being given. For example, it was a sufficient offence to take in a Confessing Church ordinand and have him work in one's parish. Werner wanted to break down the resistance of the young Confessing Church pastors by depriving them of every possibility of finding work. In this situation, many of Bonhoeffer's former students felt insecure and uncertain. But what they called a 'new situation', he called a 'smoke screen'. 'Do not let us persuade ourselves that over there, in the ranks of the consistory, we would be free to attend to our business. Once there, we shall have surrendered all internal authority, because we have not remained in the truth' (DB-ER 614).

Bonhoeffer gave a detailed position statement on 'legalization' through the consistories; this was circulated in the form of a memorandum. It was discussed, praised and, above all, vehemently attacked. But there were those who fought alongside him, and on 28 January 1939 the Confessing Church Synod in Nikolassee, west Berlin, adopted a clear resolution against 'legalization'. After that terrible year, 1938, Bonhoeffer experienced this as a liberation. He shared it in his newsletter, 'Since I last wrote, much has become clearer ...' (DBW 15, 170).

Bonhoeffer's path to joining the Resistance

From 1933 onward, Bonhoeffer was better informed than most of his colleagues about what was really going on in Germany. He got his information, as long as it was possible, from the foreign press and foreign radio broadcasts. He brought back news from his travels; but above all he made use of his family contacts. His parents, his brothers and sisters and their spouses had all been opposed to Hitler from the beginning, and each of them had friends and acquaintances who also disapproved of the Nazi regime and had access to information. Bonhoeffer's brother-in-law Hans von Dohnanyi was the Ministry of Justice staff member that worked most closely with the Minister, Dr Franz Gürtner, who protected him as long as it was at all possible, and this position allowed him to find out much sooner than most people what was being planned by the government, the SS or the Party leadership. Dohnanyi had already begun in 1933 to record and document all the legal offences of the Nazis, and he kept this file up to date.[8]

Dohnanyi was one of the first to try and recruit others to help overthrow Hitler's government. His own opposition was already no secret, since he refused to become a member of the Party. Because of this, a group of fanatical Nazis within the Ministry of Justice, including Roland

Freisler, who was later to be the death-dealing judge for conspirators, denounced Dohnanyi to Martin Bormann, Hitler's Chancellery Secretary. Bormann then forced Gürtner to remove Dohnanyi from his position in the Justice Ministry; nevertheless, Gürtner was able to have his trusted assistant appointed a supreme court judge (*Reichsgerichtsrat*) in Leipzig, even though Dohnanyi would normally have been considered too young for a seat on the highest court in the land. Bonhoeffer was afraid he was being cut off from his most important source of information, but his brother-in-law had agreed to give a weekly lecture in Berlin and thus be able to continue meeting with the persons most important to him.

On 5 November 1937, Hitler had for the first time laid out for the top officers of the three branches of his armed forces (*Wehrmacht*) his concrete plans for war. Werner Blomberg, commander in chief of the whole armed forces, and Werner von Fritsch, commander in chief of the army, had raised political and military objections to the plans and were fired from their posts. Hitler himself took over the supreme command of the *Wehrmacht* and named Field Marshal Walter von Brauchitsch as successor to Fritsch. Soon afterwards, Hans von Dohnanyi met Hitler's aide-de-camp, Captain Fritz Wiedemann. They had encountered one another often, when Dohnanyi went to the Reich Chancellery with Gürtner, and had come to trust one another. Wiedemann told Dohnanyi that, on 5 November, Hitler had said, 'Every generation needs its own war, and I shall take care that this generation gets its war.' Dohnanyi was outraged, and Wiedemann said to him, 'I grant you that nothing but a revolver is any use here, but who is to do it? I cannot help murder someone who has entrusted me with his personal safety' (DB-ER 627).

To keep General Fritsch from speaking out and to make an outcast of him, the SS had slandered him as a homosexual, by falsely attributing the homosexual acts of a cavalry captain named Frisch to the General. Hitler, who found this very convenient, handed the 'Fritsch case' over to the Minister of Justice, who passed the files on to Dohnanyi, saying, 'You will know for yourself which end of the rope to pull.'[9] Investigation soon showed that the case had been manipulated by the SS. Anger at this brought Dohnanyi together with a whole group of influential military men: Dr Karl Sack of the military judiciary, Colonel Hans Oster, chief of staff for Admiral Canaris, and other opponents of Hitler with whom he could make plans for a coup. They were counting on the army not to stand for these defamatory attacks on its commander in chief. With the support of General Ludwig Beck, Chief of the General Staff, it was decided that Fritsch should send a message to SS chief Heinrich Himmler, challenging him to a duel. The text of this message was drafted by Dohnanyi. But Fritsch hesitated, and by marching into Austria in February 1938 Hitler achieved such a massive political triumph that the army chiefs declared that the proper moment had passed. Those who had been parties to this first attempt at a coup nonetheless realized that Hitler could be overthrown, if it were possible to gain the cooperation of the right military authorities.

Bonhoeffer was initiated into all this by Hans von Dohnanyi, and because he was among those who knew about it, his attitude changed. For years he had been fighting to persuade the whole clergy to act as Pastor von Jan in Württemberg had done in response to the pogrom night. But by the time he himself heard about the pogrom, he already knew about the conspiracy, *and in it, there was only one goal;* everything depended on putting Hitler out of action. If one were to take risks at all, it must be only for this purpose. 'The use of camouflage became a moral duty', in Bethge's words. The old Latin saying, *dixi et salvavi animam meam,* 'I have said it and thus have saved my soul', which had been Bonhoeffer's watchword during the early years of the church struggle, was no longer in force for him as an initiate into the conspiracy. His course now called for him to give up public protest, to the point of raising his arm in the despised Hitler salute. And anyone who possibly could was obliged to try to work his way into a key position.

The Munich agreement between Hitler and British Prime Minister Chamberlain was celebrated at the time in many countries as a success for peace. In reality it only postponed the war, for Hitler was annoyed that his negotiating partners, by compromising with him, had taken away his reason for going to war, and he was determined to do so anyway. What few people, such as the Bonhoeffers, knew at the time was that 'Munich' had thwarted the second attempt at a coup by the Resistance group that had been brought together by the Fritsch crisis.

Franz Halder, the new Chief of General Staff, was ready to launch the coup as soon as Hitler gave the order to attack Czechoslovakia. General von Witzleben, the military commander of the Berlin-Brandenburg district, was then to march on the Reich Chancellery and have Hitler taken prisoner. What happened instead was that, after his success in Munich, Hitler altered the tasks of the General Staff, leaving it without much power, and Witzleben was moved to a lesser command in Frankfurt on the Main. So the Resistance group around Colonel Oster and Hans von Dohnanyi could now only attempt, with all necessary caution, to seek out new contacts with opponents of Hitler within the military. General Ludwig Beck, who had been Halder's predecessor, had resigned on 18 August 1938 because of Hitler's plans for war. He had submitted a memorandum to Brauchitsch which said:

The final decisions for the nation's existence are at stake here; history will charge those leaders [of the *Wehrmacht* divisions] with having blood on their hands if they do not act in accordance with their professional and political knowledge and conscience. Their obedience as soldiers must have a limit where their knowledge, their conscience and their responsibility forbid the execution of a command.

It shows a lack of stature and a failure to understand his task, if in such times a soldier in the highest position sees his duties and tasks only within the limited context of his military orders, without being conscious that his highest responsibility is to the people as a whole.

Exceptional times call for exceptional actions! (DB-ER 629)

From that point on, Beck no longer had any influence in the military, but for the military opposition he would be the future commander.

The Bonhoeffer family had discussed on many occasions whether Dietrich's twin sister Sabine and her family should stay on in Germany. Shouldn't the Leibholz parents, if only for the sake of their two young daughters, get away from the anti-Semitism and hate campaigns? But what could a German lawyer, even such a gifted one as Gerhard Leibholz, do in a foreign country? Then, in 1938, Hans von Dohnanyi reported that a new regulation on names, to identify people of Jewish origin, was expected soon. Their passports were to be stamped with a large J, and the first name 'Israel' would be imposed on men, the first name 'Sarah' on women. Thus emigration, as soon as possible, appeared unavoidable.

Dietrich Bonhoeffer travelled with his sister and her family, along with Eberhard Bethge, part of the way to Switzerland on 9 September, and with the help of his London connections did what he could to ease their move to England. Bishop Bell and other friends made special efforts to help. Gerhard Leibholz received a scholarship from the provisional World Council of Churches and was invited to lecture on political science at Magdalen College, Oxford. Bishop Bell had just become a member of the House of Lords in the British Parliament, and found in Leibholz an intelligent adviser, outstandingly well informed about all matters having to do with Germany and the danger of war.

Through his brother Hans, Gerhard Leibholz had a contact with Franz Koenigs, a banker in Amsterdam who was energetically helping emigrating Jews and also had connections with the Resistance in the

German military. Koenigs was married to Countess Anna Kalckreuth, a cousin of Paula Bonhoeffer's. He met with Klaus Bonhoeffer in Spain in 1941, and earlier the same year with Dietrich Bonhoeffer, who was so interested that he arranged a second conversation the next day (DBWE 16, 133). There was also a contact with Hans von Dohnanyi. Hans Leibholz brought reports written about Germany by Koenigs to London at regular intervals. However, this came to an end when Hitler's troops invaded the Netherlands and Hans Leibholz took his own life. In the autumn of 1941, not long after his conversations with Klaus and Dietrich Bonhoeffer, Franz Koenigs was killed at the main railway station in Cologne, under circumstances that have never been clarified.[10]

The crisis over Czechoslovakia caused the issue of Bonhoeffer's military service to become acute faster than he had expected. On 3 November 1938, along with all men of military age, he had to have his name recorded in the Military Registration Record at his place of residence. Henceforth the authorities there – in Bonhoeffer's case, in Schlawe – had to be informed of any change of address, any significant travel on holiday, and particularly any journeys abroad. In Schlawe a Major Kleist was in charge of the military registration office, so Bonhoeffer's friends in the extended Kleist family and the doughty Superintendent Block were still able, without great difficulty, to get him permission to visit his sister in England. Shortly thereafter, his father was able to be among those who helped him obtain a permit for a trip to the USA.

In the time between Bonhoeffer's entry into the Military Registration Record – from which point he had to count on being called up for induction, beginning with a medical exam – until his precipitated return from the United States, Bonhoeffer went through a severe crisis in his life. Not only did his contact with Dohnanyi appear to be at risk due to Dohnanyi's move to Leipzig, but also no progress was being seen in the rebuilding of the Resistance cell. Bonhoeffer was feeling the effects on his strength of the constant travel back and forth between Köslin and Schlawe, not to mention the many trips to Berlin. He could no longer manage to do any of the concentrated theological work to which he was accustomed. But most of all he was depressed over the setbacks which the Confessing Church had suffered: the disgrace over the oath of allegiance, the crumbling away of the 'Confessing front' after the publication of the prayer liturgy, the crippling debate about 'legalization', and the silence following the pogrom.

Bishop Bell (standing, holding a book) with a group of German pastors and their spouses of Jewish origin who were persecuted in Germany

All this seemed to confront him with the question: was it worthwhile, this struggle which was consuming the crucial years of his life? Was it right to object conscientiously to military service, at the sacrifice of his own life,[11] when no one in the Confessing Church could even understand such a sacrifice, much less approve of it? And what of his being party to the conspiracy? Wasn't that a mission in which people belonging to the military could be useful, but not a theologian?

'Only the believers obey, and only the obedient believe.' He still thought this way, but he no longer saw how it could be put into action. There was no one with whom he could talk about all of this openly. Members of his family would have been immediately concerned about saving his life, not about his theological insights. The churchmen would have pressed for more readiness to compromise on the part of this young theologian, whom they all considered highly gifted, but much too radical. There was just one person who would have an understanding for all of it, and who would give good counsel: George Bell, the Bishop of Chichester. When on 10 March 1939 Bonhoeffer took the night train to Ostend, Belgium for the Channel crossing, it was these very personal questions that he wanted to clarify, besides wanting to see his sister and her family again. In addition he had taken on some ecumenical tasks on behalf of the Confessing Church.

The weeks he spent in London were extraordinarily full. There were moving reunions with the family and with Franz Hildebrandt. Bonhoeffer saw his colleagues from his time in Sydenham, where he gave a lecture. He also met with the 40 German pastors and their families whom Bishop Bell had brought to England to protect them from the consequences of the anti-Jewish laws. During this meeting, the news was spreading that Hitler had broken the agreement made in Munich and had marched into Prague. Once again, war had come that much nearer. With his brother-in-law and Julius Rieger, Bonhoeffer travelled to Sussex, where Reinhold Niebuhr, who was by then considered the most important theologian in the United States, was on holiday. There it was decided that Niebuhr would arrange for Bonhoeffer to be invited to give some lectures in the United States.

The Confessing Church had asked Bonhoeffer to meet with Canon Leonard Hodgson in Oxford, general secretary of Faith and Order and assistant to Archbishop William Temple for ecumenical concerns.[12] He wanted to try with Hodgson to resolve the tiresome problem of how the Confessing Church could take part in ecumenical conferences without having to go through Heckel's Foreign Office. The issue was no longer to demand that the Geneva office decide in favour of the Confessing Church and against the Reich Church, but only that the church opposition in Germany be heard and be able to participate at all. Bonhoeffer wanted to get as far as having a knowledgeable person such as Franz Hildebrandt accepted as a liaison.

But Hodgson put him off with the old business of the regulations which had so often been held up to him before, according to which the Confessing Church was a group within the German Evangelical Church and the ecumenical community did not have the right to make distinctions between true church and false church. Ecumenical meetings could invite guests, but anything else would mean taking sides with one group against the other, and that could not be done. Bonhoeffer was disconsolate, for he knew that no passports would be issued for 'guests' from the Confessing Church. That Hodgson also knew this is shown by a letter he wrote to Archbishop Temple, which said that in case Heckel alone received a passport, and no one from the Confessing Church got one, the ecumenical community 'would nevertheless have maintained its impartiality' (DB-ER 644).

Fortunately the conversation with Hodgson was not the only ecumenical experience that Bonhoeffer had while in England. He heard that the successor to Henriod as head of the Geneva office, the Dutchman W. A. Visser 't Hooft, who had studied under Karl Barth, was coming to London and arranged to meet him at Paddington railway station. After the war, Visser 't Hooft described their conversation:

We had heard a great deal about each other, but it was surprising how quickly we were able to get beyond the first stage of merely feeling our way, into the deeper realm of real conversation – that, in fact, he was soon treating me as an old friend. (DB-ER 646)

As the two walked up and down the platform, Bonhoeffer portrayed the situation in Germany, and his personal dilemma: shouldn't one refuse to obey a government which was consciously heading straight for war and breaking all the commandments of God?

I remember his acute questions better than his answers; but I think I learned more from his questions than he did from my answers. In the hazy world between 'Munich' and 'Warsaw', in which hardly anyone dared to formulate the real problems clearly, this questioning voice had a liberating effect on me. (DB-ER 646–47)[13]

When Bonhoeffer later made contact with the ecumenical offices in Geneva on behalf of the Resistance movement, he had in Visser 't Hooft, from the first moment, a dependable colleague and friend.

However, the most important conversation for Bonhoeffer during this trip to England was the one with Bishop Bell. Immediately upon arriving in London, he had written to his fatherly friend of his struggle with the question of conscientious objection to military service. This was a step he felt compelled to take, but of course he could also see what such refusal would mean for the Confessing Church. The Bishop lost no time in inviting him to Chichester, where the two had a long conversation. Bonhoeffer sent Bell a sincere note of thanks before leaving London, but that is all we know about their encounter. However, it appears that Bishop Bell showed great understanding and sympathy for Bonhoeffer's question as to whether he should leave Germany. The final decision had to be made by Bonhoeffer a few months later in New York, without anyone there to advise him.

On Hitler's birthday, 18 April 1939, in the official journal of the German Evangelical Church, church president Werner published a text extolling the Führer and Reich Chancellor:

In him God has given the German people a real miracle worker; thus Luther named those who were truly great, whom God has sent out from time to time according to his free counsel and will, that they may work powerfully in the breadth and depth of history, showing their people and the world new goals, paving the way to a living future and bringing in a new age. In deepest gratitude, the German people and also German Protestant Christendom are experiencing once again this mighty event, Germany's hour, which has risen upon us with Adolf Hitler.[14]

At the same time, Werner was hemming in the work of the Confessing Church even more with further decrees. A few days before, he had signed and included in the official church journal the Godesberg declaration, a statement in which, it was claimed, pastors and local church members from different currents in the church were speaking with one voice:

With all the powers of faith and of the active life we serve the man who has brought our people out of bondage and hardship to freedom and glorious greatness ... National Socialism combats every abuse of the churches by political power and makes the National Socialist world view, the racially appropriate beliefs of the German *Volk*, obligatory for all; thus it continues the work of Martin Luther on the ideological and political side and helps us recover, in its religious aspect, a true understanding of the Christian faith ... *The Christian faith is the unbridgeable opposite to Judaism ... All supra-national or international churchliness of a Roman Catholic or World-Protestant type is a political degeneration of Christianity.* A fruitful development of genuine Christian faith is possible only within the given orders of creation.[15]

That Werner published such monstrous statements in the official church journal should not have surprised anyone; however, that Bishop Heckel adopted them and that a number of men of the Church, including Bishop Marahrens, were willing to sign them in a scarcely less venomous form was another matter. But now came a sign that, with the new General Secretary in Geneva, a new ecumenical spirit had entered in there. As a message from Geneva to the World Council member churches, a statement was sent in response to the Godesberg Declaration, initiated by Visser 't Hooft and signed by Archbishop Temple and other World Council members, as follows:

The national structure of the Christian Church is not an essential element of its life ... But the recognition of ... spiritual unity ... irrespective of race, nation or sex (Gal. 3:28, Col. 3:11) belongs to the essence of the Church. The Gospel of Jesus Christ is the fulfilment of the Jewish hope ... The Christian Church ... rejoices in maintaining fellowship with those of the Jewish race who have accepted that Gospel ... The Church is bound to proclaim [Christ's] lordship over all areas of life, including politics and ideology.[16]

Heckel, who was regarded by Hodgson and many others as the legitimate representative of the ecumenical community in Germany, wired:

Expect immediate withdrawal declaration to the churches which greatly exceeds competence, is based on wrong understanding of factual general church situation in Germany and represents an intolerable intervention in domestic German affairs. German Evangelical Church.[17]

Bonhoeffer was in London while these new developments in the German Evangelical Church were taking place. They were hardly what he needed to renew his courage, so he stayed in England longer than he had originally planned, hoping that perhaps the outbreak of war would catch him there. This was to come only months later; but in England, Bonhoeffer could sense the stark U-turn which the political mood had taken. After Hitler's triumphant march into Prague the British people no longer wanted peace at any price, but welcomed the government's guarantee to defend Poland, the next country that Hitler had in his sights.

9. New York (1939)

'One who believes will not run away'[1]

Bonhoeffer was only back in Germany for a month and a half before he left on his second journey abroad in the year 1939. He had to try to avoid being called up for induction, since after his medical exam probably his departure would no longer be allowed. And he had to convince the Council of the Confessing Church, which was very unwilling to do without him as a teacher of theology, that his intended trip was necessary, without bringing out too plainly his personal difficulties.

Saying goodbye on 2 June at Berlin's Tempelhof Airport, from where he was to fly to London and, with his brother Karl-Friedrich, board the ship for America at Southampton, England, turned out to be harder than he had expected. It had not been possible, in so little time, to find anyone to replace him as director of the collective pastorates, and Werner's latest

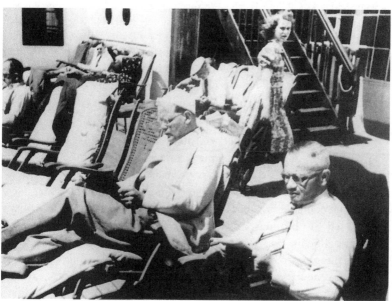

Dietrich Bonhoeffer on the deck of the SS Bremen *during the crossing to America, 1939*

decrees were robbing many of his friends of their last shreds of courage. Could he leave his church brethren in the lurch in such circumstances? In Sigurdshof, where Eberhard Bethge was holding the fort and had been obliged to shoulder the main burden of the work, a message lay on the table for Bonhoeffer's substitute: 'To my successor: He will find here one of the finest tasks in the Confessing Church' and, following requests about the subjects of instruction, a sentence was added: 'He is asked ... to go for walks with the brethren as much as possible, or to be with them in some other way' (DB-ER 649).

Bonhoeffer had scarcely landed in New York in June 1939 before he began to feel that his journey amounted to running away. His diary, which gives us a glimpse of his inner struggles, is among the most arresting texts he has left us. Reading it today, we can still experience how hard making decisions could be for him and how tormented he was by the lack of certainty as to whether he had done the right thing. Even on the ship that was taking him to New York, he began, in his travel diary, a dialogue with the Bible in which his thoughts were guided by the readings in his Moravian daily devotions (Losungen) book.[2]

8 June 1939, Zechariah 7:9 'Render true judgements, show kindness and mercy to one another.' This I beg of you, my brethren at home. I do not want to be spared, in your thoughts ... 9 June, Isaiah 41:9 'You are my servant, I have chosen you and not cast you off'... Great programmes always simply lead us to where we are; but we ought to be found only where God is ... Or have I, after all, avoided the place where God is? the place where God is *for me*? No, God says, you are my servant. 11 June, Psalm 44:21 'For [God] knows the secrets of the heart' ... If only the doubts about my own course had been overcome. (DB-ER 650)

On 13 June he had breakfast in New York with Dr Henry Smith Leiper, executive secretary of the Federal Council of Churches, who had organized his stay. Bonhoeffer told him even in this first conversation that he wanted to return to Germany in a year's time at the latest. The Americans had expected him to stay permanently.

The diary shows that these first hours in the United States were almost unendurable for Bonhoeffer. He was homesick for Germany and missed the brothers in the collective pastorates. 'The first lonely hours are difficult. I do not understand why I am here, whether it was a sensible thing to do, whether the results will be worthwhile.' He wasn't getting any news from home, and this tormented him. The next day, after prayers in the home of Dr Henry Sloane Coffin, president of Union Theological Seminary, he wrote: 'I was almost overcome by the short prayer – the whole family knelt down – in which we thought of the German brothers.'

15 June. Since yesterday evening I haven't been able to stop thinking about Germany. I would not have thought it possible that at my age, after so many years abroad, one could get so dreadfully homesick ... The whole burden of self-reproach because of a wrong decision comes back again and almost overwhelms me ... How happy I was in the evening, when I opened the *Losungen* once again and read, 'My heart rejoices that you are pleased to help me.' (DB-ER 652)

As he had done before, Bonhoeffer tried to find comfort in verses of hymns that he especially loved. But this time it was epitaphs on tombs that spoke to him. The first was a verse by the novelist Fritz Reuter which is on his tombstone in Eisenach. Bonhoeffer had quoted it in his homily at the funeral of his grandmother.

> Beginning and end, O Lord, are in thy hands,
> The span between them was my life, was mine.
> Though in the dark I sought my way in vain,
> clear light awaits me, Lord, with thee at home.
> (DBW 14, 920–25)

The second inscription reveals an even more ardent longing for the world beyond. It comes from Søren Kierkegaard's grave:

> A short while yet, and it is won
> Of painful strife there will be none.
> Refreshed by life-streams, thirsting never,
> I'll talk with Jesus for ever and ever.[3]

Bonhoeffer was trying to do some work, since he was to give some lectures in English, but he found his knowledge of English completely insufficient. 'How many years, decades even, it takes to learn German, and I still don't know it properly. I shall never learn English.' Even that was a reason to return home soon. Without the language, he felt himself lost and hopelessly lonely.

On 20 June 1939, Bonhoeffer's destiny was decided. Dr Leiper had invited him to discuss the work that was being proposed to him in the United States. The evening before, he wandered aimlessly around the streets of Manhattan for a long time.

19 June – No news from Germany the whole day, waiting in vain from one post to the next.[4] It is no use getting angry ... I want to know what is happening to the work over there, whether all is well or whether I am needed. I want to have some

sign from over there before the meeting tomorrow. Perhaps it is a good thing that it has not come ...

Visited Leiper. The decision has been made. I have refused. They were clearly disappointed, and rather upset. It probably means more for me than I can see at the moment. God alone knows what. It is remarkable how I am never quite clear about the motives for any of my decisions. Is that a sign of confusion, of inner dishonesty, or is it a sign that we are *guided* without our knowing, or is it both? ... Today's *Losung* speaks dreadfully harshly of God's incorruptible judgement. He certainly sees how much personal feeling, how much anxiety there is in today's decision, however brave it may seem. The reasons that one gives for an action to others and to oneself are certainly inadequate. One can give a reason for everything. (DB-ER 653–54)

It felt like a final decision, and Bonhoeffer entrusted it to God. 'At the end of the day I can only ask God to give a merciful judgement on today and all its decisions. It is now in his hands.' But the next day he wrote, 'Of course I still keep having second thoughts ...' Bonhoeffer wondered whether his incomprehensible homesickness was a sign that would make his return easier, or whether it was 'irresponsible, with so many other people involved, simply to say No to one's own future and that of so many others?' (DB-ER 653–4). The Catholic theologian Ernst Feil says, '[Bonhoeffer] knew of the point where our thoughts and correlative insights have their boundaries and where we must become prepared to make decisions in darkness, even in the darkness of guilt.'[5]

The journey home

On the last day, Paul Lehmann was still wrestling with him – couldn't he stay; shouldn't he really stay? – but Bonhoeffer stood firm. On 7 July he and his brother Karl-Friedrich, who had given some lectures in Chicago, boarded one of the last ships on which it was possible to return to Germany before war broke out. His diary says:

I am glad to have been over there, and glad to be on my way home again. I have perhaps learned more during this month than in the whole year nine years ago; at least I have acquired some important insight for all future personal decisions. Probably this visit will have a great effect on me ... Since I have been on the ship my inner ambiguity about the future has ceased. I can think of my shortened time in America without reproaches. (DB-ER 658, 661)

Beginning in New York, but also on the ship and later in Berlin, Bonhoeffer was busy writing an essay, 'Protestantism without Reformation'. He

Bonhoeffer's last meeting with his twin sister Sabine in Oxford in July 1939

wanted to make clear in his own mind why the Christian 'denominations' in the USA not only are so called, instead of 'confessions' as in Europe, but are actually different from 'confessions'. Did it have something to do with the fact that so many Americans had emigrated from Europe on account of their faith? For Bonhoeffer these were existential questions, in the context of the journey which had brought him to America.

Perseverance to the end can be necessary; to flee may be permissible, and even necessary. The flight of Christians under persecution does not of itself signify apostasy and disgrace, for God does not call everyone to martyrdom. Not to flee, but to disavow one's faith, is sin; that is to say, that there can be a situation where flight is equivalent to renunciation, just as on the other hand flight itself can be a part of martyrdom. The Protestant refugees who journeyed to the unknown country America did not find themselves in a paradise, but in a situation that called for hard labour. They accepted the struggle of building colonies for the sake of living out their faith in freedom, without struggle. This sheds light on the destiny of Christian refugees as such. They claimed for themselves the right to forgo the ultimate suffering, in order to be able to worship God in quietness and peace. Now, in the place of refuge, there is no more justification for the struggle to go on ...

In this way, the concept of *tolerance* becomes, for American Christians, the concept on which everything Christian is based ... Having to do without an

Bonhoeffer with Bethge and Traub

ultimate resolution of the question of truth remains, for Christian refugees, the hardest task they face all their lives long. In the last resort, it is faithfulness to their own church history that is expressed in this peculiar relativism of the question of truth in the thoughts and actions of American Christians. (DB-ER 660)

Here Bonhoeffer is seeing the ecumenical issues decidedly differently from the way he did in his essay on 'The Confessing Church and the Ecumenical Movement'. It did not disturb him much that he could not have this one published; he simply left it in his desk.

The brothers disembarked at Southampton and took the train to London. From there, Karl Friedrich Bonhoeffer flew home. Dietrich stayed a further ten days at his sister's home, planning to continue his journey by train to visit colleagues in Dortmund and friends in Elberfeld. In Dortmund it was Hans Joachim Iwand, who was still renewing his efforts to reconcile Lutherans and Dahlemites with one another, and in the process was prepared to compromise. In Elberfeld it was Hermann Albert Hesse who, along with his four sons, belonged to the small group of German theologians and pastors who refused any compromise. Thus the Hesses were men after Bonhoeffer's own heart. Hermann Albert Hesse and his youngest son, Helmuth, were later sent to Dachau because of their protests against the deportation of Jews, and Helmuth Hesse died there after 10 days in the concentration camp.

While in London, Bonhoeffer heard of the death of another unwavering witness. He was teaching his nieces English nursery rhymes when Julius Rieger came, called him outside and told him that Pastor Paul Schneider from the Rhineland, who had refused to leave his church in Hunsrück despite government expulsion orders, had been murdered in Buchenwald. This was the sort of martyrdom which Bonhoeffer had long considered necessary, a pure witness to the faith; one could not seek it out for oneself, but when one was called to it by God, it was a very particular sign of God's nearness.[6] However, since he had known about the plans to overthrow Hitler, it had seemed to Bonhoeffer that this way was no longer open to him.

He received an invitation from Edinburgh to give the 'Croall Lectures' there the next winter, a theological lecture series at the university, endowed by a wealthy Scotsman. Bonhoeffer accepted immediately and proposed the theme 'Death in the Christian Message'. Once home, he began right away preparing for these lectures, but the war put an end to this and many other plans that Bonhoeffer and his contemporaries had. To his fatherly friend the Bishop of Chichester he wrote a letter of farewell from London. It had not been possible to see him. On 25 July 1939, his sister and her family came with him to Victoria Station. That this was goodbye forever they could not yet know, but they had to reckon with the possibility. Not long afterwards, German troops invaded Poland. The Second World War had begun.

10. In the Resistance (1939–1943)

The journey towards reality

In 1914 the German people had welcomed the First World War enthusi-astically, because they saw it as a 'just war'. This time there was no such talk, and even the propaganda efforts of a Joseph Goebbels did not make much difference. Bonhoeffer's father wrote in his memoirs: 'In 1939 the people had no doubt that this was a war of aggression, prepared for and organized by Hitler, for which there was no kind of sympathy among most of the population' (DB-ER 663).

Bonhoeffer had imagined the outbreak of war as a more dramatic event. He was not called up for induction into military service, so the question of conscientious objection did not come up urgently. On the other hand, there were no new plans to overthrow Hitler, which would have allowed him to hope that the Nazi regime would soon be at an end and with it the war. The church struggle also seemed to subside; in many parts of Germany things became noticeably easier for Confessing Church pastors. There were more than a few who volunteered, having been officers in the First World War, and the consistories were willing to employ 'illegals' in their places, though without recognizing them as regular pastors. However, most 'illegals' had long since been conscripted into the army. Right at the beginning of the invasion of Poland, Bonhoeffer had to report in his newsletter the death of the first former Finkenwalde seminarian:

In reply to a card sent through the military postal service, I have received the news that our dear brother, Theodor Maaß, was killed in action in Poland on 3 September ... In him we had a good brother and a quiet, faithful pastor of the Confessing Church ... whom God had also deemed worthy to stand up for the Gospel through his suffering. (DBW 15, 267)

Theodor Maaß had been the first pastor in Pomerania to go to prison. In this letter Bonhoeffer looks back to the end of the First World War when many people were asking, where was God's justice now, since even after so many sacrifices the war was lost.

I don't know whether the question of theodicy will come up again so painfully as it did in the last war ... Christians probably know more today about the Bible's verdict upon the world and history, so they may be confirmed in their faith rather than sorely tried by present events. (DB-ER 663)

The news that Martin Niemöller in his concentration camp had volunteered for the navy combat forces was spread even abroad. Karl Barth prevailed on a friend in England to deny this emphatically. But it was actually true, and Bonhoeffer was one of those whose advice had been sought beforehand. He had counselled in favour of it, not so that Hitler would gain one more capable officer, but to save a man who would be urgently needed after the coup from being killed off beforehand by the SS.

On his own behalf, Bonhoeffer investigated the possibility of being assigned to a military chaplaincy, but was turned down; only a pastor who had already served as a soldier could be considered for a chaplaincy. So, after the invasion of Poland was over, he drove to Schlawe and from there on to Sigurdshof. There, 'protected by one of the most severe winters', as Bethge reports, he directed the fifth and last of the 'collective pastorates'. Eight ordinands had gathered there, and only one of them was conscripted into the military during that time.

During the first three years of the war Bonhoeffer was able to concentrate extraordinarily well on his theological work. This was already true of the months in Sigurdshof, where he began an exegesis of Psalm 119. This 176-verse psalm, which could have a numbing effect even on eager readers of the Bible, was Bonhoeffer's favourite. For him it was the psalm for those who had decided to 'walk in God's ways' because God had decided to call them. The Christian life is not one of 'continually beginning anew', but rather a path on which the believer goes forward because it is God's path.

'Happy are those ... who walk in the law of the Lord.' They are the ones ... who come from the beginning which God has accomplished. They are like victors after having won a battle ... Now they are reaching out toward a new future, now they go on from victory to victory, now they are on the path that is in the light. (DBW 15, 503)

The tormenting uncertainty of the days in New York, when he thought his only hope lay in the 'beyond', were behind him; he was back on earth again. Here we can see that the decision to come back to Germany had also taken Bonhoeffer a decisive step further in his theology. In his interpretation of verse 19, 'I am a sojourner on earth' (RSV), he expresses this for the first time. This exegesis became a further and especially important step in his journey to reality.

Bonhoeffer's last group of students in Sigurdshof/Pommerania

The earth that nourishes me has a right to my labour and my strength. I am not entitled to despise the earth on which I have my life. I owe it loyalty and gratitude. My lot as a stranger and a sojourner, and thus the call of God to this condition as a stranger, is not something I can escape by dreaming away my earthly life with thoughts of heaven. There is a homesickness for the world beyond which has nothing at all to do with God, and which will certainly not be granted its homecoming. I am to be a sojourner with everything that this implies. I am not to close my heart to the tasks, the sorrows and joys of the earth and remain indifferent. And I am to wait patiently for the fulfilment of God's promise, really wait, and not rob myself of it ahead of time by wishing and dreaming. (DBW 15, 530)

While in Sigurdshof, Bonhoeffer received a request from a New Testament scholar in the Rheinland, Georg Eichholz, for help in trying to compile new resources for pastors. Eichholz wanted to have Confessing Church theologians write sermon meditations for the Sundays of the church year, and to publish them as a book. Bonhoeffer remembered this colleague right away as the one Barth referred to as his 'theological masterpiece' in 1931. A lively correspondence ensued between the two of them, since Bonhoeffer, while agreeing to help, did not immediately understand the point of the proposal. He then realized, however, that his former students, especially the ones in lonely villages who had scant opportunities for conversations with one another, were very grateful for help with preparing sermons. The pastoral resource series that Eichholz began in those days is still in use today, and the contributions that Bonhoeffer made to that first edition have remained an exemplary part of it (see DBW 15, 548ff.).

On 15 March 1939, Visser 't Hooft sent a letter from Geneva to the World Council member churches, to say that in times of war there were three tasks for the churches to fulfil:

1. the task of prayer and the pure proclamation of the Word of God
2. the task of preserving brotherly relations with the churches in all countries
3. the task of preparing for a just peace

The first Christians to respond to this at the beginning of the war were those in the Nordic countries, who made efforts toward a rapid restoration of peace. As yet, the attack on Poland had not turned into a world war, so the Norwegian Bishop Eivind Berggrav carried the peace proposals, first to Lord Halifax, the British Foreign Minister, in London, then to Marshal Göring, then back to Halifax, and finally made a second visit to Göring in Berlin. In January 1940 the World Council's Provisional Committee met in the Netherlands and tried to draft an appeal for peace. But the Scandinavians and the British could not agree on it.

Bonhoeffer could not put his trust in any of this, not only because Berggrav made his contact exclusively with Heckel rather than with anyone in the Confessing Church, but especially because the Scandinavians were saying that peace must be concluded first, after which it could be decided what to do about Hitler and his regime. Bonhoeffer was convinced that Hitler must be eliminated first, because otherwise peace would not be possible. The Church Foreign Office, which thought otherwise, was in close contact with Berggrav and with Schönfeld's Research Department in Geneva, and Heckel's staff often turned up in Scandinavia and in Switzerland. However, when a man like Professor Siegmund-Schulze, who had been expelled from Germany, wanted to travel from Switzerland to Sweden, Eugen Gerstenmaier of the Church Foreign Office asked the Foreign Ministry to prevent this discreetly by telling the Swedish Embassy that granting the entry visa would be considered an unfriendly act and not in the interest of the Reich (DB-ER 670).

Colonel Hans Oster, Military Intelligence Chief of Staff under Admiral Canaris

New plans for a coup d'état

On 25 August 1939, Hans von Dohnanyi had been inducted into the military as a special aide to the chief of staff, Colonel Hans Oster, in the foreign office of Military Intelligence (*Abwehr*). The *Abwehr* office was in the Armed Forces High Command in Berlin and was headed by Admiral Wilhelm Canaris. Oster had agreed with Dohnanyi that as soon as war broke out he would request Dohnanyi's assignment to Military Intelligence. A pastor's son from Dresden, Oster was considered the most elegant officer in Berlin. 'I've never seen a more dashing horseman', said one of the conspirators of him, and with regard to Oster's efforts in 1938 to rescue the honour of General von Fritsch: 'He was a man after God's own heart.'[1]

On 27 September 1939, the day of Poland's surrender, Hitler ordered his general staff to plan invasions of the Netherlands and Belgium in preparation for attacking France. This was the decisive step towards world war. If Hitler were to be stopped in time, it had to happen now. At the same time the first reports were coming in of the SS atrocities in Poland. They were so monstrous that most people who heard them did not want to believe such things had taken place. But Canaris and General Blaskowitz, who commanded the troops in Poland, confronted a number of generals with the facts of what had happened and was still going on in the east. Blaskowitz wrote:

What the foreign radio stations have broadcast up to now is only a tiny fraction of what has actually happened ... The only possibility of fending off this pestilence lies in bringing the guilty parties and their followers under military command and military justice with all possible speed. (DB-ER 671)

Hitler reacted immediately by recalling Blaskowitz from his post. But Halder and Brauchitsch were prepared to oppose the attack on France and the invasion of the Netherlands and Belgium, and if they were looking for fellow conspirators in this they could start with General

Beck. Beck asked Dohnanyi to bring his chronicle of the regime's crimes up to date, so that it could be used to help the German people understand why Hitler had to be overthrown. Dohnanyi also obtained the SS films of the massacres they had committed in Poland, and reports that had been written for SS Director Himmler's deputy, Reinhard Heydrich. Dohnanyi showed these to generals known to be opposed to Hitler, and arranged contacts for Beck with former trade union leaders to explore the possibility of a general strike.

Admiral Wilhelm Canaris, 1940

The decisive point was, however, to gain assurances from the British government that they were prepared to keep quiet until the coup d'état had taken place. Dohnanyi and Oster entrusted this task to Dr Josef Müller, a lawyer from Munich who had close ties with the Vatican. He was able to get Pope Pius XII to vouch for the conspirators, and the seriousness of their request, to the Western powers. The prerequisite for the negotiations that would have to be carried out with them was that the overthrow of the German government must take place before Hitler launched his western offensive.

For a while it looked as though something of these plans had leaked out and that Hitler's henchmen were on the trail of the conspirators. Heydrich, now chief of the Reich SS Headquarters Office, had intercepted Vatican radio broadcasts revealing an exact knowledge of the German attack plans, and Admiral Canaris seemed likely to take the blame.[2] Eventually, however, the conspirators were reassured that the SS had not discovered anything concerning their scheme, so Oster and Dohnanyi went to work again.

Josef Müller had been taken on by Military Intelligence at the beginning of the war and was assigned to its Munich office. This made it possible for him to travel abroad without any enquiries from other offices. In January 1940 he came to Berlin several times to discuss his conversations in the Vatican with Dohnanyi. After the war, as one of the founders of the Christian Socialist Union, the conservative political party in Bavaria, he was to enjoy a certain renown under the nickname 'Ochsensepp' ('Joe the Ox').[3] He and Bonhoeffer were very different, but opposites attract, and when they met at Dohnanyi's a friendship developed between them, even before Bonhoeffer, too, was assigned to the Military Intelligence office in Munich.

Müller brought the news from Rome that the British had consented to an armistice, before an attack in the west and after the overthrow of Hitler. They also assented to peace negotiations based on Germany's remaining intact within its 1937 borders.

When Franz Halder, Chief of the General Staff in the High Command headquarters, approached Brauchitsch, the Army commander-in-chief, with a memorandum prepared by Dohnanyi, the latter refused to participate in the coup. He is said to have answered Halder, 'You ought not to have submitted that to me! What is happening here is absolute treason.' Brauchitsch demanded that Halder have the man arrested who had delivered the memo, and Halder is said to have replied, 'If anyone is to be arrested, arrest me!' (DB-ER 674).

Hans Bernd von Haeften, a boyhood friend of Bonhoeffer's and one of the conspirators in the Foreign Office, said of Brauchitsch, his mother's brother, 'And why was our dear little Walther Hitler's choice? Because he is a cadet by nature and his master's obedient pupil.' So another coup attempt had been lost. What was important now, for future attempts, was to preserve the credibility of the conspirators, after the pope had vouched for them. Josef Müller made a third trip to Rome with the information that the coup d'état had failed and the attacks on the Netherlands, Belgium and France were imminent.

There is no doubt that, according to the letter of the law, what Josef Müller and those whose missions he carried out had taken upon themselves was treason. Hans Oster even went a step further. He arranged a meeting with the Dutch military attaché, who was a friend of his, revealed the plans to attack the Netherlands, including the date, and implored him to see that the German advance was hindered by blowing up all the relevant bridges in the Netherlands. However, the government in The Hague did not believe this message. Before taking this action, Oster had held a long conversation with Bonhoeffer about what would be the responsible thing to do in such a situation; for of course it was clear to him that he was about to put the lives of German soldiers at risk. On the issue of treason, Bethge says:

Bonhoeffer regarded Oster's action on the eve of the Western offensive as a step taken on his own final responsibility ... 'Treason' had become true patriotism, and what was normally 'patriotism' had become treason. An officer saw [Hitler's] diabolical reversal of all values, and acted entirely alone to prevent new outrages in other countries, such as those he had experienced in Poland – and the pastor approved of what he did. (DB-ER 675)

When Eberhard Bethge was writing his biography of Bonhoeffer, heated discussions were still going on as to whether the men of the Resistance had betrayed their fatherland. Bethge and others were and are right to deny that they had. For us today it seems more logical to ask how the German elite, to which Brauchitsch belonged, could share in the guilt by continuing their unconditional obedience, for so long, to a regime which committed such crimes.

Bonhoeffer knew about the early coup attempts, and was in Berlin on the crucial days, but he was not yet a member of the Military Intelligence resistance group. He only began 'leading two lives', as a Confessing Church pastor on one hand and as a Military Intelligence staff member on the other – just those closest to him were allowed to know about the latter – after Hitler's surprising victory over France. That the German troops – against the predictions of military leaders, who had foreseen a long war – overran France in a few weeks, made Hitler 'the greatest commander of all time' in

At the signing of the ceasefire with France in the Forest of Compiègne, 22 June 1940. Left to right: Foreign Minister Ribbentrop, Wilhelm Keitel, Hermann Göring, Rudolf Heß, Adolf Hitler, Großadmiral Raeder (hidden behind Hitler) and General Brauchitsch

the eyes of the people, and Goebbels made plentiful use of their approval. The injustice done to Germany by the Allies in 1918, he proclaimed, had now been repaid. Hitler had restored the reign of justice. To make sure everyone 'got the picture', the French delegation was made to sign the armistice in the 'railroad car of Compiègne', the same fancy railway carriage in which the Germans had signed the armistice in 1918. Dietrich Bonhoeffer mentioned this event during a trip to Switzerland, about which we shall have more to say, in a text intended for his friends in England.

The deepest reason for the ethical confusion has ... to do with the fact that the greatest injustice, as it is embodied in the National Socialist [Nazi] regime, was able to clothe itself in the garb of relative historical and social justice. The railroad car of Compiègne is nothing less than the symbol of how evil feeds on pseudojustice. For those who do not see through the demonic nature of evil manifesting itself in the form of justice, this becomes the poisonous source of all ethical disintegration. That it has been possible for Hitler to make himself the executor of a relative historical justice derives not least from England's willingness since 1933 to extend to Hitler all those concessions it denied the Weimar Republic. Thereby England – certainly strengthened by the loyalty of broad church circles in Germany toward Hitler – took the side of Hitler against his domestic opposition. Thus both from within and without, Hitler received moral support for his claim to be the God-given executor of historical justice, and only a small remnant was able to perceive, precisely here, Satan in the form of an angel of light. (2 Cor. 11:14; DBWE 16, 530–31)

The conspirators knew, after Hitler's victory in France, that they would find people prepared to help them among the top ranks of the military only if it was plain that this victory would be followed by catastrophic defeats. And only then would the people have any understanding for a need to overthrow the government.

For a long time Bonhoeffer had simply been one of those who were 'in the know' about the plans for a coup, but now, through his close contact with Hans von Dohnanyi, he was increasingly taking on the role of an adviser. During the discussions of Josef Müller's experiences with the Vatican, Bonhoeffer's connections abroad came under consideration. Very few of the conspirators had close and reliable relationships with influential people in the countries opposed to Hitler. In the Foreign Office there was, notably, Adam von Trott, who made great personal efforts, time and again, to establish contacts between the conspirators and the Western Allies. But some of his former friends in Oxford had conceived a suspicion that he had become a Nazi supporter in disguise, and were warning highly placed people in the United States against him. The secret service there, which kept Trott under surveillance from then on, came to grotesquely false conclusions about him; but their suspicion in turn had its effect in Great Britain. Unjust though this was, it brought about the failure of all the actions undertaken by this highly gifted and steadfast member of the conspiracy.[4]

In arranging a putsch a great deal depended on the reaction of the Western powers, for only with proof that they were prepared to wait and not move against Germany could it still be possible to gain the cooperation of any high-ranking military officer. So it was logical for the resistance group in Military Intelligence to be interested in having Bonhoeffer begin working actively with it.

Visitations in East Prussia

On 18 March 1940, Bonhoeffer's collective pastorate was closed by the police. Once again it was faithful Erna Struwe, the housekeeper at Finkenwalde who had moved with the community to Sigurdshof, who was handed the police order to close the house. But this did not mean that Bonhoeffer was unemployed as a pastor. Contacts between congregations of the Confessing Church had now been made incredibly difficult. The ministers of many such congregations had been conscripted into military service, leaving them without pastoral care of any sort. 'Visiting pastorates' were therefore set up, and no one was better suited to 'ride a circuit' such as this than Bonhoeffer, who was assigned to the Confessing parishes in East Prussia.

He waited anxiously in Berlin for news of the British defeat at Dunkirk, which was really a victory since most of the British troops got across the Channel safely. But Bonhoeffer was concerned about his sister Sabine and her family, fearing that Hitler would immediately order the invasion of Britain. However, the day after Dunkirk, Bonhoeffer and Bethge set off eastwards to Tilsit and Memel. There they could preach in churches filled to overflowing; there they met pastors' wives who were carrying on with Christian education, and a farmer who, in his capacity as a local church elder, was holding worship services. So they came back from this trip with a proposal to set up training courses for lay preachers within the Confessing Church.

On 17 June 1940, during that first visitation journey, Bonhoeffer and Bethge had arrived in the village of Memel and were sitting in the garden of a café on the peninsula opposite the town, enjoying the sunshine. Suddenly Franz Liszt's fanfare came booming from every loudspeaker, signalling a special radio announcement by Goebbels: France had surrendered. Bethge, who was still having trouble behaving in such a way as to disguise his convictions, later wrote:

The people around the tables could hardly contain themselves; they jumped up, and some even climbed on the chairs. With outstretched arms they sang *Deutschland, Deutschland über alles* and the Horst Wessel song.[5] We had stood up, too. Bonhoeffer raised his arm in the regulation Hitler salute, while I stood there dazed. 'Raise your arm! Are you crazy?' he whispered to me, and later: 'We shall have to run risks for very different things now, but not for that salute!' (DB-ER 681)

On his second journey to East Prussia, on which Bethge did not go with him, Bonhoeffer ran into trouble. He was at a weekend retreat in Bloestau, sitting with some students from Königsberg, when the Gestapo appeared and asked questions, wrote down the names and addresses of the participants, and dissolved the gathering. Although Bonhoeffer had the feeling that this would not be the end of it, he continued his journey further east, where Soviet troops had been seen across the Russian border and people were worried. While Germany was celebrating Hitler's victory in the west, Stalin had taken over the areas named in his non-aggression pact with Hitler[6] as legitimately under the influence of the Soviet Union. Bonhoeffer gave up the rest of his planned visitations and a holiday at Klein-Krössin, Ruth von Kleist-Retzow's manor, and returned immediately to Berlin to seek Dohnanyi's advice.

While Bonhoeffer was in East Prussia, Dohnanyi had clarified with Oster that his brother-in-law was to be brought into the work they were doing, and Oster had secured Canaris's consent. It was now decided that during Bonhoeffer's third visitation trip, he would have the protection of a Military Intelligence assignment.

On the way to Königsberg, Bonhoeffer and all the other passengers had to get off the train at Dirschau because the bridge over the Weichsel River had been blown up during the invasion of Poland. The passengers were ferried across; on the other side another train was waiting, but it had fewer carriages and all its seats were soon full. Bonhoeffer would have had to stand in the corridor, together with 'elderly women, officers etc.', had he not firmly demanded that in each second-class compartment the six places be occupied by eight persons. 'I did this because a large number of very young people had climbed through the windows into the compartments ... Good manners are going rapidly out of circulation' (DBWE 16, 72).

In Königsberg Bonhoeffer made sure to visit the Military Intelligence officer, and was more cautious in carrying out his church work. But after only a few days, Superintendent Block telephoned from Schlawe: Bonhoeffer was to report to the police there immediately. When he arrived, a Gestapo officer informed him that, according to orders from the Reich SS Headquarters, he was now banned from public speaking throughout the Reich, on the grounds of 'activity subverting the people'. Furthermore he was to report regularly to the authorities in the town where he resided, and inform them beforehand of any travel.

It turns out that the Reich SS Headquarters was reacting to a report that was discovered 50 years later, after the overthrow of the communist East German government, in its state archives. Among the students from Königsberg with whom Bonhoeffer had met during his second East Prussian trip there was a police informer, whom the Gestapo had made a show of interrogating along with the others. His report had been forwarded directly to the SS Headquarters by the Gestapo in Königsberg (DBWE 16, 62ff). In Schlawe, Bonhoeffer wrote down the file number of the order against him, which was not given him in writing, and protested in a letter to the SS that it was not possible for him to submit to the charge of 'activity subverting the people'. He cited, as related in Chapter 1, the merits of his ancestors and their service to the fatherland in a suitably dignified manner. He never received a reply.

As a confidential agent for Military Intelligence

In a discussion with Dohnanyi in late July 1940, the final decision was made that Bonhoeffer would serve as a *V-Mann* (*Verbindungsmann*, or confidential agent) for Military Intelligence under Admiral Canaris. It was possible for Military Intelligence to have him granted a 'UK' classification – *'unabkömmlich'*, indispensable – thus making him unavailable for conscription into the army. But was it wise to employ as an agent a pastor who was already on the Gestapo's blacklist? At the time, Bonhoeffer heard Colonel Oster use words which he cleverly turned to his advantage later, during his interrogations: 'Military Intelligence works with anyone, with Communists and with Jews, so why not also with Confessing Church people?' But of course there was no point in provoking the Gestapo unnecessarily by assigning Bonhoeffer to the central office in Berlin. So it was decided to send him as far away from Schlawe as possible, to the Military Intelligence office in Munich, where other opponents of the regime, notably his friend Josef Müller, were already working.

In order to get around the Gestapo, Bonhoeffer's actual employer, the Old Prussian Council of Brethren, had to release him and at the same time continue to employ him, without telling the Council members the reasons behind this. Their legal advisor Perels, who was in on the Resistance plans, proposed to the Council that Bonhoeffer be put on leave in order to work on his *Ethics* which he had begun writing, noting that this was also necessary because he was 'needed militarily in Berlin'. The Council of Brethren agreed to be satisfied with this, since Bonhoeffer had the absolute trust of all its members. His salary was also continued; but from then on he took 30 to 50 per cent less than the full amount, since it was becoming harder and harder for the Confessing Church to fulfil its financial obligations to the pastors who had been suspended without pay from their pastorates, and to the 'illegals' and their families. Bonhoeffer was never on the Military Intelligence payroll, and would have refused any remuneration as an 'agent'. However, he was happy to accept support from his sister Sabine Leibholz and her husband, who still had a bank account in Germany which had not been discovered by the Gestapo. When this combined income was still far less then the salary to which he was entitled, Dohnanyi also helped out. He maintained a special account for the benefit of the Confessing Church, which had been set up for just such purposes, and was replenished from time to time by Carl Friedrich Goerdeler, the former mayor of Leipzig and one of the leading members of the Resistance, who collected the necessary money in his circle of friends.

Bonhoeffer was now walking a path that only those who were pursuing the same path were allowed to know about; but that did not mean he had burned all his bridges behind him. He had to lead two lives; but to him this was not a contradiction of his faith, nor did he consider his ministry as a pastor and teacher in the Confessing Church to be over. He had taken the step of joining the Resistance on the basis of an ethical decision.

Hitler, along with his countless fanatical supporters, had to be prevented from committing further crimes, and the only way of stopping him that was left was to eliminate him altogether. Not only the hordes of Germans who were carrying out his orders, but every individual and every group that quietly suffered these crimes to continue – even the Church – shared in the guilt for what was happening in Germany and in the regions its troops were occupying. The need to keep quiet in order to survive did not excuse anyone. In this situation, the conspirators needed to do everything possible to stop the crimes of the government, to 'seize the wheel itself' and bring it to a standstill, as Bonhoeffer had said in 1933.[7] In his view they were acting on behalf of all Germans, and also on behalf of the churches in Germany.

Working as an agent always means entering a twilight zone, and so it was for Bonhoeffer. He had to deceive the people around him about what he was doing. He accepted this shady aspect for himself personally, and soberly realized that the Confessing Church might someday be in a situation in which it would have to distance itself from him. Even then, he felt that his actions were legitimate for him as a servant of the Church. Until 1939 Bonhoeffer had been contemplating the idea of accepting martyrdom as a conscientious objector to military service. Now, as he took up the role of a confidential agent, it meant that from 1940 onward he was still prepared to sacrifice his life. He could no longer be concerned, now, about his own obedience and personal Christian witness; instead, he must dedicate himself to the destiny of Germany and the destiny of all persons who were threatened by the Reich's arbitrary and murderous plans.

Bonhoeffer's ability to keep his mouth shut was not the least of the reasons why he was chosen for this responsibility. None of the Finkenwaldians, with whom he had shared everything he knew about the church struggle, was allowed to know anything about his new assignment. But to him this was no reason to break contact with his former students. He continued his correspondence with them, and it remained an important part of his work until he was arrested. In the days before Christmas 1940 alone, he sent 90 letters through the military post to soldiers in the field.

No other Confessing Church pastor led such an unusual life as did Bonhoeffer in the time between his joining Military Intelligence in October 1940 and his arrest on 5 April 1943. Periods of working completely undisturbed on his theology – in the home of Ruth von Kleist-Retzow, at Ettal in Bavaria, or in his attic room in Berlin – alternated with hectic weeks in which he carried out assignments for the conspiracy, travelling in overcrowded trains that were blacked out at night, or by aeroplane or ferry. In all, he covered well over 30,000 miles.

During this time he continued, as a pastor, conducting funerals and keeping contact with those of his students who were soldiers and with the few still working as pastors in remote villages. He wrote pastoral letters to the families of his students and friends who had died at the front, and despite being banned from public speaking he held discussions in small groups and helped wherever he could. As a theologian he was not only working on his *Ethics*, but also taking part in Confessing Church committee meetings and writing expert opinions for the Church.

Through his close contact with Visser 't Hooft in Geneva, Bonhoeffer became by far the most important German partner for the ecumenical movement during these years. Political developments in the Third Reich had caused Bishop Heckel to become discredited; there was no longer any trust in him. Schönfeld on the other hand, who had been the Church Foreign Office's man in Geneva, was now a supporter of the opposition. Soon after the invasion of Poland, around Christmastime in 1939, he and Bonhoeffer had come closer together. Schönfeld and the Swede Nils Ehrenström, who also worked in Geneva, had brought Roswell Barnes, an adviser to President Roosevelt, to Germany. At that time the United States was not yet on the opposing side in the war. A secret meeting was held at the Goßner Mission in Berlin, on the invitation of its director, Hans Lokies, who was Schönfeld's brother-in-law. On the German side the participants included the teacher and theologian Oskar Hammelsbeck, Helmut Gollwitzer and Dietrich Bonhoeffer. Even more important was a second secret meeting between the American and Swedish guests and a 'retired general' whose name they were not told. He gave Barnes and Ehrenström to understand that in Germany, even in the military, there were strong Resistance movements against Hitler's policies. This was the first time that anyone on the Geneva staff had heard this.

The fact that Schönfeld was allowed to take part in both conversations showed that at that time he had already cut his inner ties to Heckel and gone over to the opposition; and Bonhoeffer must have known that he had crossed the line, for otherwise he would have refused any contact with Schönfeld.

Half a year later, Dohnanyi and Bonhoeffer met with Schönfeld in Potsdam and proposed that he, too, take on some work for Canaris's office, thus in reality for the Resistance. At that point Bonhoeffer was finally convinced that Hans Schönfeld had changed his mind, and Dohnanyi even had the impression that he was grateful to be accepted for such an assignment.[8] This must also have improved Schönfeld's relationship with Visser 't Hooft, his new boss. Furthermore, in making such a decision it must have helped him greatly that his partner in Heckel's Foreign Office, Eugen Gerstenmaier, had also quietly decided against the Nazi authorities and in favour of the Resistance group within the Reich Foreign Office.

As a member of the Resistance, Bonhoeffer had to try above all to make contacts with notable persons abroad who could exercise political influence within their countries. Contacts of this sort were easiest to come by through the good offices of Visser 't Hooft. Since the preparations for these conversations also required Bonhoeffer to engage in confidential discussions in Berlin, people increasingly came to trust his advice. He was asked to help in drawing up memoranda for the conspirators, and was included in conversations with Carl Goerdeler – whom they intended to install as Reich Chancellor after the coup d'état – and the former trade union leaders Wilhelm Leuschner and Jakob Kaiser.

Bonhoeffer's Ethics

After the war there were still reports, from Kurt Scharf, Wilhelm Niesel and others, that at a Council of Brethren meeting in early July 1940 at Nowawes (today Babelsberg) near Potsdam, Bonhoeffer bowed before Hitler's success in France as if it were the judgement of God. He is supposed to have said that after this victory it was necessary to accept a totally new situation. This memory, like the impression his words made at the time, is based on a misunderstanding. The Council of Brethren had no idea of the attempts at a putsch that had failed to come off, so it could not be clear to them what Bonhoeffer meant. He knew that, after the invasion of France, it would be a long and tortuous time before hopes of overthrowing the government could be renewed, but he could not give his friends in the Confessing Church the slightest indication that these were his thoughts. The book he was writing, *Ethics*, sheds light on the real meaning of his words at that time:

The successful create facts that cannot be reversed. What they destroy cannot be restored. What they construct has, at least in the following generation, the right of existence. No condemnation can make good the wrong that the successful commit ... The judges of history play a sad role alongside those who make history; history rolls over them. (DBWE 6, 88–89)

Yet this formulation as such is not unambiguous. It is only the next paragraph that shows clearly what Bonhoeffer wanted to say:

Where the figure of a successful person becomes especially prominent, the majority fall into *idolizing success*. They become blind to right and wrong, truth and lie, decency and malice ... Success per se is the good. This attitude is only genuine and excusable while one is intoxicated by events. After sobriety returns it can be maintained only at the cost of deep inner hypocrisy, with conscious self-deception. (DBWE 6, 89)

Bonhoeffer did not give even a moment's thought to going over to the 'successful' side. Another temptation was much greater: to withdraw into one's own inner world, and – hoping in God – to leave the outer world to the Evil One. In those days it was not only Christians who were choosing to 'migrate within'. That Bonhoeffer was not considering this option either is proven by his decision to join the conspirators. They, however, for a long time after Hitler's astonishing victory in France, were stunned and struggling to get their wind back. This was even true of Hans von Dohnanyi, who was suffering attacks of depression. It helped him during that time that Helmuth von Moltke made contact with him. Moltke had also joined the staff of Military Intelligence at the beginning of the war and was working in the department of international law.[9] He was able to turn Dohnanyi's attention to the time after Hitler's regime, for which it was essential to prepare. During that period, he and his wife often met socially with the Dohnanyis.

Because Dohnanyi did not want to take any risks in arranging Bonhoeffer's move to the Munich office, he recommended to his brother-in-law the working holiday at Ruth von Kleist's home, Klein-Krössin, which has already been mentioned, so that all might be ready ahead of time in Munich. This took place in October 1940. So when Bonhoeffer arrived on 30 October to take up his new duties, he had just completed four weeks of intensive work on his *Ethics*. Teaching Christians how to conduct themselves in the world according to the will of God had been a topic that had occupied him since his time in Barcelona. His plan to write a book on ethics seems to date from the beginning of the war.

Hitler's success in the invasion of France, as we have seen, had aroused entirely new thoughts in him, and further insights during the course of his work in the Resistance affected the conception and style of the book. Unfortunately, Bonhoeffer was never able to finish what was, to him, his most important work. Four drafts exist of the first chapter, followed by thirteen or fourteen further sections which had to be fitted together, like a jigsaw puzzle, after the war. Some are complete chapters, while others are only fragments. His work was interrupted at irregular intervals by missions on behalf of the conspiracy.[10]

Thus Bonhoeffer's *Ethics* was 'written and lived' by turns, and this makes it a fascinating book to this day. It is not a reference work in which one can 'look up' what one should do in this or that situation, but in any case that was not the sort of book Bonhoeffer wanted to write. The fragments we possess have nonetheless retained a relevance that is often astounding, even for us today.[11]

At one point Bonhoeffer had considered 'Preparing the Way and Entering in [*Wegbereitung und Einzug*]' as the title for this book. He was as much opposed to an idealistic, above-the-world, view of reality as to a positivist view that tends to divest the world of value. For him, the reality of the world was its reality as reconciled by Christ (2 Corinthians 5:19). In Christ, God accepted the world, and it is because of God's Yes to it that it can become the place in which human beings assume responsibility, make peace, protect life and overcome murder, violence and atrocities. If this is the way we see reality, we cannot uphold any principles, standards or duties as eternally valid for other persons, but can only encourage them, in every historical situation, to listen anew to God's commandments and to follow Christ. Thus during the Resistance – to name only two, very serious examples – Bonhoeffer took the view, on one hand, that Hitler must be eliminated by assassination because it had become impossible to arrest and imprison him. On the other hand, in the case of euthanasia, he adhered strictly to the commandment 'Thou shalt not kill.' Only a Christian who understands that he or she is free can make the right ethical decisions.

> The relationship between God and human beings that has been realized [*verwirklicht*] in Jesus Christ is the ultimate reason why this is the case. Jesus stands before God as the obedient one and as the free one. As the obedient one, he does the will of the Father by blindly following the law he has been commanded. As the free one, he affirms God's will out of his very own insight, with open eyes and a joyful heart; it is as if he re-creates it anew out of himself ... Obedience has tied hands, freedom is creative. In rendering obedience, human beings observe God's decalogue (Ten Commandments); in exercising freedom, they create new 'decalogues'. (DBWE 6, 287)[12]

While Bonhoeffer was at Klein-Krössin working on his *Ethics*, beginning with a section entitled 'Christ, the Reality and the Good' in which he asked basic questions about what an *Ethics* could accomplish, a generation of British fighter pilots, at the cost of tremendous sacrifices, was defeating Hermann Göring's Luftwaffe and thus preventing Germany's invasion of Britain. Only a few years before, as students at Oxford, they had declared in a spectacular battle of words that they were 'not ready to fight for king and country'.[13] Now they had beaten their German opponents in the 'Battle of Britain', of which Churchill said in Parliament that 'Never in the field of human conflict was so much owed by so many to so few.' Bonhoeffer wrote to his parents, with a veiled reference to this battle: 'While outdoors a mighty autumn storm is ripping the leaves from the trees ... I'm sitting here quietly at my work.'

With the Benedictines in Ettal

Bonhoeffer set off for Munich in the hope that he would be able to do theological work there as well. First of all, however, he had to see whether Dohnanyi's plan to fit him in there would work. An aunt, Countess Christine von Kalckreuth, whose home in the Schwabing district was a gathering place for actors and artists, took him in pro forma, since he had to be registered with the police at a Munich address in order for Military Intelligence to have him, as a new citizen of Munich, classified 'indispensable' with the Military Registration office there. 'Ninne', as his aunt was called within the family, kept a room available for him to spend the night whenever he had business in Munich. The place where he was really to stay was to be found outside the city. When he finally received his 'UK' classification on 14 January, a period of nervous tension was over, since he now no longer had to report on his movements in Schlawe.

Josef Müller had offered to find lodgings for Bonhoeffer outside Munich, and it seems to have been Paula Bonhoeffer who asked him whether the monastery in Ettal might be a possibility for her son. For several reasons, Müller found this an ideal solution. The Benedictines of Ettal were opposed to Nazism. One of them, Father Johannes, maintained a close contact with the conspirators. So Bonhoeffer would be in surroundings in which he would not have to become involved in conversations with people he did not know. Though he was good at finding his way quickly in changed situations, his new duties were unfamiliar and he needed some quiet in order to prepare for them. As for his theological work, there was no better place than the monastery, with its sizeable library. At night he would not be disturbed by air raid sirens, and no one would ask out of curiosity what a healthy young man was doing out of uniform in Munich in the middle of a war. There were eventually some questions asked, even in the little town of Ettal, but the monks knew how to handle them.

Bonhoeffer was very happy with this proposal. The abbot, who had to extend the invitation, was taken into the conspirators' confidence. The guest was given a room in the hotel Ludwig der Bayer opposite the monastery. He was invited to meals with the monks, and was even given a key for the closed area of the monastery where guests were normally not allowed. He could work in the library any time he liked.

After the weeks of tension with the ban on public speaking and obligation to report his movements, Bonhoeffer could not have found a better place to be than this monastery in the mountains, where the worship, the daily prayer offices and conversations with the Fathers were congenial and many things reminded him of Finkenwalde. He was not completely unknown to his hosts, as the abbot and some of the monks had read *Life Together* and wanted to discuss it with him. At mealtimes, silence was observed while a monk read aloud; during the Christmas season, the readings were from *Discipleship*.

In Ettal, Bonhoeffer wrote the chapter on 'Ultimate and Penultimate Things', one of the strongest parts of his *Ethics*. The distinction between 'ultimate' and 'penultimate', as we have seen, had already appeared in one of his sermons in Barcelona. By now Bonhoeffer had more experience at a personal level with this distinction and could develop the theme fully.

> The origin and essence of all Christian life are consummated in the one event that the Reformation has called the justification of the sinner by grace alone. It is not what a person is per se, but what a person is in this event, that gives us insight into the Christian life. Here the length and breadth of human life are concentrated in one moment, one point; the whole of life is embraced in this event ... The dark tunnel of human life, which was barred within and without and was disappearing ever more deeply into an abyss from which there is no exit, is powerfully torn open; the word of God bursts in. In this saving light, people recognize God and their neighbors for the first time. The labyrinth of their previous lives collapses. They become free for God and for one another. (DBWE 6, 146)

Bonhoeffer is speaking here about the faith which can never be a community experience, only an individual one. But can the person of faith live by this experience of the ultimate alone? Can faith – and that doesn't mean 'the memory of past faith, or of repeating articles of faith', but rather true faith – be 'realised daily and hourly' (DBWE 6, 152)? No; during this life there are only 'moments of the ultimate'. God lets human beings live in the penultimate. But they must always be on the lookout, throughout its length and breadth, for the ultimate. The 'penultimate' is life as human beings live it in a 'time of God's permission, waiting and preparation'. Even the person of faith lives in this 'penultimate', and for Bonhoeffer it included, not least, everything having to do with the conspiracy. It also meant that, even when one had to live in such a terrible time as the

Second World War, it was perfectly all right to enjoy one's life and happy times spent with friends, but knowing always that 'there is an ultimate time that judges and breaks off the penultimate' (DBWE 6, 151).

When we realize that Ettal very soon became anything but 'shut away from the world' for Bonhoeffer, we can only marvel that he had any time to write while he was there. Five days after he arrived, his sister Christine appeared with her three children, who were to go to boarding school in Ettal so as to be safe from the bombings. She herself immediately returned to Berlin, but when she later visited she was able to carry news back and forth. No sooner was she gone than her younger son Christoph von Dohnanyi, Bonhoeffer's godson, now a world-famous orchestral conductor, went down with a bad case of influenza. His uncle took him to his hotel room and cared for him until he was well again.

Around the same time, other 'evacuees from the bombing' arrived in Ettal – a hundred schoolgirls from Hamburg with their teachers. Bonhoeffer felt that even in Catholic Bavaria they should not do without Protestant religious instruction. He discussed the matter with Bishop Meiser in Munich, whom he would never have consulted during the Finkenwalde years because of Meiser's refusal to support the 'destroyed' churches on the Dahlem side in the church struggle. The bishop sent a member of his staff, Hermann Dietzfelbinger, to Ettal once every fortnight to hold a worship service for the youngsters and give them religious instruction. So there were constant problems, great or small, to interrupt Bonhoeffer's work. But, as in Finkenwalde, he was helped by his ability to concentrate and to write down his thoughts at speed.

Bonhoeffer was still concerned about the Confessing Church. He used his connections to try and reduce the number of Confessing pastors who were being conscripted into military service without any choice in the matter. Until then, the indescribable Mr Werner saw to it that only German Christian pastors were granted exemptions as 'indispensable'. Dohnanyi got Justice Minister Gürtner, whose son was also at the boarding school in Ettal, to enter into negotiations with Religious Affairs Minister Kerrl. When Gürtner came to visit his son at the school in December 1940, Bonhoeffer went for a long walk with him and expressed his wishes in this regard; Gürtner indicated in response that that he had already held an initial conversation with Kerrl and hoped to be able to do something for the Confessing Church. Eberhard Bethge was also present; he had come to Ettal for the Christmas holidays, and the two friends had been skiing almost every day. But the day of the conversation with Gürtner was so icy cold that he and Bonhoeffer exchanged anxious glances, because for so long the minister made no sign of being ready to turn back. Since the Gürtners also spent Christmas in Ettal with their son, a joint family celebration was held with the Dohnanyis, Bonhoeffer and Bethge at the hotel.

Gürtner's unexpected death in January 1941 was a heavy blow not only to his family, but also to his friends. Hitler's Minister of Justice was a tragic figure. He had struggled desperately to keep Germany in obedience to its own laws, but for seven years had put his signature to orders that represented violations of the law. He stayed at his post because he knew that if he resigned, he would only make way for one of Hitler's 'terrible lawyers'. To Dohnanyi he had been a fatherly friend. Gürtner was a Catholic, but to the outrage of the Benedictine fathers in Ettal the Catholic Church refused him a church burial.[14] Bishop Meiser therefore conducted a Protestant funeral, which was attended by the abbot, Father Johannes and Bonhoeffer from the Ettal monastery. Christine von Dohnanyi, whose husband was in Italy on business, came from Berlin and, with her children, stood by Mrs Gürtner and her son.

It had not been possible for Gürtner to gain agreement from Kerrl to grant exemptions from military service to pastors of the Confessing

Christmas 1940 in Ettal. Left to right: Klaus von Dohnanyi, Dietrich Bonhoeffer, Barbara and Christoph von Dohnanyi, Eberhard Bethge

Church along with the others. So the only way left was to help in individual cases. At Bonhoeffer's request, Dohnanyi and Oster were able to gain exemptions for Niesel, Perels and Rott, whose work was indispensable to the Confessing Church.

After the war the two were reproached with having endangered the Resistance movement unnecessarily by pursuing such measures, and in fact these exemptions were among the accusations raised against them after they were arrested and charged.[15] But Dohnanyi and Oster were aware of this danger and accepted it as necessary. They were thinking of the time beyond the assassination of Hitler. In a postwar Germany the Confessing Church would be needed, and therefore the people who had worked in the most responsible positions within it could not be sacrificed.

One person whose help was most important in this matter was Lieutenant Colonel Groscurth, a pastor's son from Bremen, who served as Military Intelligence's liaison officer to the Military High Command. At Bonhoeffer's request he agreed to see pastors Kurt Scharf and Wilhelm Niesel and hear their report on the lack of pastors in the Confessing Church. Afterwards, he was able to convince Army Commander in Chief Brauchitsch to help in gaining 'UK' status for a number of pastors.

Groscurth was in the inner circle of conspirators in Military Intelligence. After the invasion of Poland, he had sought out one commander after another on the western front and told them about the atrocities in Poland, in order to mobilize them to oppose such crimes. Hitler and Himmler found out about this and were furious, as Major General Jodl reported in his diary.[16] Groscurth was transferred to the western front as commander of an infantry battalion, which amounted to a demotion. This was a great loss to the conspirators in Military Intelligence. During the invasion of Russia, Groscurth was made chief of staff of an army corps, was taken prisoner in Stalingrad and died in Siberia of typhus in 1943.

The issue of 'legalization' of 'illegal' pastors also continued to occupy Bonhoeffer for a long time to come. After the first year of the war, when the majority of younger Confessing Church pastors had served half a year or more with the fighting troops (*Frontbewährung*), it became evident that those in power had no intention of honouring the dedication they had shown. 'Golden bridges' were being built for the 'illegal' pastors to entice them to the consistories, but Werner and his people would not give up insisting on their complete subjection. No pastor who refused to renounce the Confessing Church was exempted from further military service, and his family remained without support beyond what the Confessing Church could raise from donations. Younger pastors judged 'unfit' for military service, together with women pastoral assistants in the Confessing Church, were sent to work in factories. In this situation, Bonhoeffer did not break off contact with those who did go over to the consistories. But he kept counselling his former ordinands until the last to remain true to the resolutions of the Dahlem synod.

After the war, the few 'illegals' who were still living and had never submitted to the consistories of the 'official' church were welcomed by the consistories and accorded all the rights of 'legal' pastors. The view was not taken that those pastors and church officials who had sworn the oath of loyalty to Hitler, and made various other compromises, had to 'return to legality'; rather, those who had borne the burden of the church struggle were granted equal status with them.

During the years of the church struggle, hopes had been nourished in Finkenwalde and the other seminaries for a renewal of the Church and new forms of pastoral work. But the consistories made sure, in 1945, to begin again where they had left off in 1933, as indeed the Federal Republic of Germany was doing, to a large extent, in the era of Chancellor Konrad Adenauer.

The ecumenical movement had long been understood as international cooperation among churches of different confessions. The Catholic Church had never participated, as a matter of principle, and did not reverse its principled refusal until 1961. In the years before the Second World War there was no contact between Germany's two major churches. They had never considered it desirable. The persecutions that increasingly affected both after 1933, however, began to bring about changes, and it was now that the first encounters took place. Bonhoeffer's relations with Catholics while he was in Ettal were part of this development. He came into close contact with Prelate Neuhäusler in Munich, with the abbot of Metten Monastery, and above all with Father Johannes in Ettal, who became a friend of the Bonhoeffer family; when he was in Berlin he was glad to come to the Bonhoeffer parents' home for confidential conversations.

We should know nothing about all this had not the extremely lively letters exchanged between Bonhoeffer and Bethge during that time been preserved. But even these, of course, do not reveal a word of what would interest us most, that is, what was truly being discussed in each of these conversations. Prelate Neuhäusler, who was later Suffragan Bishop of Munich, enjoyed his relations with Bonhoeffer because, among other things, the latter always knew the latest political jokes. In response to Bonhoeffer's questions, Neuhäusler told him about recent developments in Catholic ethics, arranged for him to meet theologians, and helped obtain books for both him and Bethge, who had been working at the Goßner Mission in Berlin since the autumn of 1940. Bonhoeffer had advised his friend that, as 'inspector of missions', he should make contact with Catholic institutions for both foreign and home missions and study their writings. Neuhäusler was pleased, and when an important book was no longer available, he immediately sent Bethge his own copy in care of Bonhoeffer. Thus it was a blow to Bonhoeffer as well when, soon afterwards, Neuhäusler was sent to the concentration camp at Dachau, where he remained until the war was over. But it was a comfort to his many friends to hear that he not only had a cell to himself, but also shared a common sitting-room with two Catholic priests and Martin Niemöller.

Bonhoeffer was working on the problem of euthanasia for his *Ethics*; it was Nazi policy at the time to put chronically and mentally ill persons to death. This was done on personal orders from Hitler, and was terribly confusing and disturbing to the German people.[17] If a disabled family member had been placed in an institution, and soon afterwards the news arrived that the person had died suddenly of pneumonia, those who received such messages found it hard to believe them. Rumours soon began to circulate that such people were being murdered by their doctors. Goebbels had a film specially made, entitled 'I accuse [*Ich klage an*]', suggesting to audiences that it was cruel to let people with serious disabilities go on living. In Tübingen, medical students sat in the back row at the cinema and held their caps in front of the projector, so that it became impossible to show the film. As 'officers who had fought on various fronts', they wanted to force an open discussion on this topic.[18]

Bonhoeffer had arranged a conversation in Berlin between his father, Friedrich von Bodelschwingh and his colleague Paul Braune, director of the Lobethal Institute. For the two visitors, the important thing was to save their mentally ill patients in Lobethal and Bethel.[19] Braune was sent to a concentration camp shortly thereafter because of a memorandum in which he protested against the euthanasia measures. But the protests were not in vain, notably that of Count Galen, the Catholic Bishop of Münster; Hitler was obliged to order the measures stopped within the Reich.[20] Bonhoeffer's contacts with the Benedictine Monastery of Metten appear also to have had to do with the euthanasia problem. The abbot of Metten was an especially knowledgeable person with whom to discuss it. Bonhoeffer wrote to Bethge: 'I find Catholic ethics in many ways very instructive and more practical than ours. Up to now we have always dismissed it as casuistry.[21] Today we are grateful for much – precisely on the topic of my present theme' (DBWE 16, 126).

Bonhoeffer found euthanasia in any form reprehensible, with the exception of cases in which a patient of completely sound mind clearly expressed the wish to die. But, in order to avoid any chance of being misinterpreted, he treated this problem under the heading of suicide.

First journey to Switzerland

After his third trip through East Prussia, Bonhoeffer had written reports to serve as a basis for approval of his work for Military Intelligence. Not only did these reports need to be formulated with great care and checked by Dohnanyi, word for word; Bonhoeffer also had to learn how to conduct himself within Military Intelligence. In its offices there were fanatical Party members. Some of these people did not trust Oster, and trusted Dohnanyi even less, and such feelings could only be strengthened by having a politically discredited Confessing Church pastor working for them.

However, the Resistance's main opponents were not those in Military Intelligence, but rather people in the Reich SS Headquarters, whose second in command, Reinhard Heydrich, had already demanded in 1936 that the political Intelligence Service be exclusively under SS control. Admiral Canaris, according to Heydrich, should confine himself to purely military reconnaissance work outside the country. After vehement arguments and long negotiations, Canaris and Heydrich had arrived at an agreement which was referred to as the 'Ten Commandments'. Heydrich interpreted it very strictly, while Canaris had no intention of refraining from gathering 'military political information'. As a result, fresh quarrels constantly erupted, until Heydrich forced Canaris, in a meeting at the castle in Prague, to sign an agreement that defined the 'Ten Commandments' much more narrowly. A few days later, Heydrich was assassinated – he had been made Deputy High Protector of Czechoslovakia, residing in Prague Castle, and two members of the Czech Resistance threw a bomb into his open car.[22]

When Bonhoeffer, who really knew nothing about military matters, was carrying out assignments for Military Intelligence, there was always the danger that Canaris would be suspected of disregarding once again the boundaries between the jurisdiction of the Reich SS Headquarters and his own. This alone gave Bonhoeffer's superiors good reason to 'comb' his reports with the greatest care.

Bonhoeffer's first official assignment had to do with reconnaissance in Switzerland. On 24 February 1941 he travelled from Munich to Basel. It was the time of Hitler's first setbacks after his victory over France, when the conspirators' hopes were reviving. The German forces had not dared try to invade England. Mussolini, who had entered the war on Hitler's side toward the end of the invasion of France, suffered a fiasco in his attack on Greece, and German troops had to be sent to the Balkans to relieve him. This obliged Hitler to put off his planned invasion of the Soviet Union. Franklin D. Roosevelt had been re-elected President of the United States, and was showing clear sympathy for Churchill's resolute stance.

All this offered the conspirators a new opportunity to win over military command posts for an overthrow of the government. First, however, the Allies had to be informed that such an attempt was again being planned, and consulted as to what conditions they would set for a peace, both requirements of paramount importance in winning the support of military leaders. So Josef Müller was again negotiating with the Vatican, while Bonhoeffer was entrusted with making the necessary contacts through Protestant circles in the Anglo-Saxon countries.

Oster's confidential agent in Switzerland, Hans-Bernd Gisevius, the vice-consul in Zürich, was expressing grave reservations about having a pastor involved, an amateur on this difficult terrain and therefore a risk.[23] He managed to have Bonhoeffer's trip delayed considerably. Gisevius expected to have a monopoly on all contacts made by the Resistance via Switzerland, and had made several disparaging comments about Dohnanyi, who was getting in his way in this regard. Christine von Dohnanyi was right when she reproached Gisevius after the war.

Bonhoeffer's trip to Switzerland was entirely justified, since no one else among the conspirators had such good and reliable friends among British or US church people. We have already mentioned how Adam von Trott – who, like Bonhoeffer, had returned of his own free will from the United States, in 1940 – had encountered a lack of trust among his friends in Britain which he could not overcome, in all his attempts at contacts there. Even Visser 't Hooft, who supported Trott and carried a memorandum from him to London, could not help. On the contrary, the British Foreign Office proposed that such 'strange birds' as Visser 't

Hooft should no longer be granted entry visas. And when Sir Stafford Cripps asked that care be taken not to endanger Trott, the high official in the British Foreign Office who read the memorandum decided that he would probably be of more use to Great Britain as a 'martyr' than if he remained alive.[24] Trott's English biographer is right to speak of a 'German tragedy' here.

There had been no difficulty in obtaining a passport and foreign currency for Bonhoeffer's first trip to Switzerland, but the Swiss entry visa took a long time, and even when he had it, the Swiss border police asked him for a guarantor in Switzerland. Bonhoeffer named Karl Barth, who later said that the matter had seemed very odd to him. A man whom the Gestapo considered an 'enemy of the state' was crossing the Swiss border with valid papers, in the middle of a war? He sent word to Bonhoeffer to come and see him. On the way back, Bonhoeffer stopped in Basel and had a completely open and unreserved conversation with Barth, allaying the latter's fears that he had become a 'turncoat' (DB-ER 727).

But first he had carried out his assignments in Geneva and Zürich. By far the most important conversation he had was with Visser 't Hooft. As a result of the fortunate bond they had spontaneously formed in 1939 on Paddington Station, they could speak with one another as friends. Visser 't Hooft, deeply touched by this surprise visit from Bonhoeffer, wrote immediately to Bishop Bell:

Bonhoeffer was a week with us and spent most of his time extracting ecumenical information from persons and documents. It is touching to see how hungry people like him are for news about their brothers in other countries, and it is good to know that he can take back so much which will encourage his friends at home.

On the other hand, we learned a lot from him. The picture which he gave is pretty black in respect to the exterior circumstances for the community [the Confessing Church] which he represents. The pressure is greater than ever. (DB-ER 729)

However, he could also report that Christians in Germany were 'as eager as ever for fellowship' and 'really have the same reaction to all that has happened and is happening as you or I have'. Of course Bonhoeffer made use of the opportunity to correspond freely with England, and wrote not only to his sister but also to Bell.

For the ecumenical community it was crucial that Visser 't Hooft had been able to get a personal picture of the situation. After talking with Bonhoeffer he knew what had happened in Germany up to that point, that there had been plans to assassinate Hitler and why they had failed.

Siegmund-Schultze and other people Bonhoeffer knew, whom he saw again during this trip, had been finding it hard to go on believing in the opposition when there was no news of any attempt at a putsch.

When Bonhoeffer returned to Germany on 24 March – after visiting his friend Erwin Sutz, who had been making it possible for the Bonhoeffers to stay in contact with the Leibholz family since the beginning of the war – he was able to report to those who had given him his orders that the connections had been made just as they had wished. Bonhoeffer's friends in Geneva had fulfilled all the conspirators' requests, with reports going off immediately to England and the United States.

Müller's negotiations at the Vatican and Bonhoeffer's first trip to Switzerland mark the beginning of what the American historian Klemens von Klemperer termed the 'war behind the war',[25] in which not only the conspirators in Germany, but also a number of influential Christians in Western countries tried to get people to realize that, in contrast to the First World War, the Second World War was not just a conflict between opposing nations, but involved a battle of life and death between two irreconcilable world views. It is part of the tragedy of the German Resistance movement that British public opinion, Winston Churchill first and foremost, did not want to believe that the conspirators in Germany were fighting for the same principles as the peoples of Great Britain and the USA. Churchill wanted to destroy the power of the German state, and it was easier to do so if he declared that all Germans supported the Nazi government. Only in the churches, in England and the United States, were there people who saw at the time that this was not truly the case.[26]

Banned as a writer

When Bonhoeffer stopped over in Munich on the way to Berlin, two letters were waiting for him from the Reich Writers' Guild. The first informed him that he had to pay a fine because he had published writings without being a member of the Guild. The second said that his application of November 1940 for membership in the Guild had been turned down, because he was already banned from public speaking due to his 'activities subverting the people'. He was now prohibited from all activity as a writer, effective immediately.

In his application for membership Bonhoeffer had expressly referred to the clause that until then specialists writing in their fields had been excused from becoming members. The ban, as he soon discovered, was also extended to other theologians, and it did not make much of an impression on him. He nevertheless made a side trip to Halle, on the way to Berlin, to consult about this new situation with Ernst Wolf, who had published several of his essays. In any case he would clearly be unable to publish his *Ethics* as long as Hitler was in power; nevertheless he did not hesitate to continue work on the manuscript.

Bonhoeffer and the Jews

It is sometimes said that, after his essay on the 'Jewish question' in 1933, Bonhoeffer did little to help the Jews. But from the files in Geneva, and most recently from the correspondence of Gertrud Staewen,[27] we know that he must have done a great deal more than was previously known. However, since being initiated into the conspiracy he had to be extremely careful to cover his tracks when taking part in such actions.

During Bonhoeffer's first trip to Switzerland, daily discussion took place in Geneva concerning how to help persecuted Jews, and an entire day was devoted solely to this issue. To such discussions Visser 't Hooft invited dependable staff members and friends. These included Adolf Freudenberg, the former counsellor to the German Legation in London who, after being displaced by the Nazi racist policies, had come to Geneva to organize refugee work and aid to Jews for the Provisional World Council of Churches; Professor Jacques Courvoisier, who chaired the Committee for Relief of Prisoners of War; and Charles Guillon. Through Guillon, Bonhoeffer learned about the work of the French Resistance and what it was doing for Jews. Perhaps he also heard of the village of Chambon-sur-Lignon, a centre of the French Protestant Church which became famous after the war; under its pastors, André Trocmé and Édouard Théis, its entire population was organized throughout the war to rescue and shelter Jews fleeing across the border to Switzerland.[28]

When Bonhoeffer got back to Berlin he reported to a small circle of dependable friends meeting in Bethge's apartment, including Gertrud Staewen, about his experiences. She wrote to her friend Charlotte von Kirschbaum, Karl Barth's assistant, that 'Dietrich sent an invitation, and for five hours we hung on his every word ... It's been a long time since I felt so happy.'[29] Shortly before his second trip to Switzerland, Bonhoeffer must have met with Staewen in Munich or Innsbruck and asked her if she were willing to be the one who aided Jews in Berlin, and to be the contact person for Freudenberg in Geneva. Provost Heinrich Grüber, who had been directing the Confessing Church's aid office for Jewish Christians, had been sent to a concentration camp for protesting against the persecutions, the same fate shared later by his colleague, Werner Sylten. Sylten was murdered in the concentration camp by the SS.

Though shaken by the proposal that she should be the one to continue the work of Grüber and Sylten, Gertrud Staewen gave Bonhoeffer her consent, writing to her friends in Switzerland that they must surely have heard from Dietrich about her new special assignment. But she still felt hesitant. Then theologian Helmut Gollwitzer, who was doing military service as a medical orderly, came on leave and was able to advise her. She had assumed she must decide between her job on the staff of the church in Dahlem and the task of aiding persecuted Jews. Gollwitzer assured her that it was not necessary to choose, because in both cases she would be continuing her work of pastoral care.

In the years that followed, at the risk of her life, Gertrud Staewen looked after the needs of Jews and Jewish Christians. She supported those who were facing deportation. Through the contacts in Switzerland that Bonhoeffer had provided, she saw that people being deported received food packages, and, together with other courageous Berliners, she helped a number of Jews to go underground. She had women helping her, some of whom had to serve long prison sentences, but she herself never attracted the notice of the Gestapo, though Jews were going in and out of her house. Bonhoeffer and Staewen remained in contact, while observing extreme precautions. He could not allow any risks to his work in the Resistance, because he was now so far initiated into the conspiracy that his arrest would have put it in great danger.

The eastern front and the second journey to Switzerland

After his first trip to Switzerland, Bonhoeffer stayed at his parents' home and worked on his *Ethics*, except for spending Easter at Friedrichsbrunn and a summer holiday at Klein-Krössin. It was believed that the planned coup d'état was imminent and he wanted to be in Berlin for that. From March 1941, a flow of weapons and war materials was reaching the British military command from the USA under Lend-Lease. British troops landed in Greece and tied up parts of the German army in the Balkans for years to come.

Hitler was already committed to attacking the Soviet Union. He had revealed his plans to his commanders on 30 March 1941 and given them the notorious 'commissar order'. When Russian political officers or 'commissars' fell into German hands, they were to be liquidated without any legal proceedings, and the invasion in general was to be carried out with the most extreme cruelty. Field Marshal Keitel, whom people called 'Lakeitel' (lackey Keitel) because, out of principle, he would never gainsay Hitler, explained that this command was justified because Germany was fighting on behalf of its world view against that of communism. As commander of the armed forces, Brauchitsch was besieged with pleas from within them to contradict Hitler or to resign, but once again he could not bring himself to take a clear position.

Only a few commanders condemned Hitler's criminal intentions, but the number of those who were becoming more amenable to the arguments of the conspirators was increasing. On 16 June a discussion was held with General Ludwig Beck as to how best to make use of this new situation. But on 22 June, before a plan could be developed, German troops pushed eastwards across the Russian border and made enormous progress in a few days. Once again luck seemed to be on Hitler's side. This time, however, the conspirators did not become discouraged. Despite the early successes of the invasion in Russia, they were confident it would soon become clear to the more prudent army leaders where Hitler was taking them.

Nevertheless, the mutual assistance pact agreed by Churchill and Stalin on 12 June 1941, and the 'Atlantic Charter' which Roosevelt and Churchill signed on 14 August, made the aspect of the plot in which Bonhoeffer was involved that much more complicated: namely, gaining an agreement between the conspirators and Germany's enemies.

On 29 August, Bonhoeffer left on his second trip to Switzerland. Visser 't Hooft's account:

The German army was making incredible progress in Russia, and there seemed no reason why it might not march right on through Asia. So when [Bonhoeffer] entered my office and said 'Well, now it's all over, isn't it?' I couldn't believe my ears. Was he greeting me with the news of Germany's victory? He saw that I was taken aback and said: 'No, I mean, this is the beginning of the end; Hitler will never get out of there.' (DB 824)

Neither Bonhoeffer nor those who gave him his orders had any illusions about the possibilities that were still open to them at this point. Before the invasion of France, despite the atrocities in Poland, they would still have been able to negotiate an honourable peace agreement, as soon as Hitler had been overthrown and brought before a court. But after the further injustices he had committed and was continuing to commit in France, the Netherlands, Belgium, Denmark and Norway, much harsher peace conditions would certainly be demanded. And from June 1941 onwards, those who could set conditions for a peace included Joseph Stalin. Basically, the possibility of a peace agreement now seemed to have been excluded. Nevertheless, could Germany still have its place in the Allies' ideas of a Europe at peace?

In Geneva, Bonhoeffer was handed Bishop Bell's book *Christianity and World Order*. In it, he read these words, which corresponded exactly to his own thoughts: 'I have no doubt in my own mind that the results of a victory by Hitler would be so disastrous, morally and spiritually, that Christians ought to do their utmost to defeat him.' However, Bell continued, one could not call the war 'Christian' or a 'holy war', and certainly not a 'crusade'. Instead, one should take care 'not to let slip any genuine chance of a negotiated peace which observes the principles of Order and justice ...'

Links should be strengthened between the Churches in warring countries on both sides in any way that is possible through the help of the Churches in neutral countries ... It cannot be wrong for Christians in one belligerent country to seek such opportunities as may be open, to discover through neutral channels, in every way possible, from fellow-Christians in another belligerent country, what terms of peace would be likely to create a lasting peace and not lead to a further poisoning of international relationships ...[30]

Although Bell's book had already been published in 1940, it gave Bonhoeffer fresh hope, because he was doing precisely that which Bell was calling for. Once again though, his optimism was to be dampened by Siegmund-Schulze, when Bonhoeffer visited him in Zürich. The British embassy in Bern had just refused to accept a document from Goerdeler containing peace proposals, having received express orders from London not to do so.

Churchill's attitude was radically different from that of Bell, who kept insisting that Germany could not be equated with Nazism. For Churchill there was only 'Hitler Germany', the enemy which must be defeated. Lord Vansittart hammered home his message in the British press, and this opinion came increasingly to prevail, even though the British churches, at a great assembly on 10 May 1941 presided over by Cardinal Hinsley, the Archbishop of Westminster, had called for a just and honourable peace.

It was another English book which incited Bonhoeffer, as a German and a member of the Resistance movement, to intervene in the debate in Britain. William Paton, the English co-secretary of the 'Provisional World Council of Churches', published *The Church and the New Order* in July 1941.[31] Since Paton offered thoughts on a future world order, which was then the subject of a lively discussion, especially in the Anglo-Saxon countries, Bonhoeffer decided to write a response while he was in Geneva and have it sent to London.

This statement showed that Bonhoeffer's ideas of a new German state, like those of most of his fellow conspirators, had such a 'conservative and patriarchal' effect that it would not have been possible to submit his text to representatives of the Western powers. Visser 't Hooft worked with him on a thorough revision, which Bonhoeffer accepted at once, even though, unlike his Dutch friend, he believed that a democratic system on the Western model would not yet be possible for Germany so soon after the failure of its republic and the years of dictatorship under Hitler. In principle he was nevertheless in favour of a democratic form of government, as can be discovered in a letter of 20 September 1941 that he wrote from Zürich, in English, to his friend Paul Lehmann in the United States:

[You will not misunderstand me,] USA domination is indeed one of the best solutions of the present crisis. But what is to become of Europe? What, for instance, of Germany? Nothing would be worse than to impose on her any anglosaxon form of government – as much as I should like it. It simply would not work. (DBWE 16, 281)

The crucial issue for Bonhoeffer, in this context, was how a majority of Germans who were still cheering Hitler on could be brought back to respect for the law. The words 'as much as I should like it' show that he was not against democracy, but that he considered a long educational process to be indispensable. The thought that the United States could become the sole world power, which the letter also mentions in passing, did not greatly inspire him. In the English version of his position paper which he and Visser 't Hooft edited, he says:

It is no coincidence that a book like this does not come out of Germany today. The absolute insecurity of human existence there leads nearly everywhere, even among Christians, to the total abandonment of any thought of the future, which in turn results in a strongly apocalyptic stance. Under the impression that judgement day is at hand, attention to the historical future is easily lost. In turn, the German reader of Paton's book might miss the total absence of an eschato-logical perspective. (DBWE 16, 529)

In the passage that follows, however, Bonhoeffer does not shrink from making strong political statements:

It may be that consideration of the internal political situation in Germany is not possible in the official formulation of the peace aims; nevertheless, we must be clear that the demand for the unilateral disarmament of Germany, recently emphasized particularly strongly by English radio propaganda, is having an adverse effect on the internal political situation. Since, in terms of sheer power, only the military is capable of removing the present regime (any worker revolt would lead to a bloody suppression by the SS), one must take this into consideration when broadcasting these peace aims to Germany. The little that to date has reached Germany concerning the great church discussion of the new order has made a very favourable and powerful impression in important political oppostion circles. Why is English radio propaganda silent about this in its broadcasts to Germany? (DBWE 16, 529–30)

Certainly the theological aspects of the statement were important to Bonhoeffer, and at the end of his discussion he returned to expressing them. But even more important for him was to give concrete indications that there was a Resistance movement, and also of the difficulties that it had to overcome in order to succeed. Visser 't Hooft, who sent the statement on to recipients in Great Britain and the United States, especially emphasized this aspect in his covering letters, for example in this one to Hugh Martin of the Ministry of Education in London: 'You must accept my word for it that all that we say about the next steps and the urgency of the situation is not based upon wishful thinking on our part, but on actual developments in discussion with responsible people in the country concerned.'[32] An answer to this statement was absolutely necessary for these responsible people in Germany, he said. Bonhoeffer thought a reply might be received even before he left Geneva on 26 September. But William Paton and his friends didn't understand how important this communication was to Bonhoeffer and Visser 't Hooft. It took Paton until January 1942 to write back that the very influential people with whom he and others had spoken were not convinced that there was an opposition in Germany that could be taken seriously.

During this time in Switzerland, Bonhoeffer again made use of the opportunity to visit old and newer friends. After a visit to Erwin Sutz, who was to be married soon, Bonhoeffer wrote to him:

Over the years I have written many a letter for the wedding of one of the brothers and preached many a wedding sermon. The chief characteristic of such occasions essentially rested in the fact that, in the face of these 'last' times, (I do not mean this to sound quite so apocalyptic), someone dares to take a step of such affirmation of the earth and its future. It was then always very clear to me that a person could take this step as a Christian truly only from within a very strong faith and on the basis of grace. For here in the midst of the final destruction of all things, one desires to build ... in the midst of widespread misery, one desires some happiness. And the overwhelming thing is that God says yes to this strange longing ... And now I wonder whether for you here, it is something quite different, something quieter, stiller, as it once was for us as well? Yet I can scarcely believe that. How difficult it surely is to understand one another! (DBWE 16, 220–21)

This 'not understanding' did not refer to matters in the immediate foreground. Bonhoeffer's friends, united in their uncompromising disapproval of Hitler, were equally united in their conviction that not all Germans, by far, were Nazis. But then, for a German, everything had to look quite different from the way Swiss people saw it. In Zürich Bonhoeffer spent an evening at Pestalozzi's, in a group of people with whom he could speak completely openly. Visser 't Hooft, who had come especially from Geneva, asked him the question, 'What do you pray for in the present situation?' He reports that Bonhoeffer answered, 'Since you ask me, I must say that I pray for the defeat of my country, for I believe that this is the only way in which it can pay for the suffering which it has caused in the world.'[33]

In his biography of Bonhoeffer, Eberhard Bethge comments:

This was a statement people did not like to hear repeated in postwar Germany, but its essential content can hardly be denied ... More than anything, it proved how absurd and extraordinary the situation was under Hitler, when the true patriot had to speak unpatriotically to show his patriotism. It is a reaction that defies normal feelings in normal times; it may be a good thing that it has been passed on without defence or explanation, so that one confronts it directly and relives the incredible sentiments in those days. It is abundantly true that the best people of that era lived with the constant thought that they had to wish for Germany's defeat to end the injustice. (DB-ER 744)

Bethge wrote this towards the end of the 1960s, and it shows how long it took, in postwar Germany, for Germans as a people to be ready to admit the whole truth about Hitler's Germany.

The first deportations of Jews and 'Operation 7'

The news with which Bonhoeffer was greeted in Berlin on returning from his second trip to Switzerland could only dampen his high spirits over the results of his visit to Geneva. On 2 September 1941 the decree had been issued which obliged all Jews to wear a yellow star. It was in effect from 19 September onward. That something like this was coming, Bonhoeffer had heard from Dohnanyi some time previously; still, it was a shock to him to see for the first time, on the train to Berlin, people wearing such stars. Much worse, however, was to find out that deportations of Jews were imminent. These began with 'evacuation' notices sent to large numbers of Jewish families. The people who received them were taken from their homes on 16 and 17 October and transported to the occupied areas in the east.

Bonhoeffer and Perels began immediately collecting all the information they could find about these proceedings. A clue to their secret work is given by the fact that Military Intelligence sent one of them on a brief trip to the Rhineland, where deportations had also already begun; friends there seem to have had precise information about how the Gestapo and the SS were carrying out these operations. To ask about it on the telephone or in a letter would have been the height of foolishness. How closely these good friends, Bonhoeffer and Perels, were already working together can be seen from the fact that when Bonhoeffer fell ill, Perels wrote up the reports they had jointly prepared.

On 18 October 1941 the first documentation was compiled for the leaders of the military opposition, followed on 20 October by a second, more detailed report, which may possibly have been intended to be sent to Geneva as well. Dohnanyi and Bonhoeffer may have hoped for a military intervention on the basis of these reports, but it is more likely that they were just trying to do their part to hasten the plans for a coup attempt. Today, Bonhoeffer's and Perels' reports, which include one on the ominous legal situation faced by people of mixed race, the so-called 'half-breeds', are considered the earliest documents proving that the German Resistance concerned itself with the deportation policies of the SS, the Gestapo and the Reich government ministries. Since it is still being said today that the churches did not protest against the deportations of Jews, it is only right to mention these exceptions.[34]

There was also Bonhoeffer's former mentor, Superintendent Diestel, who wrote a letter of protest to the High Council of the Evangelical Church, which resulted in his being taken away and interrogated several times by the Gestapo. This was shortly before Diestel's 70th birthday, and the letter of thanks Bonhoeffer sent to him on that occasion indicates that he seems to have known about Diestel's action, since he concluded the letter with these words: 'I have heard that precisely in these days you have once again been experiencing many trials. But surely the experience of the community, love and gratitude ... will be more important and powerful for you than all the hardships that now surround you' (DBWE 16, 368).

The conspirators, in order not to put their attempt to get rid of Hitler at risk, had to keep quiet about these most recent crimes. Most other Germans were keeping quiet for other reasons. Only the Confessing Church, at the last Confessing Synod of the Old Prussian Union on 16 and 17 October 1943 in Breslau, dared to state what it thought about these monstrous proceedings. Bonhoeffer had already been in prison for months when the Synod adopted a resolution on the commandment 'Thou shalt not kill', in which it condemned racism and the 'Final Solution' of the Jewish question by murder. A pulpit proclamation for the Day of Repentance 1943 says: 'Woe be unto us and our people ... when it is considered justifiable to kill human beings because they are not considered worthy to live or because they belong to another race.'[35] As we shall see, Bonhoeffer played an important role in preparing this statement.

Aside from the Breslau Synod's declaration, for which the synod members were prepared to risk their freedom and their lives, there were only individual actions. Bishop Wurm, like Count Galen, had condemned euthanasia of human beings in his sermons; he now also took a position against the murder of the Jews. His sermons were widely circulated through clandestine channels. Harald Poelchau, a prison chaplain in Berlin, with help from people of all social classes, concealed Jews who were scheduled for deportation. Those in hiding had to to keep moving from house to house in order to look like relatives of those giving them refuge, only there for a short visit. In Württemberg some seventy pastors' families carried out similar actions, with the invaluable help of dependable members of their congregations, all at the risk of their own lives, since they were defying Nazi orders. One pastor and his wife, Eugen and Johanna Stöffler, played an outstanding role. Their parsonage had known so many visitors over the years that the Jews who stayed with them for weeks on end made no impression in their village.[36]

In the east of the country people had to work in other ways. In Naseband, Pomerania, Pastor Karl-Heinz Reimer, whom Bonhoeffer knew, had Jews hidden in his house. His patron, Ewald von Kleist, couldn't hide them on his estate, for too many people there would have asked who they were, but he arranged the provision of necessary food supplies. In Königsberg, East Prussia, Pastor Horst Symanowski and his wife saved the lives of 40 Jews.

In Essen, west Germany, Pastor Johannes Böttcher and his wife took seven Jews into their home, who managed to survive the war in their cellar; Dr Gustav Heinemann (who later became president of the Federal Republic of Germany), his wife and other acquaintances collected the needed food ration stamps. Another pastor in Essen, Heinrich Held (who after the war was the first president of the Evangelical Church in the Rhineland) and his wife hid Jews in their house. The story of these humane actions has by now been researched and documented, but only in part. The whole story will never be known, for hardly any of those involved talked about or took credit for such actions after the war, since they all felt that so much more should have been done.[37]

At the time when he heard about the deportation of Jews from the Rhineland, Bonhoeffer also found out that a trial was being prepared there of several Confessing Church pastors who had taken part in 'illegal' examinations of theological students and candidates for ordination. After his arrest, a note regarding his report on this was found among the Military Intelligence papers and used against him in interrogations. Bonhoeffer's report had in fact led to an intervention by the Armed Forces High Command to have these trials in the Rhineland put off 'until after final victory' in the war, in order not to alarm the population unduly. Bonhoeffer's writing of this report, however, represented another serious offence by Military Intelligence against Heydrich's 'Ten Commandments', according to which Canaris's office was not allowed to work inside the German Reich.

But Military Intelligence, too, became involved in saving a group of Jewish persons, on the initiative of Hans von Dohnanyi and with the express consent of Admiral Canaris. Seven persons were expected to be included at first, hence the name 'Operation 7', but eventually fourteen were rescued. 'Whoever saves one life, saves the whole world', says an old Jewish proverb. Persons who performed such acts at that time are now honoured, at the Yad Vashem Holocaust Memorial in Jerusalem, as 'the righteous among the nations'. For more than a year, Hans von Dohnanyi devoted energy, cunning and an enormous amount of work to having these 14 persons taken off the deportation lists and then having them sent, under false pretences, to Switzerland. Not only the Reich SS Headquarters, but a number of other authorities tried repeatedly to undo the plan or to delay it. Even the Swiss authorities proved less than cooperative and could only be persuaded through tough negotiations to take in these 14 refugees.

In Canaris's office Count Moltke gave his help. Bonhoeffer and Wilhelm Rott arranged for influential Christians in Switzerland, such as Karl Barth and the president of the Swiss Church Federation, Alphons Koechlin, to come forward and insist that entry visas be granted. At that time, such visas were only obtainable if travellers could prove they were not staying in Switzerland but going on further. Among those Bonhoeffer was able to include in the group and thus save from deportation was Charlotte Friedenthal, a staff member of the Confessing Church.[38]

There were people on the staff of Military Intelligence who thought that 'Operation 7' could be a pretext finally to get rid of Dohnanyi; many still hated him as an outsider who had been brought in over their heads instead of rising through the ranks. They tried to leak Military Intelligence papers on 'Operation 7' to the SS Headquarters. With people finally getting wind of a possibility for levering Canaris's entire office out of the High Command, the net began to tighten around Military Intelligence.

An involuntary rest break

At the beginning of November 1941 Bonhoeffer went down with severe pneumonia. He could not attend the Confessing Synod of the Old Prussian Union, which had to meet outside Prussia, in Hamburg, because by then many of its members were banned from various provinces in Prussia. In those days, any Confessing Church members who attracted the disapproving attention of the Gestapo were banned from residing in or visiting the province in which they were accused of carrying out illegal activities. We have already seen that Bonhoeffer could not stay anywhere in Berlin except in his parents' home. Hundreds of pastors were affected by such bans.

In absentia, Bonhoeffer was elected by the synod in Hamburg to a committee which was to prepare a draft resolution on 'The Meaning of the Signs of the Times [Zeichen der Zeit]'. The 'signs of the times' were to show, according to a saying of Jesus (Matthew 16:1–4), when the 'end time' was to come, that is, in the New Testament they had an eschatological meaning. But in Germany this concept had long ago acquired a proverbial meaning, referring to the negative characteristics of any age. The text to be prepared was to speak especially about the way the Nazi Party was de-Christianizing Germany; from the first drafts, it shows a close relationship with texts by Bonhoeffer, for example the ones he prepared for military officers about the deportations. Since he was not there to participate, another member of the committee, presumably Perels, must have had his writings available to work with in Hamburg.

Bonhoeffer was so seriously ill, in those days before antibiotics, that it took him a long time to recover. He was able to take much-needed rest in the home of his Pomeranian friends, the Kleist family in Kieckow, where he had enough to eat and could regain his strength. As soon as he was able to work again, while there, he wrote another chapter of his *Ethics*.

New hopes and the Kreisau circle

For the opposition it was a time of mighty efforts. The number of those who wanted to bring the rule of Hitler to an end was gradually increasing. Dohnanyi was hurrying from one discussion to the next. The strengthening of the opposition filled him with new hope. He and Bonhoeffer must have had a great many conversations during this period about the most crucial issues for the Resistance.

It was at this time, Bethge reports (DB-ER 625), that Dohnanyi asked his brother-in-law whether it was permissible for Christians to be involved in a murder, given that God's commandments expressly forbid it: 'For all who take the sword will perish by the sword' (Matthew 26:52). Bonhoeffer is said to have replied as follows: Murder is still murder, even when, as in the case of Hitler, it is absolutely necessary. One must be prepared to take the guilt for this sin upon oneself. Bonhoeffer added that if he could get near enough to Hitler, he would throw the bomb himself.

In his earlier lengthy conversation with Hans Oster, in 1940, Bonhoeffer had declared that 'treason' could be morally necessary, if it meant staying the hand of a criminal and thus preventing further atrocities like those Hitler had committed in Poland. But even Bonhoeffer could speak in this way only after a considerable inner struggle. This is plain from his wondering, in 1941, whether he could still be a pastor after the assassination. Even though he could not throw the bomb himself, if it succeeded he would belong to those who had Hitler's blood on their hands. He wondered whether someone who had helped plot to kill another human being should still be allowed to administer Holy Communion. Today we can hardly imagine the scruples that the conspirators had to overcome. That Bonhoeffer had fought his way to clear answers was the fruit of his work on the *Ethics*, and it made an important contribution to the inner fortitude of the co-conspirators with whom he was in contact.

The Resistance now consisted of a number of different groups, with principles and intentions that were no longer easy to coordinate. The most distinctive of these groups, and one that had only recently come together, was referred to by Judge Roland Freisler, during the trials that followed the coup attempt of 20 July 1944, as the 'Kreisau Circle'.[39] It was assembled during those months in 1941 by Count Helmuth James von Moltke (1907–1945), who held three of its meetings at his manor in Kreisau, Silesia. Many more meetings took place in Berlin, where the majority of its members were working.

While Dohnanyi's group was working towards the assassination of Hitler, that of Moltke, with Adam von Trott zu Solz (1909–1944), Count Peter Yorck von Wartenburg (1904–1944), Father Alfred Delp (1907–1945), Eugen Gerstenmaier (1906–1986), Hermann Maaß (1897–1944), Carlo Mierendorf (1897–1943) and others, was asking what Germany might be like after Hitler was gone. In trying to imagine the future, this group was developing ideas on the basis of which it was criticizing especially the thinking of men like Carl Goerdeler, whose political ideas went back to the period before Hitler, if not to the time before the First World War. Goerdeler (1884–1945) had politicians and diplomats from the Weimar Republic such as Ulrich von Hassell (1881–1944) and Johannes Popitz (1884–1945) on his side, as well as the retired generals led by General Ludwig Beck.

Thus there was an opposition between 'older' and 'younger' members of the Resistance. The Kreisau group wanted to avoid anything that might give its plans for the future a 'reactionary' character. There were also differences in thinking about the plans for the coup. Even the members of the 'Kreisau circle' were not of one mind at first. Moltke was decidedly against the assassination, and in this regard Dohnanyi and Bonhoeffer were wholly on the side of the 'older' men who were in favour of it.[40]

Among those who were untiring in their efforts, at this stage in the Resistance, to arrange contacts and reconcile differences were Bonhoeffer's brother Klaus and his sister Ursula's husband, Rüdiger Schleicher. It took time until all groups reached agreement, around the beginning of 1942, to recognize General Beck, who in 1938 had honourably resigned as Chief of the General Staff, as leader of the political opposition. Like Dohnanyi, Bonhoeffer refrained from getting involved in these discussions. As we shall see, he was indeed interested in planning for the time after Hitler, but he did not seek contact with the 'Kreisau Circle'. His reservations about Gerstenmaier as a member of Heckel's staff may have played a role in this, as well as Dohnanyi's wish not to create any more contacts than were absolutely necessary. So Bonhoeffer's place was at the side of those who, during these months, were hoping to reach their goal by assassinating Hitler.

Assassination plans and dangers – guilt and responsibility

In October 1941, Colonel Henning von Tresckow, the General Staff officer of the Central Army group in Russia, sent his adjutant, Fabian von Schlabrendorff, from Smolensk to Berlin to ask Colonel Oster whether they could jointly undertake steps towards ending the Nazi regime. Tresckow felt that the atrocities committed by SS units following the German line of advance, and Hitler's constant interference in the plans for operations, with its devastating consequences for the troops, had created a situation in which the need to overthrow him was finally beginning to make sense to many high-ranking officers. Such an enquiry was just what the conspirators had been longing to hear.

Shortly thereafter the attack on Russia was brought to a standstill, outside Moscow, by the arrival of winter weather. A number of General Staff officers swiftly recognized that the invasion was a lost cause, and even Brauchitsch seems to have aroused the impression that he had gone over to the side of Hitler's critics. The conspirators may therefore have hoped that, in the event of a successful coup d'état, he – as the only one who could do so – would be ready to give orders to the army.

So the conspiracy seemed on the threshold of success when, on 19 December 1941, the news broke that Hitler had dismissed Brauchitsch and made himself the highest commanding officer of the army. With this, the conspirators' entire plan was once again left in shambles, and needed to be rebuilt from the ground if they hoped to get anywhere. Only the army could eliminate Hitler and at the same time keep Germany from descending into chaos. But now that Hitler was commander in chief of the army, the entire High Command was ruled out as a source of order and control during the period after the assassination. The conspiracy was therefore confronted with the difficult question of how, at that point, they would gain the power to command. Although Brauchitsch had never stood high in their estimation, his fall from power came as a severe shock to them. Still, they did not give in to discouragement, but kept on working feverishly.

On 7 December 1941 the Japanese had bombed Pearl Harbor and brought the United States into the Second World War. As an ally of

Japan, Germany therefore declared war on the USA on 11 December. For the conspiracy, this meant that they had to carry out their strike against Hitler before the expected consequences of this new state of affairs got under way. The Germans were still the masters of continental Europe. But, as in the First World War, the Americans would soon be sending entire armies across the Atlantic, throwing their military superiority onto the other side of the scales.

Bonhoeffer was still in Kieckow working on his *Ethics* when the news came that Brauchitsch had been fired and the United States had entered the war. What he wrote at that point constitutes one of the deepest reflections we have from him. If, after Germany was defeated – and it was now only a matter of time – there was to be a new beginning, then the first words to be spoken must be about the guilt which had led to murder and to war. Bonhoeffer asked: What is this guilt about, and who are those who can take it upon themselves, so that justice may be restored and renewal may begin? For Bonhoeffer, the Church had to take the guilt upon itself, without any ifs or buts, because it was guilty of sin against the body of Christ.

Confession of guilt happens without a sidelong glance at the others who are also guilty. This confession is strictly exclusive in that it takes all guilt upon itself. When one still calculates and weighs things, an unfruitful self-righteous morality takes the place of confessing guilt face to face with the figure of Christ. (DBWE 6, 136)

The Church is the place where each person who counts himself or herself a member can give up looking to the left or the right at neighbours in the pews and confess that 'We have left undone those things which we ought to have done; And we have done those things which we ought not to have done'. As ever, Bonhoeffer speaks very concretely here:

The church confesses that it has witnessed the arbitrary use of brutal force, the suffering in body and soul of countless innocent people, that it has witnessed oppression, hatred and murder without raising its voice for the victims and without finding ways of rushing to help them. It has become guilty of the lives of the Weakest and most Defenceless Brothers and Sisters of Jesus Christ. (DBWE 6, 142)

He deliberately capitalized the last few words – even the adjectives, which are not usually capitalized in German – to emphasize that they referred to Jesus' brothers and sisters in the flesh, namely the Jews. As with the commandment 'Thou shalt not kill', he goes on to speak in his text about each of the Ten Commandments in turn and relates them to the guilt of the church in Germany and its members, including first and foremost his own guilt, for

in confessing its guilt, the church does not release people from their personal confession of guilt, but calls everyone into a community of confession. Only as judged by Christ can humanity that has fallen away exist before Christ. The church calls all whom it reaches to come under this judgement. The church and the individual, convicted in their guilt, are justified by the one who takes on and forgives all human guilt, namely Jesus Christ. (DBWE 6, 142)

Of course, 'the West', as Bonhoeffer calls the renewed Europe for which he hopes, cannot be justified and renewed in the same way. 'For the nations [Völker] there is only a scarring over [Vernarbung] of guilt in the return to order, justice and peace and in granting freedom to the church to proclaim Jesus Christ' (DBWE 6, 143).

While Bonhoeffer was occupied with such radical thinking, there in Kieckow, he took time to read a lecture given by Rudolf Bultmann, the New Testament scholar at the University of Marburg, for the newly founded Society for Protestant Theology. Not until the postwar years did this lecture have its chance to blow the world of theology wide open. Bonhoeffer had not been able to attend the conference on 1 June 1941, but in this era when hardly any works of theology could still be printed he had been enthusiastic about the idea of keeping scholarly debate alive through meetings. The instigator, Ernst Wolf from the University of Halle, and the members of the Society all belonged to the Confessing Church and were more or less influenced by Karl Barth. Bultmann's lecture was entitled 'New Testament and Mythology' and contained his programme for 'demythologizing the New Testament' which was later to be discussed by theologians around the world.

Bultmann's thesis was that many events reported in the New Testament, such as Christ's ascension, were actually myths. They did hold truths still valid for today, but these were to be discovered by 'existential interpretation', after being found hidden within the myths that enveloped them.

The lecture soon gave rise to a first wave of vehement criticism in Germany – Hans Asmussen apparently was especially alarmed – but Bonhoeffer, while he also had criticisms of Bultmann's fascinating programme, began by expressing agreement with it. Being under the ban, he could not have any public statement appear in print, but he wrote to one of his students in a military hospital in Marburg:

I belong to those who have welcomed [Bultmann's] writing ... To put it bluntly, Bultmann has let the cat out of the bag, not only for himself but for a great many people (the liberal cat out of the confessional bag), and in this I rejoice. He has dared to say what many repress in themselves (here I include myself) without having overcome it. He has thereby rendered a service to intellectual integrity and honesty. Many brothers oppose him with a hypocritical faith [Glaubenspharisäismus] that I find deadly. Now an account must be given. I would like to speak with Bultmann about this and open myself to the fresh air that comes from him. But then the window has to be shut again. Otherwise the susceptible will too easily catch cold. (DBWE 16, 347)

This letter, written in July 1942, proves that in spite of his new tasks Bonhoeffer remained as passionate a theologian as he had ever been. In the same way, he did not give up any opportunity for sports or music-making during this period, and his nieces and nephews remember that 'Uncle Dietrich' also managed to take time for them now and then.

We should not romanticize the 'second life' that Bonhoeffer was leading as a series of adventures out of a spy novel. For him, his activities on behalf of the conspiracy were a necessary evil, a contribution he had to make because there was no one else who could do it, and which had to be made to bring about peace and to stop the Nazis' crimes. The nervous tension with which he had to live, the fear that the plans for overthrow would be discovered, were part of the price that had to be paid, and Bonhoeffer was too intelligent to be without fear. The group around Colonel Oster knew that it had enemies very close by. In mid-February 1942 Dohnanyi received a tip from friends that his mail and telephone were under surveillance.

No less oppressive for Bonhoeffer than the danger to his own life and those of his friends in the Resistance was apprehension about what was taking place on the eastern front, the news of which was suppressed in official army reports but which people back home read aloud to one another from letters received through the military postal service. Erich Klapproth, one of the most gifted of his Finkenwalde ordinands, wrote to Bonhoeffer shortly before being killed in action:

Our clothes have been sticking to our bodies – we reckon it is minus 45° [Celsius] outside, but we keep them on even in the overheated farmhouses – since the beginning of the year. For days at a stretch we cannot even wash our hands, but go from dead bodies to a meal and from there back to the rifle. All one's energy has to be summoned up to fight against the danger of freezing, to be on the move even when one is dead tired. Sometimes when we are away from the mess hall for a long time, we invade the farmhouse after the fighting and slaughter geese,

Ruth von Kleist-Retzow

hens and sheep, get filled and overfilled with sides of bacon, honey and the nice Russian potatoes … We often dream of being relieved, but we are now reduced to forty men instead of 150, still more we dream of Germany – I dream of the 'calm and quiet life in all godliness and integrity'. But we do not, any of us, know whether we shall be allowed to go home again. (DB-ER 704)

Even more horrifying was a letter from another Finkenwaldian, who was also to be killed in action, because it showed Bonhoeffer what a destructive effect the Russian invasion was having on the thoughts and the language of his students:

Here the war has cast traditional conceptions about the treatment of others to the winds. In mid-January, a unit of our detachment had to shoot fifty prisoners in one day, because we were on the march and could not take them with us. In districts where there are partisans, women and children who are suspected of supplying partisans with provisions have to be killed by shooting them in the back of the neck. Those people have to be got rid of like that, because otherwise it means the lives of German soldiers … Over against all these experiences stands the promise, 'I have called you (faceless person [*Massenmensch*], slaughtered and shot like cattle) by your name; you are mine!' God says 'thou'[41] to each person. God has promised each one eternal life and resurrection of the body. And to us soldiers the promise comes from the Sermon on the Mount, 'Blessed are the merciful, for they will receive mercy' [Matthew 5:7]. The contradictions are enormous, for many, no doubt, unbearably great. (DBWE 16, 251–52)

Bonhoeffer spent Holy Week and Easter 1942 at Klein-Krössin with Ruth von Kleist. She had become even more passionately interested in theological questions, and was happy whenever Dietrich could visit her. At first she had questioned his being granted a draft exemption in order to work for Military Intelligence, feeling that such a man as he ought not to be sitting around while others had a much harder fate to bear. But, indomitable opponent of Hitler that she was, she revised her judgement of the matter as soon as she began to realize how things actually stood. The ideas that Bonhoeffer was developing during this period bear the stamp of a sober awareness of his responsibility at that moment in history, in which every other consideration had to be subjected to the plans for the assassination.

Extraordinary necessity appeals to the freedom of those who act responsibly. In this case there is no law behind which they could take cover. Therefore there is also no law that, in the face of such necessity, could force them to make this rather than that particular decision. Instead, in such a situation, one must let go completely of any law, knowing that here one must decide as a free venture. This must also include the open acknowledgement that here the law is being broken, violated; that the commandment is broken out of dire necessity, thereby affirming the legitimacy of the law in the very act of violating it. In thus giving up the appeal to any law, indeed only so, is there finally a surrender of one's own decision and action to the divine guidance of history. (DBWE 6, p. 274)

Bonhoeffer was saying yes to the deed on which everything now depended, and formulating the standards which now must govern the actions of the assassin himself and all his co-conspirators.

With Helmuth James von Moltke in Oslo

Bonhoeffer was expecting to make a third trip to Switzerland when Dohnanyi called him back to Berlin and told him, on the Wednesday after Easter, that he would be going to Oslo with Helmuth James von Moltke. The Norwegian Resistance against the occupation regime that had been put in place by Prime Minister Quisling, the Nazi collaborator, had brought about a church struggle. Quisling had declared Provost Fjellbu of Trondheim Cathedral deposed for making statements against the occupation. All the bishops in Norway thereupon resigned from their duties in the state church. They were followed shortly thereafter by the

Count Helmuth James von Moltke with his son Helmuth Caspar, Christmas 1938

pastors of the local churches, when it became clear that Quisling and the occupation powers which stood behind him were not prepared to listen to an appeal from the Church. When a Nazi youth organization was to be set up in Norway, a thousand Norwegian teachers resigned.

As organizer of the church Resistance movement, Bishop Eivind Berggrav was interrogated and placed under house arrest, then taken to prison. It was generally expected that he would be tried before the People's Court in Berlin, and since the charges against him were 'incitement to insurrection and contacts with the enemy' he was expected to receive a death sentence.

Theodor Steltzer, a close friend of the 'Kreisau' group, was a lieutenant colonel in the occupation army in Norway, and had agreed to telegraph Moltke immediately if Berggrav were arrested. When the telegram arrived, it was decided in the Military Intelligence central office to send Moltke and Bonhoeffer to Norway together. Bonhoeffer was known to the Norwegian bishops and could assure them that they could speak openly with Moltke. His and Moltke's official assignment, of course, was to assess the Norwegian church struggle and the possible threat it represented for the occupying German troops, as a front for their real intention to give support to the Norwegian Resistance and to save Berggrav's life.

Count Moltke considered the most important aspect of his work for Military Intelligence to be ensuring that prisoners of war were dealt with according to international treaties to which Germany was a party. He also made efforts to hinder the increasing practice of shooting hostages, which was contrary to international law. It was hardly possible any longer to do very much for prisoners of war. However, he wore himself out continuing to travel to the occupied countries, where his first move was always to gain the cooperation of the officers he knew personally. Then he worked on the commanders of the occupying armies; as the grand-nephew of the great Field Marshal Helmuth von Moltke, who won three wars for Bismarck, his name could open all doors. Among those with whom he talked, he was able to persuade many that the orders they had received to shoot hostages constituted a grave violation of international law. To those who proved immune to this argument, he described the danger to German troops from carrying out such shootings, since this could provoke acts of revenge by Resistance groups in the occupied lands. Even though he did not always succeed, there must have been thousands of people, by the end of the war, who owed their lives to Helmuth von Moltke, without knowing that he had been their advocate.[42]

Bonhoeffer and Moltke had met only once, at a large gathering. There were similarities between them: both were reserved by nature and tended to be solitary; both had trouble enduring meaningless chatter and were shrewd judges of human character. Like Bonhoeffer, Moltke had dependable and influential friends in the Anglo-Saxon countries. Since his mother's father had presided over the highest court in South Africa, he had studied law in England as well as in Germany. His closest friend at that time was Count Peter Yorck von Wartenburg, to whom Bonhoeffer was related through his mother, and whose wife, Countess Marion Yorck, had been a classmate of Bonhoeffer's in Grunewald.

It was important, in the Resistance, to be able to size up in a few moments people whom one did not know, and in doing so it helped if one knew friends of theirs. Bonhoeffer had written 'The Church and the Jewish Question' in 1933; from that time, Moltke had been an attorney working tirelessly on behalf of Jews who were in trouble. So why should not the two of them immediately feel a bond?

Some people found the tall, somewhat taciturn Count Moltke rather brusque and haughty, though his friends and the letters he left behind indicate that this was not actually so. Even if it had been, Bonhoeffer would have been comfortable with him. Countess Marion Dönhoff wrote that he was a Christian Scientist, but this is erroneous. His father had been an ardent member of that church, but the son had asked to be confirmed in the Lutheran Church, in Gräditz, near Kreisau, at age 15, and as a young adult had given up Christian Science altogether. In the late 1920s he had become associated with an unusual group of friends, including intellectual Jews, socialists, writers and scholars in the most varied fields, who for the most part did not belong to the nobility. All these persons were interested in building a new society, and like them Moltke had become convinced that Christianity had outlived its time and had nothing more to contribute to such an endeavour. But the German church struggle, from 1933 onward, taught him to think better of the

Church. On the trip back from Oslo he wrote a letter to a fatherly friend, Lionel Curtis, one of the most influential people in England though not a public servant:

Perhaps you will remember that in a conversation before the war I argued that belief in God was not essential in order to come to where we are now. Today I know that I was wrong, wholly and utterly wrong. You know that from the first day I have struggled against the Nazis, but the level of danger, and the readiness for self-sacrifice which is demanded of us today, and perhaps tomorrow, demands more than good ethical principles, especially when we know that the success of our struggle will probably mean the total collapse of national unity. But we are ready to face this ... [43]

So on this point as well, he and Bonhoeffer were in agreement; yet they did not become friends. First of all, at Saßnitz on the German island of Rügen in the Baltic Sea, they missed the ferry to Trelleborg, Sweden.

The ferry did not make the crossing the next morning either, because of drifting ice, so the two emissaries had time on 11 April 1942 to go for a five-and-a-half-hour walk, during which they did not encounter another soul except for a single woodsman. Moltke wrote to his wife that they discussed which of them would do what task in Norway, while from Bonhoeffer we have only a brief remark, as reported by Bethge (DB-ER 755): 'Stimulating, but we are not of the same opinion.' Of course it did not take them five and a half hours to agree on what was to be done in Oslo, and Bonhoeffer would have found that aspect of the conversation necessary, but certainly not 'stimulating'. Regarding their assignment, the two were in such agreement that they submitted a joint report afterwards, which only Moltke signed. During Dohnanyi's interrogations later, he was accused of not having Bonhoeffer submit a report on this assignment, suggesting that the assignment couldn't have been real intelligence work, but only a way of keeping him out of military service.

Helmut von Moltke and 'his companion', as the pastor travelling with him was referred to in Norway, did a splendid job together in Oslo, but since their conversation on Rügen a certain distance had emerged between them. Here were two of the most prominent Protestant Christians in the Resistance, but they had opposing views how to resist Hitler. We have already mentioned the 'Kreisau' group's strong reservations concerning the older men in the conspiracy, especially Goerdeler. The 'Kreisau' members were convinced that his ideas would only lead to further failure after the war, while Bonhoeffer had a high opinion of Goerdeler. The conversation during Moltke's and Bonhoeffer's walk together must have been about him and some of the other conspirators and their differing conceptions of the Resistance.

The strength of the 'Kreisau' group lay in its planning for the future, while the group around Oster and Dohnanyi concentrated on the coup d'état itself. This difference had led Moltke and Dohnanyi to break contact with each other. It may also have been a topic in that conversation between Moltke and Bonhoeffer, since lack of unity between different groups in the Resistance endangered all the conspirators. It took a long time, until a discussion on 8 January 1943, to get them all in agreement once again on recognizing the former Chief of General Staff, General Ludwig Beck, as the leader of the Resistance.[44] But the much more explosive difference between Bonhoeffer and Moltke was that Bonhoeffer was for and Moltke was against the assassination of Hitler.

We have seen how important the word 'decision' was in Bonhoeffer's life, beginning with his first sermon. But an overview of the entire 16 volumes of his works shows that from 1940 onwards Bonhoeffer scarcely used the word, not because it no longer had any significance for him, but because the central decision of his life, to which everything else had been leading, had finally been taken. For years he had gone back again and again over all his decisions – we need only remember the one in New York – and re-examined them, but not this final one. In prison, after the failed coup of 20 July 1944, Bonhoeffer wrote: 'It is the advantage and the essence of the strong that they are able to pose the great decisive questions and take clear positions on them. The weak must always decide between alternatives that are not their own' (DBWE 8, IV/184). In the face of the innumerable victims of Hitler's arbitrary state, all conscientious reservations about assassination were silenced. There was nothing more to re-examine, only the deed to be done. Bonhoeffer says in his *Ethics*: 'Here it is apt to cite Goethe's statement that the person who acts is without conscience' (DBWE 6, 259). If you let your scruples tempt you into brooding about it, you will miss the moment that calls for action.

Moltke too was of strong character and was capable of bold decisions. Everything he did in those days gives proof of his readiness to stand up unreservedly for Hitler's victims. During the 1920s, he had read these words by a politician: 'The fate of a nation might really be decided for the better by a single murder. The historical justification for believing this could be, for instance, that a people is languishing under the tyranny of some prodigious oppressor ...' But the book from which this passage comes made the young man a determined opponent of Nazism, and he could no more accept these words than any others it contained. The book was Hitler's *Mein Kampf*, and here too the author's characteristic venom is in evidence. The passage continues: 'Only the republican spirit of some guilty little scoundrel would see such a deed as detestable, whereas our nation's greatest singer of freedom knew how, in his *Tell*, to glorify such actions.' However, in December 1941 Hitler had banned Schiller's play *William Tell* from being performed at all.[45]

Let us remind ourselves that in Barcelona Bonhoeffer said, 'There are no acts that are bad in and of themselves; even murder can be sanctified' (DBWE 10, 367). These were rather dubious words, out of the mouth of a pastoral assistant, but now they had become appallingly true and had to be put into action. Even then, however – and this explains the difference between the two walking companions – Moltke could not agree with this conviction. For him there could be no such thing as a 'sanctified murder'. On the contrary, he questioned putting an end to a murderous regime precisely by committing murder. Nevertheless, his widow reported after the war that, in view of the enormous and ever-accumulating evidence of scandalous Nazi crimes, her husband no longer remained opposed in principle to the assassination. And in fact his friend Yorck joined Count Stauffenberg in the attempt on 20 July 1944. But on the day that Stauffenberg came to see Count Yorck, Moltke had been arrested. Roland Freisler, the presiding judge of the People's Court, had to admit during the trial in January 1945 that Moltke was not among those planning the assassination, but was nevertheless absolutely determined to sentence him to death. Noting that a Jesuit father, Alfred Delp, had been at the meetings in Kreisau, Freisler screamed at the defendant:

And who was there? a Jesuit father, of course – a Jesuit father! and it was with him that you were discussing civil resistance! And his Jesuit superior, you know him too ... one of the highest officials of Germany's most dangerous enemies, comes to see Graf von Moltke in Kreisau. There was a Protestant clergyman, too, three people who were later sentenced to death for taking part in the coup of 20 July! And not a single Party member! There all can I say is, the mask is off!

In Count Moltke's farewell letters to his wife, he speaks of this:

In the end, this pointed emphasis on the involvement of church people is appropriate to the inner meaning of the matter, and shows that F[reisler] is, even so, a good political judge.[46] This has the immense advantage that we are now being put to death for something that a) we have done and b) is worth doing. But that

I should die a martyr for St Ignatius of Loyola – and that is what it comes down to, because everything else was considered secondary – is really a joke, and I'm already trembling in anticipation of Papi's fatherly wrath, he was such an anti-Catholic. Otherwise he would accept everything, but that? Mami, too, would probably have a hard time with it.

We must image the writer smiling as he penned these words. Both his parents were dead, and Moltke was toying with the idea of their reproaches to him in the world beyond.[47] He was opposed to assassinating Hitler because he was deeply convinced that the German people were lost if they were taken in once again by a 'stab-in-the-back myth',[48] instead of confronting, at last, the truth of their history. For him there could only be a new beginning after the total collapse of the regime. But to make it possible, everything must be ready; this was the real aim of the 'Kreisau Circle'. During Bonhoeffer's conversations with Karl Barth in Basel, Barth had been saying similar things.

In telling his wife about the trip to Oslo, Moltke expressed his admiration for the Norwegians for whom Steltzer had arranged secret meetings with him. They included C. B. Svendsen, later a bishop, who immediately after the war was especially helpful to the churches in occupied and divided Berlin, and in the Soviet-occupied zone of the country that later became the communist German Democratic Republic (DDR). But in order for these meetings not to attract notice, Moltke had to spend a lot of time with the German officers, while his 'companion' Bonhoeffer could go on meeting with the Norwegian church representatives, who were very impressed with him. At the end of their visit, each of the two emissaries had a long talk with one of the Norwegian churchmen. That was when Moltke learned that the protesting pastors had been threatened with having to leave their parsonages if they did not end their strike. Bishop Berggrav's reaction, according to his biography:

Splendid. Just take your wives and children along and travel the roads with a handcart. Hold a parish meeting every evening. I am sure that if Norway's thousand pastors set out that way, the men in Berlin will understand fast enough how foolish this whole business is. (DBWE 16, 268)[49]

The plan to save Bishop Berggrav's life succeeded. SS leader Heinrich Himmler telegraphed German Reich Commissar Terboven in Oslo to ask why the Norwegian bishop had been arrested, and Hitler's secretary Bormann ordered Berggrav's immediate release. This was probably arranged through General Falkenhorst, who headed the German High

Command in Norway and had met several times with Moltke. Berggrav was instead placed under house arrest and had to spend the rest of the war in a remote chalet in the mountains. The two German visitors flew back to Berlin from Malmö by way of Copenhagen, without having seen the bishop at all.

Third trip to Switzerland

Soon after returning from Norway, Bonhoeffer left on the journey to Switzerland that he had actually planned to make soon after Easter. He was in Zürich on 12 May 1942 and, on the 14th, in Geneva, but he did not find the people there who were important to him. He especially missed seeing Visser 't Hooft, who had flown to England. At the end of April, Adam von Trott had given Visser 't Hooft a memorandum from the Resistance group in the Foreign Office, which he wanted to deliver personally and urgently support and recommend.

So Bonhoeffer was only able to take care of one last matter for 'Operation 7': the visa for Charlotte Friedenthal had not yet been received. This faithful servant of the Confessing Church subsequently became the first of the group to travel to Switzerland. At the beginning of September, she received word in Dahlem to go to the Gestapo office, on Alexanderplatz several miles away, to receive her completed passport. Since she could not travel on public transport wearing her yellow star, she rolled up her coat and only put it back on when she arrived. After waiting a long time, she was finally called: 'Jewess Friedenthal!' Then, on the way from Dahlem to the railway station, she was to go to the Swiss consulate to have the passport stamped; initially she was told to go 'without the star', but an hour before she left, Dohnanyi came to tell her to wear it after all. She had already taken it off her coat and had to sew it back on quickly. On the train she sat on her coat, carefully rolled up, after finding a seat in a compartment where there were 'Aryans'. After many hours the train finally left Weil, the last German station, and Charlotte Friedenthal put on her coat, to horrified looks from the other passengers in the compartment. At the Swiss border all her papers were taken away but, after a few fearful moments, returned to her. She arrived in Basel so dazed that Gisevius had to point to the yellow star still on her coat and tell her she didn't need it any more. After hearing of her safe arrival, the rest of the group successfully made the journey four weeks later.[50]

While in Zürich, Bonhoeffer obtained from Karl Barth's publisher the galley proofs of Barth's latest *Dogmatics* volume, and took them, along with other literature, to a quiet guesthouse by Lake Geneva to do some work. He wanted to be able to report to his friends and students back home on the latest developments in theology; many German theologians were eagerly awaiting the continuation of Barth's *Church Dogmatics*.

During this time in Switzerland, Bonhoeffer had a personal experience of the twilight zone in which a secret agent lives. His first two trips there had aroused doubts in many quarters. This time, in Zürich and Geneva, Bonhoeffer heard rumours that Karl Barth was among those who were to some degree suspicious of him. He wrote Barth a letter of entreaty, saying that at first he had laughed at this, but after continuing to hear it had become uncertain.

In a time when so much simply has to rest on personal trust, *everything* is lost if mistrust arises. I can, of course, understand that this curse of suspicion gradually afflicts us all, but it is difficult to bear when for the first time it affects one personally. Yet it must also be terrible for you – perhaps even worse than for me – to be compelled suddenly to be suspicious. Our conversations must have been simply unbearable for you. And I never perceived this and cannot imagine it, even in reflecting back on them. (DBWE 16, 278)

Barth's assistant, Charlotte von Kirschbaum, replied immediately: 'What a pickle to be in! Above all, please be assured that we too are laughing at this matter.' It was among the 'signs of the times' that such a tumult was even possible. 'We should be glad if you would come and see us' (DBWE 16, 279f).

While in Geneva again, Bonhoeffer heard by chance that Bishop Bell had flown to Stockholm and planned to be there for three weeks. Presumably he also heard that Schönfeld had left for Sweden, a neutral county in the war, to meet with the bishop. He decided spontaneously to leave Switzerland right away, and proposed to Dohnanyi to have him sent to Sweden. Bell was to be there only until 2 June, so it had to be arranged in the greatest hurry, and with extreme discretion. To travel to neutral Switzerland or to the army occupying Norway was one thing, but a meeting with a member of the British House of Lords was quite another, namely high treason.

On 25 May, Bonhoeffer had his last visit with Karl Barth. During their conversation in the afternoon, they heard on the BBC news from London that Molotov had arrived there to sign the British–Soviet treaty. When it was mentioned that the treaty precluded either country from making a separate peace with Germany, Bonhoeffer said, 'Well, now it's all over!' (DBWE 16, 286, note 2).

The trip to Sweden was decided, and the technicalities arranged, within three days. General Beck himself gave the order for it. The order stated that Bonhoeffer was to give Bell the names of the conspirators who were in charge of the coup: Chief of Staff General Beck, General Kurt von Hammerstein, Lord Mayor Goerdeler, and the union leaders Wilhelm Leuschner and Jakob Kaiser. None of them was in active service any longer, but their names were internationally known and their integrity was uncontested. That they could hope to have the right to give orders after Hitler's death was confirmed by the names of Günther von Kluge, Fedor von Bock and Georg von Küchler, who were still active Field Marshals, top commanders, and whose trustworthiness was vouched for by the Resistance leaders. Bonhoeffer was to make it clear that the intentions of this group were peaceful, although for camouflage purposes their names could not be made public immediately after the coup; and he was to ask Bell to convey to the British government their request not to make use of the moment of overthrow for an attack, so that the new government would be able restore order within Germany.

The meeting with Bishop Bell

On 30 May Bonhoeffer flew from Berlin to Stockholm, carrying the courier pass No. 474 that Adam von Trott had obtained for him that morning from the Foreign Office. The flight was a torment due to rough weather. In Stockholm he found out that Bell was staying in Sigtuna, the ancient Swedish royal city. It had become the centre of the church renewal movement in Sweden, with the Evangelical Academy founded by Manfred Björkquist and an adult education centre. Sigtuna was also an ecumenical centre, where efforts were being made to break through the isolation that the war had imposed on Sweden, so Bell was a very welcome guest there. Bonhoeffer travelled on there immediately, and discovered that Schönfeld had already arrived before him. There was now so much trust in Schönfeld that the Resistance group in the Foreign Office had sent him as a messenger to Bishop Bell. He must have been as surprised as the bishop when Bonhoeffer turned up in Sigtuna.

Schönfeld and Bonhoeffer were no longer adversaries, but they had very different ideas about the future of Germany. Because of his friendship with Gerstenmaier, Schönfeld was close to or affiliated with the 'Kreisau' group, but on many issues he argued more along the same lines as Goerdeler. Bonhoeffer very clearly belonged to the Resistance group in Military Intelligence. However, in the actual message that the two were carrying on this occasion there were no differences. Each of them had been given, before his departure, very precise instructions by Hans Bernd von Haeften. So each gave the bishop the same names of those involved in the conspiracy, and their accounts of how the actual putsch was to proceed also concurred.

It was only in assessing the power relationships in Europe, and in describing the aims of the conspiracy, that they showed serious differences. Schönfeld had already had two conversations with Bishop Bell before Bonhoeffer arrived, and he had raised the possibility that the conspirators' putsch might be preceded by a mutiny of the SS; the actual coup by the conspirators would then follow. He had spoken further of Germany's military strength and even of the German colonies, and seemed to think that the opposing side would regard a Germany prepared to respect human rights as a partner that they could accept without further ado.

During their first joint conversation with Bishop Bell, Bonhoeffer interrupted him to say that God must pass judgement on Germany and on the German people. He said it was wrong to hope for a seamless transition to peace, and spoke instead of repentance and assuming the guilt for what had happened, ideas he had developed in the context of his *Ethics*.

The world was to understand that the coup which the German conspirators were preparing had a theological significance transcending even Schönfeld's invocation of the dimension of human rights. The coup, then, had to take place as part of the 'punishment by God' and had thus to be recognized as the Germans' acceptance of guilt and repentance.

This was Klemens von Klemperer's comment on the discussion.[51] It makes clear once again the degree to which Bonhoeffer really lived his ethics. And for Bishop Bell, these were the thoughts that he found most persuasive. This was the young friend who, with his precise information years ago in London, had drawn Bell into the German church struggle and made him the Confessing Church's most important ally. The conspirators could not have done better than to send Bonhoeffer after Schönfeld, for through him Bishop Bell was made a spokesman on their behalf who gave his all to fighting for their cause in Great Britain. Bonhoeffer and Bell also had a private meeting. Still the fatherly friend, the bishop carried back a loving message from Bonhoeffer to his twin sister and her family and listened to all the news about the situation in the Confessing Church. He must have said to Bonhoeffer, during this conversation, that immediately after the war he would press for a meeting of representatives of the churches, and at such a conference it would be important that Germans, too, be able to contribute their ideas for a new beginning in peace and justice.

The three ecumenical visitors were hosted in Sigtuna by the theologian Harry Johansson. He followed exactly the guidelines published by Visser 't Hooft for cooperation among the churches during the war. During the conversations he was present part of the time, and offered his help as an intermediary in case there were messages to be delivered. However, his superiors subsequently decided it was too risky for a Swede to serve as contact person between Great Britain and the German conspirators. Because of its geographical position, Sweden needed to take care to remain strictly neutral, so Johansson had to withdraw his offer.[52] But after the war, he was among those who helped Bell see that the Evangelical Church in Germany was quickly taken back into the ecumenical community. Bonhoeffer signed Johansson's guest book only with his initials, DB. He was very aware of the delicacy of his mission in a neutral country like Sweden: that it was an El Dorado for spies and secret agents.

Bonhoeffer's report was eagerly awaited in Berlin. Such a direct contact between the conspirators and the government of an enemy country as Bell could make, as a member of the House of Lords, could not be hoped for even through the Vatican, where Josef Müller had been conducting further negotiations. Perhaps Oster, Dohnanyi and Bonhoeffer had too high hopes for the conversation with the bishop, but no Englishman could have been found who would represent their cause more emphatically than did Bishop Bell. Dohnanyi arranged for the report Bonhoeffer wrote for General Beck to be kept top secret. Not even Josef Müller was to be allowed to see it. But Bonhoeffer found this too rigorous a precaution, and he passed information to Müller through Bethge, so that the results of his trip to Sweden could be used in the discussions at the Vatican.

This meeting with Bishop Bell was Bonhoeffer's most important contribution to the Resistance, and also the most dangerous. But that, as a Lutheran theologian, he clarified issues of conscience for his friends in the Resistance must also have been of great importance especially to Oster and Dohnanyi. None of the conspirators carried out their missions thoughtlessly, or would have contented themselves with easy solutions to the ethical problems they were confronting.

Maria von Wedemeyer

It is characteristic of Bonhoeffer that at the beginning of June 1942, right after the debriefing of his trip to Sweden, he went back to Klein-Krössin to continue working on his *Ethics*. As always during his visits there, he had long conversations with his motherly friend Ruth von Kleist. Her 18-year-old granddaughter, Maria von Wedemeyer, was also visiting at the time, having just finished her university entrance exams at her boarding school in Wieblingen, near Heidelberg. The headmistress of Maria's school, Elisabeth von Thadden, was the sister of Reinhold Thadden, one of the staunchest supporters of the Confessing Church in Pomerania; she was later executed for her ardent opposition to Hitler.

As a child, Maria had sometimes attended church at Finkenwalde with her grandmother, and since then had occasionally seen 'Pastor Bonhoeffer' when he was visiting. When Maria was 13 her grandmother had asked him to question her to see if she was ready for confirmation class; he concluded that she wasn't. Maria felt at the time that she had failed, and also found him quite severe. But this time, when he came down from the attic room in which he worked, he and her grandmother encouraged her to join in their conversations and to say what she thought. She must have made a deeper impression on Bonhoeffer than he was ready to admit; for, once back at his desk, he found his thoughts again and again wandering away from theology and back to her.

From Christian to man for his time

Let us look back again at the stages which Bonhoeffer had traversed on his 'journey to reality' by June 1942. They were all characterized by more or less rigorous decisions he had taken. We see first the 14-year-old deciding to study theology; then the high-flyer among the theology students in Berlin, discovering Karl Barth and standing with Barth versus his teachers in Berlin, but demanding, more sternly than Barth, a 'concrete commandment'. We see the pastor who, from the beginning of the church struggle, belonged to the radical wing of the Confessing Church, and in 1933 was already confronting Christians in Germany with the question of their attitude toward the Jews. We read of his demands that the ecumenical movement support the church struggle, because no cause could be closer to that of ecumenical Christianity. We find him at Finkenwalde as director of a seminary, sharing the fate of the 'illegal' ordinands and pastors and, not least because of this, deciding not to marry. Only the path of radical obedience is the path that God wills for him. To go, 'knowingly', another way is to 'separate oneself from salvation'. We see him deciding to refuse military service, even at the cost of his life. We find him in New York in 1939, having already escaped such a consequence, but then nevertheless deciding to go back to share in Germany's fate.

We have already seen how, immediately on returning from the United States to a remote corner of East Pomerania, Bonhoeffer began working on an interpretation of Psalm 119; but we have not mentioned that this theological work marks the beginning of the third phase in the life of Dietrich Bonhoeffer. Bethge speaks here of Bonhoeffer's 'turning point from Christian to man for his times'.

To want to be only a Christian, a timeless disciple – that now became a costly privilege. To become engaged for his times, where he stood, was far more open to misinterpretation, less glorious, more confined. Yet this alone was what it now meant to be a Christian ... The earthly and national future, the realm of citizenship, demanded responsibility. (DB-ER 678)

Bonhoeffer did not simply leave the time of making 'decisions of faith' behind him. What he had discovered and learned during that time, he took with him into this new, final stage of his life. But the word 'decision' takes on a new emphasis. The earth has its rights over us, and we are not entitled to dream away the lifetime which is given to us, says Bonhoeffer's great meditation on Psalm 119. But there is much more to say about this, and it is anything but a coincidence that Bonhoeffer made the first discoveries on his new path from working with this particular Psalm, which speaks as no other does about God's law and God's commandments. A few sentences will suffice to make that clear.

With God we do not take up a stance – we walk along a path. It goes forward, otherwise we are not with God. God knows where the path goes, throughout its length; we know only the next step and the ultimate destination ... To know the way, to be going the right way, never spares us any of the responsibility and guilt, but only makes them harder to bear. God's children do not have any special rights, except that they know God's grace and that this is God's path ... (DBW 15, 508)

Even my most devout decisions and chosen paths can lead me to destruction, but never God's commands. Not my devotion, but God alone preserves me from shame and dishonour. (DBW 15, 512)

Life itself is God's aim for us. If it becomes a means to an end, then a contradiction has entered into our life which makes it a torment. For then we are seeking the aim of our life, the good of it, somewhere beyond it, and that can only be purchased by denying life itself. That is the condition we are in before we receive our life in God, and we have been taught to call this condition good. We learned to hate and despise life and to love and worship ideas. (DBW 15, 526)

[I too must ask myself:] am I perhaps already living so much on the bare bones of my own principles that I wouldn't even feel it if, some day, God were to take his living commandment away from me? Perhaps then I should still be acting in faithfulness to my principles, but the commandment of God wouldn't be with me any longer. (DBW 15, 531)

Nothing marks the change in Bonhoeffer's thinking better than the fact that, from the autumn of 1939 onward, the concepts 'earth' and 'reality' are found more and more at the centre of his thoughts, and that the 'world' in its negative meaning as the evil world, at enmity with God, fades out and the 'world that God loves' comes to the fore. It is not by chance that from now on the word 'reality' occurs almost twice as often and the word 'earth' around three times as often as previously.[53]

Bonhoeffer's decision to forgo marriage in the interest of the Confessing Church was no longer binding upon him. As a commandment he had taken upon himself, this renunciation would now only be part of the 'bare bones of his principles'. But whether the time was now right for him to become engaged to be married was another matter.

His work on the *Ethics* was now more and more closely connected with his assignments for the Resistance, rather than a separate compartment of his life. Travelling on a military train to Munich on 25 June 1942, he wrote this in a letter to Bethge:

My recent activity, which has largely been in the worldly sector, gives me much to think about. I am amazed that I am living, and can live, for days without the Bible; I would then perceive it not as obedience but as autosuggestion, if I were to force myself back to it. I understand that such autosuggestion could be and is a great help, but I fear that I would thereby falsify an authentic experience and in the end still not be experiencing authentic help. When I then open my Bible again, it is new and delightful to me as never before, and I only wish I could preach again. I know that I need only open my own books to hear all that can be said against all this. I do not wish to justify myself either, for I realize that I have had much richer times in the 'spiritual' sense. But I sense how an opposition to all that is 'religious' is growing in me. Often it amounts to an instinctive revulsion, which is surely not good either. I am not religious by nature. But I must constantly think of God, of Christ; authenticity, life, freedom and mercy mean a great deal to me. It is only that the religious clothes they wear make me so uncomfortable. Do you understand? None of these are new thoughts and insights at all. Because I believe that I am on the verge of some kind of breakthrough, I am letting things take their own course and not resisting. This is the sense in which I also understand my present work in the worldly sector. (DBWE 16, 329)

These were thoughts that Bonhoeffer was only able to pursue later, in his prison cell in Tegel. Until then he had no time. Dohnanyi came to Munich on 26 June to travel with him to Italy. During the trip, Maria von Wedemeyer continued to occupy Bonhoeffer's mind. He had spoken of her to Bethge and admitted what she meant to him. The letter quoted above, written on the train, says further:

I have not written to Maria. It is truly not time for that yet. If no further meetings are possible, the pleasant thought of a few highly charged moments will no doubt melt away again into the realm of unfulfilled fantasies that is already well populated in any case. On the other hand, I do not see how a meeting could be contrived that would be unobtrusive and inoffensive for her. One cannot expect that of Frau von Kleist either, in any case not as an idea of mine, for I am not really at all clear and decided about it as yet.

The 'war behind the war' continues

Dohnanyi and Bonhoeffer first had to discuss some matters with Wilhelm Schmidhuber, also attached to the Munich Military Intelligence office, who met them in Venice. They then travelled on with him to Rome by way of Florence. There Bonhoeffer had a long conversation with Prelate Kaas, who until 1933 had been chief of the Centrist Party in Germany. He also met with Father Leiber, the secretary of Pope Pius XII, and with Father Zeiger, Rector of the Collegium Germanicum; with both of them he had talked far into the night at Christmastime 1940 in Ettal. Josef Müller describes in his memoirs how these conversations included lively discussions as to whether it might be possible, after the war, for their two churches to make a new beginning by looking back to pre-Reformation times.[54] While Pius XII was opposed to ecumenical relations, two members of his staff who were close to him seem to have had quite different views, even at that time.

From the Vatican, Bonhoeffer wrote an optimistic letter to his twin sister: 'It won't be long until we see each other again.' But the answer from the British government to the questions Bishop Bell had conveyed to it on behalf of Bonhoeffer and Dohnanyi, and which, by unspoken agreement, they hoped to receive before they had to leave Rome, did not arrive at the Vatican. On 10 July the two brothers-in-law made their way homeward.

Again Bonhoeffer went back to Klein-Krössin to keep working on his *Ethics*, but soon the Council of Brethren called him to take part in a session in Magdeburg on 10 August 1942; a working group of which he was a member was to present an exegesis, for the present day, of the commandment 'Thou shalt not kill'. Here again, Bonhoeffer was interested in how the forthcoming synod could express and promote this commandment, not as 'eternal truth' but as a 'concrete commandment' for the year 1942, in which persecution of the Jews had worsened and 'euthanasia' killings were taking place. He therefore agreed to prepare a paper for the second session of the working group, to be held on 15 March 1943, on the doctrine of *primus usus legis*, the primary use of the law.

The expression *primus usus legis* goes back to the leaders of the Reformation, who said that the commandments were given us by God for three reasons: first, to maintain law and order among human beings according to the will of God; second, to bring humans to an awareness of their sin and guilt; third, to show humankind the way to a new life in God. However – and his friends in the Confessing Church had not expected it to be otherwise – what Bonhoeffer presented in March 1943 went far beyond what had been said previously. He addressed the situation in the Confessing Church, which was being persecuted and no longer had a public voice, saying:

But even the congregation in the catacombs never has the universality of its mission taken from it. In preaching law and Gospel, it professes this mission and thereby keeps alive its responsibility for the world. The congregation can never content itself with cultivating its own life; to do so means denying its Lord. Even in places where it can still preserve the *iustitia civilis* only among its own members, because its word is not received by the world, it does this in service to the world and as part of its universal mission. Its experience will be that the world is in trouble and that the reign of Christ is not of this world, but precisely here it will be reminded of its mission to the world; otherwise it would become a religious club. (DBWE 16, 597–98)

Here, Bonhoeffer had left far behind him the image of the Christian community as a 'sealed train in foreign territory'. His lecture became the decisive step leading to the Breslau Synod, which spoke out, half a year later, against the murder of the Jews.

The meeting at Magdeburg in August 1942 was also significant for Bonhoeffer because there he was able to see Carl Goerdeler again and to have a substantive conversation with him. Bonhoeffer knew that the 'Kreisau' group disapproved of Goerdeler. But even some of Goerdeler's close friends were becoming irritated by the optimism with which he kept saying, in spite of everything, that the opposition would soon succeed. They found this attitude rather heedless. It was the reason why Stauffenberg later left him out of the conspirators' contact network.[55] But Bonhoeffer defended Goerdeler's optimism. In his reflections on New Year's Eve 1942 there is a passage on optimism, and as Bonhoeffer wrote it he was thinking of Carl Goerdeler among others.

It is more sensible to be pessimistic; disappointments are left behind and one can face people unembarrassed. Hence, the clever frown upon optimism. In its essence, optimism is not a way of looking at the present situation, but a power of life, a power of hope when others resign, a power to hold our heads high when all seems to have come to nought, a power to put up with setbacks, a power that never abandons the future to the opponent but lays claim to it. Certainly, there is a stupid, cowardly optimism that has to be frowned upon. But no one ought to despise optimism as the will for the future, however many times it is mistaken. It is the health of life that the ill dare not infect. (DBWE 8, Prologue)

Goerdeler felt Bonhoeffer's sympathy for his views, and invited Bonhoeffer and Bethge to visit him the next day at his hotel in Berlin. He was happy to talk with anyone about the future beyond the military work that had to be done.

Toward the end of August 1942, Hans von Dohnanyi completed all the preparations for 'Operation 7' that could be done from Germany. The final agreements in Switzerland were still to be concluded, and these he also wanted to attend to himself. Bonhoeffer came especially to Berlin from Klein-Krössin to see him off. He gave his brother-in-law a letter to send to Bishop Bell, in which he indicated how hard it was becoming for him and his friends to wait so long for a reply from London. But then Dohnanyi found the answer waiting in Geneva, in the form of a telegram: 'Interest undoubted, but deeply regret no reply possible. Bell' (DB-ER 765).

It was a bitter disappointment. Dohnanyi knew better than almost anyone about the crimes being committed everywhere on the battle-fronts and behind the lines. He could well understand a government's unwillingness to settle for anything but the unconditional surrender of Germany. But a positive answer might have changed the mind of one or another of the German commanders. Now the conspirators had to go forward without such backing.

Bell had thought over very carefully every word of his telegram. What he did not and could not speak of was the various means by which he had tried to move the government in London to a positive reply. While the British Foreign Office called him 'our good German bishop', Foreign Secretary Anthony Eden spoke of him with Shakespeare's words, 'this pestilent priest'. Bell was a man who wouldn't take no for an answer. Right after returning from Sweden he had written a detailed report of his meeting with the two German pastors and visited the Foreign Office to hand it to Eden personally. The Foreign Minister appeared to be impressed, but after a time he replied: 'Without casting any reflection on the *bona fides* of your informants, I am satisfied that it would not be in the national interest' to send any reply to the German conspirators.[56] Stalin was already annoyed that the Western Allies were taking their time attacking the European mainland, and Churchill's government did not want to do anything that might further irritate their Soviet ally.

In addition, a certain scorn for the 'treasonous' actions of the German conspirators was unmistakable. London was simply not ready to acknowledge the 'war behind the war' and the German conspirators as allies in the struggle for law and human rights. That this was no longer a war between enemy nations, but rather a fight for total annihilation between irreconcilable world views, nobody in Britain saw as clearly as Bishop Bell. Bell had already witnessed during the church struggle how hard it was to defend oneself against the Nazi state, and during the war was getting an exact picture – with the help of Gerhard Leibholz, Bonhoeffer's brother-in-law – of what was going on in Germany. Leibholz wrote at the time: 'Basically, the traditional liberal democratic policy of non-intervention belongs to a world that has passed away.' This was Bell's thinking too, and because the Foreign Office refused to act, he said in a speech to the House of Bishops of the Canterbury Convocation of the Church of England:

I could wish that the British government would make it very much clearer than they have yet done that this is a war between rival philosophies of life, in which the United Nations welcome all the help they can receive from the anti-Nazis everywhere – in Germany as well as outside …[57]

Bell sought out the US ambassador in London, told him about the meeting in Sweden and asked him to transmit the conspirators' request to the government in Washington. Finally, he entered into a duel of words with Lord Vansittart in the House of Lords, whose contention that all Germans were Nazis he vehemently denied. After the coup attempt of 20 July 1944 he wrote to Eden, pointing out that after his trip to Sweden he, Bell, had named beforehand the names of the men who had now been put to death in Berlin or were on trial in the 'People's Court'. At the time, no one had wanted to give him any sign of encouragement, but couldn't something be done now, at least? In the House of Lords Bishop Bell also sharply criticized the air raids directed at the German civilian population, and Churchill never forgave him.

The Wedemeyers

Bonhoeffer spent the week 18–25 August in Klein-Krössin working on his *Ethics*. He was there when the news came that Hans von Wedemeyer, Maria's father, had been killed on 22 August, as an officer preparing for the siege of Stalingrad. Before 1933, Hans von Wedemeyer had been one of Reich Chancellor Papen's closest colleagues. When Hitler took power, Wedemeyer was disappointed in Papen's attitude and withdrew from politics to devote himself to his estate of Pätzig. The new rulers, aware of what he thought of them, had put him on trial for 'oppression of agricultural workers', but the case was thrown out. The court found working conditions at Pätzig exemplary.

Hans von Wedemeyer and his wife were ardent supporters of the 'Berneuchen Brotherhood', a church movement founded by Wilhelm Stählin which aimed to renew worship by reforming the liturgy. Several 'Berneuchen' annual conferences had been held at Pätzig. Bonhoeffer did not feel any sympathy for this renewal movement. His declaration that 'Only those who cry out for the Jews may sing Gregorian chant' has become well known. Stählin and his friends loved the ancient liturgical chants, and though in their thinking they rejected Nazism, they tried to avoid political disputes. This was not an attitude that could earn Bonhoeffer's respect. But he felt a tie to the Wedemeyers through his close friendship with Ruth von Kleist, and he had confirmed their eldest son, Max. In his condolence letter to the widow, Ruth von Kleist's daughter, he recalled her husband's visit to him at Finkenwalde to discuss the confirmation instruction for his son.

I have never forgotten that meeting. It accompanied me throughout the period of instruction. I knew that Max had already received and would continue to receive what was decisive from his parents' home. It was also clear to me what it means for a boy today to have a godly father who at the same time stands in the thick of life. When in the course of those years I then came to know almost all your children, I was often extremely impressed by the power of the blessing that emanates from a father who believes in Christ … This blessing is, of course, not something purely spiritual, but something that works its way deep into earthly life. Under the right blessing, life becomes healthy, secure, expectant, active, precisely because it is lived out of the source of life, strength, joy, activity. (DBWE 16, 351–52)

Bonhoeffer made two short visits to Klein-Krössin on 1 and 22 September. No one has recorded the reason, but it is not hard to guess. Ruth von Kleist had long been afflicted with a serious eye disease and was afraid of going blind. Presumably Bonhoeffer asked his father for the name of a doctor who could treat her. On the first visit Bonhoeffer would have noted her symptoms, and on the second he told her that she could have an operation in the next few days at St Francis Hospital in Berlin. Ruth von Wedemeyer sent her daughter Maria along to take care of her grand-mother and read to her, since after the operation her eyes had to remain bandaged for quite awhile. Maria was surprised to see how often Pastor Bonhoeffer came to visit her grandmother. He held a brief prayer service with the two of them, and Maria noted in her diary the main things he said. Then he invited Maria to an evening at the Schleichers', a farewell party for his nephew Hans-Walter, who was leaving for military service the next day. There, Bonhoeffer had a conversation with Maria about military service, about which she also wrote in her diary.

He said it was a tradition with us that young men should volunteer for military service and lay down their lives for a cause of which they mightn't approve at all. But there must also be people able to fight from conviction alone. If they approved of the grounds for war, well and good. If not, they could best serve the Fatherland by operating on the internal front, perhaps even by working against the regime ... Oh, it's all so logically clear and obvious. But isn't it terrible, when I think of my father?[58]

The Freiburg group

Hitler's early successes in the war had blinded the German people to what was truly going on. Most of the population was labouring under a fantasy, and it was only the devastating defeat at Stalingrad, and the shock wave it caused, that inclined any who were prepared to entertain second thoughts to do so. This was far from being a majority. Many still believed the propaganda about 'secret weapons' which were soon to turn the situation around. And any who didn't believe this tissue of lies had many reasons to fear even harbouring second thoughts, not to mention opening their mouths. These fears were encouraged not least by the justice system. The death penalty for listening to enemy radio stations was prescribed by law.

It was considered 'undermining military strength' even to express doubt that Germany would be victorious in the end, and one could be hanged for doing so. People were even put to death for giving a foreign worker a loaf of bread. Hundreds of thousands of people in the occupied countries had been rounded up and brought to Germany for forced labour, taking the place of soldiers in the labour force. The courts were ruthless in their sentencing and everyone knew it. Year after year German judges condemned to death not only foreigners, but thousands of Germans as well, for petty reasons.[59]

That in such a situation it would have been irresponsible to plan simply for the overthrow of the government, and not also for what needed to happen afterwards, was plain not only to the 'Kreisau' group, which was then just beginning its work, but also to the group around Oster and Dohnanyi. Negotiations with the Allied powers would be difficult even if they had the backing of the population, and there they could only count on very limited support. Within the Military Intelligence group, it was especially Bonhoeffer who stood for the idea that things could not just be allowed to happen; especially since the majority of the German population had its head in the sand, plans must be carefully made for the future. In this he came closer to the thinking of the Kreisau group than did Dohnanyi.

But his meeting in Sweden with Bishop Bell had shown him that people in the Western countries would ask about the Confessing Church as soon as the first contacts were made. In Great Britain there was a church 'Peace Aims Group',[60] and Bell must have asked Bonhoeffer whether the Confessing Church had assigned this task to a comparable working group. The partner churches abroad would listen to its ideas and plans for the renewal of Germany, and would help to make sure that Germany could not be shut out of the community of nations again, as it had been after the First World War. Bonhoeffer did know from his talks with Visser 't Hooft that there were such study groups in England, in the United States and in Sweden. But he must have been shocked to realize how much Bishop Bell was expecting of the Confessing Church, which was thinking more about the approaching armageddon than about being together with people of other nations in a Europe of the future.

As he worked on his *Ethics*, Bonhoeffer thought about these things. The 'future of the Western world' occupied him. But in this he was far ahead of the Confessing Church. Oster and Dohnanyi, however, were among those who had a sense of the importance of these reflections, and Dohnanyi must have been glad that here were people working on plans for the future who did not need to be initiated into the plans for the assassination of Adolf Hitler.

Bonhoeffer could speak with the Confessing Church leaders about what would need to be done after the war without revealing that he was talking about ideas that came from Bishop Bell, and without saying a single word about the conspiracy. Thus he was able, with the agreement of the conspirators, to accept an assignment from the Council of Brethren to speak with a group about writing a memorandum on Germany's role after the war. A group of professors in Freiburg were named as the right sort of people to do this. All of them had been members of the Confessing Church since 1933.

On 9 October 1942, Bonhoeffer was in Freiburg for a lengthy conversation with the jurist Eric Wolf, who brought along his friend Constantin von Dietze. Both were prepared to accept this assignment from the Confessing Church and to ask dependable colleagues to work with them. It was agreed that the memorandum would present, from a German viewpoint, statements on economic issues, on the new ordering of the state, on cooperation in Europe, on the role of the Church, on justice, and in particular on human rights. The historian Gerhard Ritter, professional business managers Walter Bauer and Friedrich Karrenberg, theologians Otto Dibelius and Hans Asmussen and the jurist Franz Böhm were to work with the group, as well as Walter Eucken, who like Constantin von Dietze was an economist, and Friedrich Justus Perels, who was to participate as a legal expert along with Wolf. Carl Goerdeler too, who was a friend of Gerhard Ritter's, took part in at least one session.[61]

The Freiburg group is sometimes erroneously referred to as the 'Bonhoeffer group', but Bonhoeffer was only involved in getting it started; further contact could have endangered the conspiracy. However, his initiative had a considerable long-term effect, since the text of the memorandum was presented to the founding Assembly of the World Council of Churches in Amsterdam in 1948 as a preparatory document from Germany. That its initiator had been put to death at Flossenbürg, and that other participants had been arrested by the Gestapo because of the memorandum and had only been saved by the ending of the war from meeting the same fate, gave the document a particular weight. Among those who participated, besides Bonhoeffer and Goerdeler, Friedrich Justus Perels also did not survive. He was severely tortured, and later murdered, because he was found to be in possession of a text that was part of the Freiburg memorandum.

The beginning of a difficult engagement

Only a week after 18 October, the day on which Bonhoeffer held a prayer service for Ruth von Kleist and her granddaughter, the news came that Maria's brother Max, to whom she had been especially close, had also been killed in action on the eastern front. Because Bonhoeffer had confirmed Max, Ruth von Kleist invited him to the funeral, but Ruth von Wedemeyer telephoned and asked him not to come. She was afraid the grandmother's influence on the granddaughter was becoming inappropriate at this point, so she took the risk of a conflict with her powerful, though universally beloved and respected mother. She felt that her daughter especially needed to be left in peace after the deaths of her father and brother.

But Maria found out that Bonhoeffer had been asked not to come to the funeral, and was shocked. She wrote to him spontaneously and tried to explain the ins-and-outs of her family, and added the sentence: 'But all that has nothing whatever to do with the two of us.' Bonhoeffer reacted as though all he had read was her words, 'the two of us', referring to herself and him, and wrote back that he hoped they would see each other again 'soon, very soon'. That had not been the meaning Maria had intended, so she showed the letter to her mother, and the mother asked Bonhoeffer not to write to her daughter for the time being. She said she would be glad to explain the reasons face to face. Bonhoeffer took up this invitation right away, travelled to Pätzig on 24 November 1942, spent the night there, and reported to Bethge two days later on the outcome of the conversation:

From Tuesday through Wednesday noon I was at Mrs Wedemeyer's. Contrary to my fears that the house would have an excessively spiritual tone, its style made a very pleasant impression. She herself was calm, friendly and not overwrought, as I had feared. Gist of the discussion she requested: a year of total separation to enable Maria to find some peace. No fundamental objection to the whole thing, but given the enormity of the decision, etc.... . My response: these days a year could just as well become five or ten and thus represented a postponement into the incalculable; that I understood and respected her maternal authority over her daughter, but future circumstances themselves would show whether such a stipulation could be followed ...

I am not yet decided about my next move; for now I shall remain silent. At this point there is no hurry; first the storm must pass somewhat. I think that if I wanted to, I could prevail. I can argue better than the others and could probably talk them into it. But that seems dreadful to me; it strikes me as evil, like an exploitation of the others' weakness. Through the loss of her husband, thus precisely in her weakness, Mrs Wedemeyer is stronger than if I would have had to deal with him. It would be wrong of me to give her the feeling of defencelessness now – that would be deplorable. But this makes my situation more difficult. (DBWE 16, 374–75)

Eberhard Bethge, who wanted to become engaged to marry Bonhoeffer's 17-year-old niece Renate Schleicher, was in a similar situation. Her parents were also talking of a rather long separation, at which Bonhoeffer sighed, 'Everywhere the same – old-fashioned – ideas hearkening back to past times' (DBWE 16, 375).

It was an understandable reaction, but not a fair one. The motive on the Pätzig side had not been simply to cleave to outmoded custom. Wanting only the best for her daughter, Ruth von Wedemeyer could not do otherwise than insist on a time to think it over. Her daughter had lost both of the two people to whom she was closest, her father and her elder brother. Didn't she need some time to recover? Ruth von Wedemeyer saw that her own mother longed for nothing so much as to see her granddaughter united with this Pastor Bonhoeffer whom she esteemed so highly, while the 18-year-old, very strong-willed girl herself had not yet really decided that this was what she wanted.

Bonhoeffer was almost twice Maria's age, had been in conflict with the state over his ministry, and had no secure employment. He worked as a civilian for the military, but no one was allowed to know in what role. Ruth von Wedemeyer did find it right and good that he was a pastor and that he was opposed to the Nazi state. She knew that he was a man of faith, and this must have been one of the fundamental prerequisites that she wanted to see in a son-in-law. She was deeply impressed with Bonhoeffer as a person and would be able to accept him as a son. On one point only was she not to be moved: her daughter must be allowed first of all, without influence or pressure from whomever it might be, to become clear about what she really wanted.

Though Bonhoeffer had imagined all this entirely differently, he had to go along with her wishes. And so the time passed by during which he and Maria would have had the possibility of seeing one another freely. Ruth von Wedemeyer later reproached herself severely for being the cause, but her daughter Maria and Dietrich Bonhoeffer both knew that, from her point of view, she could not have acted otherwise.

The beginning of the end for Hitler

While the Freiburg group was working on its memorandum, Dohnanyi and his comrades-in-arms, including Dietrich Bonhoeffer, entered a final period of feverish activity. Seen from outside the country, it was the time when Hitler was at the height of his power. Rommel's army in North Africa was about to reach the Nile, and would soon be able to blockade the Suez Canal and thus cut off the British supply lines. In Russia, German troops were in the Caucasus and had reached the Volga. Halder, who had urgently appealed to Hitler not to stretch the front so far, was removed from his post as General Chief of Staff. The south of France had until then not been occupied, according to the terms of the ceasefire, but these terms were violated by the total occupation of the country. Switzerland now lay exposed to attack by Hitler's forces, and its government had thus become vulnerable to blackmail.

But this zenith of Nazi power was also the beginning of its downfall. On 23 October 1942, General Montgomery attacked the German line near El Alamein. After a 12-day battle he succeeded in breaking through, and Rommel's army was lost. The Allies landed in Morocco and Algeria and pushed on towards Tunisia. On 19 November the battle for Stalingrad began. On the days when Bonhoeffer was in Pätzig talking with Ruth von Wedemeyer, the Russian city was completely encircled and 22 German divisions were caught inside the ring. Hitler had forbidden the German commander, General Paulus, to make any attempt to break out. He consciously accepted the tragedy that was about to take place, and promoted Paulus, whom he expected to fight until the last of the trapped men perished, to the rank of field marshal.

On 14 January 1943, the Allied summit at Casablanca agreed to pursue the war until Germany was forced into unconditional surrender. This also affected the conspirators. They had been fighting above all, since the the invasion of Russia was launched, to stop Hitler's murderous machinery once and for all by means of assassination. Their work must go on, even though the hopes they had held after Bonhoeffer's meeting with Bishop Bell had now vanished. In a fanatical speech at the Berlin Sports Palace on 18 February 1943, Goebbels proclaimed all-out war, and was frenetically applauded by an audience carefully selected for him by the Party, the SS and government ministries.

This was the day on which the students of the White Rose anti-Nazi movement in Munich were caught distributing their flyers and arrested. Freisler gave them short shrift at their trial. Only four days later, on 22 February, Hans and Sophie Scholl, brother and sister, were executed.[62] From that moment, every thoughtful person could see that the verdicts of Roland Freisler were judicial murders, and that he was not even following the rules for conducting trials. And the German people learned for the first time that there were persons who had the courage to confront Hitler.

In the autumn of 1942 the office of customs investigations in Prague had arrested a currency smuggler who claimed at his hearing to have been doing a job for Consul Schmidhuber. Schmidhuber was the man with whom Dohnanyi and Bonhoeffer had met and travelled in Italy; he belonged to the Military Intelligence office in Munich. Currency smuggling was not unusual among Party chiefs, but for anyone else it was an offence punishable by death. The Reich SS Headquarters immediately smelled a chance to get not only the Munich office, but the whole of Military Intelligence under Admiral Canaris, involved in this affair, and thus finally to rid itself of its rival in the military.

Neither the Admiral nor his leading colleagues realized how the net had already tightened around Canaris's office. But Hans von Dohnanyi knew that he had enemies among his colleagues, and that there was a danger that the SS, investigating Schmidhuber's case, would come across 'Operation 7'. However, in SS Headquarters itself there was at least one person associated with the conspiracy – SS Major General Arthur Nebe, the head of the Reich Criminal Investigation office. Dohnanyi and Bonhoeffer were warned by Nebe that they were in danger. In this situation, the two of them profited for a while from the jumble of jurisdictions in Hitler's system of government, which allowed the dictator to play off one institution against another and thus maintain his own power.

Currency violations were supposed to be investigated by the SS head office, but before its people could begin their probe of Military Intelligence they had to have the consent of Field Marshal Keitel as head of the Army High Command. This raised the question of whether, in a trial of Military Intelligence staff members, things might be brought to light that were supposed to remain secret in the interest of national security. While the tug-of-war over this issue dragged on for weeks, Dohnanyi and Bonhoeffer had time to arrange, as far as possible, for safeguards and could agree on how to proceed in case of hearings. Dohnanyi went to Switzerland to make sure nothing untoward could happen during interrogations of the 14 Jews who had been rescued regarding their financial affairs. Bonhoeffer had been planning a longer trip abroad and already had his visas, but Dohnanyi and Oster decided it was best for him not to go in case he should be arrested at the border.

It was crucial to make sure the exemptions from military service which Military Intelligence had granted were on record in the files and thus properly validated. When it became evident that major military defeats were on the way, all service jobs and factories were combed through for able-bodied men; the people called this 'pinching heroes'. Canaris's staff had to be able to document absolutely correctly why men like Niesel, Rott, Bethge and especially Bonhoeffer, all of whose professional qualifications were theological, had been indispensible for their work in military intelligence. For example, Bethge wrote a description of his relations with church mission circles abroad. Since Bonhoeffer could become entangled in the Schmidhuber case, great care needed to be exercised on his behalf particularly. After thoroughly discussing it with Dohnanyi, he wrote a letter to Dohnanyi on Max Krause stationery, which had not been available in the shops since 1940, and dated it 4 November 1940. This predated letter has been preserved.

Dear Hans, when we were discussing ecumenical matters recently, you asked me whether I would not be prepared, if need be, to make available my knowledge of foreign countries and my connections with people in public life in Europe and overseas, to assist in the acquisition of reliable information about foreign countries. I have been thinking the matter over. In the context of the problems you are interested in, the special feature of the ecumenical work is, of course, the fact that leading political personalities in various countries are interested in the movement, in which all the larger churches of the world, except the church of Rome, have joined together. So it really might not be difficult to learn the views and judgements of these personalities by way of such ecumenical relationships. Beyond that, I think it is quite within the realm of possibility that one might establish fresh contacts that could perhaps be of use in dealing with specialized questions ... (DB-ER, 783)

He then named a number of prominent foreign leaders such as Sir Stafford Cripps and Lord Lothian, for whose journal he had once provided an article on the church struggle. Lord Lothian was now dead, but had been living in 1940 at the time the letter was supposed to have been written, so his name helped make the false date credible.

Later in prison, Bonhoeffer wrote an essay entitled 'What does it mean to tell the truth?' This short treatise places his conduct during his hearings, and what he had already done in this fictitious letter, in the proper light. He was last person who would have assumed that he had the right to tell lies just for any reason he might think of.

If one then asserts that a lie is the conscious deception of others, to their harm, this also would include, for example, the necessary deception of the enemy in war or in analogous situations. (Kant, of course, declared that he was too proud ever to tell an untruth, yet at the same time he was compelled to extend this assertion *ad absurdum* by declaring that if a friend sought refuge with him, he would feel obliged to provide truthful information to a criminal in pursuit of the friend) ... (DBWE 16, 606–07)

How do I speak a true word? 1) by recognizing who calls on me to speak and what authorizes me to speak; 2) by recognizing the place where I am standing; 3) by putting the subject I am speaking about into this context. (DBWE 16, 608)

The fictitious letter he had written is clearly an 'analogous situation' to the necessity of deceiving the enemy in a time of war.

So that their opponents would not notice that he and Dohnanyi had been warned, Bonhoeffer had to continue preparing for his intended travel abroad. It was to begin with a brief side trip to Switzerland. The journey was now set for January 1943, to demonstrate that Bonhoeffer's contacts were indispensable to Military Intelligence. This was also part of 'deceiving the enemy'. Before the warning was received, he had been planning to travel, over three months, to Croatia, Hungary, Bulgaria, Greece, Italy and Turkey, coming back to Berlin for debriefing after each journey. Around this time, Josef Müller went to Switzerland and then on to Rome. Since the expected strike by the SS against Canaris's office seemed not to be coming, the conspirators began to feel more confident again. But this was an illusion.

The engagement

At this moment of extreme tension, Maria von Wedemeyer decided not to wait out the 'year of separation' any longer, but rather to give Bonhoeffer her Yes. It would never have occurred to her to take such a step without telling her mother, but she was determined to have her way. Ruth von Wedemeyer gave in to her strong-willed daughter, but asked the engaged couple please not to announce their engagement yet, and especially to put off setting a date for their wedding. The letter in which Maria declared to Dietrich Bonhoeffer that she had decided to share her life with him reveals a remarkable strength of mind.

Dear Pastor Bonhoeffer,

I've known ever since arriving home that I must write to you, and I've looked forward to doing so.

I spoke with my mother and my uncle [Hans-Jürgen von Kleist Retzow] from Kieckow. Now I can write to you and ask you to answer this letter.

I find it hard to have to tell you in writing what can scarcely be uttered in person.

I would rather disown every word that demands to be said on the subject, because it makes things that were better conveyed quietly sound so crude and clumsy. But, knowing from experience how well you understand me, I'm now bold enough to write to you even though I've really no right whatever to answer a question which you have never asked me.

With all my happy heart, I can now say yes.[63]

Maria von Wedemeyer after the Second World War

The day on which this letter was written, 13 January 1943, was henceforth regarded by the couple as the day they became engaged. Yet Maria von Wedemeyer had agreed to her mother's wish that they keep to the agreed-upon year of separation, because, as she wrote to Bonhoeffer, she felt she 'still needed some time to think'.

Bonhoeffer's reply, in which he wrote 'Dear Maria' instead of 'Dear Miss Wedemeyer', overflowed with joy: '... my heart is opening wide and brimming over with gratitude and confusion and still can't take it in – the "yes" that is to determine the entire future course of our lives'. And of course, he said, she must have whatever time and quiet she needed for her inner thoughts. 'With your "yes", I too can now wait patiently; without that yes I was finding it hard, and would have found it increasingly so. Now that I know what you want and need, it's easy.'[64]

The assassination attempts in March 1943

It was in October 1941 that Major General Henning von Tresckow, Chief of Staff of the Central Army Group, made the first concrete plans, together with the Resistance Group in Military Intelligence, for an overthrow of Hitler. Even as retired General Chief of Staff, General Beck was able to keep the high commanders of this portion of the front – first Field Marshal Bock and later Field Marshal Kluge – surrounded by officers whom he trusted. Tresckow had worked doggedly to convince his superior, and in October 1942 Carl Goerdeler went to Smolensk for a confidential discussion with the procrastinating Kluge. At first there had been high hopes for Halder, but since Hitler had removed him all Resistance hopes were now concentrated on the group around Tresckow, all the more so when it became known that Hitler was planning to visit the Central Army Group of the Russian front. The decisive measures that would have to be taken from Berlin after a successful assassination would be in the hands of General Olbricht, head of the army office and a friend of Oster's.

After Hitler had postponed his visit to Smolensk several times, in February 1943 Fabian von Schlabrendorff appeared in Berlin with the news that Hitler was expected in Smolensk on 13 March. Dohnanyi immediately went there to make final arrangements with Tresckow.[65] It was Bethge who drove him, in Karl Bonhoeffer's car (to which he was entitled as a doctor), to the night train to Königsberg, unaware that in Dohnanyi's suitcase was a newly developed English explosive which Military Intelligence had been able to obtain. The bomb was to be assembled in Smolensk. From East Prussia, Canaris and Dohnanyi flew to Kluge's headquarters, where the Admiral had arranged a meeting of all intelligence officers in the army group. Dohnanyi delivered the explosive, settled with Tresckow the code for notification of the plot's success, and returned immediately to Berlin.

When Hitler boarded his plane on 13 March, to fly back from Smolensk to his 'wolf's lair' in East Prussia, the conspirators had managed to smuggle aboard a small package containing the bombs disguised as two bottles of Cointreau. But although the time fuse worked, for reasons unknown to this day the bombs failed to explode, and Hitler's plane landed safely at his East Prussian headquarters. Schlabrendorff succeeded in retrieving the potentially fatal evidence, and those who knew about it celebrated this as a success in itself; but a tremendous opportunity for the conspiracy had passed. Hitler's death at such a distance from his assassins would have been nearly impossible to explain, and the centres of power in the Nazi government, the SS, the secret police and the Party apparatus would have been overwhelmed before they had a chance to protect themselves. But the conspirators did not lose a moment to discouragement. They did not even change the sequence of the plan, for only a few days later, on 21 March 1943, there would be an opportunity in Berlin for another attempt to kill Hitler.

In Bavaria meanwhile, Bonhoeffer received a summons to report for induction into the military. On 22 March he was to appear in Munich with all his papers in order. This absolutely had to be prevented so that he would not become separated from Dohnanyi in what was a critically dangerous situation. For one last time, Dohnanyi's office connections worked and the summons was withdrawn. What the conspirators did not know, however, was that the SS had finally prevailed over the military and gained the consent of Keitel, chief of the Army High Command, for an investigation into the Schmidhuber case under the rubric 'deposit account'.

The 21st of March was Heroes' Remembrance Day, a Sunday. At the Schleichers' house in Marienburger Allee, the Bonhoeffer children, their spouses and the grandchildren, led by Eberhard Bethge, were rehearsing the cantata by the blind organist Helmuth Walcha, *Lobe den Herrn, den mächtigen König der Ehren* (Praise to the Lord, the Almighty, the King of Creation), for Karl Bonhoeffer's 75th birthday. In many Christian families at the time, the original chorale of 1680 by Joachim Neander of Düsseldorf was sung as a birthday hymn. On 31 March the Bonhoeffers were to perfom the cantata with instrumental accompaniment. Dietrich Bonhoeffer was at the grand piano, Rüdiger Schleicher and Emmi Bonhoeffer played violin, Klaus Bonhoeffer cello, and everyone else made up the choir. A year later, Bonhoeffer wrote in a letter, smuggled out of the prison, to Bethge: 'That you succeeded, for instance, in getting Hans and Christel to sing with us is one of your best and most amazing accomplishments, and truly also a form of asserting yourself!' (DBWE 8, II/117)

> Praise to the Lord, who o'er all things so wondrously reigneth,
> Shieldeth thee under his wings, yea, so gently sustaineth,
> Hast thou not seen how thy desires have been
> Granted in what he ordaineth ...[66]

So sang the little choir, while Hans von Dohnanyi kept looking at his watch, and his wife Christel whispered to her sister Ursula, 'It must go off any moment now!' In front of the house, Dohnanyi's official car was waiting to take him to the operations centre.

In the *Zeughaus*, the Prussian war museum in the city centre, Hitler had arrived for a state ceremony. The conspirators had obtained his timetable beforehand. The solemnities were to be followed by an inspection tour of the Central Army unit's trophies. Colonel Gersdorff, Military Intelligence officer for the unit, was to conduct Hitler. He had a bomb hidden in his coat pocket, and planned to jump on the dictator and blow himself up with him. Gersdorff was one of several officers who had said they were prepared to carry out such an attack at the sacrifice of their own lives. But

Hitler hurried through the exhibition in a few minutes, and left before the 10-minute fuse had time to work. Gersdorff had only a couple of minutes to reach the lavatory and defuse the bomb.

For Bonhoeffer and Dohnanyi, that Sunday morning was the high point in their lives. They had given their all to 'seize the spokes and stop the wheel', to change decisively the course of Germany's history. On that day, Hitler's fate hung on a knife's edge. Everything that was to take place after his death was planned in detail. After that morning, nothing was the same any longer. The cantata was performed for Karl Bonhoeffer's 75th birthday; but five days later, on 5 April 1943, Hans and Christine von Dohnanyi and Dietrich Bonhoeffer were arrested. From then on they had to fight not only for their own lives, but above all to keep the conspiracy from being discovered. As Bethge says:

The most promising period of the German resistance was over. Costly work had been done in vain, while fresh crimes and suffering mounted. What Stauffenberg was to say shortly before 20 July 1944 was already true: the overthrow can no longer change anything in the hopeless political and military situation. (DB-ER 780)

11. In Prison (1943–1945)

The arrests and first interrogations

The head of the army legal department, Dr Lehmann, had assured Canaris at the beginning of April that nothing serious would happen in Dohnanyi's case in the next few days; he was hoping to get the matter out of the hands of the Gestapo. What he did not say was that, in February, Criminal Commissioner Franz-Xaver Sonderegger had written a report on the Schmidhuber case in which Josef Müller, Dohnanyi and Bonhoeffer were all significantly implicated.

Heinrich Müller, the Gestapo chief, had agreed with Colonel Manfred Roeder, the investigating judge in the War Court, that he himself would pass this report to Himmler at the SS, while Roeder was to pass it on to Field Marshal Keitel, chief of the Army High Command. On the way to Keitel the report came first to Lehmann, who had two colleagues read it, and they concurred with him that the real target was Canaris. Lehmann telephoned Keitel, who agreed that the matter must be pursued, but if at all possible it should be done through the military justice system and not through the Reich SS Headquarters. Lehmann recommended to Keitel that the case be assigned to Roeder, because the SS would be satisfied and in this way the matter would stay within the jurisdiction of the War Court.

On the morning of 5 April, Roeder appeared with Sonderegger at Canaris's office and announced that he had come to arrest Dohnanyi. Visibly shaken, the Military Intelligence chief showed him the way, and since Dohnanyi's office could only be entered through Oster's office, Oster also learned what Roeder's business was. He curtly demanded that Roeder arrest him as well, since Dohnanyi had not done anything without his knowledge. Dohnanyi, for his part, had cleared out his office thoroughly – a fairly large sum of money belonging to the Confessing Church had been taken away to safety only a few days previously – but it was a terrible shock to him when Roeder, Sonderegger, Oster and Canaris appeared in his office unannounced. His secretary later reported that he was still quite pale when he was led away.

Criminal Commissioner Franz-Xaver Sonderegger directed the preliminary investigations and was assigned to work with the investigating judge, Roeder

Roeder told Dohnanyi briefly that he was under arrest, and began to search the room. In the process something happened which was referred to, in the accounts that circulated after the war, as the 'Zettel affair'. A Zettel, in German, is a slip of paper used for brief notes. Although Dohnanyi had cleared all incriminating papers out of his office, Roeder found, and laid on Dohnanyi's desk with a bundle of other files, a grey file folder marked with a Z, with notes on three topics that Dohnanyi had prepared for a meeting that afternoon. One concerned the situation of the Confessing Church; the second was the authorization by Military Intelligence of Müller's and Bonhoeffer's trip to Rome, planned for 9 April; the third appeared to give more details about Bonhoeffer's assignment there, though for those 'in the know' it was really about the work of the professors in Freiburg. The two emissaries were to explain in Rome that the coup attempts on 13 and 21 March had failed; what the note gave was their cover story, that the 'representative of a group of German Protestant clergymen who were discussing the concept of peace was to seek to influence the pope's Christmas peace message, which was expected to set forth the Catholic Church's ideas about peace, respected worldwide'.[1]

Dohnanyi wanted to have this 'code message' approved by Canaris, and tried to pull the grey folder with these notes out of the pile Roeder had put on his desk, but Roeder stopped him. However, because a few minutes earlier Dohnanyi had whispered to Oster, 'Send my wife a note [Zettel]!' and Oster apparently caught only the word 'Zettel', the latter tried to pick up the note unobserved and put it in his coat pocket. Sonderegger saw him and pointed this out to Roeder, who ordered Oster to hand over the note and leave the room. The same day Roeder was able, with Keitel's consent, to have Oster suspended from his office on suspicion of being an accessory after the fact, and placed under house arrest.[2] On 16 April he was dismissed as chief of staff for Military Intelligence and transferred to the officer reserves. Without realizing it, Roeder had paralysed the centre of the Resistance.

Senior Military Prosecutor Manfred Roeder

Dohnanyi was taken to the military officers' prison, next to the Lehrter Railway Station, under top secret arrangements and confined there under a false name. The proceedings against him were to be classified and carried out as top secret. Roeder thought that in these 'Zettel' he had proof of high treason on Dohnanyi's part, a suspicion that seemed confirmed when Oster stated during an interrogation that he had never seen these notes, and had never signed the one he had tried to take, although it was found to have an initial O. on the back.

At noon that day, 5 April, at his parents' home, Bonhoeffer had tried to telephone his sister Christine; when an unfamiliar voice answered the phone, the thought flashed through his mind: her house is being searched! Without disturbing his parents, he went next door, where his sister Ursula prepared a hearty midday meal for him. Then he went to his study in the attic to ensure that every precaution had been taken should it be searched, and thereafter waited, with Ursula and Rüdiger Schleicher as well as Eberhard Bethge, for whatever was to happen. About four o'clock in the afternoon, his father came over and said, 'There are two men up in your room who would like to speak to you.' The two, Roeder and Sonderegger, had already arrested Christine von Dohnanyi, and they soon drove away with Bonhoeffer. In Munich that same day, Josef and Anni Müller were also arrested.

Maria von Wedemeyer was at the time in training as a nurse with the Red Cross in Hanover. Soon after that day she sealed the diary she had been keeping, and it was not opened again until after her death, when her correspondence with Bonhoeffer, the *Love Letters from Cell 92*, was being prepared for publication. On 5 April 1943 she had written, 'Has something bad happened? I'm afraid it must be something very bad.'[3] On 18 April she had leave to go to Pätzig for the confirmation of her brother Hans-Werner. While out for a walk with her brother-in-law, Klaus von Bismarck, she told him that despite the promise to her mother she was determined to see Dietrich. When the two of them returned to the house they met Maria's uncle, Hans-Jürgen von Kleist, who told them that Bonhoeffer had been arrested. As a sign of her commitment to her fiancé, Maria then insisted that their engagement be made public. Her mother agreed to this; she understood that her daughter could not now do otherwise.

The conspirators' centre of operations had been destroyed in an instant by Dohnanyi's arrest and Oster's house arrest, and with others also arrested, they knew that their personal safety depended on how the prisoners stood up to interrogation. They could depend on the legal skills of Hans von Dohnanyi and Josef Müller, and their wives could credibly affirm that they themselves had known nothing. But would a clergyman, who could not deny that he had been involved, see through the cunning questions that a man like Roeder might ask in order to trap him? Bonhoeffer had been present at important discussions. His meeting with Bell had not only been approved by Beck; the general had himself ordered Bonhoeffer to give the names of all the Resistance leaders to the English bishop.

Roeder was known to be both clever and brutal. There was no doubt that the other conspirators would now have regarded Bonhoeffer as the weakest link in the chain. Only if he reacted correctly during interrogation could they construct a new centre of operations and begin their plans over again. If he failed to do so, they would all find themselves in Freisler's People's Court. Would Bonhoeffer stand up to physical pressure? As soon as Roeder found out that he had someone before him who was hiding important knowledge while pretending to be an unsuspecting pastor, he would have this prisoner tortured. Bonhoeffer would by no means be the first of Roeder's victims to receive such treatment. For the next few weeks, the fate of the Resistance movement depended upon Dietrich Bonhoeffer.

Manfred Roeder, the man to whom the 'Dohnanyi case' had been assigned, and with whom Bonhoeffer too would have to fight out his case, belonged to the Air Force and liked to mention in passing that he was a regular visitor to Karinhall, Göring's country palace. He had been the chief prosecutor against the 'Rote Kapelle', a Resistance group that had contacted the Soviet Union in the hope of overthrowing Hitler with the help of Russia. Only by mentioning Roeder's name had Göring been able to get Hitler's consent to holding their trial in the War Court instead of the People's Court. Dohnanyi and Bonhoeffer, too, were to be tried in the War Court, but the SS promised in advance to give Roeder its full support. For the SS Headquarters, it was only a side issue to get rid of these men as 'enemies of the State'. The crucial goal was to eliminate Canaris's office, so as to incorporate Military Intelligence at last into the

SS Headquarters. For this purpose a room in the SS Headquarters had been assigned to Roeder, who had ties to several high-ranking SS officers; Sonderegger, who had investigated the Schmidhuber case in Munich, had been assigned to work for him.

Roeder had secured 45 death sentences in the trial of the 'Rote Kapelle', and was still proud of it after the war. He was unscrupulous to the point of having Liane Berkowitz beheaded only a few days after the birth of her first child, and after the war it was said that he had even had pregnant women put to death. The former Prussian Minister of Culture and later director of Northwest German Radio, Adolf Grimme, was also caught up in this trial. He said after the war that Roeder proved to be 'one of the most inhuman, cynical and brutal Nazis' he had ever encountered.[4]

The 'Rote Kapelle' was not recognized as a Resistance group until long after 1945, because it had maintained contacts with the Soviet Union. The group had operated through secret radio transmitters; such operators were known among newscasters as 'pianists',[5] hence the nickname 'Rote Kapelle [Red Band]'. The group had been broken up because of inadequately coded Soviet messages containing addresses, which the Gestapo had been able to decode. The first 12 death sentences were handed down on 19 December 1942 and carried out rapidly, one every three minutes, three days later at Plötzensee Prison. Hitler had had the trials of Mildred Harnack and Countess Erika Brockdorff transferred to another panel of judges in the War Court, so that their sentences could be changed from the penitentiary to death sentences.

The prosecution of subgroups of the 'Rote Kapelle' was still going on while Dohnanyi and Bonhoeffer were being interrogated. So Dohnanyi had to resolve to face a hard struggle, and everything depended on Bonhoeffer's keeping exactly to the rules on which they had agreed for such an eventuality. One of these was that whenever a subject looked to him like dangerous territory, he must say it was Dohnanyi's responsibility; the latter would be best able to see through and defend himself against the question.

Roeder saw Dohnanyi as his real opponent, and presumably thought that a clergyman would in any case be no match for him. In this way he played into the hands of both prisoners. The first stage of Bonhoeffer's imprisonment mirrored the situation of his brother-in-law, who became the subject of his first interrogations. To make it clear that he was to be considered the truly responsible party, Dohnanyi gave up his chance to write an Easter letter to his family and wrote instead, on 23 April, a letter to Bonhoeffer which was really intended for Roeder's censoring eyes:

My dear Dietrich, I don't know if I'll be allowed to send you this greeting, but I'll try. Outside, the church bells are ringing for the service ... You can't imagine how unhappy I am to be the reason that you, Christel, the children and our parents should have to suffer like this, and that my dear wife and you should have your freedom taken away ... If I knew that you all – that you personally – did not think badly of me, I'd feel so relieved. What wouldn't I give to know that you were all free again; what wouldn't I take upon myself if you could be spared this affliction. It was wonderful to be able to see you. I've been allowed to see Christel too – but what can you say in front of other people ... No one can know what it means not to be able to be with her in this time of trial. It certainly does not help in the matter ... (DB-ER 800–1)

The style of the letters Dohnanyi and Bonhoeffer wrote in prison is nothing if not admirable. They had to admit what their position was as captives in the hands of their persecutors. At the same time, they wanted to show the recipients of their letters: we are keeping our composure, just as you are. What we shall have to endure, we can bear, and we are not giving up the fight for our future. Karl and Paula Bonhoeffer replied in the same vein. After their first visit to Dietrich, his father wrote:

It has definitely been very reassuring for us to be able to speak with you the other day, to see with our own eyes that you are physically quite well, and that you are bearing the awful trial that has been imposed upon you with internal composure and the confidence that comes from a clear conscience. (DBWE 8, I/21)

Roeder treated Dohnanyi from the beginning as a criminal who was guilty of high treason. He gave hints that there was interest in this case at the highest levels of the Reich, and indeed not only Keitel had been informed, but also Gestapo chief Müller, Central Security chief Kaltenbrunner and Himmler as head of the SS, the Party general secretary Bormann and even Hitler himself – not just about the investigation leading to the prosecution but equally about the course of the proceedings themselves. Roeder refused to have Dohnanyi's statements correctly recorded, took documents away from him that were intended for his defence and even tried to keep him from engaging a defence lawyer. Even so, after months of effort, Roeder still had not succeeded in bringing charges against him that would hold water. As a jurist he was simply not Dohnanyi's equal.

Christine von Dohnanyi was released from the women's prison, sick and miserable, on 30 April. As her husband's closest confidante she had such an exceptional knowledge of his affairs that she could mobilize help immediately when it was needed. First she gave her attention to the 'Zettel affair'. There had been precise discussion and agreement as to how communications were to be maintained in such a situation, so it was not long until Oster was informed, through a secret message from Dohnanyi, as to why it was crucial for all concerned that he acknowledge the content of the notes about Bonhoeffer's intended trip to Rome. He immediately retracted his former statement and acknowledged the *Zettel* with the 'O.' on the back as having been initialled by him. Soon afterwards, Dohnanyi, Oster and Canaris were able to make Roeder accept the version that the *Zettel* was a normal, encoded Military Intelligence document.

In the background the struggle was continuing between the two opposing groups within Military Intelligence. Oster's and Dohnanyi's main opponents among their colleagues were the office manager, Colonel Johannes Toeppen, and the director of the legal affairs group, Walter Herzlieb. Both these men hated Oster, and especially Dohnanyi, because of the position of trust they enjoyed with Admiral Canaris, so Toeppen repeatedly provided Roeder with material that would arouse fresh suspicions against Dohnanyi. Meanwhile Klaus Bonhoeffer's brother-in-law Justus Delbrück, Baron Karl-Ludwig von Guttenberg and others were helping Canaris to refute Roeder's points for his charges against Dohnanyi. Roeder was not in the good graces of his superior, Dr Lehmann, head of the Army legal department, who was able to keep the accused prisoners from being expelled from the military. This was important, because otherwise they would have been turned over to the SS immediately.

The members of the ZB (Foreign Policy Reporting) office in the Military Intelligence Central Office: (left to right) Baron Karl-Ludwig von Guttenberg, Hans von Dohnanyi and Justus Delbrück. Photo from Hans Oster's birthday party in 1942

What was simply decisive, however, was the help of Justice Karl Sack of the General Staff, with whom Dohnanyi had already collaborated on the Fritsch case. Rüdiger Schleicher, in his uniform as a member of the Air Force legal department, could go in and out of Sack's office without attracting attention. It was more dangerous for Perels as a civilian, but he too received information and warnings from Sack, on an ongoing basis, to take to the Bonhoeffer family for concealment in books and food packages destined for the two prisoners.

Nevertheless, over the course of time Sack and Dohnanyi came to assess the situation differently. Dohnanyi, and Bonhoeffer too, were trying to obtain the earliest possible dates for their trials, both hoping to be acquitted. Sack, however, could see more clearly than Dohnanyi could in prison the danger to Admiral Canaris's Military Intelligence office. He was afraid that the entire case would be submitted to Hitler for his decision, if there were no success in depoliticizing the proceedings. He wanted to get Roeder removed from the case; moreover, he wanted to let the whole business 'run out of steam' until the coup, which was once again being feverishly prepared.[6] A new centre for the conspiracy was taking shape in the office of General Olbricht, chief of the General Army office, with Count Claus von Stauffenberg as its driving force.

Roeder had thought at first that in the suspect 'Zettel' he had proof that Dohnanyi and Bonhoeffer had committed high treason. But nothing he did – not allowing Dohnanyi to read, write or smoke; threatening to 'finish him off' and that Hitler would make 'short work' of him if he didn't open up – brought anything more than Dohnanyi's insistence that the note was normal Military Intelligence material. When Oster confirmed this on 17 June, and Canaris had repudiated every suspicion cast on his staff, not much was left of this first line of attack. So Roeder seized upon 'Operation 7'. He succeeded in having a lawyer sent to Switzerland to interrogate the rescued Jews, but they were not deceived. And when the lawyer saw for what purpose his services had been used, he told Klaus Bonhoeffer, with whom he was acquainted, about his trip and its outcome. When Canaris found out that Toeppen had engineered the sending of this lawyer, he dismissed Toeppen from Military Intelligence.

It would be characteristic of Roeder that he could not imagine why Dohnanyi had organized 'Operation 7', since there was no indication he had profited financially by it. It was Toeppen who had repeatedly insinuated that he had, though Toeppen had to be careful because he and some friends had themselves engaged in transfers of currency, which they did not want brought to light. As an official who was meticulous to a fault, Dohnanyi found these suspicions especially distasteful even though they did not lead anywhere. Meanwhile, investigation of exemptions of Confessing Church pastors from military service proved laborious, as we shall see in Bonhoeffer's case. Furthermore, in pursuing this line Roeder had moved rather far afield from charges like high treason. In the end he got tangled up in trying to prove irregularities in Dohnanyi's accounting for currency exchanges, taxes, travel expenses and interest charges.

At this point Sack succeeded in convincing Keitel that Roeder and the SS Headquarters actually had Canaris in their sights instead of Dohnanyi, and that their aim was to weaken the military to the advantage of the SS. Keitel had Dr Lehmann examine the files and, on receiving his report, gave the order on 23 July 1943 that this case was not to be continued on charges of high treason. That did not leave anything very weighty to pursue.

Dohnanyi's imprisonment was a period of unparalleled suffering. He had a much harder time of it than Bonhoeffer. It began with a bad case of phlebitis in both legs. His family wanted to bring in the leading Berlin physician Dr Ferdinand Sauerbruch, but Roeder prevented them. During an air raid in November 1943, in which Roeder's court files were destroyed by fire, a firebomb struck Dohnanyi's cell, and when the guards finally came to check on his welfare he had suffered an embolism in his brain. Sack and Lehmann could not reach Roeder by telephone and decided to have Dohnanyi taken to the Charité Hospital under Sauerbruch's care. Roeder turned up there two days later, raging to have his victim returned to him, but Sauerbruch would not release Dohnanyi, saying he was in danger of further embolisms.

Roeder ordered that no one but Dohnanyi's wife and children was to see or speak with him; but Sauerbruch and his assistant allowed all visitors who were important to the patient to visit him at night during blackouts. Roeder must have suspected this, for after a time he sent an ambulance with medical orderlies to move Dohnanyi to a prison hospital. Sauerbruch sent them away. But in January he had to go out of town, and Roeder immediately appeared at the Charité Hospital and took Dohnanyi to the prison hospital in Buch on the north side of Berlin.

There, Roeder obtained Keitel's permission for Professor Max de Crinis to examine Dohnanyi, to certify whether he was fit for normal imprisonment and for interrogations. De Crinis was the successor to Karl Bonhoeffer, who had retired as head of the Charité Hospital's Psychiatric department in 1938, and his first act as the new chief had been to have a large bust of Hitler installed in the foyer. He was a civilian SS member and had friends among the SS leaders. He provided a report exactly to Roeder's liking, sent a notice to SS Headquarters that his recommendations had been carried out, and asked that Central Security chief Kaltenbrunner be informed.

In the Tegel military prison

Bonhoeffer was brought to the Tegel prison in the early evening of 5 April 1943. As soon as he was allowed to write to his parents, he assured them that he was all right and didn't really need anything, but he later gave quite another description of his situation to his friend Eberhard Bethge. In December 1943 he wrote a letter imagining that the two of them were sitting together in the evening as they used to do.

Then I would first have infinitely many questions for you ... And finally I would begin to tell you, e.g., that, despite everything I have written it is horrible here, that the dreadful impressions often pursue me well into the night, and that I can cope with them only by reciting countless verses of hymns, and that then my awakening sometimes begins with a sigh instead of with the praise of God. (DBWE 8, II/86)

This was written after he had been in prison for eight months. Outwardly he was always composed, but he asked his friend, 'What does composure [*Haltung*] mean, actually? ... one knows less about oneself than ever, and one no longer cares to know.'

Around this time he wrote an official report in which he described the beginning of his imprisonment in such detail that we today can still feel how abominable it was.

For the first night I was locked in a reception cell; the blankets on the cot stank so abominably that in spite of the cold, it was impossible to cover oneself with them. The next morning a piece of bread was thrown into my cell, so that I had to pick it up off the floor ... For the first time my cell was invaded by the foul curses inflicted on persons detained for interrogation by the prison staff; since then I have heard the abuse daily from morning till night. (DBWE 8, II/131)

There were 800 prisoners awaiting trial in Tegel. Week after week, some twenty of them were condemned to death, mostly on convictions of 'undermining Germany's defences' (i.e. talking against the regime).

Dietrich Bonhoeffer in Tegel Prison, Berlin, summer 1944

Then new prisoners would arrive. Those condemned to death were confined on the top floor, where Bonhoeffer also was assigned at first. In the daytime the prison was noisy, but at night he could hear the prisoners under death sentences, who occasionally wept. He learned how to communicate with his neighbours by knocking, and like all the inmates he could tell when the condemned ones were being taken away for execution. In his poem 'Night Voices in Tegel', written in prison, he described this:

> A low voice reads something, brusque and cold.
> Compose yourself, Brother, soon it will be finished,
> soon! soon!
> Courageous and proud are your steps I now hear.
> No longer mindful of the moment that's near,
> you see future times coming clear.
> (DBWE 8, III/175)[7]

It is not by chance that the word 'decision' was one of the most important words in Bonhoeffer's life and theology. That people he did not know, who were hostile to his way of thinking, now had the power to decide what happened to him was hard to bear. He had known handcuffs only from the cinema; now they were put on him whenever he was taken from his cell to Roeder's interrogations in the War Court. One of the guards called him a 'scoundrel', and it was all so unaccustomed and humiliating that during the first phase of the interrogations Bonhoeffer must have been going through 'prison shock'. Roeder knew how to exploit this condition, which made the situation more dangerous.

Bonhoeffer wrote notes on such slips of paper as he could find, often single words. On one, 'discontent', 'tension', 'impatience', are followed by 'suicide, not out of a sense of guilt, but because I am practically dead already, the closing of the book, sum total' (DBWE 8, I/12). These must stand for a great deal more. No human being knows how he or she would react to being wounded and tortured. But Bonhoeffer knew how much depended on his not revealing the real context of his draft exemption as a secret agent. In case of doubt, taking his own life would be preferable to betraying his friends. Suicide would be the ultimate consequence of the decision he had made in 1940 to work for the conspiracy; it would be dictated by his ethical convictions. Moreover, the depression which followed his 'prison shock' would have played a role in the idea of 'ending it all'. But Bonhoeffer soon put this thought aside and never mentioned it again.

During this early phase of his imprisonment, nothing helped Bonhoeffer more than his acquaintance with the monastic life and his own experiences of it in Finkenwalde and Ettal. A monk also lives in a 'cell', and knows life in two modes, the *vita activa* and the *vita contemplativa*, the active life and the life of contemplation and prayer. Bonhoeffer had been torn from his active life from one day to the next. He had not chosen to live in a cell as he now was obliged to do; but he succeeded in transforming the *vita contemplativa* that had been forced upon him into one that he could affirm with his inner being, and thus overcame the 'prison shock'.

His Bible had been returned to him on the third day. Now he could go back to reading regularly, as he had done in Finkenwalde, the daily texts indicated in his Moravian devotional book, meditate on them, commit Bible texts to memory and say aloud the hymns of the great German poet Paul Gerhardt that he already knew by heart. He began to observe carefully what went on around him and how this affected his thoughts and feelings; he devised a daily schedule, including physical exercises, and kept to it with an iron will. He knew he had to show himself to be equal to a formidable opponent, and had to prepare himself in body and spirit for the struggle. Bonhoeffer realized right away that Roeder 'would have liked

to finish me off' (DBWE 8, II/79), but he never gave any outward indication that he knew this. Since politeness was second nature to him, he was able to play the role of the guileless pastor who doesn't know how to defend himself in court. Roeder had a reputation for vanity, so he was probably flattered when Bonhoeffer wrote that he couldn't keep up with the tempo set by the 'honourable Senior Military Prosecutor' during the interrogations.

Since Roeder was treating Bonhoeffer like a convicted criminal, he could never have gained a true picture of the man in front of him during these interrogations. Though he did not treat

Bonhoeffer's cell in Tegel Prison, Berlin

Bonhoeffer quite as brutally as Dohnanyi, he used coarse language and tried in all sorts of ways to hoodwink his prisoner. Bonhoeffer had no experience in dealing with the justice system, and the interrogations must have made him somewhat apprehensive. Yet even so, he thwarted Roeder's attempts to lure him into serious contradictions, thanks initially to his strict observance of Dohnanyi's warning to plead ignorance and assign all responsibility to him, Dohnanyi. Later, when Bonhoeffer was allowed visits from his parents, the family network helped. Concealed messages let him in on Roeder's strategy, so that he could coordinate his statements with Dohnanyi's line of defence. No one played a greater role in this than Christine von Dohnanyi, who would find out from her husband how Bonhoeffer should conduct himself and then get the answer to him without ever making the slightest mistake.

Bonhoeffer was soon allowed to have books of his own brought to him, with his name written on the flyleaf. If the family had underlined the name, the book contained a message. Beginning at the back, on every tenth page a single letter was marked lightly with a pencil. On noting these letters in order, Bonhoeffer would have a sentence before him, such as 'Oster now acknowledges *Zettel.*' Bonhoeffer could also return books in which he concealed replies or questions in the same way.

The conditions of his imprisonment were greatly eased when his mother asked her cousin, General Paul von Hase, who happened to be the city commander of Berlin, to ring up the Tegel prison and ask how his nephew, imprisoned there, was getting along. Since the prison was under Hase's command, his telephone call caused great excitement. From one day to the next, Bonhoeffer became a sort of 'star prisoner'. The prison commander stretched his visitation privileges as far as they would go, and all packages delivered by his family were received by the prisoner, which greatly improved his diet. Bonhoeffer was allowed to go to the infirmary, at first because he needed treatment himself, later in order to help out there. Guards who had treated him badly now tried to flatter him, to his boundless disgust. But there were at least three who were anti-Nazi and who, he soon found, were honest through and through. They were prepared to help him in any way. It was they who made possible his 'illegal correspondence' with Eberhard Bethge, containing his new theological reflections while in Tegel, and carried news back and forth between him and his family, although they were putting themselves in danger by doing so.

Of course the books brought to Bonhoeffer from home had another use as well. He had known and loved German literature since his schooldays, and now it helped him escape from Tegel into another and better world. At no other time of his life did he read so many novels, stories and plays as in the first months of his imprisonment. A few books he had been allowed, as early as April, to borrow from the prison library. Roeder, since he was in charge of investigating Bonhoeffer, read what he said about his reading in his letters, and prison officials listened to his conversations with his visitors. Here, exchanges of opinion on nineteenth-century literature became an elevated and non-incriminating topic, and also helped Bonhoeffer to shield his parents from the reality of Tegel Prison.

The situation as such, that is the individual moment, is in fact often not so different from being someplace else. I read, reflect, work, write, pace the room – and I really do so without rubbing myself sore on the wall like a polar bear ... By the way, I have my Bible and reading material from the library here ... I am treated well and read a lot, besides the newspaper and novels especially the Bible. (DBWE 8, I/17, 2 and 6)

Bonhoeffer must have read the Party newspapers in the way pastors read *Neues Deutschland* later in communist East Germany – quickly and knowing exactly the real conditions they concealed – but he mentioned reading the papers especially for Roeder's benefit. The novels he mentioned were also named for the benefit of the man who wanted to 'finish him off', since novels are so unthreatening. But even they quickly gained their own importance, as we can see from Bonhoeffer's comments. We learn that in the prison library he found works by the great Austrian poet Adalbert Stifter, and by Jeremias Gotthelf, K. L. Immermann, Theodor Fontane and Gottfried Keller, and that he read these authors 'with new admiration' because of their beautifully clear language. Unfortunately we are not always given the exact titles he read, but as soon as his family was allowed to bring books, he asked for Fontane's *The Stechlin, Jenny Treibel* and *Entanglements*. The period of Bonhoeffer's interrogations, during which he was also trying to write a play himself, seems to be the time when he did by far the most reading. From 23 May 1943 onwards, his parents were allowed to visit at regular intervals. The first book he asked them to bring was a volume from a set of Stifter. After that, they brought books by Gotthelf, a Swiss pastor and poet, about whom he remarked in the draft for a letter:

I greatly enjoyed reading Jeremias Gotthelf again, whom, in his clear, healthy, quiet style, I consider to be one of our very great writers. Someone ought to publish a selection of his writings [*Brevier*] sometime ... Adalbert Stifter's background is also primarily Christian – his forest descriptions, by the way, often make me yearn for the quiet forest meadows near Friedrichsbrunn. Stifter is not as strong as Gotthelf, yet he has a wonderful simplicity and clarity that gives me great joy. (DBWE 8, I/9, note 6 and I/17)

In time, Stifter was to become his favourite author:

Actually I am reading some Stifter nearly every day. The sheltered and concealed life of his characters – he is so pleasantly old fashioned in exclusively portraying sympathetic characters – has something very soothing in this atmosphere, and focuses one's thoughts on the essential purposes in life. Here in the cell, one is both outwardly and inwardly led back to the most basic things in life; thus, for example, Rilke was no help at all. But maybe one's intellect also suffers somewhat from the constriction under which one lives? (DBWE 8, I/25)

Bonhoeffer's comment about Rilke led to a lively exchange about literature in letters between him and his fiancée, as we shall see.

That he left us drafts of letters, in addition to the letters themselves, has to do with the fact that prisoners were only allowed to write one letter every ten days, of a length which could not exceed precise limits. Since Bonhoeffer had so much he wanted to say, he made drafts of almost all his letters before writing final versions. During the interrogations his letters landed first on Roeder's desk, and the latter could decide whether to keep them or send them on. Later they were read by another censor. Bonhoeffer kept his drafts and, along with his other writings, turned them over to his father for safekeeping.

Among the most important of Bonhoeffer's writings are the drafts for his letters to Roeder, in which he corrected some of his statements and re-emphasized others. These make it possible, still today, to follow the lines along which Roeder proceeded and Bonhoeffer defended himself. The drafts are now preserved in the Federal Archives in Berlin. These pages, written in pencil which has now faded, show how a prisoner, decades ago, pursued a struggle in which a single word could make the difference between life and death.

Further interrogations and the defeat of Roeder

During the early weeks of the interrogations Roeder had given orders that Bonhoeffer could write his one letter to his parents every ten days, but otherwise could have no contact with the outside world. Since at this time the guards were still mistreating him, it was hard to bear. But Bonhoeffer did not give any hint of this in his letters home, not only to spare his parents, but because in his family one did not whine or complain over one's hard lot. Instead he wrote, 'I am now learning daily how good my life with you has always been, and besides, I now have to practise myself what I have told others in my sermons and books' (DBWE 8, I/9). This sentence both conceals the disgust he felt at the conditions in Tegel during the phase of the interrogations, and says to his parents, but most of all to himself, that the time in prison was going to be a trial of his faith. Everything he had said previously about the Church, about life as a disciple of Jesus and the reality of God, was now being put to the test. He recognized this at the beginning of his imprisonment and it guided his life all the way until 9 April 1945. In this way he became the 'witness to Jesus Christ among his brothers', as the simple tablet says in the church at Flossenbürg.

Since Bonhoeffer's case was closely connected to that of his brother-in-law Dohnanyi, his interrogations dealt with the same topics in the same order. The first, however, was Bonhoeffer's exemption from military service. Roeder claimed that he had really only been motivated by the desire to escape from his duty to report his movements as ordered by the Gestapo, and from his ban on public speaking. Bonhoeffer countered that the orders from the Gestapo had been a routine matter and also involved six other clergymen.

... in order to avoid all further grounds for dispute, I had withdrawn to the Bavarian Alps to work on an extensive scholarly project and as required had reported this to the State Police ... Despite considerable inner reservations, I seized the possibility, opened to me by my brother-in-law, of entering into Military Intelligence service and utilizing my church connections, because it promised me the engagement in the war effort I had sought since the beginning of the war and in fact in my role as a theologian. (DBWE 16, 417)

He described the exemption obtained for him by Military Intelligence as a relief to him, coming as it did immediately after the orders received from the Gestapo, since he saw it as an opportunity to rehabilitate himself in the eyes of the authorities. The knowledge that he was needed by a department of the military had, he emphasized, been very important to him, and he couldn't imagine that there could be any objection to a draft exemption to allow him to work for Military Intelligence, since he had been told that it was Admiral Canaris's wish and was done on his orders.

To my occasional question whether difficulties might not arise for either Military Intelligence or for me because of my state police record, I was told that these things did not mean anything for military duty and, in addition, Military Intelligence works with all sorts of people who are useful to it. So I felt quite reassured. (DBWE 16, 419)

His notes for the draft of this statement included what Oster had said: 'We work with enemies, Communists, Jews – why not with the Confessing Church as well?' but this would have been an unnecessary provocation for Roeder.

Roeder now produced another suspicion: that Bonhoeffer had only made use of the draft exemption in order to continue working for the Church, and that this had been confirmed by General Superintendent Dibelius. This was a lie which Bonhoeffer could easily see through, since he had told Dibelius and Diestel that he was working for the Army High Command in Munich and abroad. Thus they could not have been counting on him for any ongoing employment in the Church. Roeder then told him that Consul Schmidhuber had testified in quite other terms than these, about his draft exemption, but Bonhoeffer replied that he had been told that the admiral did not want Schmidhuber to be informed about the assignments that he, Bonhoeffer, had personally undertaken. So such a statement could only represent very inexact knowledge, if not simply suppositions.

Shortly before the charge of treason was dropped, Bonhoeffer summed up his defence in a letter to Roeder, beginning as always with the salutation 'Dear Senior Military Prosecutor Roeder':

For you there can certainly be nothing conclusive (but perhaps you will believe it of me personally, and in this hope I will express it) about the fact that it is very painful for me to see how my early conflicts with the secret police which, I am deeply convinced, arose from conduct strictly confined to church affairs, have now led to my being considered capable of so serious a crime against the obvious duty of a German towards my people [*Volk*] and Reich. I also still cannot believe that this accusation has actually been made against me. If this were my attitude, would I then have found my fiancée, who herself has lost father and brother at the front, from within a long-standing family of officers, all of whose fathers and sons have served in the field as officers since the beginning of the war, many serving with the highest decorations and making the ultimate blood sacrifice? Would I then, immediately before outbreak of war, severing all the commitments I had made in America, have returned to Germany, where of course I had to reckon with my immediate induction? Would I then, immediately following the outbreak of the war, have volunteered as a military chaplain? Anyone who wishes to become acquainted with my conception of the Christian obligation of duty towards the governing authorities should read my exegesis of Romans 13 in my book *Discipleship*. The appeal to submit oneself to the will and the demands of the governing authorities for the sake of Christian conscience has probably seldom been expressed more strongly than there. (DBWE 16, 422)

If Roeder had bothered to obtain the book himself, he would not, of course, have found very much about being 'subject to the governing authorities' (Romans 13:1). Instead, Bonhoeffer had written: 'No authority can legitimately interpret Paul's words as a divine justification of its existence ... Those in authority ... could never interpret it as a divine authorization of their conduct in office' (DBWE 4, 241–42). When he wrote this, he had intended it not only to oppose a false understanding of Luther's 'doctrine of the two kingdoms', but also to oppose Hitler's acts of violence disguised in religious language.

In June 1943 Roeder decided to look into 'Operation 7'. Here Bonhoeffer had to be especially careful to avoid unintentionally contradicting testimony by Dohnanyi or Canaris. But his part in this matter only amounted to a side issue. He had arranged for Charlotte Friedenthal to be rescued, and also arranged the decisive conversation in Basel between Consul Schmidhuber and Alphons Koechlin, president of the Swiss Protestant Church Federation which was aiding these Jewish refugees. He did not deny that it had been personally very important to him to help Charlotte Friedenthal. He also recalled that she had asked him whether he thought she could responsibly accept the spying assignment that Military Intelligence was giving her, and he had said that she could. But he added that he had never learned specifically what her assignment was to be. This he could say truly, since it had never existed.

What Roeder was actually looking for was evidence that this was a rescue operation to get around the SS deportations of Jews. Therefore the accused had to show that Military Intelligence had actually begun working on it long before the beginning of the deportations, and here Bonhoeffer, who had not seen this at first, had to retract a statement he had made. He therefore wrote to Roeder correcting his testimony that he had asked Schmidhuber in the spring of 1942 to speak with Koechlin; he had now remembered that it must have been soon after August 1941. Canaris, however, was able to cover the entire operation in such a commanding way that Roeder had to let the matter drop.

It is still amazing to consider that Roeder scarcely asked Bonhoeffer anything about his trips abroad. If he had 'put the screws on' his victim here, Bonhoeffer could possibly have encountered difficulties. As it turned out, the travel only played a role in Roeder's claim that Bonhoeffer had violated the Gestapo's ban on his visiting Berlin. But there Bonhoeffer knew easily which card to play: that he had to be available to the Berlin office before and after each journey, in particular when it was a special assignment directly from the admiral. He also pointed out that he had earlier been granted specific permission to visit his parents, and that when he had double pneumonia in the winter of 1941 they had insisted on having him cared for at home.

That Roeder aimed his attacks only at Bonhoeffer's draft exemption and not at his travels shows how precisely the network of family and friends was functioning. Roeder's methods of investigation didn't take him anywhere near the real problem. He had two opponents of the regime in his hands, who knew about all the assassination attempts; Dohnanyi had even obtained the explosive for one attempt and brought it to Schlabrendorff, so had been actively involved. But Roeder never found the slightest hint that there was a conspiracy against Hitler.

On 5 April 1943 in Dohnanyi's office, Roeder had also found a letter from Bonhoeffer asking his brother-in-law to prevent the call-up to military service 'threatening' Wilhelm Niesel, an important member of the Council of Brethren who had been Bonhoeffer's superior when he was director of the 'illegal' seminary at Finkenwalde. Such a request could possibly lead to a death sentence, since 'undermining Germany's defences', even by talking against the draft, was a capital crime. Death sentences were handed down for much less serious 'crimes'. All Bonhoeffer could do was write another of his letters to Roeder, attempting at least to get out of this trap as well.

Dear Senior Military Prosecutor Roeder:

I am truly sorry to trouble you repeatedly in this way, but I dare not neglect to tell you something that seems important to me, and so I beg you sincerely to excuse this claim on your time as well. Yesterday when you read to me from my long-forgotten letter to my brother-in-law, I myself was initially profoundly shocked by the word 'threat' in connection with Niesel's being drafted, and did not understand how I could have arrived at this sort of expression; and I must confess that this language, in and of itself, does truly make a very unpleasant impression. (DBWE 16, 422)

But he then went on to explain that Niesel, if he had been a staff member of a church authority recognized by the state, would certainly have been classified as worthy of an exemption. Only a church which stands firm in its faith can carry out the difficult task which it owes its homeland during a war; it is called to unwavering trust in God, strong inner resistance, steadfastness, firm confidence and offering person-to-person pastoral care to those fighting to defend the homeland. One might think whatever one likes of the Confessing Church, he continued, but certainly it could not be reproached with speaking of the call-up to military service as a threat. He said that the Confessing Church pastors he had met considered their call-up as a liberation from heavy inner pressure, because at last they could give proof that they too were ready to sacrifice themselves; thus even Martin Niemöller had volunteered.

I know that even religious persons can judge the church very differently, but especially in wartime no one dare desire to deny that the motive for another's conviction and action is love of the German people and the wish to serve them during the war as much as possible. (DBWE 16, 424)

Then he spoke of his conversation with Justice Minister Gürtner in Ettal, when Gürtner had said he would do what he could to gain exemptions for Confessing Church pastors. Bonhoeffer therefore felt himself obliged to make every effort on Niesel's behalf, in order to enable the church's response to the war effort to be the strongest and most fluent within its power (DBWE 16, 422ff). Of course this letter would hardly have stopped Roeder from demanding that Bonhoeffer be put to death for 'undermining Germany's defences', but before he could do so the opposition succeeded in taking the trial out of his hands and having him promoted away from Berlin.

During the interrogations, Bonhoeffer wrote the short essay 'What does it mean to tell the truth?' of which we have already spoken. Only by his ensuring that he did not take a single step away from the path on which he and Dohnanyi had agreed could the conspirators keep working to end Hitler's system of injustice. To have told the 'truth' that Roeder was trying to get from him would have been utter betrayal. That Bonhoeffer withstood this period of interrogation, and the way in which he did it, were his last and most important contributions to the story of the German Resistance.

Despite the serious and very painful handicaps from which Dohnanyi suffered, he kept fighting against Roeder's accusations and trying to make his defence watertight. As soon as he was ready, he filed an official complaint against Roeder in the War Court. There were also complaints from others about Roeder and his conduct. This led to his being transferred as a 'judge with the rank of general', on 1 January 1944, to Air Fleet Four; in other words, he was 'kicked upstairs' to Lemberg in occupied Poland. He had actually already received his orders at the time when he had Dohnanyi moved from the Charité Hospital to the one at Buch and brought in de Crinis for an opinion. In this way he ensured that the investigation of Dohnanyi could be continued and that eventually the SS would get its hands on him.

But Roeder's goal had been to have both Dohnanyi and Bonhoeffer condemned to death, and in this he had not succeeded, so he must have regarded his being taken off their cases as a defeat. During the interrogations he had foolishly referred to the 'Brandenburg' division, which belonged to Military Intelligence, as a 'crowd of shirkers'. The division commander, General Pfuhlstein, heard about this, had it confirmed by Dohnanyi, and flew out to Lemberg to box Roeder's ears. Keitel sentenced Pfuhlstein to a mere seven days' detention.[8]

Roeder was succeeded by a prosecutor named Kutzner, who conducted Dohnanyi's case without ideological zeal, even when the SS tried to put him under pressure. As Sack advised him to do, he was working towards depoliticizing the trial. It was Christine von Dohnanyi's impression that Kutzner had an inkling of the real lie of the land. During this phase, Dohnanyi and Bonhoeffer were both pushing for their actual day in court, because they were counting on being acquitted. But their friends outside wanted to prevent them at any cost from being turned over to the SS. It seemed much safer simply to let the case 'run out of steam', especially because there were now renewed hopes for a coup. Hitler was to be shown some new uniforms, and several young officers, including Axel von Bussche and Ewald Heinrich von Kleist, the eldest son of Ewald von Kleist-Schmenzin, had volunteered for a suicide attack on Hitler during this occasion. But shortly before they were due to be presented, the uniforms were burnt up during an air raid.

'Dreaming of heaven on earth' – the love letters

It was depressing for Bonhoeffer that he could not personally present his fiancée to his parents. All his brothers and sisters had married friends who had long been regular visitors in their parents' home. But Maria came from a conservative milieu, that of the landed nobility east of the Oder River, now part of Poland, where sons grew up to be military officers or to farm their inherited estates, while daughters married such estate-owners, officers or higher-ranking government officials. Bonhoeffer had come to know these families, and to appreciate them for their basic convictions and their piety, but for his family it was another world and he knew how critical his parents and especially his brothers and sisters could be. Maria was 15 years younger than Bonhoeffer's youngest sister, closer to the grandchildren's generation. How would she be received in Marienburger Allee?

As it turned out, he could have spared himself these worries; the family was simply delighted with his choice. His eldest brother Karl Friedrich wrote him an especially warm letter of congratulations on 23 April:

From your letters, I have now also learned that you are secretly engaged. You cannot imagine how happy this made me. I basically feel sorry for every unmarried man, even if this confession sounds ridiculous. But of course, in your case, as I see it, there were special circumstances. You do not belong to those who by disposition are destined to remain bachelors. Especially with the difficulties your profession entails nowadays, you need a good, astute and competent wife. (DBWE 8, I/16)

Karl Friedrich, who lived in Leipzig, happened to be in Berlin and met Maria on May 23 when she and her mother made their first visit to his parents. He was impressed that she talked very naturally and without a trace of embarrassment about her work in Hanover as a Red Cross nursing student.

She is apparently one of those people who always pick the most difficult and exhausting tasks, and who pay no attention at all to themselves. The modest and matter-of-fact way she talked about it impressed me very much. I thoroughly scolded her for saving up her weekly ration of butter for you, and for not setting aside the few coffee beans she had been given by a patient for her own night shifts. I trust it was what you would have wanted me to do. (DBWE 8, I/23)

Maria and Bonhoeffer's mother got on well together from the first moment. Paula Bonhoeffer wrote to her son how quickly Maria had learned the names of the 18 Bonhoeffer grandchildren, and that she had asked to see his room.

Of course I had tidied it up a little, although not too much, so that she will know what to expect later on. But she found it fabulously neat. Mothers are apparently more critical than fiancées, and that's how it should be ... Even though she is still very young, her entire attitude already speaks of being very dependable, hardworking and warmhearted. Her mother who during this year has experienced so much hardship is indeed to be admired in the way she attends to her responsibilities for the household and children, which she now faces alone, and how through this she is coping with the grief for her husband and son. (DBWE 8, I/22)

Both Paula Bonhoeffer and Maria von Wedemeyer were women of energetic character and were soon helping one another to mobilize friends, relatives and acquaintances for the benefit of the imprisoned family members. Not the least of these efforts was Maria's untiring provision of food so that both Hans and Dietrich could be better nourished in prison.

That Bonhoeffer was only allowed to write to his fiancée after the interrogations were over, and then only censored letters, must have been a torment for both. On 26 June Roeder decided to bring them face to face in his office at the War Court, and Bonhoeffer was only told immediately beforehand. This was undoubtedly intended to throw him off balance. He wrote to his parents:

I've just come back to my cell after seeing Maria – an indescribable surprise and joy! I had been told just one minute beforehand. It is still like a dream – really an almost incomprehensible situation – how we shall remember this some day! Everything one is able to utter in such a moment is of course so trivial, but that's not the most important thing. It was so brave of her to come. I had not dared at all to suggest she should ... (DBWE 8, I/31)

Throughout their engagement, the two of them never met or spoke except in the presence of supervisory personnel. Even before Bonhoeffer's arrest, they had hardly ever had a chance to be alone together. But as she was being shown the way out, Maria tore herself away from the men leading her and ran back to Bonhoeffer to give him a hug and a kiss for the very first time. From then on that was how they greeted each other whenever they met and when they had to say goodbye.

Probably literature had never been, even in passing, a subject of conversation for them, but – given that the only letters they could write would first be read by Roeder – it came quite naturally to write about books they were reading or that they loved. Since his schooldays Bonhoeffer had been very well read, but apart from a few propaganda-free books that people had managed to obtain and pass around at that time, his fiancée knew only the books she had read at school. Bonhoeffer had already experienced what this was like with his students in Finkenwalde, but he must have been expecting something different from Maria von Wedemeyer; and so the two of them discovered that they were not of the same opinion about everything. Bonhoeffer seems to have been genuinely shocked, for on 28 November 1943, after they had exchanged quite a few letters, he wrote to Eberhard Bethge:

Unfortunately I am not yet of one mind with Maria in the area of literature. She writes me such truly good, unselfconscious letters, but she reads and sends me and loves, of all people, Rilke, Bergengruen, Binding, Wiechert, of whom I consider the latter three beneath our level and the first outright unhealthy. Thus actually none of them suits her at all. Yet something draws her to them. One would need to be able to talk about such things to one another, and I am not convinced they're so unimportant. I would very much like for my wife to be in agreement with me as fully as possible in such matters ... I don't like it at all when wives and husbands are of different opinions. They must stand together like an unassailable bulwark. Don't you agree? Or does this also belong in some way to my 'tyrannical' nature that you know so intimately? (DBWE 8, II/79)

His friend replied on 9 January 1944:

But I'm an example of how easily this can be corrected, the more so with such an intelligent person as Maria who, according to my observation, is very attentive to persuasions and nuances of taste ... Even with us, you had to wait awhile until we realized that Frank Thieß wasn't the ultimate and most exciting author! (DBWE 8, II/96)

Some passages in Bonhoeffer's letters to Maria seem more like suggestions for reading that a lecturer in German literature might make to his favourite student. We have to remember how terribly hard it was for him to write love letters when Roeder was the one who saw them first, before they reached Maria. She, however, was able to disregard Roeder and all other annoyances and be superbly herself, so that her letters are among the most unusual and beautiful love letters of the twentieth century. With regard to literature, but other matters as well, they show how Maria was able to stand up to her highly educated fiancé, 18 years older than she and with rather fixed opinions, because of her superior sense of humour. On 7 February 1944 she wrote:

Just in case you read my letters standing up, you'd better sit down – with all due deference to your equilibrium, stone floors are no joking matter. The fact is, I'm in the middle of a theological tome! What's more, I don't find it half as boring as I expected. You weren't supposed to know, really. I started it to be a little closer to you, not to become a 'Burckhardthaus type', but now I'm reading it eagerly and greedily. It's *Das Evangelium* [The Gospel] by Paul Schütz. (If you don't like the book, that'll be the last straw.)[9]

The reply came 11 days later:

I'm delighted that you're reading Schütz! But forgive me for chuckling a little, because I've seldom inveighed against any book as fiercely in recent times – though solely and exclusively in the company of theologians! But I think it's only a danger to theologians – why, it would take too long to explain – and not to you. However, I'd welcome it if you took a strong dose of Kierkegaard (*Fear and Trembling, Practice in Christianity, Sickness unto Death*) as an antidote. Have you by any chance read Jeremias Gotthelf's *Berner Geist*? It's time you read that too. I wonder if you would care for *Don Quixote*, which I love so much. Or *Wilhelm Meister*? That would be far more important to me than Fontane, who can wait awhile. Do you know Stifter's *Aus der Mappe m[eines] Urgroßvaters?*[10]

Maria replied on 2 March 1944 from Bundorf Castle in Franconia in the south of Germany, where she was now staying with her cousin and helping to care for several children:

I laughed so much at your aversion to Schütz that Hesi came running upstairs and thought I'd gone off my head. The first thing I did was stow the big book in my trunk with a sigh of relief, and there may it remain to all eternity! You're putting me through the mill where books are concerned. I'll soon be timidly consulting you first every time, and end by reading nothing but Kierkegaard with 'fear and trembling' and 'sickness unto death'.[11]

Then she defended Werner Bergengruen, a romantic contemporary author, even more than Rilke, of whom she says in another letter '... I can admire him perfectly well on my own.'[12] In every case she humorously refused to be 'tyrannized' by Bonhoeffer's superiority; she just laughed it off. But she eagerly took his suggestions for her reading, read Goethe's *Wilhelm Meister* with enthusiasm, and of course also got hold of a copy of Bonhoeffer's favourite book, Adalbert Stifter's *Witiko*. After Bonhoeffer had read all of Stifter's books in the set his family owned, he asked them to look for Stifter's last book on which he had worked for almost twenty years, but they couldn't find it anywhere. On 9 November 1943 he wrote to his parents:

The last ten days have unfolded for me entirely under the spell of *Witiko* which – after I had pestered you so long to find it – turned out to be right here in the prison library, where I had truly not expected to find it! With its thousand pages, which can't be skimmed through but must be read when one has leisure, it is presumably not accessible to more than a few people today and for this reason I don't know if I ought to recommend it to you. For me it belongs among the most beautiful books of all I know; by its purity of language and of the characters it transports one into a quite rare and curious feeling of happiness. Actually one should read it for the first time at age 14, instead of the *Battle for Rome*, and then grow up with it. Among all the novels I've read to date, I have had an equally strong impression only of *Don Quixote* and Gotthelf's *Berner Geist*.[13] (DBWE 8, II/71)

In his biography of Bonhoeffer, Eberhard Bethge cites words written by Hermann Bahr in 1922, which make it clear why Bonhoeffer was so moved by Stifter's major works:

... then Witiko starts doing injustice for the sake of good and helps to bring out of this a new justice ... Where there has been a [lasting] victory for revolution it has always been the victory of legitimacy, the victory of justice outside the law over a law that had become unjust ... New justice must always first expiate its defects through profound suffering; it must first be purified by fire, with the wrongdoing burned away. Only then, through penance, will justice finally emerge from good injustice. (DB-ER 845–46)

These are ideas which can be found in Bonhoeffer's *Ethics*, in passages where he is speaking of the conspiracy without saying so in so many words. Maria von Wedemeyer knew this instinctively when she responded to this long novel, which many young people even in those days found distasteful, as the loving young woman she was:

[*Witiko*] gets more and more beautiful, right up to the end. I quite understand why you couldn't help liking the book; if I'd read it first, I'd have sent it to you. It reminds me of you, somehow. That's why I can't help liking it too, even though it's very different from anything I've read in the past.[14]

'She writes me such good, natural letters', Bonhoeffer had written to Bethge. And indeed his fiancée was showing him her love, simply by letting him share in her life:

Pätzig, 19 October 1943 – There's a shooting party here today – a strange occasion in wartime, and without Father. Masses of guests have turned up. They think it's wonderful to be able to take their tails and evening gowns out of mothballs, have a good time and enjoy making small talk. I'm the only one with a great big hole beside me all the time, and it's so hard to talk across a hole like that. It's better to write into it, even if one only imagines one can fill it a little.

Altenburg, 13 January 1944 – I'm so wistful, Dietrich, wistful as can be. I so love to sit curled up on the windowsill, gazing at the sky. Then I have a little piece of it all to myself. And I send my dreams up to heaven and dream heaven down to me, until I know exactly how various things stand, and how they'll be one day for us both: heaven on earth.

Bundorf, 26 April 1944 – I've chalked a line around my bed roughly the size of your cell. There are a table and a chair standing there, the way I picture it, and when I sit there I almost believe I'm with you.[15]

But the letter from Bundorf also tells about a crisis that was very distressing for the engaged couple. Maria's cousin in Bundorf, Hedwig (Hesi) von Truchseß, and her husband belonged, like the Wedemeyers, to the 'Berneuchen' movement. Its leader, Wilhelm Stählin, came to their mansion with numerous invited guests to celebrate an elaborate monastic liturgy for Easter week, and told the lady of the house to 'just send Maria away' so that she would not have to take part in this Easter observance. He claimed that, as he knew her, she would not be able to endure making 'the choice between her father and her fiancé' that would be required of her afterwards. Maria's cousin did not tell her about this until after Easter. Maria wrote about it to Bonhoeffer and described the intensive worship services to him. He was beside himself about it: 'I'm glad you told me everything, including Stählin's unpleasant remark. He shouldn't have made it, and he can hardly hope to justify it. Where lies the fanaticism for which we're so fiercely vilified, on his side or on mine?' She would certainly not have to choose between her father and himself, he assured her: he and her father had regarded themselves as brothers in Christ. Even if they had had a disagreement, they would have been ready to learn from one another.

I'm all in favour of unequivocal decisions where they are needed, certainly, but it's wrong – for God's sake! – in this age of necessary decisions, to bully people into making decisions that are neither genuine nor necessary! I'm glad this Holy Week reinforced your belief in Christ, which would also imply that you don't allow yourself to be influenced, either by other people or by considerations of taste. However sure it is that one owes one's faith to certain people, every Christian should judge for him or herself and be obedient solely to God and his word, not to other people and their ideas.[16]

As pastor and author in cell 92

Maria von Wedemeyer at home in Pätzig Even during the interrogations, Bonhoeffer was already beginning to create a world of his own in his cell. He was trying to write a play. He wrote to his parents early on that, after hours of concentrated work on it, he had some difficulty in returning to the reality around him. He must have felt that drama was the appropriate form in which to express himself, since he was living under dramatic circumstances. But here he was already in difficulty, since he could not write about his own situation, much less about his hopes for an overthrow of the government. So he set his story in the immediate post-First World War period, and his characters were soldiers returning from the war.

This material, however, was not nearly as exciting as the author's own situation, so after a time he put the manuscript aside and made an attempt instead at a novel showing the development of two families. This, too, he had given up by the time the guards who had become his friends made possible his secret correspondence with Eberhard Bethge. Some time later he mentioned his two literary experiments disparagingly to Bethge, calling them 'crazy mucked-up stuff', but in this he did himself some injustice. Both fragments contain less successful passages, but also some rather successful ones, and in both manuscripts these best parts occur, characteristically, in scenes of childhood. And in the midst of each text, sentences suddenly crop up which express directly Bonhoeffer's attitude toward the Resistance; for example: 'What well-meaning person today can still utter the besmirched words freedom, brotherhood, or even the word Germany? ... Let us honour the highest values by silence for a while. Let us learn to do what is right without words for a while' (DBWE 7, 50).[17]

It is no surprise that the novel borrows very much from the world of the Bonhoeffer family, and understandable that the imprisoned author idealizes this world from which he is now separated. What has been irritating to Bonhoeffer researchers, however, is the author's conservative, some would even say reactionary, world view; he even gives his allegiance to elitist concepts in a way that no one today would do. So his fragmentary literary efforts in Tegel seem precisely opposed to the 'new theology' that Bonhoeffer began to develop soon afterwards in his letters to Eberhard Bethge. This has indeed been rather confusing.

Both texts are, however, immediate reactions to the shock of imprisonment and to the world of Tegel. Bonhoeffer was writing under the sway of a regressive phase that he had to overcome.[18] And his effort to set an entirely different elite in contrast to the Nazi elite represented by Roeder was legitimate. The most telling assessment of these texts comes from Ulrich Kabitz:

As an archer has to pull back the string of his bow in order to send the arrow straight to its goal, so Bonhoeffer concentrated on his past, the world from which he came, in order to draw strength from it. This made it possible for him then to turn to his new theology for the future.[19]

When one considers how political prisoners were treated in Adolf Hitler's Germany from 1933 onward, and what Hans von Dohnanyi was made to suffer, it is clear that Bonhoeffer's lot in Tegel was unusual. He had been arrested and taken there under top-secret conditions, and until Roeder lost interest in him there was plenty of harassment. But a telephone call from General Hase had sufficed to make Bonhoeffer a privileged prisoner, with whom the prison commander, Captain Maetz, went for walks in the courtyard, and for whom visiting times with his parents and fiancée were stretched as far as possible.

Some further easing of his situation was brought about by Bonhoeffer himself, through his manner towards others. When guards took the liberty of speaking disrespectfully to him, he corrected them sharply and had success in doing so. People felt that here was someone with whom they could talk. When the heavy air raids on Berlin began, the inmate from cell 92 proved to be a man who emanated calm and could help others. In the infirmary, where he had been treated occasionally for illness, Bonhoeffer became like one of the staff. His approach to a sick person was energetic; like his mother, he could always decide quickly what to do.

Guards soon began coming to him with their problems, and among them Bonhoeffer found the helpers to which modern theology owes so much, Sergeants Holzendorf (whom the Bonhoeffers called his 'angel'), Knobloch and Linke. These were men who had seen through the systematic injustice being practised in their country and especially in Tegel. Without regard for their own safety, they smuggled out the letters to Bethge which, after the Second World War, made Bonhoeffer famous far beyond Germany. He enjoyed listening to concerts with these friends in the infirmary, where there was a radio, and with great caution they also listened to 'enemy' radio stations (a capital offence in wartime Nazi Germany). When Bethge, on leave from the front in June 1944, was allowed to visit Bonhoeffer, Sergeant Linke went so far as to lock the two of them in the visiting room alone for a whole hour so that they could talk undisturbed. It was the last time they saw each other. A year earlier, in May 1943, it was also Linke who brought Eberhard and Renate Bethge the homily that Bonhoeffer had prepared for their wedding and, in May 1944, the baptismal homily for their son Dietrich.

Bonhoeffer and some fellow Italian prisoners

All three of these helpful friends died in air raids or disappeared during the fall of Berlin.

Fellow prisoners also tried to approach Bonhoeffer, as soon as he could move about a bit more freely in the prison, the word quickly passing among them that he was someone whom it was good to know. They could meet him in the infirmary or during air raids and immediately afterwards. He began playing chess again and had a book on chess theory sent to him. He also revived, after many years, his gift for handwriting analysis.

He was often asked by prisoners to pray for them. Pious words he used most sparingly, yet he was ready to help immediately with practical matters. For example, when young soldiers had wandered away from their unit – sometimes solely due to the shock of battle – and now stood accused of desertion, Bonhoeffer would find a lawyer to defend them and more than once arranged for the lawyer's compensation. At the request of Captain Maetz, after a heavy attack in which not only the nearby Borsig locomotive factories were damaged, but also the military prison itself, Bonhoeffer wrote an expert opinion on possible measures of protection during air raids (DBWE 8, II/80). He had heard prisoners kept locked in their cells screaming in fear of death, and those who were wounded had to wait much too long even for first aid. A second opinion, having to do with the reform of the penal system, was written for City Commander Hase (DBWE 8, II/131).

A few of the prisoners, like the helpful guards, became good friends of his, and these friendships would certainly have continued after the war. The most interesting of these persons was probably Gaetano Latmiral, an Italian engineer who had been inspecting radar installations in Berlin at the point when Italy went over to the western Allies. He and several of his countrymen were arrested because they had security clearance for military secrets. Latmiral spent much time with Bonhoeffer, and right after the war he came to see the Bonhoeffer family, becoming the first to tell them about the role Dietrich had played among his fellow prisoners in Tegel.

The most amazing moment in Bonhoeffer's unusual life as a prisoner was undoubtedly the visit of City Commander Paul von Hase, on 30 June 1944. Bonhoeffer told Bethge about it in a letter written the same day:

U[ncle] Paul was here, had me brought downstairs immediately and stayed – Maetz and Maaß were there – more than five hours! He had four bottles of sparkling wine served up, probably the only time in the annals of this place, and behaved in a way more generous and kind than I would ever have expected of him. He no doubt wanted to make it ostentatiously clear what his attitude is toward me and what he expects of that timid pedant M[aetz]. I was impressed with this independence, which would probably be unthinkable in civilian life. (DBWE 8, II/170)

Maaß was the much more cooperative commander of the first prison in which Dohnanyi had been held. Like Bonhoeffer, and Paul von Hase, he was hoping for the success of the coup attempt which was expected very soon; no one could yet know how it would turn out. Less than six weeks after his visit to Tegel prison, Paul von Hase was hanged as a party to the conspiracy. His wife, after being turned away by her closest relatives, found refuge with Rüdiger and Ursula Schleicher in Marienburger Allee.

Right to the end of the war, the regime failed in its efforts to do away completely with prison chaplaincies in Germany. So Tegel still had two Catholic and two Protestant chaplains serving the military and civilian departments of the prison. Hans Dannenbaum, the military chaplain, was director of the Berlin City Mission, knew who Bonhoeffer was and was grateful for his unexpected help. Harald Poelchau, who has already been mentioned, was not actually supposed to visit the military wing of the prison, but was so well regarded in Tegel that he had no trouble gaining access to Bonhoeffer in his cell. It was at his request that Bonhoeffer wrote his 'Prayers for Prisoners', which the pastors had duplicated and could distribute to people who asked for them. Here Bonhoeffer, usually so reserved about using religious language, speaks from an almost childlike piety (see pp. 412–14). Poelchau visited Bonhoeffer once a week and told him a great deal about how prisoners condemned to death and their executions were handled. Poelchau and the Italian Latmiral were the first persons with whom he talked about his new theological ideas.

Although there was a large church building in the middle of the prison grounds, it had been a long time since any worship services were held there; so from the spring of 1943 onwards, Bonhoeffer was never able to go to church again. He therefore kept that much more strictly to his times of prayer in his cell and even blessed himself with the sign of the cross, as Luther had done. At the time, Protestants regarded such things as 'falling back into Catholicism'; for Bonhoeffer it expressed his inner attitude, in which his cell became a place apart from the power of the state and was instead placed under God's protection. In Thomas à Kempis's *Imitation of Christ*, which he owned in the original Latin, he found good counsel: *custodi diligenter cellam tuam, et custodiet te*, as he wrote with delight to Bethge: 'Keep watch diligently over your cell, and it will keep watch over you.' A few times it even sounds as though he was getting used to living in a cell, but didn't really want to let that happen. No one in the prison noticed anything having to do with his 'spiritual life'; he took care there to remain one inmate among others. This was also the reason he scarcely ever spoke of God or used religious language with people while in prison.

As bearable as Bonhoeffer's prison situation was, compared with that endured by other opponents of the Hitler regime, he longed for freedom like every other prisoner. He wanted to get married and live together with his wife. He wanted a child. Often he had to force himself to stop thinking about these things, because otherwise his four walls would have become unendurable for him. But Bonhoeffer was accustomed to disciplining himself.

Isn't it an essential part of human maturity, as opposed to immaturity, that your centre of gravity is always wherever you happen to be at the moment, and that even longing for the fulfilment of your wishes can't pull you off balance, away from being your complete self wherever you are? (DBWE 8, II/122)

It was easy enough to say that, but hard to stay the course. He had to admit to himself that 'nothing is more tormenting than one's longings'; and this torment was what lay behind his poem, 'The Past', written immediately after a visit from his fiancée.

> You left, beloved bliss and pain so hard to love.
> What shall I call you? Life, Anguish, Ecstasy,

my Heart, of my own self a part – the past?
The door slammed shut and locked,
I hear your steps depart, resound, then slowly fade.
What remains for me? Joy, torment, longing?
I know just this: You left – and all is past.

This 110-line poem (DBWE 8, III/158) is the first of the ten poems
Bonhoeffer wrote in prison. It betrays his suffering so clearly that he did
not dare at first to send it to Maria, to whom it is addressed. So it went
first, questioningly, to Eberhard Bethge. But before his friend could reply
that yes, it must be sent to the one for whom it was meant, Bonhoeffer
himself had realized that he must take that risk. It was to Maria that he
was revealing his innermost self here – even though veiled, in the form
of poetry.

Do you feel how I reach for you now,
how I clutch you as with claws,
so tightly that it must hurt?
How I wound your flesh
till your blood oozes out,
just to be assured you are near,
you bodily, earthly fullness of life?
Do you sense my terrible longing for pain of my own?
that I yearn to see my own blood
just so that all will not fade away
into the past?

Bonhoeffer was quite shaken by his own burst of creativity.[20] Writing a
novel – or any book – is a long and wearisome task, which takes a lot of
thinking and involves crossing out much of what one has already written.
He in any case had found it so. But with this poem he had simply written,
felt compelled to write down, what came welling up from within himself.
The violence and passion of the language recalls his sermon on Jeremiah
in January 1934 (DBWE 13, 349ff.). Only this time it is not about the
Church to which his zeal is dedicated, but rather about his passionate
love for a woman. 'When you are in love you want to live, above all
things, and you hate everything that represents a threat to your life', he
wrote in a letter to Bethge (DBWE 8, III/147). The 'world' was not a new
theme that Bonhoeffer had discovered for his theology; instead, he had
himself arrived in the reality of the world.

He tells Bethge in some embarrassment, 'I feel like a silly kid, keeping
from you that I've been trying my hand at poetry here from time to time.'

Even this was a sort of justifcation, for as far as we know he had not previously tried to write any poetry. 'I've kept it a secret from everyone until now – even Maria, who would be the one it concerns most! – simply because I was embarrassed somehow …' (DBWE 8, III/157). He asks his friend to tell him to forget it, to leave it alone, if necessary. But perhaps Bethge, who was then a soldier at the Italian front and thus also separated from his wife, had similar feelings and could therefore understand him. Bethge himself had once written to him, 'In saying goodbye, practice is pretty useless.'

For me, this confrontation with the past, this attempt to hold onto it and to get it back, and above all the fear of losing it, is almost the daily background music of my life here, which at times – especially after brief visits, which are always followed by long partings – becomes a theme with variations. (DBWE 8, III/157)

Bonhoeffer was not in the dark about the fact that his fiancée was going through a crisis. How hard it was for her, she must have revealed to him in a letter which has not been preserved. She was much too intelligent not to have realized that their prospects for a life together were continually dwindling, and whenever she went to see him in Tegel she came back to Bundorf exhausted and in despair. She began to suffer from dizziness and fainting spells. Her visits to Berlin and her life in Bundorf did not really fit together, but she had been so happy there. All this and more she must have written to Bonhoeffer. She would not have told him outright that her cousin Hesi thought, and said, that it was fundamentally wrong for her to be engaged to a man twice her age who was in prison, but perhaps Bonhoeffer sensed it. He responded carefully and lovingly to her letter, and then said: 'On Whit Monday you felt you "couldn't go on". So tell me, *can* you go on without me? And, if you feel you can, can you still do so if you know that *I* can't go on without *you*?'[21] Bonhoeffer had always believed that he must spare Maria whatever he could. Now he was asking for her help, and this call for help brought her to a decision. She left Bundorf and moved to his parents' home, and because she must of course have an occupation to justify her being in Berlin, she worked as receptionist for her future father-in-law, who still had a private medical practice at home.

Eighteen times Maria von Wedemeyer was able to visit her fiancé in Tegel Prison, from 24 June 1943 to 23 August 1944. Their engagement was made up of 18 tormenting farewells. These and their letters were all they had, fanning the flame, over and over again, of their longing for a life together. Maria received the poem 'The Past' in a letter smuggled out of the prison at the beginning of June 1944. On 27 June she was with him again in Tegel, and after the failed coup of 20 July 1944 they saw each other one last time, on 23 August.[22]

'Letters became Bonhoeffer's elixir of life in Tegel' – those he received and those he wrote himself (DB-ER 838). Through them, his imprisonment became a time of the liveliest exchanges with his parents, brothers and sisters, with his fiancée, and above all with Eberhard Bethge, to whom he wrote jokingly on 1 February 1944:

Carpe diem – in this case that means I use every opportunity to write you a letter. First, I could go on writing for weeks without coming to the end of everything I have to tell you, and second, one never knows how long it will still be possible. And since you will some day be called upon to write my biography, I want to make sure the material you have is as complete as possible! (DBWE 8, II/108)

Bethge did become Bonhoeffer's biographer, and dedicated the rest of his life to the works of his friend; without him, only a few traces of Bonhoeffer's work would be left to us. But Eberhard Bethge was much more than a biographer. The Letters and Papers from Prison that he published in 1951 contained only Bonhoeffer's side of the correspondence. Only when an enlarged edition appeared many years later, containing Bethge's letters to Bonhoeffer as well, did we discover that Bonhoeffer developed his ideas in dialogue with Bethge. This was possible because they had been in ongoing conversation with one another since 1935. Thus, during the time Bonhoeffer was in Tegel, they could have said, like another, very different pair of friends, 'I do my thinking in you, and you do yours in me.'[23] And the praise Bethge accorded Bonhoeffer's letters, he also deserves himself, although he stayed so modestly hidden behind his friend for many years:

Letters and essays are the literary form, apart from his theological style, in which Bonhoeffer speaks directly and convinces. Summer evenings over the prison walls, Karl Barth's cigar, memories of Berlin concert halls, the rhythm of the church year or the surprise at holding a knife and fork in his hands again, the privileges of mothers-in-law, Berlin beer, the anger at shabby cowardice – all this, unintentionally, makes fascinating reading. It is serious, has touches of humour, and conveys the joy in earthly things that surprised the friends of the earlier Bonhoeffer, the theologian; they wrongly imagined him to be a fierce and radical teacher of eschatology. Instead, his praise was for 'a beauty that is neither classical nor demonic, but simply earthly, though it has its own proper place. For myself, I must say that this is the only kind of beauty that really appeals to me.' (DB-ER 842)

Bonhoeffer's arrest did not cause Eberhard Bethge's ties to the Resistance to be discovered. So, on 8–10 July 1943, Bethge was still an agent for Military Intelligence and in that capacity was sent to Switzerland – as an 'expert on India' due to his work for the Goßner Mission – where he was able to see Visser 't Hooft and to pay a visit to Karl Barth. The latter sent his regards to Bonhoeffer and gave Bethge a cigar to take back to him.

Theology for a 'religionless' time

The contact that Bonhoeffer was able to regain with Bethge after being imprisoned, beginning on 18 November 1943, brought a change of direction both theological and political. As he had been doing before he was arrested, Bonhoeffer was again increasingly looking ahead. He no longer needed to seek security by looking back to German literature, because he was now well in command of his situation in Tegel. In April 1944 he came to a watershed; the style and content of his letters changed so fundamentally that not even the 20th of July, with the news that once again the coup d'état had failed, could alter them any longer.

There was another reason for this new focus. Sack had sent word to Bonhoeffer that he should no longer count on a court trial, but should rather adjust to the idea of staying in Tegel for some time to come. This was the news that released in him a new phase in his theological work. He wrote to Bethge, 'It is just as you say, that "recognition" (Erkenntnis) is the most exciting thing in the world and this is why I am quite riveted by my work now' (DBWE 8, IV/188).

From Stifter, he turned to reading philosophers and scientists like Carl Friedrich von Weizsäcker, José Ortega y Gasset and Wilhelm Dilthey, and instead of theological books he read The Homeric Gods by W. F. Otto and Die Geschichte der preußischen Akademie (History of the Prussian Academy) by his teacher, Adolf von Harnack. It is striking that the results of his research into the nineteenth century consciously entered into his attempts to express what Christian faith is today. But he also made use of his observations of himself and others there in Tegel:

Last night was pretty lively again. The view of the city from the roof was appalling ... To me it's crazy when they announce the arrival of bombers and we are immediately tempted ... instinctively to wish the horror on other cities, anyone's neck but our own ... At such moments one is very aware of our natura corrupta and peccatum orginale; to that extent it is perhaps a healthy development. (DBWE 8, II/124)[24]

Both inmates and guards would say, 'Keep your fingers crossed for me.' Do we mean by this that thinking of someone else actually has power? Bonhoeffer wondered whether this and other superstitious sayings like 'touch wood' or 'you can't escape your fate' are leftover memories of intercessions and church community, of God's anger and mercy, of divine guidance.[25] 'What I don't see at all is any relic of an eschatological sort. Or have you noticed any?' (DBWE 8, II/121). He asked his father for a book on superstition, and wrote to Bethge: 'Here I'm surrounded almost entirely by people clinging to their desires, so that they're not there for anyone else; they don't listen any more and aren't able to love their neighbour' (DBWE 8, II/122). He observed how few persons are able to keep several things in mind at the same time. If aeroplanes were heard, people were overcome by fear; on seeing something good to eat, they were given over to greed; if something they wished for didn't happen, they fell into complete despair. Thus, he concluded, instead of living fully, they had only pieces of their potential existence (DBWE 8, III/152). So, he asked, how can one speak the word of God to human beings who can no longer hear? Religious declarations wouldn't do any good here.

Many commentators after the Second World War, including even Karl Barth, wanted to ascribe Bonhoeffer's new theological ideas to the shock of his arrest and imprisonment; but he had already left that far behind when he began expressing his new insights. One of the earliest essays in response to *Letters and Papers from Prison*, the book in which Bonhoeffer's letters from Tegel were first published, says:

Anyone who knew Bonhoeffer's earlier work most likely knew him as the author of *The Cost of Discipleship* and *Life Together*. In his letters from prison, the emotional tone of those two books seems to have given way to a very different one. There he had sought to define Christianity with a sharpness reminiscent of Kierkegaard, in contrast to the deadly reservations, half-measures and self-deceptions which he saw infecting the churches of the Reformation ... When one is placed by God in a Christian community, one is placed in a spiritual, divine reality which lives by its own laws and could not be more sharply distinct from every merely psychological human reality. That Christians belong nonetheless in the world means they belong 'in the midst of their enemies' ... To the last, Bonhoeffer never gave up this attitude of a fighter at the front. But the letters from his time in prison, and the fragments of the *Ethics* he left us, show that he saw himself surrounded more and more, with the passage of time, by a great danger, to which even the reawakening Church was blind ... To his deep unease, he was finding that the Confessing Church, in defending itself against violation by a regime of terror and lies, was leaving others threatened by that regime to their fate ... In this situation, it was a great discovery for Bonhoeffer to find that the only Gospel in the Bible is a Gospel turned toward the whole world. This world is, even though at enmity with God or far away from God, still the world that God loves. So there can only be a church which turns toward the world.[26]

This early review defines exactly the change in Bonhoeffer's thinking. He had not given up his stance at the front on behalf of the Church; but he no longer saw the church itself in the foreground, but rather the world that God loves. 'Christianity entails a decision', he had said in his first sermon. But, impressive as Bonhoeffer's focus had always been, and remained, on the obedience implied in faith and on following Christ, all his statements from this time show a trace of calling himself to order: this is the way it must be, and this way only! The man in prison still spoke of the obedience of faith; but even in his *Ethics*, and that much more so in the letters from prison, the language had clearly changed. His vision had broadened, because in the Resistance he had come to know people who did 'the right thing' without being consciously Christians, and because he was now seeing the world that he was learning to know in Tegel through the eyes of Jesus, whose cross and resurrection are the fundamental facts for every human life. He wrote to Eberhard and Renate Bethge in June 1944, in an interpretation of 1 Peter 3:9:

God does not repay evil for evil, and thus the righteous should not do so either. No judgement, no abuse, but blessing. The world would have no hope if this were not the case. The world lives by the blessing of God and of the righteous and thus has a future. Blessing means laying one's hand on something and saying, Despite everything, you belong to God. This is what we do with the world that inflicts such suffering on us. We do not abandon it; we do not repudiate, despise or condemn it. Instead we call it back to God, we give it hope, we lay our hand on it and say: may God's blessing come upon you, may God renew you; be blessed, world created by God, you who belong to your Creator and Redeemer. We have received God's blessing in happiness and in suffering. Yet those who have been blessed can do nothing but pass on this blessing; indeed, they must be a blessing wherever they are. (DBWE 16, p. 632)

We can see that the 'new theology', as we now have it before us, could only have emerged in the 'world of Tegel', in which Bonhoeffer not only developed but also experienced it. It revolves especially around one theme:

What keeps gnawing at me is the question, what is Christianity, or who is Christ actually for us today? The age when we could tell people that with words – whether with theological or pious words – is past, as is the age of inwardness and of conscience, and that means the age of religion altogether. (DBWE 8, III/137)

Bonhoeffer found it salutary that, in the religionless world of Tegel, he was getting to know the world 'from below', 'from the perspective of the outcasts, the suspects, the maltreated, the powerless, the oppressed and reviled, in short from the perspective of the suffering' (DBWE 8, Prologue), but he did not want to get pulled into the undertow of this world. He remained who he was; yet neither did he want, when people turned to him, to exploit their situations for religious purposes. His distrust of 'religious words' kept growing as long as he was in Tegel. 'That the Israelites never pronounce the name of God is something I think about over and over again, and I understand it better and better' (DBWE 8, II/73).

He came to prefer the Old Testament for his reading. By the time he could begin writing to Bethge, he reported that he had already read it two and a half times since he had been in Tegel (DBWE 8, II/73). And what impressed him in the Old Testament, much more than in previous years, was the profound 'this-worldliness' of the Jews' Bible. Now he no longer clung to Kierkegaard's epitaph [see page 229], but rather wrote, as early as January 1944: 'I'm still doing fine, working and waiting. By the way, I'm still optimistic in every regard . . .' (DBWE 8, II/102).

Bonhoeffer's concept of 'religionlessness' is regarded by many theologians today as a prophecy that has not come true. But he did not at all mean to say that the world religions were going to come to an end, nor that there could no longer be any new styles of religion. Instead, this concept contains first of all a two-pronged criticism of his own church. Not only had the church recognized by the state, against which Bonhoeffer had struggled so passionately, approved of Hitler's war – in this regard there were pulpit proclamations from bishops, even after 20 July 1944, which can only make our hair stand on end – but even the Confessing Church had far too seldom issued clear statements. For Bonhoeffer, religious language in Germany had been discredited, in political and human terms, by the conduct of the Church between 1933 and 1945.

Besides this, there was a much older problem. The Church had dug in its heels against the Enlightenment and entered into a defensive war against the triumphant progress of the modern natural sciences, which were explaining how the world worked 'without God as a working hypothesis'. Theologians had thus been fighting a 'rearguard action' against the secularization of the world and society, trying to keep at least marginal areas of human life open for God. In this way, God was turned into a sort of 'stopgap'. Against this strategy, Bonhoeffer says: 'God wants to be grasped by us not in unsolved questions, but in those that have been solved' (DBWE 8, III/152). In any case, there should be no attempt to keep God within bounds as a 'private' or 'personal' God.[27]

What used to be the servants' secrets – to put it crudely – i.e. the intimate areas of life (from prayer to sexuality) – became the hunting ground of modern pastors. The intention ... is religious blackmail ... It is not the sins of weakness, but rather the sins of strength that matter. There is no need to go spying around. Nowhere does the Bible do this ... What I am driving at is that God should not be smuggled in somewhere, in the very last secret place that is left. Instead, one must simply recognize that the world and humankind have come of age. One must not find fault with people in their worldliness, but rather confront them with God where they are strongest. (DBWE 8, III/172)

Bonhoeffer determinedly drops the word 'secularization' and instead speaks of the modern world's 'coming of age' and the 'coming of age' of humankind.

And we cannot be honest, unless we recognize that we have to live in the world – *etsi deus non daretur*. And this is precisely what we do recognize – before God! God himself compels us to recognize it. Thus our coming of age leads us to a truer recognition of our situation before God. God would have us know that we must live as those who manage their lives without God. The same God who is with us is the God who forsakes us (Mark 15:34!). The same God who makes us live in the world without the working hypothesis of God, is the God before whom we stand continually. Before God, and with God, we live without God. God consents to be pushed out of the world and onto the cross, God is weak and powerless in the world, and in precisely this way, and only so, is at our side and helps us. (DBWE 8, III/177)

This development toward thinking of the world's coming of age lets us see clearly the God of the Bible, whose powerlessness in the world becomes paradoxically the source of power and space there for God. However, in solidarity with the godless world, Christians must confront the question 'What do we really believe?' Here no one can take refuge any longer behind the faith of the Church. Even in the Confessing Church, Bonhoeffer was convinced there was more 'standing up for the "cause" of the Church, etc., but little personal faith in Christ. "Jesus" disappears from view.' Yet everything depended on the encounter with him, on the experience that there is here a 'turning around of all human existence' (DBWE 8, IV/187).

Jesus' 'being-for-others' is the experience of transcendence! Only through this liberation from self, through this 'being-for-others' unto death, does omnipotence, omniscience and omnipresence come into being. Faith is participating in this being of Jesus ... Our relationship to God is ... a new life in being there-for-others', through participation in the being of Jesus. Transcendence is not the infinite, unattainable tasks, but the neighbour within reach in any given situation. God in human form! (DBWE 8, IV/187)

Bonhoeffer is not speaking 'out of the human condition' about faith here. (This is why, after the publication of the *Letters and Papers from Prison* [the original German title is *Widerstand und Ergebung*, Resistance and Submission], there were those who wanted to make use of him against Karl Barth.) Instead, he can speak only 'out of' the nature of the Son of God who became a human being, who was closest to those farthest away and still is so, again and again, today. Of Rudolf Bultmann, to whose thinking there are several positive references by Bonhoeffer in Tegel, but from whom he also distances himself, he says that one cannot 'demythologize' anything here. 'This mythology (resurrection and so forth) is the thing itself!' (DBWE 8, III/161). The review we have already quoted above says further:

It is the image of Jesus himself which disturbs Bonhoeffer, encourages him and shows him the way forward ...

The Son of God reveals his divinity in his lowliness, and this is the way, thought by the religious master teachers to be impossible, by which we come to faith. It is a faith incredibly lacking in prerequisites. Jesus Christ himself is its only prerequisite.[28]

It cannot be the task of the Church to overwhelm persons who have come of age with a language that they can neither understand nor speak. As 'church which is there for others', the Church must go back to having an arcane discipline. That means that in every case where the revelations of the Bible cherished by the Church could be discouraging for people outside the Church, it may, and should, treat these matters as secret. In so doing it is betraying neither its task nor its Lord himself, but instead is inviting others to know him in the self-abnegation which he practised himself.

Ever since the publication of the *Letters and Papers from Prison*, the baptismal homily written in May 1944 for Eberhard and Renate Bethge's son Dietrich has rightly been considered an outstanding part of Bonhoeffer's legacy. In it he summarizes his new theological ideas:

You are being baptized today as a Christian. All those great and ancient words of the Christian proclamation will be pronounced over you, and the command of Jesus Christ to baptize will be carried out, without your understanding any of it. But we too are being thrown back all the way to the beginnings of our understanding. What reconciliation and redemption mean, rebirth and Holy Spirit, love for one's enemies, cross and resurrection, what it means to live in Christ and follow Christ, all that is so difficult and remote that we hardly dare speak of it anymore.[29] In these words and actions handed down to us we sense something totally new and revolutionary, but we cannot yet grasp it and express it. This is our own fault. Our church has been fighting, during these years, only for its self-preservation, as if that were an end in itself. It has become incapable of bringing the word of reconciliation and redemption to humankind and to the world. So the words we used before must lose their power, be silenced, and we can be Christians today in only two ways, through prayer and in doing justice among human beings. All Christian thinking, talking and organizing must be born anew, out of that prayer and action. By the time you grow up, the form of the Church will have changed considerably. It is still being melted and remolded, and every attempt to help it develop prematurely into a powerful organization again will only delay its conversion [Umkehr] and purification. It is not for us to predict the day – but the day will come – when people will once more be called to speak the word of God in such a way that the world is changed and renewed. It will be in a new language, perhaps quite nonreligious language, but liberating and redeeming like Jesus' language, so that people will be alarmed, but overcome by its power – the language of a new righteousness and truth, a language proclaiming that God makes peace with humankind and that God's kingdom is drawing near ... Until then, the Christian cause will be a quiet and hidden one; but there will be people who pray and do justice and wait for God's own time. (DBWE 8, III/145)

Ernst Lange says that the greatness of Dietrich Bonhoeffer is that he reflected upon the way in which he himself was a *homo religiosus*, expounded the problems he discovered, and overcame them; in doing so he did not in fact create a religionless Christianity, but rather became the originator of a new way of being religious.[30] His image of the Church to come is a prophetic image, particularly because it has so little in common with the Church that was actually restored after the Second World War. A great deal of what Bonhoeffer foretold still lies ahead of us.

A person who draws such a picture must have experienced the presence of God; as Bonhoeffer puts it in his *Ethics*, such a person must have experienced, in the 'penultimate', moments of the 'ultimate'. The mystics knew that the certainty of God's presence comes in a moment, in its own time. It cannot be compelled, and it is never something that lasts. Bonhoeffer knew this as well. He wrote early on, 'One has only the decisive moment'

(DBWE 10, 365). His baptismal homily was written out of such an experience of the 'ultimate'. He was talking here of the faith which can never become a community experience, but only that of an individual person. In times of loneliness, and during his imprisonment in Tegel, this faith took on a new form for him. Bonhoeffer was speaking with the calm of the mystic, out of the experience of the 'ultimate', when he wrote to Eberhard Bethge on 21 July 1944, the day after the failure of the coup d'état:

Later on I discovered, and am still discovering to this day, that one only learns to have faith by living in the full this-worldliness of life. If one has completely renounced making something of oneself ... then one throws oneself completely into the arms of God ... then one no longer takes one's own sufferings seriously, but rather the suffering of God in the world. Then one stays awake with Christ in Gethsemane. And I think this is faith, this is *metanoia* [conversion]; and this is how one becomes a human being, a Christian.

How should one become arrogant over successes or shaken by one's failures when one shares in God's suffering in the life of this world? You understand what I mean even when I put it so briefly. I am grateful that I have been allowed this insight, and I know that it is only on the path that I have finally taken that I was able to learn this. So I am thinking gratefully and with peace of mind about past as well as present things. (DBWE 8, IV/178)

The last sentence of this quotation is the first, and by far the shortest, reaction we know of to the 20th of July 1944.

The 20th of July 1944

On 20 July Count Claus von Stauffenberg left a bomb in a briefcase in a conference room at the *Wolfsschanze* (Wolf's Lair) field headquarters at Rastenburg, East Prussia, where Hitler was meeting with top military aides. Stauffenberg slipped from the room, witnessed the explosion at 12:42 p.m. and, convinced that Hitler had been killed, flew to Berlin to join the other plotters, who were to have seized the Supreme Command Headquarters there ... A stenographer and three officers died, but Hitler escaped with only minor injury ... Rumours of Hitler's survival melted the resolve of many of the key officers. In a countercoup at the Berlin headquarters, General Friedrich Fromm, who had known about and condoned the plot, sought to prove his allegiance by arresting a few of the chief conspirators, who were promptly shot (Stauffenberg, Olbricht and two aides) or forced to commit suicide (Beck). In subsequent days, Hitler's police rounded up the remaining conspirators, many of whom were tortured by the Gestapo to reveal their confederates and hauled before the *Volksgericht* (People's Court) to be excoriated by the dreaded Nazi judge Roland Freisler. About 180 to 200 plotters were shot or hanged, or viciously strangled with piano wire.[31]

Bonhoeffer was among those who knew when this last assassination attempt was about to take place. He had great hopes for it, so his quiet reaction to its failure was remarkable. He scarcely allowed it to interrupt his ongoing theological work. He did know that from then on his life was in even greater danger than it had already been.

> Come now, highest of feasts on the way to freedom eternal,
> Death, lay down your ponderous chains and earthen enclosures
> walls that deceive our souls and fetter our mortal bodies,
> that we might at last behold what here we are hindered from seeing.
> Freedom, long have we sought you through discipline, action and
>   suffering.
> Dying, now we discern in the countenance of God your own face.
> (DBWE 8, IV/191)

These are the words of one who is determined to fight for his life up to the last moment, who has already done so, yet who looks with complete calm into the face of his approaching death. 'Come now, highest of feasts ...'[32]

Nothing shows how calm Bonhoeffer remained, despite the failure of the coup, so clearly as the continuation of his theological efforts. He wanted to put his new insights into a book. It would take him no more than a hundred pages to put down his new ideas, since they were not a new doctrine but rather theses for a discussion on fundamentals. He wrote to Bethge:

The church must get out of its stagnation. We must also get back out into the fresh air of intellectual discourse with the world. We also have to risk saying controversial things, if that will stir up discussion of the important issues in life. As a 'modern' theologian who has nevertheless inherited the legacy of liberal theology, I feel responsible to address these questions. (DBWE 8, IV/186)

In his small book, the first chapter was to be 'Taking Stock of Christianity'. Here he would speak of the coming of age of humankind and of its religionlessness, in which it no longer needs God as a 'stopgap for when we come up short', but also about the human illusion that we can 'organize' our lives so as to make ourselves safe from all strokes of fate. In the second chapter he meant to pursue the question, 'What is Christian faith really, and who is God?' This was to be about the insight that Jesus' 'being-there-for-others' is the quintessential experience of transcendence.

Here he was also to ask the question of what we really believe, and of the contradictions among the confessions, which Bonhoeffer no longer believed were really genuine. And in the third chapter he intended to draw the conclusions from the above. 'Church is church only when it is there for others.'

It will have to speak of moderation, authenticity, trust, faithfulness, steadfastness, patience, discipline, humility, modesty, contentment. It will have to see that it does not underestimate the significance of the human 'example' (which has its origin in the humanity of Jesus and is so important in Paul's writings!); the church's word gains weight and power not through concepts but by example. (DBWE 8, IV/187)

This he intended to develop more fully, since he felt that in his time people had almost lost the concept of following the New Testament example. Undoubtedly this book would not have fitted people's expectations amid the 'economic miracle' of postwar Germany. We today would have liked it better. Bonhoeffer was working on it right up to April 1945, but with his death it was lost forever.

After surviving the assassination attempt of 20 July, Hitler seems to have thought it was 'a tiny clique of treasonous officers' who had tried to murder him. He had his mistress, Eva von Braun, present his bloodstained uniform tunic as proof that the 'Providence' which he was so fond of invoking had declared once again that he was its instrument. His attackers were to be 'liquidated' as rapidly as possible.

The SS headquarters, however, suspected right away following the attack that the number of Hitler's opponents who had taken part in it was much larger. SS chief Ernst Kaltenbrunner appointed a staff of 400 officials to an investigating committee, which resulted in a wave of arrests. The proof that a conspiracy had existed for some time was discovered by officials of this special 20 July Commission, on 22 September 1944 at a branch office of the Armed Forces High Command, in Zossen near Berlin. There they found parts of a secret archive belonging to Hans von Dohnanyi, which he had originally kept in a bank but had later moved to the bunker at Zossen for safety.

Several times since his imprisonment Dohnanyi had enquired about these files and begged to have them destroyed, because their discovery would be a catastrophe for the conspirators. But General Beck had ordered that they be preserved; he wanted to use them to prove to the German public that Hitler's regime had been committing crimes from the beginning. Christine von Dohnanyi had passed on the warnings from her husband and had been assured that everything necessary had been taken into consideration.

After the files had been discovered there was no longer any question of 'making short shrift of the traitors'. The trials already taking place in the People's Court were suspended, and the executions already ordered were postponed, so that the conspirators under arrest could be tortured and the names of further participants and accessories unearthed. For the next three months Kaltenbrunner's Commission carried on working in 11 groups. He sifted through their findings and passed them on to Freisler. Summaries were sent to Hitler through the Party general secretary, Martin Bormann.

A rescue plan

Since Bonhoeffer in Tegel was not immediately in the Gestapo's sights, a plan was devised to save his life. One of the friendly guards, Sergeant Knobloch, a factory worker from north Berlin, offered to smuggle Bonhoeffer out of Tegel Prison disguised as a mechanic, and to hide with him in a colony of garden allotments on the edge of the city until the end of the war. Bonhoeffer and his family accepted this offer immediately. The mechanic's uniform was obtained, and – together with money and food ration coupons – brought by Rüdiger and Ursula Schleicher, with their daughter Renate Bethge, on 24 September to Knobloch at his home in Berlin's Niederschönhausen district. He concealed everything in the garden colony and planned to escape with Bonhoeffer during the first days of October. But things turned out otherwise.

On 30 September Klaus Bonhoeffer came home from work to see a suspicious-looking black car parked in front of his house. He turned round and went to his sister Ursula's house in Marienburger Allee, where the widow of City Commander Hase had found refuge that very day. When he got there, Knobloch had just arrived also, to make the final arrangements. All the family could do was to ask him to inform Dietrich of this latest development.

All that night in the Schleicher home, they struggled to decide what Klaus Bonhoeffer should do: flee, commit suicide, or allow himself to be arrested. He and Rüdiger Schleicher had been actively involved only in later stages of the conspiracy, when it was reorganized after the arrests of Dohnanyi and Bonhoeffer. His wife happened just then to be away visiting their children, who had been evacuated to Schleswig-Holstein, Germany's northernmost province. He himself was inclined to take his own life, but the family held him back. Ursula Schleicher later reproached herself bitterly on this account, since this brother of hers was cruelly tortured in prison. On 1 October the Gestapo came to the house on Marienburger Allee to arrest him. The next day, Sergeant Knobloch returned with the news that Dietrich had decided to give up the escape plan, in order not to put his family and fiancée in even greater danger. Two days later, Rüdiger Schleicher was arrested at his office, and the day afterwards, Friedrich Justus Perels. Their arrests were followed by those of the university professors who had written the Freiburg Memorandum, and by those of the 'Kreisau Circle' members.

In the power of the Gestapo

On Sunday, 8 October 1944, Bonhoeffer was removed from Tegel Prison to the cellar prison of the Reich SS Headquarters in Prince Albrecht Street. During the two and a half months since 20 July, he had been concentrating on the draft of his new book. Before leaving Tegel he had been able to turn over to his father all his important papers except this last book manuscript, which he took with him. According to fellow prisoners who survived, he kept working on it until shortly before his death.

In the infamous Gestapo cellar he was reunited with his friend and comrade-in-arms Josef Müller, who had been held there since 27 September, and later also with other conspirators; in February he even saw Hans von Dohnanyi. But this was far from being the only Gestapo prison. The SS leadership had taken over a wing of the officers' prison on Lehrter Street, to which Canaris, Oster, Sack and many others were taken – even, some time later, Eberhard Bethge.

Bethge was clerk for his army unit on the Italian front, where his normal duties included sorting the mail and opening the letters for the major, his superior. Suddenly he had before him a telegram which said that Corporal Bethge was to be sent back to Berlin under guard. Before bringing the major his mail, Bethge burned all of Bonhoeffer's letters that he still had, not yet having sent them as usual to his wife for safekeeping.

He got along so well with the two soldiers guarding him on the way to Berlin that they were willing to take him first to the Schleichers' in Marienburger Allee, where his mother-in-law Ursula gave them all a good dinner. There it was agreed that the two guards would deliver Bethge to the prison the next day at the exact moment when Ursula Schleicher came there to enquire about her husband. In this way Bethge would have time to get all the information he needed to be prepared for his interrogations. During the reunion scenes at the prison, his wife Renate, his mother-in-law and he himself all pretended to be surprised at meeting each other there, and the prison personnel could see that they would not gain anything by unexpectedly confronting him with his loved ones.[33]

Much more is known about the interrogations undergone by Klaus Bonhoeffer and Rüdiger Schleicher than about those which Dohnanyi and Bonhoeffer now had to face under changed conditions. This may seem surprising at first, but the reason for it makes sense. Kaltenbrunner's reports to Hitler and Himmler have been preserved.[34] Their content must have passed through many hands before it came to Kaltenbrunner in the form of transcripts of interrogations. However, this had to be avoided in the investigations of Canaris's office because, in the interrogations of Military Intelligence people, highly secret reports could surface that needed to be seen by as few people as possible. The interrogations of the Oster–Dohnanyi Resistance group are therefore only marginally referred to in the Kaltenbrunner reports.

When Oster had been placed under house arrest, followed by Canaris on 26 February 1944, Canaris's office was incorporated into the Reich SS Headquarters with all its staff, except for a small unit which remained with the Armed Forces High Command. Of course its secret service work was not to be broken up, but rather to be continued by the same experienced professionals under the supervision of the SS. Not least, the SS was interested in probing the conspirators' enemy contacts to see if it could make use of them itself. This is why none of the conspirators in Military Intelligence were brought before Freisler in the People's Court.

The Foreign News Service, which the SS Headquarters had maintained in parallel to that of Admiral Canaris, was directed by SS Brigadier General Walter Schellenberg. He had working under him SS Colonel Walter Huppenkothen, who since 1935 had made his career with the Gestapo and was now the new chief of the Military Intelligence police. It was to Huppenkothen that the former Military Intelligence staff members who were now under suspicion of being involved in the coup attempt were assigned for investigation. Because the results of these investigations were kept strictly secret, he was allowed to work independently of the other investigating groups. The member of his staff with whom he worked most closely was Criminal Commissioner Franz-Xaver Sonderegger.

After the Second World War the two of them were put on trial, and their testimony showed that Kaltenbrunner treated their reports differently from those of the other 10 investigating groups. Huppenkothen stated during a later trial that, from the archives discovered in Zossen, he and Sonderegger put together a special 160-page 'report to the Führer', along with two volumes of documentation, of which only three copies are said to have existed: one each for Hitler and Himmler, and a joint one for Kaltenbrunner and Gestapo Chief Müller. These three copies are said to have been destroyed before the end of the war. It is presumed that, at his hearings, Huppenkothen did not reveal anywhere near everything he knew, and certainly not anything self-incriminating. This is why there are no official documents, with one exception as we shall soon see, about what was done with Bonhoeffer during the time from 8 October 1944 to 9 April 1945.

On instructions from Schellenberg, who at that time was supposed to be making contacts in Sweden for Himmler, Huppenkothen focused for a time, while interrogating Bonhoeffer in the prison in Prince Albrecht Street, on his contacts abroad. This is known through a letter from Kaltenbrunner to the Reich Foreign Ministry, in which he reported in detail on Bonhoeffer's conversations with Bishop Bell in Sweden. The letter shows that Bonhoeffer succeeded in having his trip to Sweden accepted as an assignment in the national interest. The letter does not say that it was General Beck who had actually given him his orders, but it does describe in detail Bishop Bell's role in Britain and portrays him as a friend of Germany. It says that Bell had been 'on familiar terms' with Rudolf Heß, and had first sought an understanding with the 'Reich Church' before turning to the Confessing Church. The purpose of his trip to Sweden, it continues, had been to find out about Sweden's relationship with the Soviet Union and about what was going on in the Scandinavian churches. According to Bonhoeffer, Kaltenbrunner wrote further, Bell

explained that he had spoken at length with Eden before leaving England, and had asked what he should do if peace feelers were extended from any particular direction in Sweden. Eden had told him quite bluntly that there was no question of England discussing peace terms before it had won the war. In this matter Eden was totally in agreement with Churchill. The attitude of Sir Stafford Cripps to these problems was quite different from that of Eden, according to Bell. It was quite wrong to say that Sir Stafford was a Bolshevik; he was more of a Christian socialist. Sir Stafford evidently spoke with great concern about the power of Russia, which almost everyone in England underestimated ... During the course of the interview Bell had commented on the visit which evidently Lord Beaverbrook had recently made to Switzerland. Beaverbrook had held meetings with German industrialists and had discussed with them the possibilities of negotiating peace terms, with a view to forming a common front between the Western powers and Germany against Russia. (DB-ER 903–4)

Sonderegger testified at his trial that Bonhoeffer had dictated this information into his machine. According to him, Bonhoeffer had admitted that, on orders from Canaris, he had violated Heydrich's 'Ten Commandments'; nevertheless he had been able to avoid speaking of his role in the conspiracy, and by referring to Lord Beaverbrook's visit to Switzerland had shown Huppenkothen that it might be useful to keep the Military Intelligence members alive for awhile longer.

The work of Huppenkothen's investigating group was made considerably more difficult by air raids. The Americans and British were advancing from the west, and on 12 January 1945 the Red Army launched its major offensive on the eastern front. Bonhoeffer believed that there was no important evidence being held against him, and that he would still be able to drag out his case long enough.

The prison in Prince Albert Street was a different world from that of Tegel. No visitors were allowed, and contact by mail was forbidden; however, three letters exist that Bonhoeffer wrote during this time, as we shall see. Not a single word

Walter Huppenkothen, Bonhoeffer's interrogator in the Gestapo prison

was supposed to reach the outside world from this dreaded cellar, and no one was allowed to find out what the prisoners looked like. According to all information we have, Bonhoeffer himself would have been presentable. He had been threatened with torture by the SS, but was never actually tortured. Denying outsiders any contact with prisoners, however, added to the terror associated with this centre of power. The inmates were each entitled to receive one package every Wednesday. This was the only possibility of making their lot any easier.

While we know little from official sources about this final phase of Bonhoeffer's life, there are quite a few witnesses whose testimony is more valuable to us than any SS documents could be. Fellow prisoners who managed to escape Freisler's death sentences reported after the war about their encounters with Bonhoeffer. After a few days he was moved from cell 19 to cell 25, next door to Fabian von Schlabrendorff, who was a cousin of Maria von Wedemeyer's. It was Schlabrendorff who, together with Tresckow, had carried out the assassination attempt in Smolensk, and had removed the evidence after it failed. Bonhoeffer and he had seen each other even before the war at one time or another.

Now, since there was only a single toilet for all the prisoners, and one bathroom at the end of the corridor where several had to wash at once, there were opportunities to communicate. Talking was of course strictly forbidden, but they could whisper to each other while the cold shower was running. There were even guards who no longer believed in Germany's 'final victory' and may have looked the other way now and then. Schlabrendorff reported that under the shower Bonhoeffer had tersely described his interrogations as 'repulsive'; but it was astonishing how, even in the Gestapo's cellar, he was able to win over some of the guards.[35] Huppenkothen's interrogations were repulsive because, although he did not torture anyone himself, he ordered it done by others. When he appeared again afterwards he would offer his victim a cigarette and act the perfect gentleman.

The best opportunities for sustained conversations among the inmates came during air raids, which now occurred ever more frequently. Not to protect their lives but in the hope that there were still confessions to be extracted from them, the prisoners were driven like cattle into the so-called Himmler Bunker, where they had to stand closely packed until the all-clear was given. Schlabrendorff wrote that this was actually helpful for men who had been brought there after long periods of solitary confinement. Here, for example, Bonhoeffer met Goerdeler and was able to speak with him; and when Hans von Dohnanyi was brought to the prison on 1 February, paralysed by diphtheria, Bonhoeffer managed in the jostling during the next air raid warning to dive into his brother-in-law's cell unnoticed for a few moments, and then still to get in line with the group coming out of the bunker. This, on 3 February 1945, was the heaviest bombing Berlin had yet seen, and also turned the SS Headquarters buildings into a burnt-out shell. Schlabrendorff wrote about it:

We were standing tightly squeezed together ... when a bomb hit [the bunker] with an enormous explosion. For a second it seemed as if the bunker were bursting and the ceiling crashing down on top of us. It rocked like a ship tossing in the storm, but it held. At that moment Dietrich Bonhoeffer showed his mettle. He remained quite calm, he did not move a muscle ... as if nothing had happened.[36]

Schlabrendorff noted that in their conversations it was often he who was depressed, while Bonhoeffer was always hopeful. Unlike his fellow inmates, Bonhoeffer had recovered long ago from the shock of his imprisonment. Because his courage and will to live could no longer be broken, it could influence others around him. When he received a food package, he would look for opportunities to pass bread, apples or cigars to other prisoners, happy that even in prison there were still opportunities to share with others and help one's neighbour. Dohnanyi soon had to be moved to a military hospital because of his illness. On 25 February 1945 he said in a secret message to his wife: 'I have seen Dietrich; he looks cheerful ... Runge [an SS lawyer] has a soft spot for Maria ... he thought Dietrich was a decent fellow' (DB-ER 908).

Maria von Wedemeyer had come to Berlin to stay with Bonhoeffer's parents and help them, and to take part in efforts to ease the situation of the family members in prison; in one attempt to be allowed to see Bonhoeffer, she got as far as an audience with Huppenkothen. This had been made possible by Countess Maria Bredow, who had a certain influence on higher-ranking SS leaders.[37] But Huppenkothen kept his iron mien and did not allow her to see her fiancé.

However, Runge was not the only one in Central Security on whom Maria von Wedemeyer had made an impression. It was Sonderegger especially who also had a 'soft spot' for her, and allowed her to bring, to him personally, packages for Bonhoeffer whenever she wanted. Thus the third and last letter which Bonhoeffer was allowed to write from Prince Albrecht Street says, 'Unfortunately no books were handed in for me today. Commissar Sonderegger would accept them on another day if Maria brings them' (DBWE 8, IV/202). A secret message from Dohnanyi to his wife also says, 'Sonderegger loves people to play to the gentleman in him, and is not wholly heartless, but he's shifty.' Against regulations, Sonderegger handed over to Maria von Wedemeyer each of the last three letters Bonhoeffer's loved ones received from him. The first was for Maria herself, a Christmas letter written on 19 December 1944. Bonhoeffer wrote to her that the days of Christmas would be very quiet for him, but it had always been his experience that the deeper the stillness around him, the more clearly he felt the bond to those he loved. 'It's as if, in solitude, the soul develops organs of which we're hardly aware in everyday life.' With this letter he enclosed the poem 'By Powers of

Good', and asked her to copy it out for his parents, brothers and sisters. Today German Protestants have it in their hymnals as Bonhoeffer's legacy (see pp. 415–16). What he meant by 'powers of good', he wrote in the letter to his fiancée:

I haven't for an instant felt lonely and forlorn. You yourself, my parents – all of you, including my friends and students on active service – are my constant companions. Your prayers and kind thoughts, passages from the Bible, long-forgotten conversations, pieces of music, books – all are invested with life and reality as never before. I live in a great, unseen realm of whose real existence I'm in no doubt. The old children's song about the angels says 'two to cover me, two to wake me', and today we grown-ups are no less in need than children are of preservation, night and morning, by kindly unseen powers.[38]

The second letter of Bonhoeffer's that Sonderegger handed to Maria was for his mother, for her 68th birthday. It says in part:

I know that you have always lived only for us, and that there has never been a life you could call your own. This is why everything that I experience, I can only experience as if together with you. It is a very great comfort to me that Maria is with you. I thank you, Mama, for all the love that has come from you to me in my cell in the past year and made every day easier for me. I believe that these difficult years have forged an even closer bond between us than ever before. (DBWE 8, IV/201)

The third letter mentioned, among other requests, some books he hoped Maria could bring to Sonderegger. This letter Bonhoeffer intended not least as a sign to reassure his family that he was still alive and still in Berlin.

From December 1944 onwards, the Bonhoeffers experienced a time of suffering that had become almost unbearable by the time it was over. Klaus Bonhoeffer and brother-in-law Rüdiger Schleicher had had contacts with the Resistance even before Dietrich Bonhoeffer and Hans von Dohnanyi were arrested, but had not participated actively until afterwards. Both had said they were ready to work with a new regime after the coup d'état, and important meetings of the conspirators had been held in their homes. Formal charges were brought against them on 20 December 1944. During this time Dohnanyi lay seriously ill in the Sachsenhausen concentration camp, but he was brought to Prince Albrecht Street on 1 February 1945 because Huppenkothen was not getting anywhere in his interrogations of the Military Intelligence people. Dohnanyi was turned over to a Commissioner Stawitzky, who tried to wear him down through neglect; the guards were forbidden to take him to the washroom or even the toilet. In his helplessness he was soon in a bad state.

On 2 February Freisler brought his verdict in the People's Court against Klaus Bonhoeffer, Rüdiger Schleicher, Friedrich Justus Perels, and Schleicher's colleague Hans John who had facilitated many of the contacts among the conspirators. All were sentenced to death. The following day Ursula Schleicher had arranged to speak with Reich Attorney General Ernst Lautz about an appeal for clemency.

With the same purpose in mind, Rüdiger's brother Rolf Schleicher, a military doctor, who had come from Stuttgart for the conclusion of the trial, also set out the next morning. He was caught in that same air raid, the most severe the Allies had yet inflicted on Berlin by daylight, and had to wait until the all-clear in the Potsdamer Platz Underground station. When he arrived on foot at the People's Court, the building was on fire. Someone saw by his uniform that he was a doctor and took him to a man who was severely injured. But all he could do was assure them that the man was dead; it was Roland Freisler. Rolf Schleicher said he would not issue the death certificate, however, until he had first spoken with Justice Minister Thierack. Shaken by this odd coincidence, the Minister said he would have the executions delayed and would entertain an appeal for clemency.

That same morning, Bonhoeffer's parents, together with Klaus Bonhoeffer's wife Emmi, had set out for the prison to bring their son Dietrich a birthday package. They had to wait out the air raid in the Underground under the Anhalter railway station. After that they were not allowed to approach the heavily damaged SS Headquarters building in Prince Albrecht Street; they were desperate with anxiety, but there was nothing to do but go home again. However, they were able to deliver the parcel the following Wednesday, with at least one of the requested books, having learned that nothing had happened to the prisoners in the bunker. The letter accompanying the package, however, was refused. Karl Bonhoeffer had written, hiding his fears behind his usual laconic style: '... it wasn't a very pretty sight. Apart from the fact that we looked like chimney sweeps afterward, we came away unscathed' (DBWE 8, IV/204).

This air raid also severely diminished Huppenkothen's resources for carrying on his investigation. The SS Headquarters and the cellar prison in Prince Albrecht Street had been largely destroyed. Only the prisoners who were expected to appear in court in the next few days were left in the bunker; the others were forced to 'decamp' along with the various branches of SS Headquarters operations.

12. The End

Buchenwald

While a group including Canaris and Oster was being taken to Flossenbürg concentration camp, Bonhoeffer found himself in an eight-seat prison van with eleven other prisoners, on the way to Buchenwald. When he protested against being handcuffed again, his friend Josef Müller, who had plenty of experience with torture, consoled him, 'Dietrich, don't take it so hard. We're doing this for our Christian convictions.' But the interrogations of the Canaris group were definitively over. Even Huppenkothen seemed to have run out of possibilities to continue them.

At Buchenwald the group from Berlin was not put into the concentration camp itself, but rather in the cellar of an SS barracks in front of it; this cellar had been used as a jail for guards who were being punished. Because this area outside the actual camp had already been bombed several times by the Allies, the inmates were locked in during air raids, while those guarding them fled into the woods nearby where trenches had been dug. The rooms in the cellar were damp and the food meagre. At midday, normal dinner-time in Germany, there was soup, and for supper, bread with a little pork fat and jam. Anyone who wanted breakfast had to save some of this for the next morning.

The Americans were advancing from the west, making the guards visibly nervous. They refused ever to let the prisoners outdoors for some fresh air, but after some humming and hawing allowed them out of their cells once a day to walk in the cellar corridor, which was divided lengthwise into three narrow passages. There were a few gaps in the walls between these, so that the inmates were able to meet and talk with one another. And since the guards found it too much effort to supervise them while the cell doors were open, these were really sociable times. One or another of the guards would be selling black market tobacco, which made the atmosphere a bit more relaxed. The prisoners could get to know one another and share any books they still had with them. Bonhoeffer's neighbour in the next cell was Hermann Pünder from the Rhineland, a Catholic who as a young man had been Chancellor Brüning's chief of staff before 1933. Bonhoeffer enjoyed political and cultural discussions with Pünder, especially about the future relations they both hoped for between Catholics and Protestants in Germany.

After a time further prisoners arrived in Buchenwald, including two English officers, Hugh Falconer and Sigismund Payne Best. Best had been lured by an SS commando into an ambush in the Dutch border town of Venlo in 1939 and taken to the Sachsenhausen concentration camp. His book *The Venlo Incident*, written soon after the war, is the only reliable source we have for the last weeks of Dietrich Bonhoeffer's life.[1] All other testimonies were written a long time after the war. The new group also included a Russian, Vassily Kokorin, a nephew of Soviet Foreign Minister Molotov, Generals Falkenhausen and Rabenau, and a few more.

Friedrich von Rabenau was put into Bonhoeffer's cell, and Payne Best had the impression that they were the only two cell-mates who got along together without any problems. General Rabenau was a friend of Goerdeler's. He had been director of the Army archives, and since his retirement had studied theology in Berlin and earned his doctorate in it. He had been arrested when it became known that he had enabled contacts between Goerdeler and several generals. He and Bonhoeffer were worlds apart in their theological thinking, but that did not prevent them from having lively theological conversations, to which their neighbour Pünder listened with great interest.

Rabenau introduced Payne Best to Bonhoeffer in the washroom, and Bonhoeffer enjoyed the opportunity to speak English again. Best had ample luggage with him, and when he discovered that Bonhoeffer lacked warm clothes and was wearing wooden prison clogs instead of shoes, he gave him his golf shoes and a warm sweater. Best also had two chess sets, one of which he offered to the two theologians, to their delight. Thus life in the cell next to the stairs was far from monotonous, especially since Bonhoeffer and Rabenau also had pencils and paper and each could continue working on a manuscript which he had brought with him. Best later described his fellow prisoners half-humorously, half-caustically. About Bonhoeffer he wrote:

Bonhoeffer was all humility and sweetness; he always seemed to diffuse an atmosphere of happiness, of joy in every smallest event in life, and of deep gratitude for the mere fact that he was alive. There was something doglike in the look of fidelity in his eyes and his gladness if you showed that you liked him. He was one of the very few men I have ever met to whom his God was real and ever close to him.[2]

In a letter to Sabine and Gerhard Leibholz he later expressed himself more fully, and no doubt found that his animal comparison was no longer appropriate. 'In fact my feeling was far stronger than these words imply. He was, without exception, the finest and most lovable man I have ever met.'

The original letter seemed to have been lost, but in 2008 Stephanie Schlingensiepen (the author's daughter) discovered a copy in the Imperial War Museum in London. It contains such a lively description of the conditions in Buchenwald that it is included in the Appendix of this book (see pp. 417–21).

Best reported that most inmates complained a lot, but that Falkenhausen and Bonhoeffer never did. Bonhoeffer was always composed and master of his situation. 'His soul really shone in the dark desperation of our prison ... [we were] in complete agreement that our warders and guards needed pity far more than we and that it was absurd to blame them for their actions.'³ Payne Best had spent five years in the Sachsenhausen concentration camp and had developed there a similar sort of expertise, in dealing with the guards, to that of Bonhoeffer in Tegel. This short statement shows that they had talked about it. When, in the Buchenwald cellar, the inmates began hearing the artillery of the advancing Americans from the Werra River area, Best had the feeling that he could persuade the wardens to escape with the prisoners; but the German prisoners would all have had to take part in this, and before they could reach agreement the opportunity had been missed.

The destruction of Pätzig

During Bonhoeffer's imprisonment in Prince Albrecht Street, the Red Army had conquered large stretches of eastern Germany and had almost reached the Oder River. On 30 January 1945, Ruth von Wedemeyer wrote to Bonhoeffer's mother that she had had to be very hard on her, asking her daughter Maria to come back to Pätzig immediately.

Despite twelve degrees of frost and an icy east wind, I've sent Maria in a covered wagon with my three other children, Mrs Döpke and her own two children, Miss Rath, who has a high temperature, and Mrs Dimel who's very delicate, their destination being a village in the west, in the neighbourhood of Celle ... I need her help very badly now. It's really far too much for her. She has a Polish driver and the three best plough horses. Join me in praying that she proves equal to her difficult task. They should be there in two weeks, if all goes well, but the snow and wind have been very severe since then.[4]

Maria had set out on this journey on 29 January. Her mother later reported that when they said goodbye, she had a feeling of great strength flowing to her from her daughter. Shortly after the wagon had departed, the state authorities, just before taking their own departure, had announced a strict ban on trekking, although the Russians were now very nearby. Ruth von Wedemeyer had actually been determined to stay at Pätzig, but at the last moment was persuaded to flee on foot. From the edge of the village, she saw her manor house enveloped in flames.

Almost as soon as she had arrived safely at the home of relatives in the west, Maria set off once again to find out where her fiancé had been taken. Suspecting that he might have been transferred to the concentration camp at Dachau or at Flossenbürg, she travelled to both places, and on 19 February wrote to her mother from the Upper Palatinate (near Flossenbürg) that she had not been able to find Dietrich at either place. 'I'm feeling utterly miserable, but that's only because I've been on the train for two days now, had to walk seven kilometers to get there, and then, without any prospect of hearing anything, had to trudge the same seven kilometres back again' (DBWE 8, IV/205). She did not mention that she had done all this while carrying a suitcase full of warm clothing and food for Dietrich. Since Pätzig was no more, and she didn't want to return to Berlin because the Russians were expected there, she ended up, exhausted and miserable, in Bundorf.

The last seven days

On the first of April, which in 1945 was Easter Sunday, the American artillery was thunderous as they advanced beyond the Werra River. In the cellar at Buchenwald, one of the guards arrived with orders for the prisoners to get ready to march. Another guard confirmed that they would be leaving on foot, which made them afraid that they would be taken into the woods and shot. In this uncertainty, on 3 April the last week of Dietrich Bonhoeffer's life began.

But in the evening of that day, the Tuesday after Easter, an enormous closed van appeared, with a motor that used wood for fuel. The prisoners had to squeeze past a great stack of wood and huddle together inside. The van departed that night, headed southward. Everyone now travelled at night if at all possible, since the Allies had long dominated Germany's air space and military transports were a prized target for bombers. This lorry could only manage twenty miles an hour at most, and had to keep stopping to be serviced. While the air filters were being cleaned, the boiler refilled with chopped wood and the whole engine reheated, the air inside the van became almost unbreathable, yet the prisoners were not allowed to get out, and they had no water and nothing to eat during these stops. Payne Best, a heavy smoker, remembers that in this situation Bonhoeffer found the last of his tobacco in his pocket and insisted on sharing it with everyone. 'He was a good and saintly man.'

As the woodpile grew smaller, two prisoners at a time could climb past it to breathe some fresh air through the crack at the edge of the tailgate. In this way those who knew the area saw that they had arrived in northeastern Bavaria. At noon on 4 April they were supposed to stop at the town of Weiden, but there were already so many refugees there that the transport was turned away. Now they would find out where they were going; if they turned left, it would be Flossenbürg and almost certain death, but if they continued southward, were they possibly headed for freedom? The journey continued toward the south.

A few miles further on they were stopped by two military policemen on motorcycles; Josef Müller and Franz Liedig were ordered to get out. Bonhoeffer leaned back so as not to be noticed. But Ludwig Gehre, who had been Müller's cell-mate at Buchenwald, jumped out after Müller. He was jumping to his death, since he thence became one of those who were hanged a few days later with Canaris and his group.

It took a while until the wood-burning lorry started up again. Were there no further orders for its guards? In any case it was striking how much friendlier they became from this moment on. They made a stop at a farmhouse and let the prisoners get out. There was a pump in working order, and they could all drink water and freshen up. The farmer's wife brought out a loaf of rye bread and a pitcher of milk. Then they continued onwards, arriving in Regensburg that evening. The transporter drove into the yard of the courthouse there.

'Aristocrats again,' grumbled a jailer when the new group objected to being rudely ordered about. The Regensburg city jail was full of *Sippenhäftlinge*, family members of accused prisoners, who were being kept in the corridors. Bonhoeffer and his companions in suffering met people of all ages bearing the names Stauffenberg, Goerdeler, Hammerstein, Hassell and so forth. The new group was locked up for the night, five to a cell, but they were hungry and protested noisily until a kind-hearted warden managed to get them some soup.

The scene on the morning of 5 April, according to Payne Best, must have been more like a festive reception than the beginning of a day in prison. It was very lively, and the guards had quite a struggle to herd the group from Buchenwald back into their cells. Bonhoeffer remained standing at the little window in the cell door, telling the inmates in the corridor about people he had seen in the Prince Albrecht Street prison under the SS Headquarters. In this way Mrs Goerdeler found out what he knew about the last weeks of her husband's life, and that he had been executed on 2 February.

Suddenly this joyful reunion of people who had almost reached safety was interrupted by an air raid siren. All the inmates were herded into the courthouse cellar, where they survived an attack on the nearby railroad marshalling yard. Payne Best got a look at it through a window, and remembered: 'Engines and coaches lying on their backs with their legs in the air, burnt-out coaches in long rows, and railway lines sticking up in great loops like pieces of wire ...' Hearing this destruction from inside the cellar must have been frightful. But when the prisoners came back upstairs it was the same scene as in the morning, all over again. When finally everyone was ready to settle down for the night, one of the Buchenwald guards appeared and called for his group; they were going further.

This was the day, 5 April, the Thursday after Easter, on which Bonhoeffer's fate was decided. By chance, the SS General Walter Buhle had discovered in Zossen some further material from Dohnanyi's secret archive, including diaries belonging to Admiral Canaris. Kaltenbrunner immediately passed on their fully revealing content to Hitler, who worked himself up into a frenzied rage. At a noon meeting in his headquarters, he ordered the 'liquidation' of Canaris and the other conspirators from Military Intelligence.

By this time it was no longer possible for anyone to believe that Germany would be victorious. The watchword everywhere had already been for some time, 'every man for himself' – save yourself if you can. Nevertheless, it took only a single command from Hitler to start up the official machinery of judicial murder in a far corner of the Reich. He still had henchmen who shared his fury and blindly carried out their orders to the very last. Thus, on the evening of this same day, the SS judge Otto Thorbeck in Nuremberg was summoned to preside over a court-martial at Flossenbürg. On the Sunday he found an open coal train that took him as far as Weiden. From there no further transport was available, so he got hold a bicycle for the last twelve miles or so, intent on carrying out Hitler's judicial murders as if they had been lawful acts.*

In Berlin, Dr Tietze in the State Hospital received orders to prepare Dohnanyi for transport to Sachsenhausen the next morning. He immediately sent for Christine von Dohnanyi, and at Hans's bedside they discussed escape plans with him, but were forced to accept that it was too late. The next morning Sonderegger came to collect the prisoner, and left no doubt in anyone's mind that Dohnanyi's fate was sealed. Huppenkothen, together with an unknown SS judge and the camp commander at Sachsenhausen, proclaimed the death sentence for Hans von Dohnanyi, who was already lying only half-conscious on a stretcher before them. The sentence was carried out on 9 April.

Klaus Bonhoeffer, Rüdiger Schleicher, Hans John, Friedrich Justus Perels, Albrecht Haushofer and 11 other prisoners were told on 22 April that they were to be moved from the prison in Lehrter Street to another building, where they were to be released. Instead, they were taken out that night behind Lehrter Railway Station and murdered by machine pistol shots in the back. One prisoner escaped and was able to bring the news of their death to their families on 31 May. At a bomb crater in the Dorotheenstadt Cemetery, which had been used as a shallow grave for these victims and many others, Eberhard Bethge, who had been freed in the meantime by Soviet troops, held a funeral service with the families of the dead on 11 June. The Bonhoeffer family was then still waiting for Dietrich to come home.

---

* For anyone who has not experienced it, it is hard to realize what it means to condemn one's own government as criminal. In the United States in 2009, for example, only a small group is ready to prosecute the Bush administration for its serious violations of our laws over eight years. In Germany the first reaction after the war was to condemn the 'Valkyrie' group and the other resisters as having committed treason. Only a generation or two later, when the animosity towards Germany from outside had faded somewhat, the country had been rebuilt and the fear and horror of the war remained only in the memories of older people, were Germans themselves ready to begin confronting publicly the evil and the illegality of Nazi actions. Around 1980, the German supreme court and the Bundestag were able to declare that Hitler's many hasty 'liquidations' of his opponents within the Reich were really 'judicial murders', committed with the apparatus of the state but against its laws, and to label them with the German word *ermordet*, literally 'murdered'.

Bonhoeffer and his group had arrived in Schönberg, 25 miles north of Passau, in the afternoon of 6 April. The journey there from Regensburg had been an adventure. In heavy rain and mud it had not been long until the steering of the old wood-burning van broke down and could not be repaired. The guards asked passers-by to report this to Regensburg Jail and request that another vehicle be sent. Despite being armed with machine pistols they were extremely tense and nervous. The rain was drumming on the roof of the van, in which the prisoners still huddled. Towards morning they were allowed out to stretch their legs. It was nearly noon before a new team of 10 SS guards showed up with a bus. The guards from Buchenwald, who had become friendlier as time passed, had to stay with their van, while the group of prisoners was treated to a pleasant trip, by daylight, in the much more comfortable bus. They passed by Metten Monastery and continued up into the hills of north-eastern Bavaria.

In the meantime the family members of those who had planned the coup had also been sent to Schönberg from Regensburg. They had moved into the ground floor of the school there, while Bonhoeffer's group was placed in the large classroom upstairs. On three sides they could see from the windows the beautiful landscape of the Ilz River valley. They had freshly made beds, but nothing to eat. But what the guards could not do, the prisoners' families downstairs could. They made contact with sympathetic people in the village, who brought a huge pot of steaming unpeeled potatoes and even made potato salad the next day.

Bonhoeffer's bed was next to that of the Russian, Kokorin. Hugh Falconer later wrote to Sabine Leibholz:

He did a great deal to keep some of the weaker brethren from depression and anxiety. He spent a good deal of time with Wasily Wasiliev Kokorin, Molotov's nephew, who was a delightful young man although an atheist. I think your brother divided his time with him between instilling the foundations of Christianity and learning Russian. (DB-ER 924)

Saturday, 7 April 1945, was the most pleasant day the prisoners had had since they were taken to Buchenwald. They found an electric outlet in the classroom, and Payne Best got out his electric razor and passed it around. Bonhoeffer still had his books with him, and probably also his manuscript, which had grown considerably since he left Tegel. The search for it has continued to this day. But it must have been lost on the way to Flossenbürg or destroyed at the camp there: an irreparable loss in the true sense of the word.

Bonhoeffer is said to have spent much of this day sitting in conversation with others at one of the open windows. The rain had stopped, and the valley was green and springlike. In the bright sunshine the prisoners' spirits rose as they looked forward to freedom and new life.

The night before, Walter Huppenkothen and his wife had packed several large suitcases with things that they hoped to save until after the war. He was to be the prosecutor at Flossenbürg, making sure that the Military Intelligence group of Resistance members was liquidated before the Americans got there. When the couple joined the convoy led by an SS leader named Gogalla next morning, Huppenkothen had two purposes in mind: carrying out the Führer's orders, and preparing to flee the capital before it was taken by the Russians. He was to return only once, briefly, to Berlin, where he was entrusted with some more files, and then he escaped to Austria. By bringing death to a final group of Hitler's opponents he was given the chance to survive himself.

Gogalla and Huppenkothen were both carrying 'Reich Secret Business' files with them, which were to guarantee them the support of the military police in case their journey to the south should be interrupted by accidents or delays. The documents specified exactly what they were to do in Flossenbürg, Dachau and Schönberg. Himmler seems to have hoped to the last that if he had internationally respected prisoners well treated and handed them over to the Allies, he could save his own life. It was, oddly enough, Payne Best who got hold one of these 'Reich Secret Business' documents. Somebody gave it to him when they had arrived in the Tyrolean Mountains. It said that Georg Elser, who had tried in 1939 to assassinate Hitler in the Bürgerbräu Cellar in Munich, was to be 'liquidated', but others such as Schacht, Halder, former Austrian Chancellor Schuschnigg and his wife, and Martin Niemöller were to be treated politely and transported on towards the Alps. Gogalla, who was responsible for carrying out these orders, picked up General Falkenhausen, Payne Best and Vassily Kokorin at Schönberg.

Huppenkothen arrived in Flossenbürg on Saturday evening, and together with the camp commander, Max Kögl, prepared the summary court-martial that was to pass the death sentences on Military Intelligence's Resistance group and Army Judge Karl Sack as their protector. As they were doing so, someone realized that prisoner Bonhoeffer was missing. A feverish search for him began. Other prisoners, including Schlabrendorff and Josef Müller, were shouted at in their cells during the night, 'Surely you are Bonhoeffer!' Finally the conclusion was reached that, by mistake,

Bonhoeffer must have been transported onwards to Schönberg. While Germany's fighting forces were abandoning their vehicles on both the eastern and western fronts for lack of petrol, Concentration Camp Commander Kögl was able to send a car on the 100-mile journey, by way of Weiden, Cham and Regen, to Schönberg.

It arrived there on White Sunday,[6] where the prisoners were in high spirits. After breakfast, Pünder suggested that Bonhoeffer lead them in Morning Prayer. Bonhoeffer objected at first, saying that most of the group were Catholics and Kokorin did not belong to any church. But then Kokorin himself joined the others in requesting a worship service. So Bonhoeffer read the Bible texts for that Sunday, led the group in prayer, and spoke on the texts for that day, 'With his stripes we are healed' (Isaiah 53:5) and 'Blessed be the God and Father of our Lord Jesus Christ! By his great mercy we have been born anew to a living hope through the resurrection of Jesus Christ from the dead' (1 Peter 1:3).[7]

The prisoners' families on the ground floor could hear that a service was being held upstairs, and were considering how to smuggle Bonhoeffer

The execution grounds at Flossenbürg. Here, on the morning of 9 April 1945, Dietrich Bonhoeffer, Wilhelm Canaris, Ludwig Gehre, Hans Oster, Karl Sack, Theodor Strünck and Friedrich von Rabenau were put to death

downstairs to lead one for them as well, when two men dressed as civilians appeared and called him: 'Prisoner Bonhoeffer, get ready and come with us!' They also called for Rabenau. Both men quickly packed their things. The Plutarch book that his brother Karl Friedrich had sent to Bonhoeffer in the prison in Prince Albrecht Street was later found on a table in the middle of the classroom. Dietrich Bonhoeffer had written his name in it in three places, to leave a trace of where he had been.

Payne Best described their farewell: 'We bade him goodbye. He drew me aside. "This is the end," he said, "for me, the beginning of life," and then he gave me a message to give, if I could, to the Bishop of Chichester, a friend to all evangelical pastors in Germany.'[8] As Bonhoeffer ran hurriedly down the stairs, Mrs Goerdeler called out a final goodbye. It was her son who later brought the Plutarch book to Bonhoeffer's family.

In the meantime, SS Judge Thorbeck had arrived in Flossenbürg by bicycle. Though he later insisted that he, Huppenkothen and Kögl had held a proper trial, at which the prisoners were thoroughly questioned and were allowed to respond, it only had the appearance of a trial. The verdict had already been given before this court was called to order.[9]

During the morning hours of 9 April, Wilhelm Canaris, Hans Oster, his colleagues Theodor Strünck and Ludwig Gehre, Karl Sack and Dietrich Bonhoeffer were hanged and cremated. Friedrich von Rabenau was to follow them a few days later. Their ashes, together with those of many thousands of other victims of Hitler's regime, form the now grass-grown pyramid in the middle of the former concentration camp at Flossenbürg.

Epilogue

Above the west portal of Westminster Abbey, the national shrine of the English people, 10 new statues carved in stone were installed some years ago, portraying martyrs of the twentieth century. In the middle stands Dietrich Bonhoeffer, holding an open Bible. For many people, far beyond the borders of Germany, he has become a model of the Christian life.

How this came about is a story in itself, for when Josef Müller and Fabian von Schlabrendorff brought the news of Bonhoeffer's death from Flossenbürg, he was hardly a publicly known figure. The two conspirators had been taken, with a larger group of prominent prisoners of the SS, including Martin Niemöller, former Austrian Chancellor Schuschnigg and his wife, Halder, Falkenhausen, Payne Best, Falconer and Kokorin, as far as the Puster Valley in the Tyrolean Alps of northern Italy, where a

Statue of Dietrich Bonhoeffer (far right) among other martyrs of the twentieth century at Westminster Abbey in London

German army unit released them and US troops brought them to Venice and Capri. From there they were able to send a message to Visser 't Hooft and his staff in Geneva. Visser 't Hooft himself, however, had flown to the USA together with Bishop Bell, to help prepare for a meeting of ecumenical leaders. They were especially hoping to have Bonhoeffer participate on behalf of Germany. It was only on returning to Europe that they learned he had been hanged at Flossenbürg.

Julius Rieger, who received a telegram from Freudenberg, Visser 't Hooft's collegue in Geneva, had to bring Sabine Leibholz the news that her brothers Klaus and Dietrich had been murdered during the last days of the war. Maria von Wedemeyer heard it in June, at her cousin's in Bundorf; but there was still no communication from the outside with Berlin.

In July, all British newspapers carried the shocking photos of the liberation of Bergen-Belsen concentration camp and the mounds of corpses that had been found there. These images went beyond what anyone had ever imagined of the atrocities in Germany, and after that hardly anyone in Britain could or would envision receiving Germany back into the community of nations. Even Payne Best waited more than a year before writing to Bishop Bell that he had a message for him from Dietrich Bonhoeffer.[1]

It was on 27 July, during this time of shock when Germany and Germans were regarded with abhorrence, that Bishop Bell, Franz Hildebrandt and Julius Rieger held a public memorial service for Dietrich Bonhoeffer at Holy Trinity Church in Kingsway in London – a service that was broadcast by the BBC. Bonhoeffer's parents, who had finally learned only a few days earlier that their son Dietrich had also perished, listened on the radio in Berlin. Sabine Leibholz came to the service with her family, as did members of Bonhoeffer's former parishes and friends from his time in London, German émigrés and British Christians, filling every pew in the church. In his sermon, the bishop spoke of his friend as hardly anyone else would have dared to do at that time:

His death is a death for Germany – indeed for Europe too … his death, like his life, marks a fact of the deepest value in the witness of the Confessing Church. As one of a noble company of martyrs of differing traditions, he represents both the resistance of the believing soul, in the name of God, to the assault of evil, and also the moral and political revolt of the human conscience against injustice and cruelty. He and his fellows are indeed built upon the foundation of the Apostles and the Prophets. And it was this passion for justice that brought him, and so many others ... into close partnership with other resisters, who, though outside the Church, shared the same humanitarian and liberal ideals ...

For him and Klaus ... there is the resurrection from the dead; for Germany redemption and resurrection, if God pleases to lead the nation through men animated by his spirit, holy and humble and brave like him; for the Church, not only in that Germany which he loved, but the Church Universal which was greater to him than nations, the hope of a new life. (DB-ER 931)

Long before the Marshall Plan or even the currency reform, before the economy rose again under the Federal Republic of Germany, Christians in the Scandinavian countries, Britain and the United States began rescuing those who were starving and aiding the hosts of German refugees. The Scandinavians, who were nearest, also worked fervently within East Germany, the Russian-occupied zone. Bonhoeffer had known since his meeting with Bell in Sweden that the bishop and his fellow campaigners would bring the 'war behind the war' to a peaceful conclusion and urge that Germany not remain an outcast from the community of nations. He had foreseen this in his poem 'The Death of Moses' (DBWE 8, IV/197).[2]

The Old Testament (Deuteronomy 34:1–4) relates that Moses, who had led the Israelites out of captivity in Egypt, was not allowed to enter the Promised Land with them. But before his death, God showed him that land from the summit of Mount Nebo. Bonhoeffer tells this story in simple verse, without any overt reference to the present. Yet we can hear that he was thinking of himself and the others who were prepared to pay with their lives for their patriotism.

> Faithful Lord, your faithless servant's sure
> that your righteousness shall e'er endure ...
> Wondrous deeds with me you have arranged,
> bitterness to sweetness you have changed.
>
> Through death's veil you let me see at least
> this, my people, go to highest feast.
> They stride into freedom, God, I see,
> as I sink to your eternity.
> To punish sin, to forgive you are moved;
> O God, this people have I truly loved.[3]

Notes

Chapter 1

1 Julius Rieger, *Dietrich Bonhoeffer in England*, 1966.
2 A field marshal is the equivalent of a five-star general.
3 The unpublished memoirs of Susanne Dreß were available to the author. They portray vividly the youth of her brother Dietrich, three years older than she.
4 Where not otherwise indicated, all following information about Bonhoeffer's early life comes from the memoirs of Susanne Dreß.
5 Carl Friedrich von Weizsäcker, 'Thoughts of a Non-Theologian on Dietrich Bonhoeffer's Theological Development', presented at a Bonhoeffer symposium in Geneva (Switzerland), 1976, trans. World Council of Churches Language Service, *Ecumenical Review*, Vol. 28, No. 2, April 1976, pp. 156–73, here p. 157.
6 Maria Horn belonged to the Moravian 'Brüdergemeine' community founded at Herrnhut, Germany by Nikolaus von Zinzendorf, which shares pulpit and table fellowship with the Evangelical Church in Germany. Its *Losungen* ('watchword' for the day), the daily devotions book, played an important role in Bonhoeffer's life and is still widely used today. For each day of the year the book has a verse from the Old Testament as *Losung* (text for the day) and a verse from the New Testament as *Lehrtext* (instruction), followed by a brief prayer.
7 The USPD, or Independent Socialist Party of Germany, had split off from the Socialist Party in 1917 and was fighting against continuing the war.
8 Marion Yorck von Wartenburg, *Die Stärke der Stille*, 1984, pp. 14ff.
9 Weizsäcker, 'Thoughts of a Non-Theologian', p. 162.

Chapter 2

1 Memoirs of Bonhoeffer's student friend Theodor Pfizer, later mayor of the city of Ulm: *Im Schatten der Zeit* (In the Shadow of the Time), *1940–1948*, 1979, pp. 77ff.
2 There is an impressive description of this episode also by Theodor Pfizer.
3 On Easter Sunday 1928, in a sermon in Barcelona, Bonhoeffer told the story of the death of Pan at some length (DBWE 10, [p. 464]).

4 Bonhoeffer erroneously wrote 'June 1923'.
5 Cf. Karl Barth, *The Epistle to the Romans*, 6th edn, trans. Edwyn C. Hoskins, Oxford, Oxford University Press, 1933. Barth had never felt that it made sense to express himself briefly and precisely in his lectures. What was important to him is especially clear in the chapter 'Concerning the Value of History', pp. 140–8.
6 Adolf von Harnack, 'Fünfzehn Fragen an die Verächter der wissenschaftlichen Theologie unter den Theologen [Fifteen Questions for Theologians Who Despise Scientific Theology]', in *Die Christliche Welt*, 37/1923, cols 6–8, here col. 8. Karl Barth, 'Sechzehn Antworten an Herrn Professor von Harnack (Sixteen Answers for Professor Harnack)', in *Die Christliche Welt*, 37/1923, cols 89–91, here col. 91.
7 Allusion to Friedrich Schiller's saying, in the epigrams of the *Musenalmanach* for 1797, p. 212, referring to Kant and his interpreters: 'Just look how many beggars a single rich person can feed! When kings build, the cart drivers have work.'
8 Cf. his Bible study on Ezra–Nehemiah in DBWE 14, 930.
9 *Beiderwand* cloth: homespun linen and wool; lederhosen with leather braces were either 'short shorts' for hiking or knee-length for more formal wear; the *Wandervogel* was a 'back-to-nature' youth movement in Germany.
10 Cf. H. Pfeifer, 'Die Bedeutung der Jugendbewegung für Dietrich Bonhoeffer (The Significance of the Youth Movement for Dietrich Bonhoeffer)', in *Dietrich-Bonhoeffer-Jahrbuch*, ed. Christoph Gremmels *et al.*, 2003, pp. 74ff.
11 Cf. Emmi Bonhoeffer, *Essay, Gespräch, Erinnerung* (Essays, Conversations, Memories), ed. S. Gabner and H. Röder, p. 64. This contains many accounts of experiences and observations on the Bonhoeffer family style.
12 In continental Europe, 'St Nicholas' is celebrated on 6 December, rather than at Christmas, with a visit from Father Christmas (Santa Claus) appropriately disguised, bringing treats for children.
13 Bonhoeffer had originally planned to have the customary word order, *Communio Sanctorum*, for his title. But then the professor of systematic theology at Erlangen, Paul Althaus, published a book with that title, so Bonhoeffer changed his word order.
14 Bishop Otto Dibelius had proposed a third, consciously positive view in his book *Das Jahrhundert der Kirche* (The Century of the Church), but it had been rejected by all critically minded theologians.
15 Cf. M. Honecker, *Kirche als Gestalt und Ereignis* (The Church as Form and Event), 1963, p. 47.
16 Cf. Karl Barth, *The Word of God and the Word of Man*, trans. Douglas Horton. Boston, The Pilgrim Press, 1928, p. 213.

17 Dietrich Bonhoeffer, *Sanctorum Communio: A Dogmatic Inquiry into the Sociology of the Church*, trans. R. Gregor Smith, London, Collins, 1963, p. 213.

18 Ibid., p. 193. (Translator's note: In Germany in the 1920s, as today, the terms 'bourgeois' and 'proletariat' could be used by everybody. They were not seen as 'communist' language.)

19 Weizsäcker, 'Thoughts of a Non-Theologian', p. 163.

20 Philosopher Georg Wilhelm Friedrich Hegel, 1770–1831. On the expression 'God existing as community', see Bonhoeffer's notes in DBWE 1, pp. 132f.

21 Dietrich Bonhoeffer and Maria von Wedemeyer, *Love Letters from Cell 92, 1943–1945*, ed. Ruth-Alice von Bismarck and Ulrich Kabitz, postscript by Eberhard Bethge, trans. John Brownjohn, London, HarperCollins, 1994, p. 139.

22 Ibid., p. 153.

23 Karl Barth called the first volume of his Dogmatics 'Christian Dogmatics', but later completely reworked this volume and published it anew with the title *Church Dogmatics*. Thus he conceded Bonhoeffer's point, but presumably without knowing of it.

Chapter 3

1 Tauentzien Street was Berlin's 'red-light district'.

2 The Bonhoeffers of course were Lutheran, and no Lutheran church calls its governing body a 'presbytery', but the origin of the Barcelona congregation was apparently Reformed. As usual in expatriate situations, Protestant denominational distinctions faded; it was being able to worship in one's home language that was important.

3 Cf. J. van Norden, *'Heim ins neue Deutschland Adolf Hitlers'. Die Evakuierung der Spaniendeutschen während des spanischen Bürgerkrieges* ('Home to Adolf Hitler's new Germany': The Evacuation of Germans from Spain during the Spanish Civil War), 1998.

4 Spain was actually under Islamic (Moorish) influence for over seven hundred years.

5 Though Barth was Swiss, he belonged to the German-speaking culture that prevails in Switzerland and Austria as well as Germany, within which university professors can move about freely. In Bonhoeffer's mind, to live 'abroad' would have meant in a country outside this cultural realm.

6 The Stahlhelm [Steel Helmet] federation, formed in 1918 by veterans of the First World War front lines, was at first conservative and clung to prewar ideals, but became increasingly radical as it rejected the Republic. The majority of its members were integrated into the SA in 1933.

7 Weizsäcker, 'Thoughts of a Non-Theologian', p. 164.

8 Cf. C. Tietz-Steiding, *Bonhoeffers Kritik der verkrümmten Vernunft. Eine erken-*

ntnistheoretische Untersuchung (Bonhoeffer's Critique of Crooked Reason: An Investigation in the Theory of Knowledge), 1999, and J. Boomgarden, *Das Verständnis der Wirklichkeit. Dietrich Bonhoeffers systematische Theologie und ihr philosophischer Hintergrund in 'Akt und Sein'* (Understanding Reality: Dietrich Bonhoeffer's Systematic Theology and Its Philosophical Background in 'Act and Being'), 1999.

9 Prohibition of 'intoxicating liquors … for beverage purposes' was established by an amendment to the US Constitution in 1919. This amendment was repealed in 1933. It was at first promoted by the churches to try and mitigate alcoholism, a severe problem because the cultural norms that used to prevent 'binge' drinking in Europe were lacking in America.

10 Martin Luther King Jr used it in 1964 in his famous speech in Washington, 'I Have a Dream'.

11 Hans Pfeifer in his dissertation at the University of Heidelberg: *Das Kirchenverständnis Dietrich Bonhoeffers. Ein Beitrag zur theologischen Prinzipienlehre* (Dietrich Bonhoeffer's Understanding of the Church: A Contribution to the Theological Teaching of Fundamental Principles), 1964, p. 79.

12 William James, *The Varieties of Religious Experience: A Study in Human Nature*, 1928. See also DBWE 11, II/9, 4.V. 1932 and 4.VI. 1932.

13 See Chapter 1, p. 15, for the exact wording.

14 Bonhoeffer took courses in ethics from this famous German-born theologian and ethicist.

15 In German and other northern European languages, *Engel*, the word for angel, is close to the words for England and English.

16 General Superintendent Otto Dibelius, who later took the side of the church struggle against Nazism.

17 Hans Pfeifer, "Learning Faith and Ethical Commitment in the Context of Spiritual Training Groups. Consequences of Dietrich Bonhoeffer's Postdoctoral Year in New York City, 1930–31", in *Dietrich Bonhoeffer Yearbook*, vol. 3. Edited by Clifford Green, Kirsten Busch Nielsen, Hans Pfeifer and Christiane Tietz. Gütersloh: Gütersloher Verlagshaus 2008, 251–79, here 278–79.

Chapter 4

1 This was Bonhoeffer's first encounter with the Benedictine order, which was to play an important role in his future life. At the time he also visited the abbey of Maria Laach.

2 Deuteronomy 10:19.

3 Like their professors, all university students in Germany and Austria were considered 'German', since they shared the same language and culture.

4 *Das Volk* in German normally means 'the nation' or 'the people' as a whole. In the Third Reich it became a term for distinguishing 'us' from 'them': the

Volk had to be of racially pure Aryan origin, the 'master race', and dedicated to making the German people, under its *Führer* Hitler, the greatest and most powerful in the world, as in the Nazi view it had the right to be. Aryan meant of northern Caucasian, Nordic stock.

⁵ Both in songs by Rudolf Alexander Schröder, who was opposed to Nazism.

⁶ From Nazism's earliest days its uniforms were brown.

⁷ The book of poetry is entitled *Das Kreuz auf Golgotha. Gedichtkreis eines Ketzers* (The Cross on Golgotha: Poetry by a Heretic). Cf. H. Chr. Brandenburg, *Die Geschichte der HJ. Wege und Irrwege einer Generation* (The History of the Hitler Youth; a Generation Losing its Way), 1968, p. 61.

⁸ Brandenburg, *Die Geschichte der HJ*, p. 112.

⁹ See *No Rusty Swords: Letters, Lectures and Notes, 1928–1936, from the Collected Works of Dietrich Bonhoeffer*, edited and introduced by Edwin H. Robertson, translated by Edwin H. Robertson and John Bowden, London, Collins, 1965, p. 142. Luther's confession was translated from 30 I 94 in the German Weimar edition of Luther's works. For the experience of forgiveness of sins, these translators used the word 'sanctify', in an older sense, instead of 'justify' for the German *heiligen*. The German word means either, and Luther is known throughout Christendom for his teaching of 'justification by faith'.

¹⁰ See *A History of the Ecumenical Movement 1517–1948*, ed. Ruth Rouse and Stephen Charles Neill, Philadelphia, Westminster Press, 1954, and London (published on behalf of the Ecumenical Institute by SPCK), 1954.

¹¹ Bonhoeffer also attended another preparatory meeting in England on which he did not report. See DB-ER 199.

¹² The statement's (preceding) description of the 'situation' was that the Allies had openly broken the promises made to Germany at the time of its surrender in 1918. Germany had been robbed of space in which to live and breathe *das Volk ohne Raum*, a theme of Hitler's) and was being depleted by payments falsely depicted as reparations. The Allied disarmament obligation undertaken in the peace treaty had been flagrantly broken. Cf. DB-ER 963.

¹³ See S. Grotefeld, *Friedrich Siegmund-Schulze. Ein deutscher Ökumeniker und christlicher Pazifist* (Friedrich Siegmund-Schulze: German Ecumenicist and Christian Pacifist), 1995.

¹⁴ Quoted in DB-ER 250, from F. A. Iremonger, *William Temple*, p. 376. Temple was one of the most well-known early ecumenical leaders. The 60-nation World Disarmament Conference in Geneva had been called by the League of Nations (a forerunner of the United Nations that lasted only until the Second World War); the ideal was for all nations to give up weapons of attack, in order to prevent war. The United States and the Soviet Union participated although they had not joined the League of Nations.

15 Some of this seems also to have been included in a letter of 27 January 1936 from Finkenwalde, according to Bethge, who also quotes it from DBW 14, 112–44.

16 See an interpretation of this poem by Jürgen Henkys, *Geheimnis der Freiheit. Die Gedichte Dietrich Bonhoeffers aus der Haft. Biographie, Poesie, Theologie* (The Mystery of Freedom: Dietrich Bonhoeffer's Prison Poems). Gütersloh, Gütersloher Verlagshaus, 2005, pp. 121ff.

17 Wolf-Dieter Zimmermann and Ronald Gregor Smith (eds), *I Knew Dietrich Bonhoeffer: Reminiscences by His Friends*, translated by Käthe Gregor Smith, New York, Harper and Row, 1966, pp. 126, 128.

18 Ibid., p. 69 (Mark 8:19).

19 Cf. Hans Pfeifer, 'Bonhoeffer und die Jugendbewegung (Bonhoeffer and the Youth Movement)', in *Dietrich-Bonhoeffer-Jahrbuch*, ed. Christian Gremmels *et al.*, 2003, p. 80.

20 Cf. Marlies Flesch-Thebesius, *Zu den Aussenseitern gestellt. Die Geschichte der Gertrud Staewen* (Marginalized: Gertrud Staewen's Story), 2004, pp. 51ff.

21 Günter Dehn, *Die alte Zeit, die vorigen Jahre. Lebenserinnerungen* (Old Times, Past Years: Reminiscences), 1962, pp. 247–362.

22 Flesch-Thebesius, *Zu den Aussenseitern gestellt*, pp. 181ff.

23 Robert Frick, the author's predecessor in 'Kaiserswerth', responded thus in 1981 to a speech by the then City Superintendent of Düsseldorf.

24 This idea was taken up by Karow; cf. his letter of 2 January 1934, to the Consistory (DBWE 13, 1/43).

25 Cf. Jürgen Glenthoj (ed.), *Dokumente zur Bonhoeffer-Forschung* (Documents for Research on Bonhoeffer) *1928–1945*, 1969, p. 29.

26 The Baltic states, Latvia, Estonia and Lithuania, had become independent of Russia after the First World War. Until then they had for centuries been governed by a German speaking nobility.

27 Glenthoj, *Dokumente zur Bonhoeffer-Forschung*, p. 31.

28 On the following, cf. the detailed interpretation by Jürgen Henkys in *Geheimnis der Freiheit* (see note 16 above), pp. 33–40.

29 Gottfried Benn, '*Das Unaufhörliche* (The Unceasing)', from his collected works, 1. *Gedichte* (Poems), 1960, pp. 145–6.

30 Cf. Pinchas Lapide, 'Bonhoeffer und das Judentum (Bonhoeffer and Judaism)', in *Verspieltes Erbe*, ed. Ernst Feil (Second International Bonhoeffer Forum), 1979, p. 122.

Chapter 5

1 Cf. Karl Dietrich Bracher, *The German Dictatorship: The Origin, Structure and Effects of National Socialism*, trans. Jean Steinberg, New York, Praeger, 1970, pp. 169–214.

2   For a summary of further developments after *Mein Kampf* was published, see Ian Kershaw, *Hitler 1936–1945: Nemesis*, London, Norton, 2000, pp. 127–53.

3   Cf. Bracher, *The German Dictatorship*, pp. 229–72.

4   Letter of 11 January 1945 from Count Moltke to his wife, Freya; in *Dying We Live*, the final messages and records of some Germans who defied Hitler, ed. Helmut Gollwitzer, Käthe Kuhn and Reinhold Schneider, trans. Reinhard C. Kuhn, Glasgow, Collins, 1958, p. 119.

5   The names and the historical and cultural origins of Germany's provincial Protestant churches go back to the independent, mostly small states of which the country was composed until the beginning of the nineteenth century. Germany was not united until 1870.

6   An indispensable account of the church struggle in 1933–1934 is found in Klaus Scholder's *The Churches and the Third Reich*, trans. John Bowden, Vol. 1: *Preliminary History and the Time of Illusions, 1918–1934*, Philadelphia, Fortress Press, 1988 and Vol. 2, *The Year of Disillusionment 1934: Barmen and Rome*, London, SCM Press, 1988. Another is J. S. Conway's *The Nazi Persecution of the Churches, 1933–1945*, London, Weidenfeld & Nicolson, 1968.

7   In the original German version. See *Dietrich Bonhoeffer: A Biography*, rev. edn by Victoria J. Barnett (DB-ER), Minneapolis, Fortress Press, 2000, pp. 257–323. This is the first complete English translation of Bethge's original.

8   Like many a dictator, Hitler professed to offer the German people leadership in which they needed only to put their entire confidence and everything would go well for them. However, in developing the *Führer* (single leader) concept into a principle of government, he pushed it to its absolute limits. Every thought and word of his was to be regarded as godlike, and his every command was to be obeyed absolutely without question. So, at least in theory, the entire responsibility for thinking and decision-making on behalf of the nation rested solely on the shoulders of the *Führer*.

9   The German word here is *Verführer*, which in its more usual sense means 'seducer'.

10   Cf. Max Domarus, ed. *Hitler: Speeches and Proclamations, 1932–1945; The Chronicle of a Dictatorship*, with commentary by a contemporary German, Vol. 1 (1932–1934), trans. Mary Fran Gilbert, London, I. B. Tauris, 1990, p. 235.

11   Ibid., p. 250.

12   At the time, Marinus van der Lubbe was put on trial as the accused arsonist. Among those who believe he acted alone are Fritz Tobias and Hans Mommsen. The latest to deny this are Alexander Bahar and Winfried Kugel, in *Der Reichstagsbrand. Wie Geschichte gemacht wird* (The Reichstag Fire: How History is Created), Berlin, edition q, 2001. See a review of this book in English by Wilhelm Klein on the World Socialist Website, www.wsws. org/articles/2001/jul2001/reic-j05.shtml (this review was used by David Ray Griffin on 28 April 2006 in a historical comparison to claim US

responsibility for the 11 September 2001 attacks: www.911truth.org/article. php?story=20060501003040487).

13. The district where Bonhoeffer had worked at Zion Church. The name has nothing to do with the English word 'wedding'.

14. Klaus Scholder, *The Churches and the Third Reich*, Vol. 1: *Preliminary History and the Time of Illusions, 1918–1934*, trans. John Bowden, Philadelphia, Fortress Press, 1988, pp. 261–3.

15. Renate Wind, *Dietrich Bonhoeffer: A Spoke in the Wheel*, trans. John Bowden. Grand Rapids, MI, W. B. Eerdmans, 1991, p. 66. Early writers on Bonhoeffer in English were unfamiliar with the German expression *dem Rad in die Speichen fallen*, which means to bring a wheel to a standstill by seizing its spokes. See the quotation from Bonhoeffer's essay on 'The Church and the Jewish Question', p. 126 below.

16. Radio speech by General Superintendent Otto Dibelius to the people of the USA, 4 April 1933; English text in a pamphlet, 'The Strange Case of Bishop Dibelius', Berlin, Rütten and Loening, 1961.

17. Cf. Ferdinand Schlingensiepen (ed.), *Theologisches Studium im Dritten Reich* (Studying Theology under the Third Reich), 1998, p. 138.

18. Domarus, *Hitler*, p. 279.

19. Schlingensiepen, *Theologisches Studium im Dritten Reich*, p. 142.

20. Kurt Meier, *Der evangelische Kirchenkampf: Gesamtdarstellung in drei Bänden* (The Protestant Church Struggle: An Overview in Three Volumes), Vol. 1: *Der Kampf um die 'Reichskirche'* (The Struggle for the 'Reich Church'), Göttingen, Vandenhoeck & Ruprecht, 1976, pp. 56–76, 85.

21. *Gleichschaltung* was a new Nazi word to indicate that the whole society in its every aspect must conform to Nazi ideology.

22. Gauleiter (leader of a province in the Nazi party) Kube was among those few Nazi officials, like Hans Kerrl, Hitler's Minister of Church Affairs from 1935, who did not want to keep the churches out of public affairs but wanted instead to make them into a supra-confessional Reich Church which would help to impart Nazi ideology.

23. Cf. Renate Bethge, 'Bonhoeffers Familie in der NS-Zeit', in E. H. Robertson, *Dietrich Bonhoeffer, Leben und Verkündigung*, Göttingen, Vandenhoeck & Ruprecht, c1989, pp. 15–24 (NB: The original English version of Robertson's book, *The Shame and the Sacrifice*, does not contain the introduction by R. Bethge).

24. Especially taken together with Bonhoeffer's writings (DBWE 12, I/95, 101, 102, 105; II/16) against the Aryan paragraph in the same year, the expression 'call to action' is appropriate for 'The Church and the Jewish Question'. Cf. Timo Rainer Peters, *Die Präsenz des Politischen in der Theologie Dietrich Bonhoeffers*, 1976, pp. 44ff.

25. Hans Christian Brandenburg, *Die Geschichte der HJ*, p. 129.

[26] Ibid., p. 130.

[27] Communication from Heinz Zimmermann, a school headmaster in Bad Godesberg (near Bonn), whose son had belonged to a Hitler Youth group.

[28] Wolf Dieter Zimmermann, *I Knew Dietrich Bonhoeffer*, p. 71.

[29] Quoted by Bethge from *Junge Kirche*, the successor to *Vormarsch*.

[30] For the original and revised texts of the Bethel Confession, see DBWE 12, II, No. 15, as well as the editorial note on the Bethel Confession at the beginning of the Appendices. On the participation of Georg Merz, see M. M. Lichtenfeld, *Georg Merz, Pastoraltheologe zwischen den Zeiten. Leben und Werk in Weimarer Republik und Kirchenkampf* (Pastoral Theologian between the Times: Life and Work in the Weimar Republic and the Church Struggle), 1997, pp. 327–409.

[31] Kurt Scharf, *Für ein politisches Gewissen der Kirche. Aus Reden und Schriften* (For a Political Conscience in the Church: Selected Speeches and Writings) *1932–1972*, with prefaces by Ludwig Raiser and Philip Potter and an introduction by Martin Fischer, ed. Wolfgang Erk, Stuttgart, J. F. Steinkopf, 1972.

[32] Scholder, *The Churches and the Third Reich*, p. 484.

[33] Ibid., p. 484.

[34] Ibid., p. 485.

[35] Ibid., p. 492.

[36] Cf. Jürgen Glenthoj (ed.), *Dokumente zur Bonhoeffer-Forschung*, p. 127.

Chapter 6

[1] Julius Rieger, *Bonhoeffer in England*, Berlin, Lettner Press, 1966, p. 17. Unless otherwise indicated, this publication is the source of the other information given here about Bonhoeffer's life in London. See also Keith W. Clements, *Bonhoeffer in Britain*, London, Churches Together in Britain and Ireland, 2006, which contains many photographs.

[2] See DBWE 13, pp. 321ff.

[3] Exact source not known, but Hitler is similarly quoted in Max Domarus, ed., *Hitler: Reden und Proklamationen 1932–1945*, with commentary by a contemporary German, Vol. 1, 1962, p. 724.

[4] There are two cities called Frankfurt in Germany: the big metropolis of Frankfurt am Main (on the Main river) in West Germany, the home of American military installations for many years since the Second World War; the other, smaller city of Frankfurt lies on the Oder River, which later became the boundary between East Germany and present-day Poland.

[5] Scholder, *The Churches and the Third Reich*, Vol. 1, p. 526.

[6] Hans Christian Brandenburg, *Geschichte der Hitler Jugend. Wege und Irrwege einer Generation* (The History of the Hitler Youth: A Generation Led Astray),

Köln, Verlag Wissenschaft und Politik, 1968, p. 102. The Protestant youth federations had over 700,000 members, which the Hitler Youth came nowhere near; when the Reich youth commission was set up, the Hitler Youth accounted for only 1 per cent of the combined memberships. Ibid., pp. 132, 156.

7   Scholder, *The Churches and the Third Reich*, Vol. 1, pp. 261–3.

8   Ibid., p. 540. *Der Hauptmann von Köpenick* (The Captain from Köpenick) was a popular comedy by Carl Zuckmaier, based on a true incident following the First World War. A cobbler and petty thief in Köpenick, then a suburb of Berlin, bought a captain's uniform secondhand and immediately put it on in a public toilet. To his delight, soldiers in uniform whom he met in the street followed his orders. He marched them to the Town Hall, where he successfully 'requisitioned' the cash box, then dismissed 'his' troops. He was caught and briefly imprisoned in Tegel, but everyone laughed, including the King.

9   Ibid., p. 678.

10 Klemens von Klemperer, *German Resistance Against Hitler: The Search for Allies Abroad, 1938–1945*, Oxford, Clarendon Press and New York, Oxford University Press, 1992, p. 11.

11 On Hitler's reception and the story leading up to it, cf. Scholder, *The Churches and the Third Reich*, Vol. 2, pp. 22–52.

12 Cf. Werner Kallen, *In der Gewissheit seiner Gegenwart. Dietrich Bonhoeffer und die Spur des vermißten Gottes* (Certain of His Presence: Dietrich Bonhoeffer and the Trace of the Absent God), Mainz, Matthias-Grünewald-Verlag, 1997, pp. 64–79.

13 H. Pickert, *Hitlers Tischgespräche im Führerhauptquartier* (Table Conversations in Hitler's Headquarters) *1941–1942*, 1951, p. 357.

14 Scharf, *Für ein politisches Gewissen der Kirche*, p. 34.

15 Scholder, *The Churches and the Third Reich*, Vol. 2, pp. 73–4.

16 These membership cards came in different colours. Today we speak of them as red because it was a 'red card' which played a role in Bonhoeffer's story. Cf. pp. 189 and 202 of the present volume.

17 For the full text of the Barmen Declaration, see pp. 407–11 in the Appendix. Cf. also Scholder, *The Churches and the Third Reich*, Vol. 2, pp. 142–71. Scholder discusses here in detail the reservations of Lutherans toward 'Barmen', reservations against which Bonhoeffer was soon battling energetically.

18 Ibid., p. 150.

19 'Thinking believers' is an expression used by (the German poet and critic) Heinrich Heine among others. Heine divided Protestants into three groups: 'rigid believers', pietists and 'thinking believers'. Cf. Heine, *Brief an* (Letter to) *Varnhagen von Ense, Säkularausgabe*, Vol. 20, 1974, pp. 227–8.

20 Translated by Arthur C. Cochrane in his *The Church's Confession under Hitler*, Philadephia, The Westminster Press, 1962, pp. 237–42. Also at www.sacred-texts.com/chr/barmen.htm.

21 Scharf, *Für ein politisches Gewissen der Kirche*, p. 37.

22 On the so-called 'Röhm-Putsch', the coup that never actually took place, cf. William L. Shirer, *The Rise and Fall of the Third Reich: A History of Nazi Germany*. New York, Simon & Schuster, 1960, pp. 68–79, 213–26.

23 Domarus, *Hitler*, Vol. 1, p. 498.

24 Cf. Fritz Günther von Tschirschsky, *Erinnerungen eines Hochverräters* (A Traitor's Memoir), Stuttgart, 1972, p. 227.

25 Scholder, *The Churches and the Third Reich*, Vol. 2, pp. 267 and 272 (lines in italics; the rest trans. IB). Cf. also Wilhelm Niemöller, *Kampf und Zeugnis der Bekennenden Kirche* (The Struggle and Witness of the Confessing Church), 1947, pp. 184ff.

26 Joachim Beckmann (ed.), *Kirchliches Jahrbuch* (Church Yearbook) *1933–1945*, 2nd edn 1976, pp. 82ff.

27 Reconstructed from Foreign Ministry files, Az. R 42 II 162: 182 and Az. R 42 II 163: 113 with a handwritten note: 'The Führer has been informed'.

28 In Germany and many other European countries, there are one or two state churches, i.e. majority churches established as the 'religion of state', to which most Christians belong. All other denominations, such as Baptists, Methodists etc., are much smaller and, to the extent they are not considered sects, are regarded as 'free churches' (*Freikirchen* in German).

29 Here Bonhoeffer's German text has the sentence: 'As a member of the ecumenical movement, the World Alliance for Promoting International Friendship through the Churches has taken up God's call to peace and sends this command out to all peoples.' For Bonhoeffer, the ecumenical movement had to act as 'church', if God confronted it with a situation in which the member churches were called to make a decision. Of course the movement wasn't 'a' church as such; but as an assembly representing God's people on earth 'in such a time as this', it was called to do what was right in God's eyes.

30 Karl Barth also had doubts about Bonhoeffer's admiration for Gandhi; cf. DBWE 14.

31 Zimmermann, *I Knew Dietrich Bonhoeffer*, p. 74.

32 For the resolution of the pastors' meeting on secession, according to minutes taken by Bonhoeffer, as well as minutes of the meeting at which it was discussed, see DBWE 13, pp. 230ff.

33 For Rößler's letter, see DBWE 13, pp. 245ff.

34 These figures reflect the great hopes of Bonhoeffer and his friends at this time. Cf. Larry Rassmussen, 'Interview with Herbert Jehle', *Bonhoeffer Jahrbuch*, 2, pp. 115–16.

35 For Wegner's story, see www.armenian-genocide.org/wegnerbio.html.

Chapter 7

1 The German churches of the Reformation had been state churches in the various principalities. The local princes were the heads of the territorial churches and acted as *summus episcopus*, or highest bishop. This arrangement ceased with the end of the monarchy in 1918. In the Weimar Republic, concordats were signed between the churches and the states of the Weimar Republic which specified their right to collect taxes from their members. They nominated their own bishops or presidents. The process of qualification for the ordained clergy, who kept the status of civil servants, was agreed upon in the concordats, including the First and Second Theological Examinations and training at a state university and a preachers' seminary. Benefits included care of their widows and orphans, though not exemption from military service. From 1935 onwards the Confessing Church clergy and its candidates for ordination were taking a major legal risk by bypassing the seminaries that were part of this system.

2 Many have wanted to know more about this extraordinary friendship. Eberhard Bethge himself wrote about it:

> After the first edition of Bonhoeffer's *Letters and Papers from Prison* was published in the 1950s, without revealing the names of his correspondents, someone asked me if I knew who the friend was with whom he had exchanged so many letters in that book; they 'must have been homosexuals' to have had such an intense correspondence. No, we were actually pretty straight. Of course we know more today about the fact that even friendships between persons of the same sex are not without some measure of homoerotic elements. In our case, our friendship was deepened at its beginning by Dietrich's sharing with me that he had ended a relationship of several years' duration with a woman, and the pain this had caused, and my revealing to him that my engagement to be married had just ended in bitterness. And towards the end of our friendship it brought each of us a new commitment to a most vital woman partner, and we shared the development of these relationships, and difficulties due to the war, in the way that men do, before anyone else knew about them ... Both of our love stories ... couldn't have been more intense, even though we expressed this in ways that seem unimaginably prudish today. However, we could really understand the Song of Solomon, which has been in the Bible for two thousand years. (Quoted in Christian Gremmels and Wolfgang Huber (eds), *Theologie und Freundschaft: Wechselwirkungen, Eberhard Bethge und Dietrich Bonhoeffer*, Gütersloh, Kaiser, Gütersloher Verlagshaus, 1994, pp. 15–16)

3   See J. Pejsa's biography of her, *Mit dem Mut einer Frau. Matriarchin des Widerstands* (A Woman's Courage: Matriarch of the Resistance), 2nd edn 1999; also the letters from Ruth von Kleist to Werner Koch, in Zimmermann, *I Knew Dietrich Bonhoeffer*.

4   Zimmermann, *I Knew Dietrich Bonhoeffer*, p. 108.

5   See DBWE 5, *Life Together* and *The Prayerbook of the Bible: An Introduction to the Psalms*, in one volume, trans. Daniel W. Bloesch and James H. Burtness, ed. Geoffrey B. Kelly. Minneapolis, Fortress Press, 1996.

6   Zimmermann, *I Knew Dietrich Bonhoeffer*, p. 133.

7   Paul de Lagarde, Heinrich von Treitschke and Richard Wagner were among those who had propagated this idea in the nineteenth century; 'religion and *Volk*-oriented' groups had brought their influence to bear on elements within the Nazi Party.

8   Dietrich Bonhoeffer, *No Rusty Swords. Letters, Lectures and Notes 1928–1936*, Vol. 12, ed. Edwin H. Robertson, trans. Edwin H. Robertson and John Bowden, London, Collins, 1965, p. 326.

9   Ibid., pp. 329–30.

10 Ibid., p. 333.

11 Timo Rainer Peters, *Die politische Relevanz der Theologie Bonhoeffers* (The Political Relevance of Bonhoeffer's Theology), 1976, p. 55: 'Bonhoeffer had never applied his theological-political hermeneutics more directly and with such a fighting spirit, nor in a more exposed and awkward manner … Here was a brilliant opportunity for those opposed to his church politics.' And on p. 180: 'Within his powerful exegeses … elements of that dangerous lack of scholarship could be found, against which Adolf von Harnack had warned him with regard to (Barth's) theology of revelation.'

12 W. Niemöller, *Kampf und Zeugnis der Bekennenden Kirche*, p. 304.

13 Cf. Meier, *Der evangelische Kirchenkampf*, Vol. 2, pp. 88–9.

14 From the author's memories of his own youth. (In Germany, composing doggerel to speak or sing in a teasing vein is a usual part of a birthday or other personal celebration.)

15 From J. Beckman (ed.), *Kirchliches Jahrbuch* (Church Yearbook) *1933–1945*, 1976, pp. 132–7.

16 Heinz E. Tödt (ed.), *Wie ein Flaschenpost. Ökumenische Briefe und Beiträge für Eberhard Bethge* (Like a Message in a Bottle: Ecumenical Letters and Articles for Eberhard Bethge), Munich, Kaiser, 1979, pp. 331–2.

17 One participant in this course was the later Professor of Systematic Theology, Gerhard Ebeling, who was prepared at that time, due to the difficult situation of the Confessing Church, to give up his plans for a doctorate. This was most agreeable to the Council of Brethren of Berlin-Brandenburg, but Bonhoeffer managed to have Ebeling freed to continue

his studies instead of being sent to a pastorate because, especially in its hour of need, the church needed scholarly theologians.

18 Beckmann, *Kirchliches Jahrbuch 1933–1945*, pp. 158ff.

19 Hans-Ulrich Wehler, *Deutsche Gesellschaftsgeschichte* (German Social History), Vol. 4, 2003, p. 797. That Dibelius had already clearly distanced himself (from Hitler) in 1933 is documented by Scholder in *The Churches and the Third Reich*, Vol. 1, pp. 232–4.

20 Meier, *Der evangelische Kirchenkampf*, Vol. 2, pp. 12–15.

21 This title has remained influential among Christians worldwide. See the titles of reports from three World Council of Churches meetings in its 'Ecclesiology and Ethics' study series: *Costly Unity* (1993), *Costly Commitment* (1994) and *Costly Obedience* (1996).

22 In the 1960s and 70s there were intensive discussions on the place of *Discipleship* in Bonhoeffer's theology. See for example Ernst Feil, *The Theology of Dietrich Bonhoeffer*, trans. Martin Rumscheidt, Philadelphia, Fortress Press, 1985, pp. 128–38.

23 On Hermann Stöhr, see E. Röhm, *Sterben für den Frieden. Hermann Stöhr (1898–1940) und die ökumenische Friedensbewegung* (To Die for Peace: Hermann Stöhr and the Ecumenical Peace Movement), 1985. (In English, an account may be found at http://soc.kuleuven.be/iieb/ipraweb/papers/Martyrfor%20 Peace%20%20The%20German%20Protestant%20Conscientious%20 Objector%20Hermann%20Stoehr%201898–40.pdf.)

Chapter 8

1 In most European countries, local authorities are routinely expected to keep records on all persons residing in their jurisdictions; when moving, residents are expected to cancel their registrations and re-register at their new addresses as soon as possible. This system could prove a resident's right to city services, and so forth. So it had nothing to do with Hitler's police state, although the Gestapo made plenteous use of it.

2 Beckmann, *Kirchliches Jahrbuch*, 1976, pp. 282ff.

3 Meier, *Der evangelische Kirchenkampf*, Vol. 3, pp. 51–2.

4 J. Seim, *Hans Joachim Iwand. Eine Biographie*, 1999, pp. 222ff.

5 W. Niemöller, *Kampf und Zeugnis der Bekennenden Kirche* (Struggle and Witness of the Confessing Church), p. 462.

6 M. Kahle, *Was hätten Sie getan? Die Flucht der Familie Kahle aus Nazi-Deutschland* (What Would You have Done? The Kahle Family's Flight from Nazi Germany), 1998, p. 193. For the judgement against the eldest son, signed by the rector of the University of Bonn, see pp. 32–3.

7 See Helmut Gollwitzer, *Dennoch bleibe ich stets bei dir. Predigten aus dem Kirchenkampf* (Nevertheless I Am Continually with You: Sermons from the

Church Struggle) *1937–1944*, ed. J. Hoppe, 1988, pp. 52–61 (see Psalm 73:23).

8   Cf. M. Smid, *Hans von Dohnanyi–Christine Bonhoeffer. Eine Ehe im Widerstand gegen Hitler* (Hans von Dohnanyi–Christine Bonhoeffer: A Couple in the Resistance against Hitler), 2002, pp. 178–81.

9   To this day German historians still argue as to whether the Fritsch crisis was a game set up in advance or a chain of unpredicted occurrences. André François-Poncet spoke for the first thesis in his memoir, *The Fateful Years; Memoirs of a French Ambassador in Berlin, 1931–1938*, London, Victor Gollancz, 1949. Historian Ian Kershaw, however, sees the chain of events as coincidences from which Hitler, Göring, Himmler and Heydrich profited. Kershaw describes Gürtner's position as 'devastating for Fritsch' (Ian Kershaw, *Hitler 1936–45: Nemesis*, New York, Norton, 2000, pp. 54–6). But that can be seen in another way. Hitler wanted to hush up the whole thing, but Gürtner, by taking a public position, made it necessary to put Fritsch on trial, so that his innocence was proved and he had to be acquitted. Precisely this way of proceeding could have been proposed by Dohnanyi.

10   The support which Franz Koenigs and Hans Leibholz gave to the German Resistance should be thoroughly investigated. My information is based on the detailed and documented account by Koenigs' granddaughter, Christine F. Koenigs, in Amsterdam. Sabine Leibholz-Bonhoeffer tells about her family's exile in *Vergangen, erlebt, überwunden* (It's over, we lived through it, we overcame it), Gutersloh, Verlagshaus Mohn, 1976.

11   The Nazi regime made no provision for conscientious objectors. Refusal of military service was treated as a crime against the Reich, punishable by death.

12   At that time a Provisional Committee was preparing for a World Council of Churches, which eventually held its founding Assembly, delayed by the war, in 1948 in Amsterdam. Only then did the Faith and Order movement become part of it. Due to the church struggle in Germany and problems of representation, German participation in the Provisional Committee was minimal.

13   Cf. W. A. Visser 't Hooft, *Das Zeugnis eines Boten. Zum Gedächtnis von Dietrich Bonhoeffer* (The Witness of a Messenger: In Memory of Dietrich Bonhoeffer), Geneva, WCC, 1945, pp. 6–7. In English, see also the *Memoirs* of W. A. Visser 't Hooft, Geneva, WCC, 1976, pp. 107–9.

14   Beckmann, *Kirchliches Jahrbuch*, 1976, p. 289.

15   Key sentences in italics quoted from Visser 't Hooft, *Memoirs*, p. 95, otherwise trans. IB.

16   Visser 't Hooft, *Memoirs*, p. 96.

17   Ibid., p. 96.

Chapter 9

1. Isaiah 28:16. English translations of the Bible do not have 'run away' (*flieht*). The Revised Standard Version has 'He who believes will not be in haste.'
2. See Chapter 1, note 6.
3. Bonhoeffer had quoted this at the end of a sermon in London in September 1934 (cf. DBWE 13, 375), in a somewhat free German version of the original Danish. This translation from his German version is by Isabel Best and Keith Clements.
4. In urban areas of Europe and the US until the late twentieth century, post offices made at least two deliveries on weekdays.
5. Feil, *The Theology of Dietrich Bonhoeffer*, p. 45. (When the International Bonhoeffer Society was founded in 1972, Ernst Feil was elected first president of the section in the Federal Republic of Germany, then West Germany.)
6. See Bonhoeffer's sermon in London on Jeremiah 20:7, 21 January 1934 (DBWE 13, 349ff).

Chapter 10

1. Fabian von Schlabrendorff, quoted in F. G. de Beus, *Morgen bei Tagesanbruch. Dramatische Stunden im Leben eines Diplomaten* (Tomorrow at Daybreak: Dramatic Moments in the Life of a Diplomat), 1982, p. 134.
2. Cf. Walter Schellenberg, *Aufzeichnungen* (Notes), 1979, p. 327.
3. Josef Müller came from a family of modest means, and had once been observed by his schoolmates driving a team of oxen; this was the origin of his nickname.
4. Cf. Christopher Sykes: *Troubled Loyalty – A Biography of Adam von Trott zu Solz*, Collins, London, 1968. The relationship between Bonhoeffer and Adam von Trott seems to have been closer than indicated by the documents at hand. For example, at Sigtuna it was agreed that 'in future Trott instead of Bonhoeffer would operate in the Swedish contact sector'. Cf. Glenthoj, *Dokumente zur Bonhoeffer-Forschung*, pp. 273ff.
5. *Die Fahne Hoch* was a very popular Nazi song written by an SA militia leader, Horst Wessel, who was held up as an example to the Hitler youth.
6. The non-aggression pact between Hitler and Stalin had been concluded in August 1939.
7. See Chapter 5, Bonhoeffer's essay on 'The Church and the Jewish Question'.
8. M. Smid, *Hans von Dohnanyi–Christine Bonhoeffer*, p. 263.
9. Cf. G. van Roon, 'Graf Moltke als Völkerrechtler im OKW (Count Moltke as an Expert in International Law)', *Vierteljahrshefte für Zeitgeschichte* (Contemporary History Quarterly), No. 18 (1970), pp. 12ff.

10 See the Foreword by Ilse Tödt on the writing of Bonhoeffer's *Ethik*, pp. 467–76 in DBWE 6.

11 See for example, Clifford Green, 'Editor's Introduction', DBWE 6, pp. 1ff; Hans Pfeifer, 'Ethics for the Renewal of Life: A Reconstruction of its Concept', in John W. de Gruchy (ed.), *Bonhoeffer for a New Day: Theology in a Time of Transition*, Grand Rapids, Eerdmans, 1997, pp. 137–54; Heinz Eduard Toedt, *Authentic Faith: Bonhoeffer's Theological Ethics in Context*, Grand Rapids, Eerdmans, 1997; Larry Rasmussen, 'The Ethics of Responsible Action', in John W. de Gruchy (ed.), *The Cambridge Companion to Dietrich Bonhoeffer*. Cambridge University Press, 1999, pp. 206–25; Ilse Tödt, 'Paradoxical Obedience: Dietrich Bonhoeffer's Theological Ethics, 1933–1945', *Lutheran Theological Journal*, Vol. 35, No. 1 (2001), pp. 3–16.

12 Based on a statement in Luther's *Disputationen*, of which Bonhoeffer said in 1926: 'The new person ... could create new decalogues, which would be clearer than that of Moses' (DBWE 9, 381).

13 This is the way the story was told in England, although of course it was not only those who had participated in the notorious debate at the Oxford Union who were among the fighter pilots; there were many others, including Poles. There was also the fact that Germany's navy was not strong enough for an invasion of Britain.

14 The author has been unable to ascertain the reason for this refusal. Most likely it was because Mrs Gürtner was a Protestant and their wedding had been in a Protestant church. It was customary for the Catholic Church to refuse Catholic burial under such circumstances.

15 Hans-Bernd Gisevius, who as German vice-consul in Zürich, Switzerland, was part of the conspiracy, was among those who made this postwar complaint. He felt that Bonhoeffer, as a clergyman, had tended not to think politically enough.

16 Cf. Helmuth Groscurth, *Tagebücher eines Abwehroffiziers* (Diaries of a Military Intelligence Officer) *1938–1940*, ed. H. Krausnick and H. C. Deutsch, 1970, p. 245.

17 On the history of this order of Hitler's, see Ian Kershaw, *Hitler, 1936–1945*, pp. 252–61.

18 From a direct communication with Dr Hans Schadewald, professor of medical history in Düsseldorf.

19 Cf. U. Gerrens, *Medizinisches Ethos und theologische Ethik. Karl und Dietrich Bonhoeffer in der Auseinandersetzung um Zwangssterilisation und 'Euthanasie' im Nationalsozialismus* (Medical Ethos and Theological Ethics: Karl and Dietrich Bonhoeffer in the Debate over Forced Sterilization and 'Euthanasia' under Nazism), 1996. The patients in Bethel were left undisturbed, but from almost all the other church social service institutions for the disabled and mentally ill, innumerable patients were taken away and murdered.

20 However, this only affected the use of gas. Killings by injection continued, and many disabled patients were simply left to starve.

21 'Casuistry' is the treatment of individual cases, sometimes approaching hair-splitting, in Catholic moral theology (DBWE 16, 126).

22 In revenge, the SS destroyed the nearby village of Lidice and massacred all its inhabitants, including small children. Heydrich is also known for having organized the plans for the Holocaust.

23 Cf. P. Steinbach's introduction to Smid, *Hans von Dohnanyi–Christine Bonhoeffer*, p. xvii.

24 Armin Boyens, *Kirchenkampf und Ökumene* (The Church Struggle and the Ecumenical Movement), Munich, C. Kaiser, 1973, pp. 210–13.

25 Klemens von Klemperer, *German Resistance against Hitler: The Search for Allies Abroad, 1938–1945*. Oxford, Clarendon Press; New York, Oxford University Press, 1992, pp. 264–314.

26 Among the conspirators there were indeed those, especially Goerdeler, who wanted to retain an authoritarian state. But since all were prepared to negotiate, and Moltke and Bonhoeffer among others emphatically thought otherwise, there could have been a meaningful meeting point with Germany's opponents. Churchill later revised his opinion.

27 M. Flesch-Thebesius, *Zu den Aussenseitern gestellt*, pp. 172ff. (see Chapter 4, note 19).

28 Cf. Philip Paul Hallie, *Lest Innocent Blood Be Shed: The Story of the Village of Le Chambon, and How Goodness Happened There*. New York, Harper and Row, 1979.

29 M. Flesch-Thebesius, *Zu den Aussenseitern gestellt*, pp. 171ff.

30 G. K. A. Bell, *Christianity and World Order*, Harmondsworth and New York, Penguin Books, 1940, quoted in DB-ER, p. 736.

31 In this book, Paton presented the concept on which the British 'Peace Aims Group' was founded under the leadership of Archbishop William Temple. Cf. DBWE 16, 172, and the references to other works there.

32 See the account of Bonhoeffer's second trip to Switzerland in DBWE 16; letter to Martin quoted here from excerpt in Visser 't Hooft's *Memoirs*, p. 154.

33 W. A. Visser 't Hooft, *Memoirs*, p. 153. Eberhard Bethge mentions this and comments on it in DB-ER, p. 744.

34 In Munich in 1943, a group of people including the publisher Albert Lempp implored Bishop Meiser that the church must protest against the persecution of the Jews, not only out of compassion, but also in order to remain the church. Cf. M. Wurster, 'Der Münchener Laienbrief (Letter from Laypersons in Munich) 1943', in Günther van Norden and Volkmar Wittmutz (eds), *Evangelische Kirche im Zweiten Weltkrieg* (The Protestant Church in the Second World War), Köln, Rheinland-Verlag, 1991, pp. 77–102.

35 Beckmann, *Kirchliches Jahrbuch*, p. 387. The autumn Day of Repentance (*Buß und Bettag*) is a regular part of the church calendar year in Germany, and was until recently also a national holiday.

36 Max Krakauer, one of those who were so aided and survived, wrote a book about it, *Licht im Dunkeln* (Light in the Darkness). He and his wife stayed not only with the Stöfflers, but also – disguised as guests – in some seventy other pastors' homes in Württemberg. Cf. E. Röhm and J. Thierfelder, *Juden, Christen, Deutsche*, Vol. 4, (1941–1945), 2004.

37 Wolfgang Benz, *Überleben im Dritten Reich: Juden im Untergrund und ihre Helfer* (Surviving the Third Reich: Jews in the Underground and Their Helpers), 2003. This carefully researched book shows how impossible it is to account for all such cases. The specifics are no longer known. Of the helpers I have named, Benz mentions only Poelchau, who was without doubt the most important of them in Berlin. A new memorial centre to 'Silent Heroes', gentile Germans who helped hide Jews during the Second World War, has recently opened in Berlin. See news story in English at http://www.philly. com/inquirer/sports/20081102_Berlin_center_honors_Nazi-defying__ quot_Silent_Heroes__quot_.html.

38 See DB-ER, pp. 747–9.

39 More information on the 'Kreisau Circle' is available in two works in German by Günter Brakelmann: *Der Kreisauer Kreis. Chronologien, Kurzbiographien und Texte aus dem Widerstand*, Vol. 3, 2004, and *Die Kreisauer: folgenreiche Begegnungen* [Momentous Encounters]: *biographische Skizzen zu Helmuth James von Moltke, Peter Yorck von Wartenburg, Carlo Mierendorff und Theodor Haubach*, 2nd rev. edn, Münster and London, Lang, 2004.

40 There are different opinions on this matter. For example, Eugen Gerstenmaier declared after the war that the members of the 'Kreisau' group had not been at all opposed to the assassination ('Der Kreisauer Kreis', in *Vierteljahrshefte für Zeitgeschichte*, No. 15 (1967), pp. 221–46). However, it has been clearly established that Moltke was against the use of force, and Freisler even had to grant him this during his trial. Cf. Helmuth James von Moltke, *Letters to Freya 1939–1945*, trans. and ed. by Beate Ruhm von Oppen, New York, Alfred A. Knopf.

41 In German, the singular pronoun *Du*, for 'you', is used in intimate human relationships; English lacks this distinction, since we no longer say 'thou', except perhaps to God. See also note 63 below.

42 Moltke, *Letters to Freya*, Introduction by Beate Ruhm von Oppen.

43 Freya von Moltke *et al.*, *Helmuth James von Moltke 1907–1945*, Anwalt der Zukunft Stuttgart, 1975, p. 176.

44 Baron Friedrich von Gaertingen (ed.), *Die Hassell-Tagebücher* (Hassell's Diaries) *1938–1944*, 2nd edn 1989, p. 347.

45 Adolf Hitler, *Mein Kampf*, p. 609.

46 This is meant ironically, since a 'political judge' actually offends against the judge's duty to give impartial opinions. In following Nazi Party directives, Freisler had no equal. NB: St Ignatius of Loyola was the founder of the Jesuit order (Society of Jesus).

47 Dietrich Bonhoeffer, in his poem 'Stations on the Way to Freedom', called death 'the highest of feasts'. A help in understanding what he meant would be Moltke's farewell letters, smuggled out of the prison by Chaplain Harald Poelchau. They are a commentary, which can take one's breath away, on the image of death as the final feast. See Moltke's *Letters to Freya*, note 40 above, or the excerpts in *Dying We Live* (cf. Chapter 5, note 4).

48 This refers to General Ludendorff's false contention after the First World War that the war would have been won had the fighting soldiers not been been 'stabbed in the back' by civilians, especially the Social Democrats. Hitler made great use of the myth thereby created.

49 Quoted from Alex Johnson, *Eivind Berggrav, God's Man of Suspense*, trans. Kjell Jordheim with Harriet L. Overholt, Minneapolis, Augsburg, 1960, p. 167.

50 See DB-ER, p. 749.

51 Klemperer, *German Resistance Against Hitler*, p. 286.

52 However, at this time the Swedes were facilitating a lively exchange of news within the ecumenical community. See Boyens, *Kirchenkampf und Ökumene*, pp. 164ff.

53 It would not be meaningful to calculate the frequency of the word 'decision', since in each case it makes a difference what the decision is about.

54 Josef Müller, *Bis zur letzten Konsequenz. Ein Leben für Friede und Freiheit* (Going All the Way: A Life Lived for Peace and Freedom), 1975, p. 241.

55 Cf. H. Mommsen: 'Gesellschaftsbild und Verfassungspläne des deutschen Widerstandes', in W. Schmitthenner and H. Buchheim (eds), *Der deutsche Widerstand gegen Hitler. Vier historisch-kritische Studien*, 1966, pp. 132–46; M. Krüger-Charlé: 'Carl Goerdeler. Versuche zur Durchsetzung einer alternativen Politik 1933–1937', in *Der Widerstand gegen den Nationalsozialismus. Die deutsche Gesellschaft und der Widerstand gegen Hitler*, ed. J. Schmädeke and P. Steinbach, 1985, pp. 383–404. Both of these articles take a more critical attitude than the original biography by Gerhard Ritter, *The German Resistance: Carl Goerdeler's Struggle against Tyranny*, trans. R. T. Clark, Freeport, NY, Books for Libraries Press, 1970.

56 See Bell's 'Memorandum of Conversations', and the documents which follow, in DBWE 16.

57 G. K. A. Bell, *The Church and Humanity (1939–1946)*, London and New York etc., Longmans, Green, 1946, p. 84.

58 *Love Letters from Cell 92: Dietrich Bonhoeffer and Maria von Wedemeyer 1943–1945*, ed. Ruth-Alice von Bismarck and Ulrich Kabitz, with a postscript by Eberhard Bethge, trans. John Brownjohn, London, HarperCollins, 1994, p. 285.

[59] The author remembers a conversation in the former Evangelical High Church Council building in Berlin during the 1960s. Four of us were eating together in the canteen, two lawyers and two clergymen. A trial was causing heated arguments at that time, in which a widow whose husband had been executed during the war for giving a loaf of bread to a 'Polish foreign worker' wanted the judgment annulled so that she could receive a pension. The day before our conversation, the court had ruled against the plaintiff. We who were younger were outraged, but the elder of the two lawyers said, 'What are you so excited about? That was the law then. No other verdict was possible. Why do you think I went into the church judicial system in 1934? I didn't want to be involved in the sort of state justice which I saw coming. The judge in that case didn't have any choice.' The well-known words of the former prime minister of Baden-Württemberg, 'What was justice then can't be called injustice today', must still have been, in the 1960s, the opinion of most older lawyers and judges.

[60] See DBWE, p. 172. For information on the British 'Peace Aims Group', see E. M. Jackson, *Red Tape and the Gospel*, pp. 267–70.

[61] The contribution of another working group in Stuttgart, around the theologian Helmut Thielicke among others, in connection with the one in Freiburg, needs to be investigated. Contemporary German assessments of the Freiburg memorandum show that it is still considered controversial by some.

[62] For their story as told by their sister, see Inge Scholl, *The White Rose: Munich, 1942–1943*; with an introduction by Dorothee Sölle; translated from the German by Arthur R. Schultz, Middletown, CT, Wesleyan University Press; also Scranton, PA, distributed by Harper & Row, 1983.

[63] *Love Letters from Cell 92*, p. 290.

[64] *Love Letters from Cell 92*, p. 291. In European languages other than English, the singular form of 'you' (*Du* in German) is not felt to be archaic as 'thou' is in English. People use it with someone they have decided is a friend, with whom they agree to have a more intimate relationship. (It is also used for family members and for any child.) In prewar Germany this custom was more strictly observed than it is now, and usually people only began using first names along with it.

[65] Fabian von Schlabrendorff, *The Secret War against Hitler*, trans. Hilda Simon, new introduction by Beate Ruhm von Oppen, with a foreword by John J. McCloy, Boulder, Westview Press, 1994.

[66] Translation by Catherine Winkworth, 1863.

Chapter 11

[1] W. Meyer, *Unternehmen 7, Eine Rettungsaktion für vom Holocaust Bedrohte aus dem Amt Ausland/Abwehr im Oberkommando der Wehrmacht* (Operation 7: A Rescue

Action by the Military Intelligence Foreign Office in the Army High Command on Behalf of Persons Threatened by the Holocaust), 1993, p. 383. See also note 316 with regard to Gisevius's adverse statement about Bonhoeffer's military exemption. Cf. note 2 for the present chapter, below.

2   On 12 May 1943, Hans-Bernd Gisevius testified as a witness at Dohnanyi's hearing and proved all too cooperative. Canaris and Oster called him to order the next day and he had to change his statements. He does not mention it in his book, but he had portrayed the scene in Dohnanyi's office, at which he was not present, as though Dohnanyi had whispered '*die Zettel, die Zettel*' so excitedly that Oster thought it must be a matter of life and death. In this way, Gisevius could blame Dohnanyi for Oster's removal from Canaris's office. Cf. H.-B. Gisevius, *Bis zum bitteren Ende*, 1946, pp. 267–8. Especially incriminating was his statement during the hearing that he had already pointed out to Dohnanyi, early on, that Bonhoeffer's military classification was not justified. On this, see also note 1 above.

3   *Love Letters from Cell 92*, p. 11.

4   Quoted from H. Vinke, *Cato Bontjes van Beek*, 2003, p. 120.

5   This was actually a misnomer; the *Rote Kapelle* in fact had only two Russian radio transmitters, neither of which was in working order.

6   See Bonhoeffer's letter of 22 December 1943 to Eberhard Bethge, DBWE 8, II/88.

7   Jürgen Henkys' interpretations of Bonhoeffer's poetry offer deep insight into his thoughts and feelings while in prison, for those able to consult them: Henkys, *Geheimnis der Freiheit. Die Gedichte Dietrich Bonhoeffers aus der Haft. Biographie, Poesie, Theologie* (The Mystery of Freedom: Dietrich Bonhoeffer's Prison Poems). Gütersloh, Gütersloher Verlagshaus, 2005.

8   Cf. W. Meyer, *Unternehmen 7* (Operation 7), p. 557, note 412. Canaris and Pfuhlstein must have agreed on this in order to prevent Roeder being brought back.

9   *Love Letters from Cell 92*, p. 146. The Burckhardt House in Berlin was a training school for female parish workers, of whom it was said superficially that they looked and acted too much alike.

10 Bonhoeffer said elsewhere of Schütz: 'Schütz's book softens one up terribly, it just leaves us in our human condition.' But also: 'the joke is that our hearts are supposed to become *firm*, and that happens by grace' (DBW 15, 32). Cf. also Gotthelf, *Zeitgeist und Berner Geist*, a novel in two parts; J. W. Goethe, *Wilhelm Meister's Apprenticeship* (1795–6), New York, Suhrkamp, 1989, and *Wilhelm Meister's Travels* (1821–9), London, G. Bell, 1911; and Adalbert Stifter, *Die Mappe meines Urgroßvaters* (My Great-Grandfather's Album), 1841.

11 *Love Letters from Cell 92*, p. 161.

12 Ibid., p. 146.

13 Dahn, *Ein Kampf um Rom*; on Don Quixote, see Chapter 3, p. 52ff.

14 *Love Letters from Cell 92*, pp. 131–2.

15 *Love Letters from Cell 92*, pp. 85–6, 131–2 and 191. On the second passage, see Regine Schindler's worthwhile essay 'Verhaftet und Verlobt (Imprisoned and Engaged to be Married)', in *Theologie und Freundschaft, Wechselwirkungen zwischen* (Theology and Friendship, Interactions Between) *Eberhard Bethge und Dietrich Bonhoeffer*, Chr. Gremmels and W. Huber (eds), 1994, pp. 160–1.

16 *Love Letters from Cell 92*, p. 192.

17 On 'arcane discipline', see Bonhoeffer's words in DBWE 7, 50 (also DBWE 8, 415).

18 Cf. the sensitive essay by the American Bonhoeffer researcher Ruth Zerner, 'Dietrich Bonhoeffer's Prison Fiction: A Commentary', included as an afterword (pp. 139–67) in Bonhoeffer's *Fiction from Prison: Gathering up the Past*, ed. Renate and Eberhard Bethge, trans. Ursula Hoffmann, Philadephia, Fortress, 1981. A section of the essay is entitled 'Artistic Regression and Theological Insights', pp. 152–4.

19 Ulrich Kabitz, former lector at Chr. Kaiser Verlag, who worked with both Bethge and the present author on their biographies, in a letter to the author.

20 See Henkys, *Geheimnis der Freiheit*, pp. 93ff. regarding the poem 'The Past'.

21 *Love Letters from Cell 92*, pp. 215–16.

22 There are unusually lively descriptions by Bonhoeffer's youngest sister, Susanne Dreß, of visits she made by legal permission as well as 'illegally' with the help of the friendly guards. Cf. Zimmermann, *I Knew Dietrich Bonhoeffer*, pp. 215–21.

23 Marx is supposed to have said this to Engels.

24 *Natura corrupta* = human nature after the Fall; *peccatum originale* = original sin.

25 Germans actually say 'Hold your thumbs for me', but the meaning is the same. Touch wood = knock on wood.

26 Cf. Hermann Schlingensiepen (the author's father): 'Zum Vermächtnis Dietrich Bonhoeffers (On the Legacy of Dietrich Bonhoeffer)', in *Die Mündige Welt*, ed. Jørgen Glenthoj, 2nd edn. Munich, Kaiser Verlag, 1955, pp. 96ff.

27 That Bonhoeffer's 'new theology' is still fertile ground today can be seen in the lectures presented at the Eighth International Bonhoeffer Congress in 2000 in Berlin. These may be found in Christian Gremmels and Wolfgang Huber (eds), *Religion im Erbe. Dietrich Bonhoeffer und die Zukunftsfähigkeit des Christentums* (Religious Heritage: Bonhoeffer and the Future Viability of Christianity), 2002. See, for example, under the heading 'Religionslosigkeit und multireligiöse Gesellschaft (Religionlessness and Multireligious Society)', the essay by John de Gruchy, 'God's Desire for a Community of Human Beings', pp. 147ff. Taken together, the lectures provide a good overview of discussions on Bonhoeffer in recent years.

28 H. Schlingensiepen, 'Zum Vermächtnis Dietrich Bonhoeffers', p. 105.

29 Cf. Bonhoeffer's letter to Ruth-Roberta Stahlberg, DBWE 16, I/3.

30 Cf. Ernst Lange: 'Notizen zu (Notes on) Theodore A. Gill's "Memo for a Movie"', in Ernst Feil (ed.), *Verspieltes Erbe?* (Squandered Inheritance?), Munich, Kaiser, 1979, p. 135. Ernst Lange's essays and lectures on Bonhoeffer's theology are among the most sensitive interpretations we have of him. See, for example, in Lange's *Kirche für die Welt. Aufsätze zur Theorie kirchlichen Handelns* (The Church for the World: Essays on the Theory of Church Action), ed. Rüdiger Schloz, München, Kaiser, and Gelnhausen, Burckhardthaus, 1981, the study on 'Kirche für andere (The Church for Others)', pp. 19–62.

31 Excerpted from Britannica Online Encyclopedia, www.britannica.com/EBchecked/topic/308021/July-Plot.

32 On this poem of Bonhoeffer's, *'Stationen auf dem Wege zur Freiheit* (Stations on the Way to Freedom)', see Henkys, *Geheimnis der Freiheit*, pp. 180ff.

33 Eberhard Bethge, *In Zitz gab es keine Juden: Erinnerungen aus meinen ersten vierzig Jahren* (There Were No Jews in Zitz: Memories from My First Forty Years), München, Kaiser, 1989, pp. 151–7.

34 K. H. Peter (ed.), *Spiegelbild einer Verschwörung. Die Kaltenbrunner-Berichte an Bormann und Hitler vom 20. Juli 1944* (Mirror Image of a Conspiracy: The Kaltenbrunner Reports on 20 July 1944 to Bormann and Hitler), 1961.

35 Fabian von Schlabrendorff, *Offiziere gegen Hitler* (Officers against Hitler), pp. 144–5. See also Schlabrendorff's contribution in Zimmermann, *I Knew Dietrich Bonhoeffer*.

36 Schlabrendorff, in *I Knew Dietrich Bonhoeffer*, pp. 229–30.

37 See Ulrich Kabitz, 'Eine "Randfigur". Vom politischen Engagement zum Therapiezentrum [A "Marginal Figure": From Political Activism to Therapy Centre]; Countess Maria Bredow', *Newsletter of the International Bonhoeffer Society*, No. 62, June 2000, pp. 55–60

38 *Love Letters from Cell 92*, p. 227.

Chapter 12

1 See S. Payne Best, *The Venlo Incident*, London and New York, Hutchinson, 1950.

2 Ibid., p. 180.

3 Letter from Payne Best to Sabine and Gerhard Leibholz, 2 March 1951.

4 *Love Letters from Cell 92*, p. 233.

5 White Sunday is the Sunday after Easter, which in some Christian confessions is the traditional day for children to receive their First Communion, all dressed in white.

6 Revised Standard Version.

7 Best, *The Venlo Incident*, p. 200.

8 The report by the SS doctor H. Fischer-Hüllstrung, in Zimmermann (ed.), *I Knew Dietrich Bonhoeffer*, is unfortunately a lie (DB-ER 927f.). The doctor could not have seen Bonhoeffer kneeling in his cell, neither could Bonhoeffer have said a prayer before his execution and then climbed the steps to the gallows. There were no steps. Fischer-Hüllstrung had the job of reviving political prisoners after they had been hanged until they were almost dead, in order to prolong the agony of their dying. According to a Danish prisoner, L. F. Mogenson, the executions of Admiral Canaris and his group were drawn out from 6 a.m. until almost noon. Cf. Mogenson, 'Ein Zeuge aus dem KZ Flossenbürg (A Testimony from Flossenbürg Concentration Camp)', in R. Mayer and P. Zimmerling (eds), *Dietrich Bonhoeffer – Mensch hinter Mauern. Theologie und Spiritualität in den Gefängnisjahren* (Man Behind Walls: Theology and Spirituality in His Years in Prison), 1993, p. 107

Epilogue

1 Due to an unfortunate chain of circumstances, Payne Best could only transmit Bonhoeffer's words of farewell to the bishop in 1953 from memory. But the message Best delivered then, according to Bell himself, was more complete than it appears in the book: 'Tell him [the bishop], that this is for me the end, but also the beginning – with him I believe in the principle of our Universal Christian brotherhood which rises above all national interests, and that our victory is certain – tell him too that I have never forgotten his words at our last meeting' (Cf. DBWE 16, 468).

2 On the poem 'The Death of Moses', as with the other poems, see the commentary of Jürgen Henkys, *Geheimnis der Freiheit*, p. 226.

3 Cf. DBWE 8, IV/191, 'Stations on the Way to Freedom', Death: the 'highest of feasts on the way to freedom eternal'. Cf. also Rothfels (ed.), *I Loved This People*. Rothfels' anthology of Bonhoeffer's writings was published in Germany in 1961 when anti-Nazi conspirators were still widely considered traitors.

Appendix 1: Theological Declaration of Barmen

Written by Karl Barth and the confessing church in Nazi Germany in response to Hitler's national church. Its central doctrines concern the sin of idolatry and the lordship of Christ.

I. An Appeal to the Evangelical Congregations and Christians in Germany

8.01 The Confessional Synod of the German Evangelical Church met in Barmen, May 29–31, 1934. Here representatives from all the German Confessional Churches met with one accord in a confession of the one Lord of the one, holy, apostolic Church. In fidelity to their Confession of Faith, members of Lutheran, Reformed, and United Churches sought a common message for the need and temptation of the Church in our day. With gratitude to God they are convinced that they have been given a common word to utter. It was not their intention to found a new Church or to form a union. For nothing was farther from their minds than the abolition of the confessional status of our Churches. Their intention was, rather, to withstand in faith and unanimity the destruction of the Confession of Faith, and thus of the Evangelical Church in Germany. In opposition to attempts to establish the unity of the German Evangelical Church by means of false doctrine, by the use of force and insincere practices, the Confessional Synod insists that the unity of the Evangelical Churches in Germany can come only from the Word of God in faith through the Holy Spirit. Thus alone is the Church renewed.

8.02 Therefore the Confessional Synod calls upon the congregations to range themselves behind it in prayer, and steadfastly to gather around those pastors and teachers who are loyal to the Confessions.

8.03 Be not deceived by loose talk, as if we meant to oppose the unity of the German nation! Do not listen to the seducers who pervert our intentions, as if we wanted to break up the unity of the German Evangelical Church or to forsake the Confessions of the Fathers!

8.04 Try the spirits whether they are of God! Prove also the words of the Confessional Synod of the German Evangelical Church to see whether they agree with Holy Scripture and with the Confessions of the Fathers. If you find that we are speaking contrary to Scripture, then do not listen to us! But if you find that we are taking our stand upon Scripture, then let no fear or temptation keep you from treading with us the path of faith and obedience to the Word of God, in order that God's people be of one mind upon earth and that we in faith experience what he himself has said: 'I will never leave you, nor forsake you.' Therefore, 'Fear not, little flock, for it is your Father's good pleasure to give you the kingdom.'

II. Theological Declaration Concerning the Present Situation of the German Evangelical Church

8.05 According to the opening words of its constitution of July 11, 1933, the German Evangelical Church is a federation of Confessional Churches that grew our of the Reformation and that enjoy equal rights. The theological basis for the unification of these Churches is laid down in Article 1 and Article 2(1) of the constitution of the German Evangelical Church that was recognized by the Reich Government on July 14, 1933:
* Article 1. The inviolable foundation of the German Evangelical Church is the gospel of Jesus Christ as it is attested for us in Holy Scripture and brought to light again in the Confessions of the Reformation. The full powers that the Church needs for its mission are hereby determined and limited.
* Article 2 (1). The German Evangelical Church is divided into member Churches Landeskirchen).

8.06 We, the representatives of Lutheran, Reformed, and United Churches, of free synods, Church assemblies, and parish organizations united in the Confessional Synod of the German Evangelical Church, declare that we stand together on the ground of the German Evangelical Church as a federation of German Confessional Churches. We are bound together by the confession of the one Lord of the one, holy, catholic, and apostolic Church.

8.07 We publicly declare before all evangelical Churches in Germany that what they hold in common in this Confession is grievously imperiled, and with it the unity of the German Evangelical Church. It is threatened by the teaching methods and actions of the ruling Church party of the 'German Christians' and of the Church administration carried on by them. These have become more and more apparent during the first year of the existence of the German Evangelical Church. This threat consists in the fact that the theological basis, in which the German Evangelical Church is united, has been continually and systematically thwarted and rendered ineffective by alien principles, on the part of the leaders and spokesmen of the 'German Christians' as well as on the part of the Church administration. When these principles are held to be valid, then, according to all the Confessions in force among us, the Church ceases to be the Church and th German Evangelical Church, as a federation of Confessional Churches, becomes intrinsically impossible.

8.08 As members of Lutheran, Reformed, and United Churches we may and must speak with one voice in this matter today. Precisely because we want to be and to remain faithful to our various Confessions, we may not keep silent, since we believe that we have been given a common message to utter in a time of common need and temptation. We commend to God what this may mean for the intrrelations of the Confessional Churches.

8.09 In view of the errors of the 'German Christians' of the present Reich Church government which are devastating the Church and also therefore breaking up the unity of the German Evangelical Church, we confess the following evangelical truths:

8.10 – 1. 'I am the way, and the truth, and the life; no one comes to the Father, but by me.' (John 14.6). 'Truly, truly, I say to you, he who does not enter the sheepfold by the door, but climbs in by another way, that man is a thief and a robber. . . . I am the door; if anyone enters by me, he will be saved.' (John 10:1, 9.)

8.11 Jesus Christ, as he is attested for us in Holy Scripture, is the one Word of God which we have to hear and which we have to trust and obey in life and in death.

8.12 We reiect the false doctrine, as though the church could and would have to acknowledge as a source of its proclamation, apart from and besides this one Word of God, still other events and powers, figures and truths, as God's revelation.

8.13 – 2. 'Christ Jesus, whom God has made our wisdom, our righteousness and sanctification and redemption.' (1 Cor. 1:30.)

8.14 As Jesus Christ is God's assurance of the forgiveness of all our sins, so, in the same way and with the same seriousness he is also God's mighty claim upon our whole life. Through him befalls us a joyful deliverance from the godless fetters of this world for a free, grateful service to his creatures.

8.15 We reiect the false doctrine, as though there were areas of our life in which we would not belong to Jesus Christ, but to other lords--areas in which we would not need justification and sanctification through him.

8.16 – 3. 'Rather, speaking the truth in love, we are to grow up in every way into him who is the head, into Christ, from whom the whole body [is] joined and knit together.' (Eph. 4:15,16.)

8.17 The Christian Church is the congregation of the brethren in which Jesus Christ acts presently as the Lord in Word and sacrament through the Holy Spirit. As the Church of pardoned sinners, it has to testify in the midst of a sinful world, with its faith as with its obedience, with its message as with its order, that it is solely his property, and that it lives and wants to live solely from his comfort and from his direction in the expectation of his appearance.

8.18 We reject the false doctrine, as though the Church were permitted to abandon the form of its message and order to its own pleasure or to changes in prevailing ideological and political convictions.

8.19 – 4. 'You know that the rulers of the Gentiles lord it over them, and their great men excercise authority over them. It shall not be so among you; but whoever would be great among you must be your srvant.' (Matt. 20:25,26.)

8.20 The various offices in the Church do not establish a dominion of some over the others; on the contrary, they are for the excercise of the ministry entrusted to and enjoined upon the whole congregation.

8.21 We reject the false doctrine, as though the Church, apart from this ministry, could and were permitted to give itself, or allow to be given to it, special leaders vested with ruling powers.

8.22 – 5. 'Fear God. Honor the emperor.' (1 Peter 2:17.)
Scripture tells us that, in the as yet unredeemed world in which the Church also exists, the State has by divine appointment the task of providing for justice and peace. [It fulfills this task] by means of the threat and exercise of force, according to the measure of human judgment and human ability. The Church acknowledges the benefit of this divine

appointment in gratitude and reverence before him. It calls to mind the Kingdom of God, God's commandment and righteousness, and thereby the responsibility both of rulers and of the ruled. It trusts and obeys the power of the Word by which God upholds all things.

8.23 We reject the false doctrine, as though the State, over and beyond its special commision, should and could become the single and totalitarian order of human life, thus fulfilling the Church's vocation as well.

8.24 We reject the false doctrine, as though the Church, over and beyond its special commission, should and could appropriate the characteristics, the tasks, and the dignity of the State, thus itself becoming an organ of the State.

8.25 – 6. 'Lo, I am with you always, to the close of the age.' (Matt. 28:20.) 'The word of God is not fettered.' (2 Tim. 2:9.)

8.26 The Church's commission, upon which its freedom is founded, consists in delivering the message of th free grace of God to all people in Christ's stead, and therefore in the ministry of his own Word and work through sermon and sacrament.

8.27 We reject the false doctrine, as though the Church in human arrogance could place the Word and work of the Lord in the service of any arbitrarily chosen desires, purposes, and plans.

8.28 The Confessional Synod of the German Evangelical Church declares that it sees in the acknowledgment of these truths and in the rejection of these errors the indispensable theological basis of the German Evangelical Church as a federation of Confessional Churches. It invites all who are able to accept its declaration to be mindful of these theological principles in their decisions in Church politics. It entreats all whom it concerns to return to the unity of faith, love, and hope.

From: The Church's Confession Under Hitler by Arthur C. Cochrane. Philadelphia: Westminster Press, 1962, pp. 237–242.

Appendix 2: Prayers for Prisoners

Dietrich Bonhoeffer

The following translation of Bonhoeffer's 'Gebete für Gefangene' will be published in the forthcoming Volume 8 (*Letters and Papers from Prison*) of the Dietrich Bonhoeffer Works, English Edition. Translation is by Lisa E. Dahill.

1. Morning Prayer

God, I call to you early in the morning
help me pray and collect my thoughts;
I cannot do so alone

In me it is dark, but with you there is light.
I am lonely, but you do not abandon me.
I am faint-hearted, but from You comes my help.
I am restless, but with you is peace.
In me is bitterness, but with you is patience.
I do not understand Your ways, but you know [the] right way for me.

Father in heaven,
Praise and thanks be to you for the quiet of the night
Praise and thanks be to you for the new day
Praise and thanks be to you for all your goodness and faithfulness
in my life thus far.

You have granted me much good,
now let me also accept hardship from your hand.
You will not lay on me more than I can bear.
You make all things serve your children for the best.

Lord Jesus Christ,
you were poor and miserable, imprisoned and abandoned as I am.
You know all human need,
you remain with me when no human being stands by me
you do not forget me and you seek me,
you want me to recognize you and turn back to you

Lord, I hear your call and follow.
Help me!

Holy Spirit,
Grant me the faith
that saves me from despair and vice
Grant me the love for God and others
that purges all hate and bitterness,
grant me the hope
that frees me from fear and despondency.

Teach me to discern Jesus Christ and to do his will.
Triune God,
my creator and my savior,
this day belongs to you. My time is in your hands.

Holy, merciful God
my creator and my savior
my judge and my redeemer
you know me and all my ways and actions.

You hate and punish evil in this and every world
without regard for person,
you forgive sins
for anyone who asks you sincerely
and you love the good and reward it
on this earth with a clear conscience
and in the world to come with the crown of righteousness.

Before you I remember all those I love,
my fellow prisoners, and all
who in this house perform their difficult duty.
Lord, have mercy
Grant me freedom again
and in the meantime let me live in such a way
that I can give account before [you] and others.

Lord, whatever this day may bring – your name be praised.

2. *Evening Prayer*

Lord my God,
I thank you that you have brought this day to an end.

I thank you that you allow body and soul to come to rest
Your hand was over me and has protected and preserved me.

Forgive all weakness of faith and wrong of this day
and help me gladly to forgive those
who have done wrong to me.

Let me sleep in peace beneath your protection
And preserve me from the assaults of darkness.

I commend to you those dear to me,
I commend to you this house,
I commend to you my body and my soul
God, your holy name be praised.

Amen.

3. Prayer in Particular Need

Lord God,
misery has come over me.
My afflictions are about to crush me;
I don't know which way to turn.

God, be gracious and help me.
Give me strength to bear what you send.
do not let fear rule over me.
give fatherly care to those I love,
especially my wife and children,
protect them with your strong hand
from all evil and all danger.

Merciful God,
forgive me everything in which I have sinned
against you and others.
I trust in your grace
and commit my life entirely into your hand

Do with me
as pleases you and as is good for me.
Whether I live or die,
I am with you and you are with me, my God
Lord I await your salvation and your kingdom.

Amen

414   *Dietrich Bonhoeffer (1906–1945)*

Appendix 3: By Powers of Good

Dietrich Bonhoeffer

The following translation will be published in the forthcoming Volume 8 (*Letters and Papers from Prison*) of the Dietrich Bonhoeffer Works, English Edition. Translation is by Nancy Lukens.

1. By faithful, quiet powers of good surrounded
so wondrously consoled and sheltered here,
I wish to live these days with you in spirit
and with you enter into a new year.

2. The old year still would try our hearts to torment,
of evil times we still do bear the weight;
o Lord, do grant our souls, now terror-stricken,
salvation for which you did us create.

3. And should you offer us the cup of suffering,
though heavy, brimming full and bitter brand,
we'll thankfully accept it, never flinching,
from your good heart and your beloved hand.

4. But should you wish now once again to give us
the joys of this world and its glorious sun,
then we'll recall anew what past times brought us
and then our life belongs to you alone.

5. The candles you have brought into our darkness,
let them today be burning warm and bright,
and if it's possible, do reunite us!
We know your light is shining through the night.

6. When now the quiet deepens all around us,
o, let our ears that fullest sound amaze
of this, your world, invisibly expanding
as all your children sing high hymns of praise.

7. By powers of good so wondrously protected,
we wait with confidence, befall what may.
God is with us at night and in the morning
and oh, most certainly on each new day.

Appendix 4: Letter from S. Payne Best to Professor Leibholz

2nd March 1951

My dear Professor Leibholz,

I was extremely happy to receive your letter this morning (hutchinson's [sic] are always dilatory about forwarding letters) not only because of your very kind remarks about my book, but mainly, because I am delighted to have this contact with a close relative of Dietrich Bonnhöfer [sic, throughout]. You are quite right in saying that I liked him though in fact my feeling was far stronger than these words imply. He was, without exception, the finest and most lovable man I have ever met. I fear though, that there is very little that I can add by way of information which might be useful to you beyond what is contained in my book.

You must understand that our meetings in the passage of our prison at Buchenwald were always surreptitious and liable to interruption. As General von Rabenau had been a passenger in the prison van which brought me from Berlin to Buchenwald I was no stranger to him. I think that is was a day after my arrival when I met him in the lavatory and he introduced me to Bonnhofer [sic] saying, 'I am sure that you will like my friend, he is the son of the famous neurologist Professor Bonnhöfer'. He then whispered to me 'Er ist durch den Volksgericht zum Tode verurteilt aber er hat die Hoffnung nicht aufgegeben'. He then went on to tell me about himself; that he had written a life of General von Seeckt, that he had retired from the army as a full general and had since taken two degrees in philology and divinity. Then he went on to tell me how much weight he had lost and of his fear that one day he might lose his trousers. Bonnhöfer did not say much on this occasion but I had quite a long talk with him when we met a day or two later. I noticed that he was wearing a pair of prison wooden clogs and when he told me that he had no other foot-gear I gave him a pair of black-and-white golf shoes which fitted him perfectly and with which he was highly delighted. Von Rabenau mentioned chess and said how he wishes they could play this or some other game to while away the tedium of the hours in their cell.

As I had a small travelling chess set I lent this to them and also various books.

As you will understand, it was not etiquette amongst prisoners to ask questions as to the reasons of their imprisonment, nor even to seek information of this nature. The Gestapo frequently had spies disguised as prisoners and in any case, no one was safe from being called up for interrogation and therefore, the less one knew and could give away, the better. Old Werner von Alvensleben was, however, very talkative and it was from him that most of my information about my companions was derived. He told me on one of our first meetings 'Wir haben viele Todeskandidaten hier' and went on to say that Müller, Liedig, Bonnhöfer, Gehre, and von Rabenau had all been sentenced to death by the Volksgericht. Later, von Rabenau told me that he had never been tried and interrogated only once, but that his young friend (Bonnhöfer) had been before the Volksgericht and sentenced to death. He did not, however, think that the sentence would be carried out as, if there had been this intention, he would have never been sent to Buchenwald. On another occasion, Josef Müller, warning me against his room mate Gehre whom he said was a Gestapo spy, told me about how he had shot his wife and attempted to commit suicide. He said that Gehre had given all his comrades away and, having been sentenced to death by the Volksgericht had been given a chance of life if he could obtain evidence which would lead to his (Müller's) conviction. Please don't take this seriously – I didn't at the time. All these people had been held in prison for a long time without news of any kind from the outside world and were in a pretty bad state of nerves. You see, I had been a prisoner for so many years that I had quite got used to the life and so rather tended to father all the rest of the flock even to the extent of seeing that they were properly dressed. Bonnhöfer went to execution in my shoes and sweater, Gehre, in my overcoat, and von Rabenau in my trousers. Curiously enough, I had a letter yesterday from the Dr. Schäfer who was my interrogator at the Gestapo H. A. in 1939. He wrote:– 'Nach Kriegsende erzählte mir ein deutscher Oberstleutnant, der in einen amerikanischen Lager das Bett über mir bewohnte, dass er als Gestapo-Hälfling mit Ihnen zusammen die letzten Kriegswochen, das Kriegs-Ende und auch den Aufenthalt in Italien geteilt habe. Er zeigte mir seine Pantoffel, die angeblich Ihnen gehörten. Den Namen des Mannes habe ich vergessen; er war ein Adeliger mit einen lähmen Arm. – So wusste ich, dass Sie den Krieg überlebt hatten'. This was Horst von Petersdorff.

But, I am getting far from the subject about which I intended to write. Arrest II at Buchenwald was a most miserable place and personally I never expected to get away from there alive. I had, however, lived so long under such conditions that I had reached the point where I did not much care one way or another; my comrades were though, with the exception of von Falkenhausen and Bonnhöfer; oh yes, I forget to include Margot Heberlein who was always unafraid, in an extremely jumpy condition and very much inclined to look upon the dark side of things. Falkenhausen was the Chinese philosopher and Margot Heberlein a very brave woman but Bonnhöfer was different. Just quite calm and normal; seemingly perfectly at his ease. It is a funny thing, but when I think of him I always seem to see him with a halo of light round his head – his soul really shone in the dark desperation of our prison. I don't suppose I spoke to him more than three times whilst we were at Buchenwald but when we left he sat for a time next to me in the prison van. He told me then how happy prison had made him. He had always been afraid that he would not be strong enough to stand such a test but now he knew that there was nothing in life of which one need ever be afraid. He also expressed complete agreement with my view that our warders and guards needed pity far more than we and that it was absurd to blame them for their actions. The journey in the prison van, first to Regensburg and then on to Schöneberg was a nightmare of which little remains in my memory except the few details given in my book. I can't remember whether I had any more connected conversation with Bonnhöfer, nor indeed any further close association with him except for his most moving sermon on Easter Sunday shortly after which he was taken from us to Flossenberg.

His sister will probably wish to know how he looked. He always looked extremely well with a good colour and with plenty of flesh on his bones. He did not look in the least like a man who had spent months in prison and who went in fear of his life – on the contrary, he was cheerful. [sic] ready to respond to a joke, and apparently completely care-free. I am sure that he went to his death in just such a spirit. In a sense, he was materially disembodied. His little poem 'Wer bin ich' expresses, I think, not only his own feelings but also those of many others of us.

At Buchenwald, Bonnhöfer was a cell-mate of von Rabenau and I do not know whether he had much contact with any of the other prisoners besides myself. You might, however, like to make enquiries of some of them as possible they may be able to tell you more than I can. Here are some names and addresses:–

Donna Margot Heberlein, 'El Rincon', Cristo de la Parra, 8. Toledo
Dr. H. Pünder, Altenburgerstrasse, 404. Cologne
Franz Liedig, Planegg bei München, Heimstätterallee, 13
Dr. Josef Müller, Gedonstrasse, 4. München
General von Falkenhausen, Prison de St. Gilles, Brussels

As regards the execution of your brother-in-law and of so many others at Flossenburg on 8th and 9th April 1945 I do not believe that there can ever have been any trial there and I think that it is safe to say that the orders for their liquidation were brought from Berlin by Gogalla just as he brought the order for the liquidation of Georg Elser to Dachau. What part was played by Huppenkothen I do not know but I am inclined to think that he really only had quite a minor role and that the executions are carried out either on the direct orders of Hitler or Himmler, or by instructions from them transmitted by either Obergruppenführers Müller or Pohle. Sepp Müller was in London last July and I talked over the whole matter with him and with Staatsanwalt Ferid. I also gave him the original of the letter reproduced between pages 208/209 of my book. Müller wanted revenge for the death of Canaris and Oster and as Huppenkothen was the only man in his power he wished at all costs to have him punished. I did not, however, consider the case against him verystrong [sic].

During these last weeks of the war there seemed to be a large number of death sentences floating round, some issued as much as three months earlier. From what I could learn, of the two men who were with us when we reached Niederdorf, Stiller and Bader, the former had a specified list of those to be liquidated whilst Bader relied upon a general routine order given many months earlier according to which no prisoners were to be allowed to fall alive into the hands of the enemy. Leutnant [sic] von Alvensleen, the officer commanding the first Wehrmacht troops sent to our rescue says in his report: 'Ich befragte dort den Führer des S.D. ohne mich zunächst zu erkennen zu geben, seinem nach Aufträge [sic], die Häftlinge irgenwo in die Berge zu leiten. Auf weiteres Befragen gab er zu, dass sein Auftrag erledigt sei, 'Wenn die Gefangenen gertorben seien'.[']

I am sorry to have bothered you with so long a letter which contains so little information of the nature which you require. Please take it as a sign of my deep interest. Perhaps some day, when I am on my way to or from London you will permit me to call on you, for I should so much like to meet Dietrich's sister to whom I hope you will convey my deep respects. I heard a lot about Dietrich and Klaus from Otto John whom I occasionally met in London before his return to Germany.

Again thanking you for your letter and with my very kind regards

Yours sincerely
S. Payne Best

Appendix 5: Chronology

4 February 1906	Dietrich Bonhoeffer born in Breslau
1912	Father becomes head of psychiatry and neurology at the University of Berlin; the family moves to Berlin.
1918	Brother Walter Bonhoeffer killed at the front in World War 1
1923	Begins theology studies at the University of Tübingen
1924	Trip to Italy, Holy Week in Rome an especially formative experience; continues undergraduate studies in Berlin, takes examinations
1925	Discovers the writings of Karl Barth
17 December 1927	Completes doctorate in theology under Reinhold Seeberg, with thesis *Sanctorum Communio*
1928	First qualifying examination for the ministry under the church consistory in Berlin
Feb. 1928 – Feb. 1929	Pastoral assistant in Barcelona
July 1929 – July 1930	Academic assistant to Prof. Wilhelm Lütgert in Berlin
8 July 1930	Second qualifying examination under the consistory
18 July 1930	Completes postdoctoral degree with thesis *Act and Being*
Sept. 1930 – June 1931	Year of study at Union Theological Seminary, New York; youth work at Abyssinian Baptist Church in Harlem
December 1930	Trip to Cuba with Erwin Sutz
May-June 1931	Trip to Mexico with Jean Lasserre
July 1931	Two weeks in Bonn to meet Karl Barth
1 August 1931	Begins work as adjunct lecturer in systematic theology in Berlin: lectures on 'History of 20th-Century Systematic Theology', seminar

	on 'The Concept of Philosophy and Protestant Theology'
13 November 1931	Ordained as Lutheran pastor; chaplain to students at the Technical University; takes over confirmation class of 42 boys
1–5 September 1931	World Alliance Conference in Cambridge; elected an international youth secretary
January 1932	Moves to Oderberger Street in east Berlin to be closer to his confirmands
19–29 March 1932	Confirmation class retreat in Friedrichsbrunn
Summer 1932	Lectures on 'The Nature of the Church'; seminar 'Is There a Christian Ethic?'
Spring 1932	Bonhoeffer acquires a hut in Biesenthal, north of Berlin, for retreats with his students and confirmands
July-August 1932	Takes part in ecumenical conferences at Westerburg, Germany, (July 12–14), Ciernohorské Kúpele, Czechoslovakia (July 20–30) and Gland, Switzerland (August 25–31)
Winter 1932–33	Lectures on 'Creation and Sin' (published as *Creation and Fall*) and 'Recent Theology'; seminar 'Problems of a Theological Anthropology'
1 February 1933	Radio lecture 'The Younger Generation's Altered View of the Concept of Führer'
April 1933	Essay 'The Church and the Jewish Question'
6–10 March 1933	Ecumenical meeting in Dassel
May 1933	Beginning of summer semester: lectures on 'Christology'; seminar 'Hegel's Philosophy of Religion'; works with the 'Young Reformation' movement; preparations for the church elections ordered by Hitler
22 June 1933	Student assembly on 'The Struggle for the Church' with 2000 participants, organized by Bonhoeffer and a colleague
14 July 1933	Theodor Heckel (Church Foreign Office) offers Bonhoeffer a pastorate in London.
28 July 1933	Interviews at Sydenham Church and St. George Church in London
15–25 August 1933	Works with others on the 'Bethel Confession'

	opposing the false doctrines of the 'German Christians'
Late August 1933	Publishes theses on 'The Aryan Paragraph in the Churches', leading to a dispute with Heckel
12 September 1933	Bonhoeffer, Martin Niemöller and others found the 'Pastors' Emergency League'
15–20 September 1933	At the World Alliance conference in Sofia, Bulgaria, Bonhoeffer confidentially informs prominent participants about what is taking place in Germany
27 September 1933	Bonhoeffer and others protest against the 'National Synod' of the church, dominated by 'German Christians', in Wittenberg
4 October 1933	Informs Heckel that he will not represent the position of the 'Reich' church while in London
17 October 1933	Begins his ministry to the two parishes in London
21 November 1933	First meeting with George Bell, Bishop of Chichester
27–30 November 1933	Conference of pastors of expatriate German congregations at Bradford, England. Bonhoeffer tells his colleagues about the situation in Germany
1934	Efforts by Bonhoeffer and his colleages to intervene in the church struggle in Germany and to have Ludwig Müller removed from his position as 'Reich Bishop'.
21 January 1934	Sermon on Jeremiah 20:7
8–9 February 1934	Heckel in London with two colleagues, fails to persuade the German pastors in England and Bishop Bell to keep out of the church struggle
13 February 1934	Bonhoeffer in Hanover for a meeting of the Pastors' Emergency League Council of Brethren
6–7 March 1934	Heckel, having been named 'Bishop abroad', summons Bonhoeffer to Berlin and demands that he give up his ecumenical contacts; Bonhoeffer refuses; attends first Berlin-Brandenburg Confessing Church synod as a guest

10 May 1934	Bishop Bell, after detailed consultation with Bonhoeffer, sends his 'Ascensiontide Pastoral Letter' on the situation in the German church to the member churches of the Universal Council for Life and Work
18–30 August 1934	Ecumenical conference on the island of Fanø, Denmark, at which Bonhoeffer gives a speech on peace (28 August)
4–8 September 1934	French-German-British youth conference in Bruay-en-Artois, France, hosted by Jean Lasserre
October 1934	At Bonhoeffer's urging, Bishop Bell and Archbishop Lang protest against aggravation of the German church struggle by church 'legal administrator' August Jäger. Jäger dismissed on orders from Hitler
1 November 1934	Bonhoeffer invited to India by Mahatma Gandhi, but unable to accept due to lack of time
5 November 1934	Under Bonhoeffer's leadership, the German congregations in England resolve to secede from the Reich Church government
January 1935	Begins refugee work in London, aided by Bishop Bell; final sermon in London; accepts call as director of a pastoral training seminary of the Confessing Church
26 March 1935	Begins visits, with Julius Rieger, to three Anglican monasteries
15 April 1935	Farewell visit to Bishop Bell
26 April 1935	Begins work with Confessing Church seminary, temporarily at Zingsthof (first course 26 April – 16 October)
24 June 1935	Seminary moves to Finkenwalde estate near Stettin
3–12 August 1935	Bonhoeffer officially takes leave of the congregations in London
23 August 1935	Lectures on 'Recalling New Testament Texts'; essay on 'The Confessing Church and the Ecumenical Movement'

4 November 1935 – 15 March 1936	Second seminary course at Finkenwalde
February 1936	Last lecture at the University of Berlin
29 Feb.– 10 March 1936	Seminary study trip to Denmark and Sweden
April 1936	Essay on 'The Church Community'
20 August – early September 1936	Travels with Eberhard Bethge to the Chamby ecumenical conference in Switzerland, then to Rome
February 1937	Bonhoeffer resigns as ecumenical youth secretary; attends his last ecumenical conference, in London
August 1937	Bonhoeffer's right to teach at the university revoked
late September 1937	Seminary at Finkenwalde closed and sealed by the police
November 1937	Twenty-seven of Bonhoeffer's former seminary students in prison. Bonhoeffer's fourth book, *Discipleship*, published by Kaiser Verlag
5 December 1937	The first of five half-year 'collective pastorates' in Köslin and Schlawe (Groß Schlönwitz), East Pomerania, begins
11 January 1938	Bonhoeffer and other Confessing Church educators banned from Berlin. His father obtains exceptional permission for him to visit his parents.
February 1938	Hans von Dohnanyi arranges Bonhoeffer's first contacts with Resistance members (Dr. Karl Sack and Col. Hans Oster)
20 June 1938	Reunion of former Finkenwaldians at Zingst
9 September 1938	Twin sister Sabine Leibholz emigrates with her family. In her house in Göttingen, Bonhoeffer writes his book *Life Together*
March 1939	Trip to see his sister in London, also conversations with Bishop Bell, Visser 't Hooft, Canon Hodgson, Reinhold Niebuhr and Gerhard Leibholz
2 June 1939	Leaves for the USA, originally planning to stay a year, but returns on 27 July
August 1939	Beginning of the war. Applies without success for a military chaplaincy

25 August 1939	Hans von Dohnanyi appointed 'Sonderführer' in the Military Intelligence department of the Army High Command, under Admiral Canaris
Late October 1939	Last collective pastorate begins at Sigurdshof near Schlawe
15 March 1940	Last collective pastorate course ends
18 March 1940	The Gestapo closes and seals Sigurdshof
24 March 1940	Bonhoeffer meets with Hans Oster
6 June 1940	First of three visitation journeys to East Prussia begins
17 June 1940	France capitulates – Bonhoeffer and Bethge in Memel
September 1940	A decree by the SS bans Bonhoeffer from public speaking anywhere in the Reich, and obliges him to report his movements in Schlawe. Meanwhile Canaris' Military Intelligence office discusses employing him as an agent. Begins work on his Ethics.
30 October 1940	Bonhoeffer becomes a Military Intelligence secret agent attached to the Munich office
Nov. 1940 – Feb. 1941	Guest at the Benedictine Abbey in Ettal
24 Feb. – 24 March 1941	First journey to Switzerland for Military Intelligence
19 March 1941	Bonhoeffer banned from publishing and printing throughout the Reich by the Reich Writers' Guild
29 Aug. – 26 Sept. 1941	Second journey to Switzerland; takes part in 'Operation 7', rescue of 14 Jews through Military Intelligence
November 1941	Suffers severe pneumonia; cared for in his parents' home
10–18 April 1942	Trip to Norway with Helmuth James von Moltke
11–26 May 1942	Third trip to Switzerland
30 May – 2 June 1942	Travels to Sweden; meets with Bishop Bell in Sigtuna and Stockholm
June 1942	Journey to Italy with Dohnanyi; Bonhoeffer has conversations with Vatican contacts
17 January 1943	Becomes engaged to Maria von Wedemeyer

13 and 21 March 1943	Failed attempts by the Resistance to assassinate Hitler
5 April 1943	Bonhoeffer's room searched; Bonhoeffer arrested and imprisoned in Tegel military prison. Josef Müller, Hans von Dohnanyi and their wives arrested the same day.
June 1943 – Aug. 1944	Maria von Wedemeyer allowed 18 visits to Bonhoeffer at Tegel, on 21 June, 30 July, 26 Aug., 7 Oct., 10 Nov., 26 Nov., 10 Dec., 21 Dec. 1943, and 5 Jan., 24 Jan., 4 Feb., 20 Feb., 30 March, 18 April, 25 April, 22 May, 27 June and 23 Aug. 1944
18 November 1943	Beginning of 'illegal' correspondence with Eberhard Bethge, through letters smuggled by friendly prison wardens
January 1944	Investigating judge Manfred Roeder taken off Bonhoeffer's case
6 March 1944	First major air raid on Tegel
30 April 1944	Bonhoeffer's first letter to Bethge about his new theological ideas
May 1944	Case against Dohnanyi and Bonhoeffer postponed indefinitely
20 July 1944	Final, unsuccessful attempt by Stauffenberg to assassinate Hitler
23 August 1944	Last prison visit to Bonhoeffer by Maria von Wedemeyer
22 September 1944	Zossen files discovered; Bonhoeffer's and Dohnanyi's lives in immediate danger
5 October 1944	Following the arrests of his brother Klaus and brother-in-law Rüdiger Schleicher, Bonhoeffer gives up the escape plan proposed by one of the guards
8 October 1944	Transferred to the Gestapo prison on Prince Albrecht Street
7 February 1945	Moved to Buchenwald concentration camp following heavy air raids on Berlin
4 April 1945	Transported to Regensburg
5 April 1945	Hitler orders liquidation of the Resistance group in Military Intelligence

6 April 1945	The prisoners travel on to Schönberg in the Bavarian mountains
8–9 April 1945	Bonhoeffer brought to Flossenbürg and, following a sham trial during the night, put to death together with the other members of the Canaris group. Brother-in-law Hans von Dohnanyi at Sachsenhausen meets the same fate.
23 April 1945	Klaus Bonhoeffer, Rüdiger Schleicher, Friedrich Justus Perels and others shot in the back by firing squad in Berlin

Volumes 9–16 of the Dietrich Bonhoeffer Works in English (DBWE) contain much more detailed chronologies, in some cases updating the information that was available for publication in the German original Dietrich Bonhoeffer Works (DBW).

Appendix 6: Bonhoeffer Family Tree

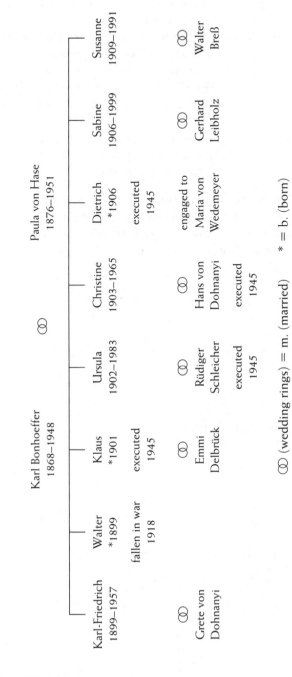

⚭ (wedding rings) = m. (married)   * = b. (born)

Index of Names

Page numbers in italics denote images